AF334722

# Painting the Ancient Land of Australia

Dedicated to Psiche Hughes

# Painting the Ancient Land of Australia

## PHILIP HUGHES

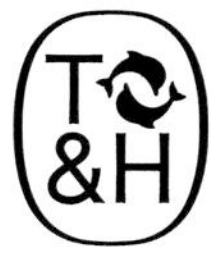

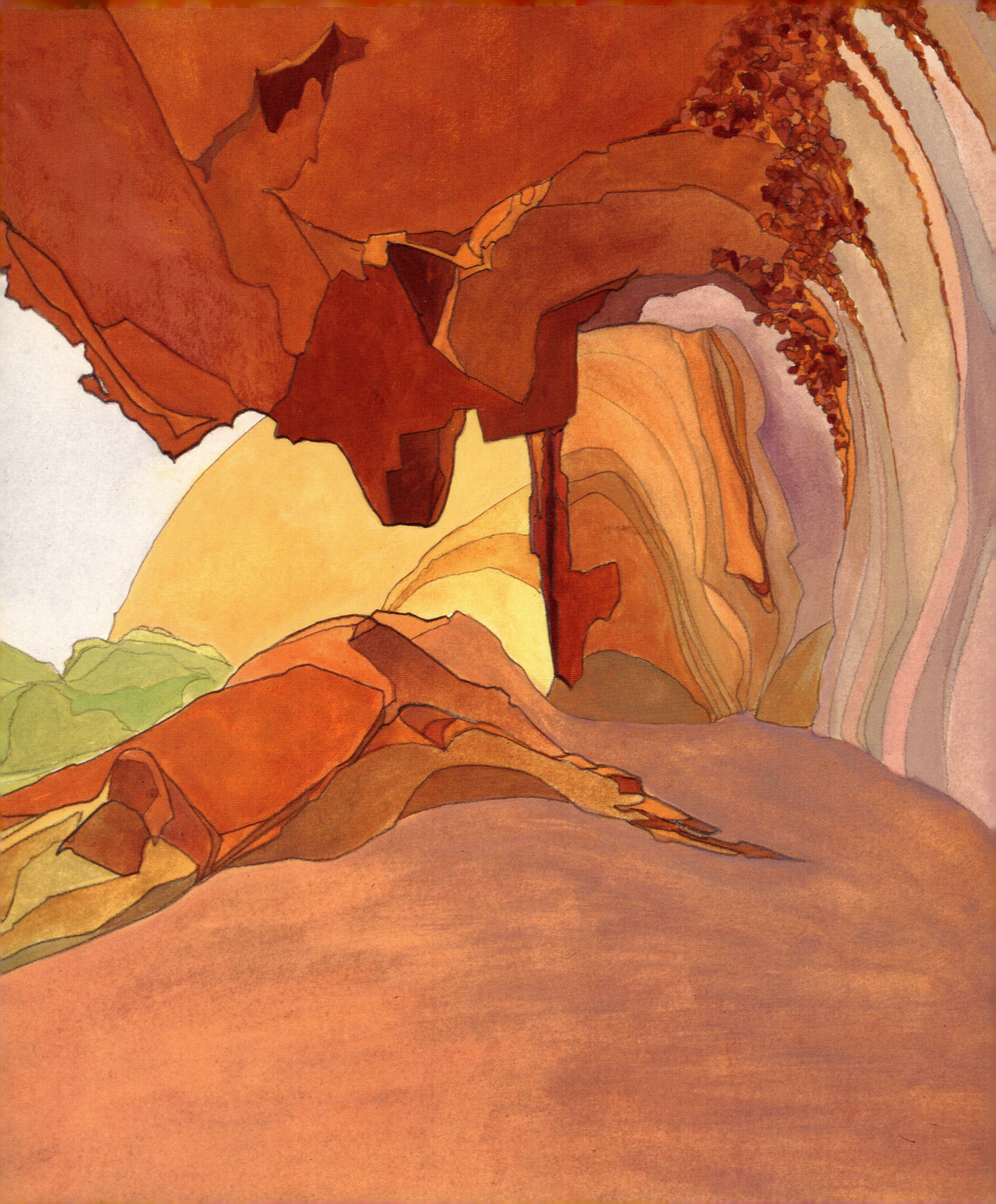

# Contents

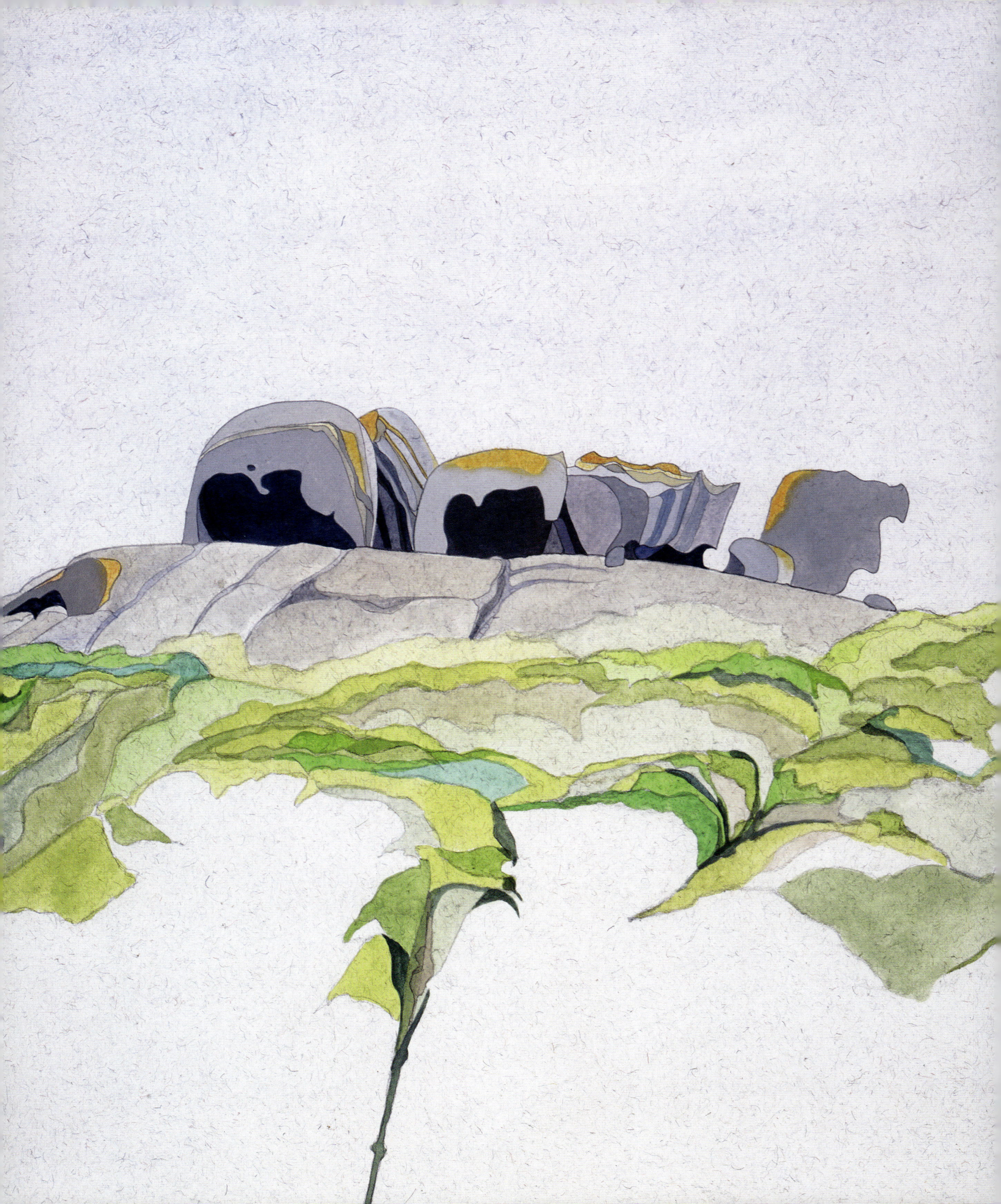

# Preface

BY GLENN MURCUTT

I became aware of Philip Hughes's deep interest in topography when on a visit to his studio in London many years ago. There, among layers of maps, were the most wonderful documents that defined topography through the beauty of reading contours – in the land, in the form of rock outcrops, in the structure of tree cover. Philip's work at the time developed with and through topographic maps. That love of geological form continues, and his Australian works show that Philip's art is made through a topographer's eye.

The island continent of Australia is about 7.7 million square kilometres in area, almost as large as the USA. This immense landmass, with a huge coastline of approximately 59,700 kilometres, extends some 3860 kilometres north to south and 4000 kilometres east to west. Australia lies south of the equator: its northernmost coastline, Cape York Peninsula in Queensland, at a latitude of just over 10 degrees south, and its southernmost point, South East Cape in Tasmania, at a latitude of 43 degrees south. Ours is the flattest, driest continent on the planet, with certain areas in northern South Australia, such as Kati Thanda/Lake Eyre, lying below sea level. Australia's highest peak, Mount Kosciuszko in New South Wales – part of the Great Dividing Range that extends from northern Queensland to Victoria – reaches only 2228 metres.

From coastal areas and flood plains to mountain ranges and deserts, Australia possesses a diversity of geographical regions, with the unique geology, soil, humidity, temperature, wind velocity and rainfall of each area determining the species of its native flora and the habitat of its native fauna. Most significantly, however, the relationship between Australia's landmass and the currents and varying temperatures of the oceans surrounding it produces a climate that is – or can be – extraordinarily dry. While rainforest, both 'dry' and 'wet', is found in areas with good rainfall, it is dry sclerophyll forest that predominates on this island continent.

Its flora is tough and legible. All flora is wonderful, but Australia's is especially extraordinary in the way it responds to varying climatic and geological conditions. Most of our trees are evergreen – a few are semideciduous – and it's possible to 'read' the life of the tree. Branches tend to be at the higher elevation of large trees, exposing the power of the tree trunk and creating an effect of delicacy as each branch sends out leaves that feather at their junction with the sky. During long periods of drought, the ends of the branches die, limiting nutrient delivery at a time when the tree is under stress. When rain finally arrives, the tree sends out new shoots, at a different angle from the shed section of branch. The varying stages of regression and growth, and the systems at work within the tree, are written in the changing direction of the tree's branches. Australia's landscape too is legible, viewed through and well beyond its native trees. Many of the eucalypts provide a beautiful visual connection between the land and the sky.

In Europe, the foliage of deciduous trees in summer is dense, solid, obscuring both the plant's structure and the landscape beyond, and producing deep shade – resembling our rainforest as it appears in all seasons. In Australia, the foliage of much of our dry-climate flora is sparse, the thin, hard leaves hanging down and away from the heat of the summer sun. It could be said that Australian trees behave throughout the year like much of the deciduous flora of the world in winter, when trees lose their leaves. Sunlight penetrates the canopy of our trees, casting shadows that are dappled, translucent and seemingly luminous. The light that passes through reveals the strength, structure and delicacy of the foliage and flowers.

In the Australian winter, our semideciduous trees shed their foliage for only a couple of weeks before producing a new flush, and in the case of the *Brachychiton* genus – which includes the kurrajong and the Illawarra flame tree – the beautiful flowers arrive as the leaves are falling.

But beyond these comparisons, our flora's relationship to Australia's geography and climate is particular and unique. Some plants in the hot, arid regions have leaves that rotate on their stems: beginning with their edges positioned towards the early morning sun, they track its movement through the daylight hours to sunset, thereby reducing the amount of sunlight on the face of each leaf and, ultimately, reducing transpiration.

There has been a clear shift in climate in Australia. The average temperature across the country over the past three decades has risen 1.52 °C. Coupled with a severe drought and very early seasonal heat, the conditions during the spring and summer of 2019–20 made for catastrophic, uncontrollable wildfires on a scale never before experienced by Australians. According to the New South Wales Department of Planning, Industry and Environment's report on the fires, some 5.4 million hectares of land was affected in New South Wales alone, and many fires occurred within the country's national parks. An estimated one billion native animals perished, together with their habitat. Rainforests burnt for the first time ever, and most are unlikely to recover, as the intense heat of the fires destroyed the seed bank distributed across the forest floor. Then, finally, came the heavy rains that extinguished the bushfires – and delivered floods.

———————

This ancient landmass has been occupied by the longest continuing living culture on Earth for between 50,000 and 120,000 years. At this point, Aboriginal people are thought to have lived in Australia for 60,000 years – but estimates as to the length of habitation extend as more evidence is uncovered.

Aboriginal people have been modifying the Australian landscape for millennia through fire-stick technology, or 'cool burns': the annual regimen of low-intensity burning of the landscape, limiting the outbreak of bushfires by eliminating the year-upon-year build-up of leaf and forest-litter fuel. The fire regimen is also structured to round up native animals so they can be harvested for food. This traditional system of annual burning has, of course, caused huge changes to the landscape, especially the flora, as a burnt-out area of forest will inevitably be replaced by a different vegetation type; for example, after a rainforest burn, the affected site might be revegetated with dry sclerophyll forest.

Since the arrival of Europeans, the landscape has largely been – and continues to be – disrespected through the irresponsible consumption of prime native bushland and farmland, lost to infrastructure, housing, industry and mining. Having said that, Australia was the second nation, behind the USA, to establish a national park, the Royal National Park in New South Wales, in 1879, and successive governments have since secured the greatest area of national parks per capita of any country in the world.

There are also some modern human interventions made in the landscape that are visually remarkable, however, such as the sites of the opal-mining fields at Lightning Ridge in New South Wales. The excavated tailings form hundreds of white-earth cones above each mining lease; a few metres in diameter and rising to a similar height, they look like large-scale anthills. Each mound is accompanied by an intricate metal frame housing the bucket-tip that removes the excavated material, together with a 3-metre-high black ventilation tube that, when heated by the sun, draws air and dust from the cool working area set many metres below ground. Then there is the immense excavation of the iron-ore mine at Mount Tom Price in Western Australia. The cutting exposes the extraordinary upheavals and folds in the structure of the earth, revealing not only geological form but superb colours. It's all strangely beautiful, reminiscent of a lunar landscape.

———————

Philip Hughes's parents and younger sister emigrated to New South Wales when he was sixteen. Having remained in England to complete his schooling, Philip spent a gap year in Australia before beginning his studies at Cambridge University. Based in the UK, over subsequent years he has often returned to this country, where his interest in landscape has become the focus of his work. This interest has led him to innumerable extraordinary sites in Australia, investigating the geology and structure of the land, recording it in drawings and notes, capturing the essence of place in each painting.

During turbulent political times, he joined the significant and hugely successful 1980s protest in south-western Tasmania that stopped the

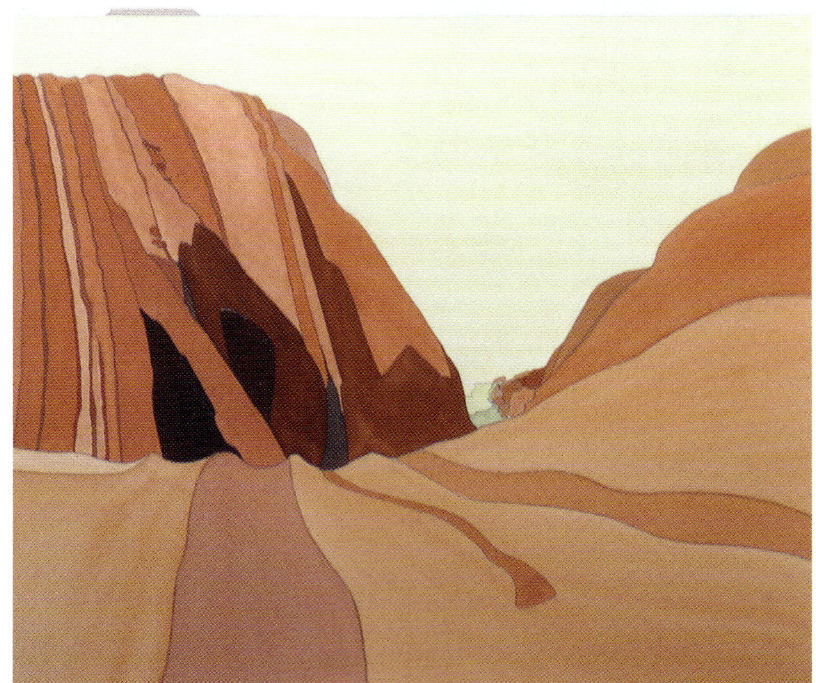

Gordon-below-Franklin dam project. The incredibly beautiful and significant World Heritage-listed Franklin-Gordon region remains a milestone in conservation history.

Philip has a deep affinity for Australia's diverse landscapes and its ancient geology – especially its rock formations – and an abiding interest in this country's endemic flora and fauna and the conservation of species. He has an equal fascination with the impact of human intervention on the Earth's forms, such as mining, excavating and tunnelling for minerals and gems – whether carried out using heavy machinery or by individual labour, as is the case with opals. His subjects and his travels span the arid deserts of Central and Western Australia, and extend from the climatically equatorial north and the subtropical north-east to the warm-temperate grasslands of the east and beyond. On his travels to the remote, cool-temperate region of south-western Tasmania, he visited the breeding grounds of the extremely rare and critically endangered ground-dwelling orange-bellied parrot, which each year migrates from the mainland across Bass Strait to breed in that one area only.

Philip has also recorded many of Australia's World Heritage-listed sites, including Kakadu National Park in the Northern Territory, with its ancient rock art, sacred sites and other areas of great cultural significance for Aboriginal people, and Purnululu National Park in Western Australia, where he has profiled the extraordinary geological 'beehive' formations and striated layers of the Bungle Bungles. He has also sketched and painted the remarkable topography, landscape and flora of Lord Howe Island, lying 780 kilometres north-east of Sydney, and the Blue Mountains National Park, replete with 600-metre-deep sunken valleys, located some 130 kilometres west of Sydney.

The diversity and breadth of his work provide a window into the immense scale of this land. With the clarification of the essential through his art, Philip has expressed his love of the Australian landscape.



*The Head of Olga Gorge*, 1981



*Meeting Tent in TWS Camp*
(detail), 1983

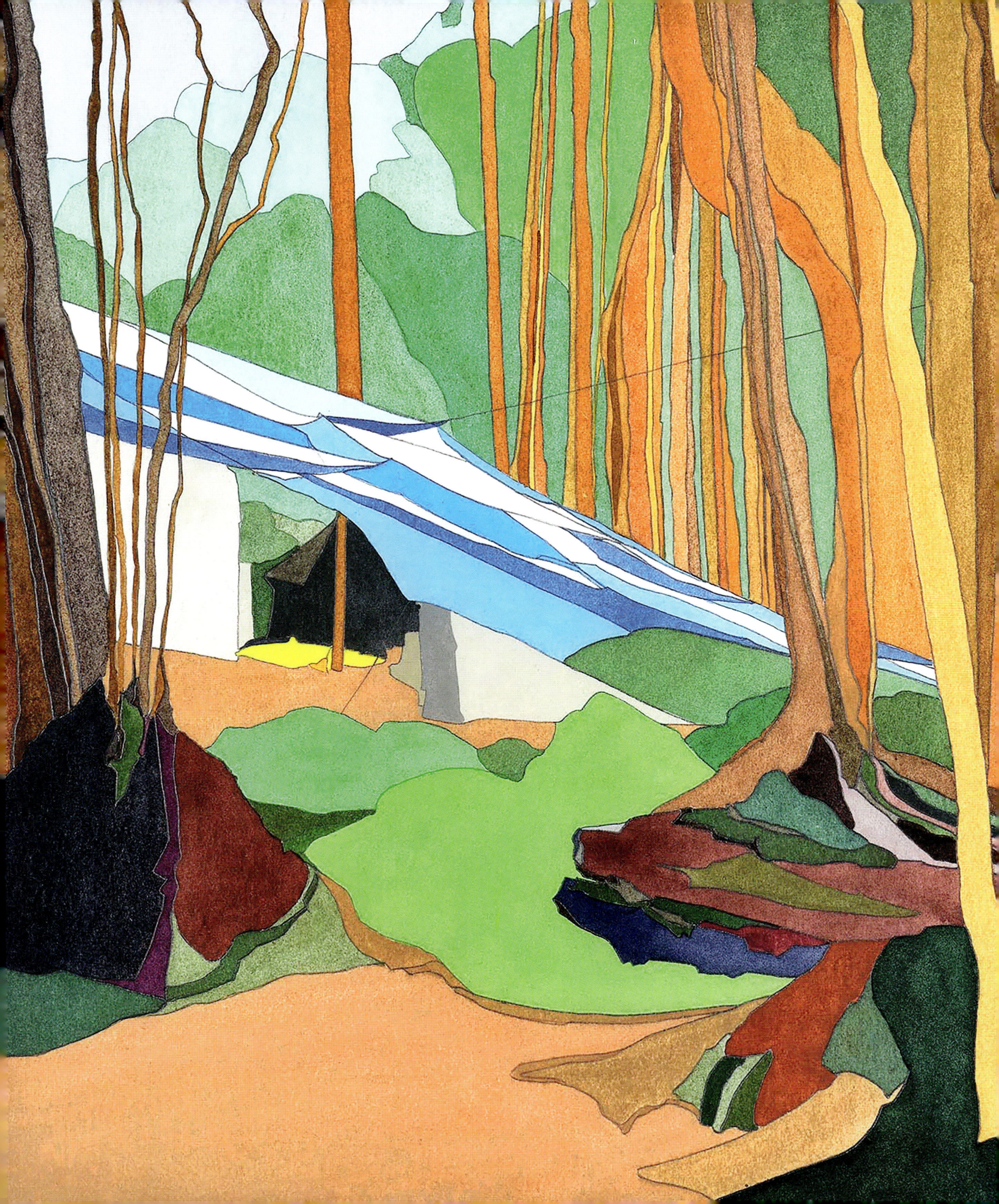

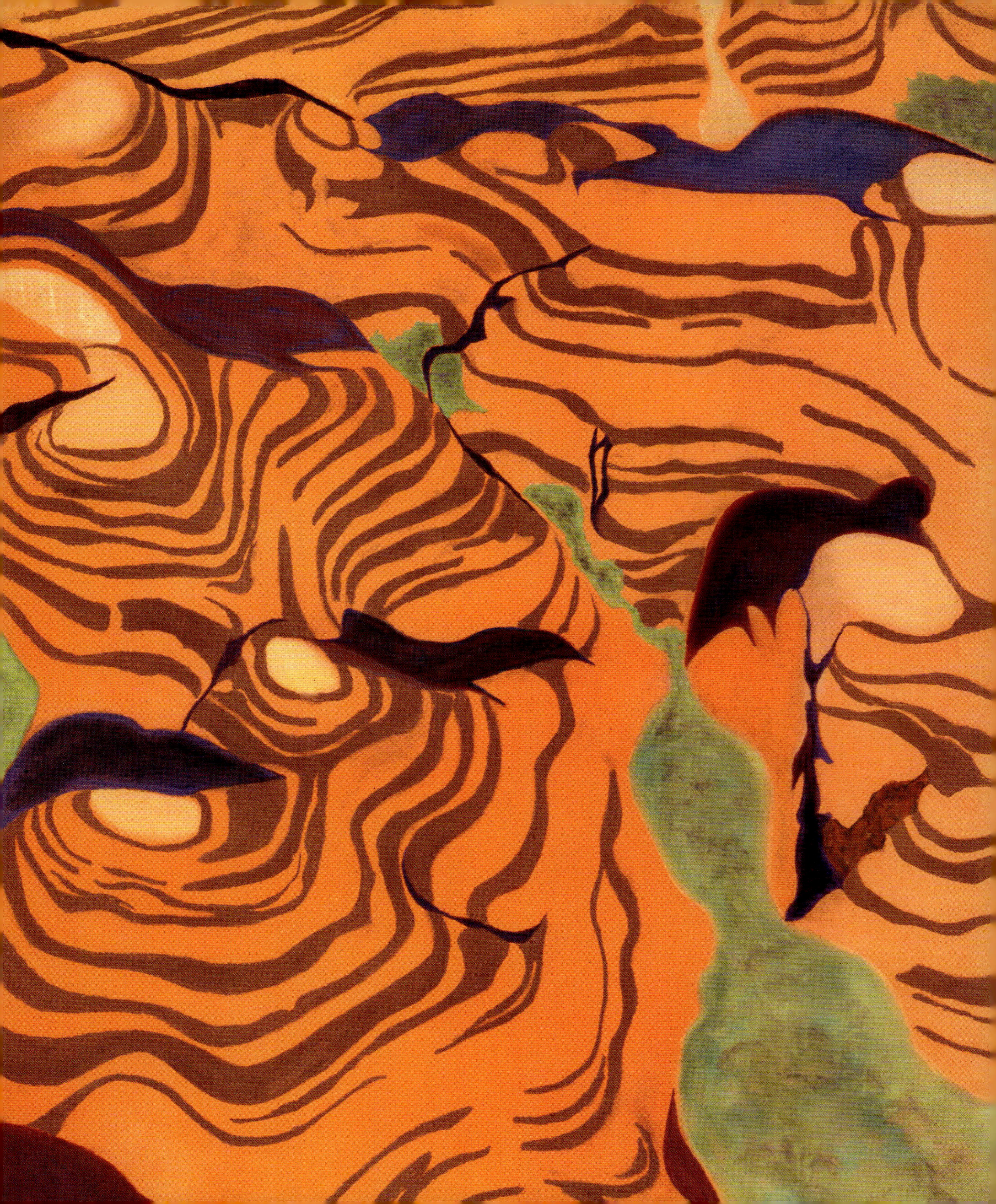

# Ways of Working

**BY PHILIP HUGHES**

The foundation of all of my work is drawing, with the majority of drawings made on site, in the land. There are broadly three categories:

The first is large-format drawings. These are made in situ on sheets of large, heavyweight paper. Sometimes colour is added later, in the studio, but they remain essentially drawings. Those made in Bouddi National Park (shown on pages 154–5) exemplify this category.

The second is drawings that are destined to become paintings. I sketch in the landscape, and then paint is added once I'm back in the studio. All areas of the image are painted, the line drawing largely lost as the pencil line becomes a framework for painted spaces. Examples of this type are shown in my Lightning Ridge paintings (pages 136–7).

The third category is my work in notebooks, the main 'canvas' for my drawings. Usually, when walking in the land, a notebook is with me.

Over the past thirty years, I have used just two types of notebook, both of which were bought in France. The first, now no longer available, was made with recycled paper. An earlier Thames and Hudson publication – *Patterns in the Landscape* – was devoted exclusively to facsimiles from these notebooks. The examples shown in this book are from Cabbage Tree Creek (pages 34–7).

The second notebook design uses a fine Fabriano paper. This model is still used. The drawings of my flight from Alice Springs (pages 88–9) and train journey across the Nullarbor Plain (pages 48–53) were made in this type of notebook. These two sequences show different ways the notebook works can develop.

Sometimes, the notebook drawings are scanned, printed as enlargements and collaged to make larger works. An example of this technique is the room divider/screen shown on page 37. At other times, the notebook entries are the final works – those from the train journey across the Nullarbor are, again, a good example.

By far the greatest use for notebook drawings, however, is when they are the basis for separate, larger paintings. Usually, colour is already selected and marked in the notebook before I begin painting. These early, foundational colours help to define the larger final painting.

I am often asked how I choose colour. This is difficult to explain, except to say that I use what I think will work. To a certain extent they are 'real', by which I mean come directly as I see the land. At other times, they are chosen to create a balanced final work. I am often not trying to copy the impression of the landscape; I aim instead to create paintings that inspire ways of looking. This concept also provides a framework to better understand my incorporation of source material, such as aerial photography or maps, into some paintings.

One approach holds them side by side, as on page 60, where the aerial image of Gosse Bluff is incorporated into the final work, or on page 17, where the relevant maps are presented alongside my paintings of Mount Bruce and Joffre Gorge. Another is to simply use the aerial image as direct inspiration for a piece, as was the case for my Fraser Island painting on page 181.

For aerial-perspective works I usually use photography as my source, as sketching is seldom possible. I prefer to use photographs taken by myself, either from helicopters (as done for my image of the Bungle Bungles on page 32) or from small aeroplanes (as on my flight to Melaleuca, Tasmania, shown on page 119), but I do also use professional photographs from higher altitudes.

Each source is important in its own way. The view from the air shows the structure of the land in ways not possible from the ground – this is especially relevant in Australia, a land most striking when seen from above. And I consider both topographical and geological maps to be the key to the land, as well as often being beautiful images in their own right.

I have chosen to show maps and/or aerial images at the beginning of each section to reflect my great interest in these materials. However, my approach in such works is not intended to compare the maps or photographs to my paintings or to define the landscape I portray, but rather to express the different ways one can see the land.

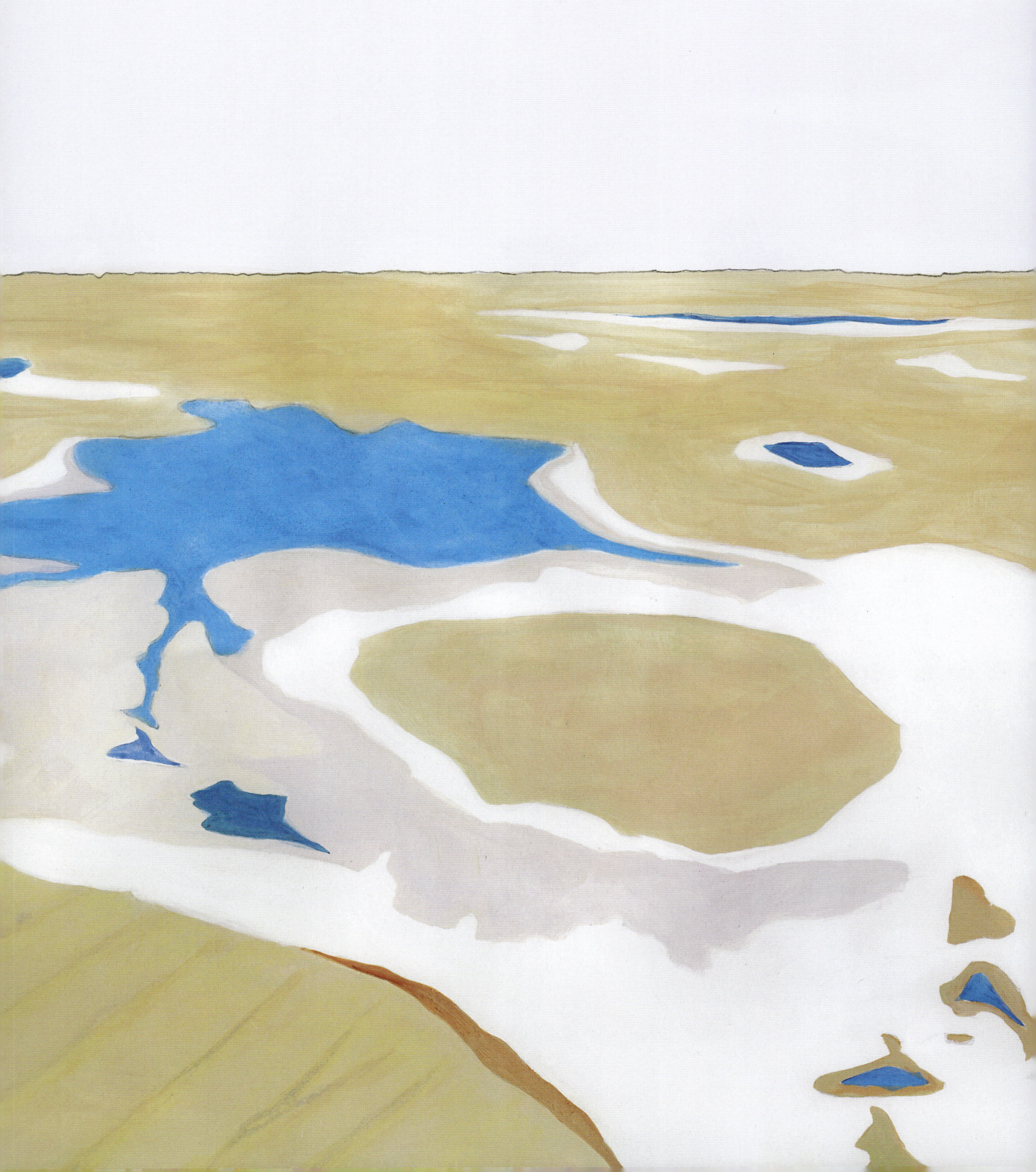

# Introduction

BY JONATHAN MEYER

An unfamiliar landscape is initially inscrutable. We all have ways of locating ourselves, of becoming acclimatised to our surroundings, but are necessarily lost on first arriving in a new place. The art of Philip Hughes is in many ways a record of the act of his finding himself in new places, learning to read the signs that allow the transition from bewilderment to comprehension. It is this adaptive vision, the ability to take the ambient cues from an environment, that must exist first and foremost in a landscape painter, far in advance of the tasks of representation.[1]

In much of Hughes's early work, these cues are directly tied to previous inhabitation – history is called upon to make a first reading, with a focused examination of humankind's physical impact upon the land acting as a structuring device. Thus do walls, agricultural fields, terraces and ancient routes mark out and define the elements in many of his early paintings of Europe, a landscape greatly affected and shaped by the duration and intensity of its inhabitation.

There is in the same manner a fascination with sacred sites: ancient settlements display a de facto sensitivity to the landscape that can only be instructive. Hughes's early works from significant cultural sites – ranging from Machu Picchu to Skara Brae, from the pre-Columbian desert city-states of Yagul and Monte Albán to the Anasazi cliff palaces at Canyon de Chelly and Mesa Verde, from the stone circles of Stonehenge and Avebury to the jungle temples of Tikal and Palenque – all present the viewer with an already palpable atavistic sense of how humankind relates to the lie of the land. In these 'archaeological' works, it is important to note the implication of trust embedded within them. These are not cases of the artist inflicting his personal vision on an existing sacred place, but acknowledgements of our indebtedness to the physical heritage of cultures that have lived before us, and with respect to the crucial notion that they have done so in full communion with the land.

But what happens when the signs of inhabitation are not immediately visible? When the observer is confronted with a place that, because of its remoteness or severe climate, has not been intensively occupied or farmed – or, pertinently, a place where the built material record of the Indigenous occupants is not conspicuous or has not endured?[2] In these circumstances, Hughes seeks out other structural systems that organise the seemingly chaotic nature of wilderness, illuminating how the Earth's surface has been formed and how it has become worn and weathered over time, how water storage and dispersal have given rise to climatic thresholds, and how these have in turn influenced the behaviour and distribution of flora and fauna – the realms of geology, geomorphology and ecology.

These are large subjects, whole disciplines in the world of science, the sheer scale and complexity of which may seem daunting to the painter. But Hughes is content to look closely and record; his intention is not to delve too deeply into the data or to produce a definitive study, but, rather, to find a way in.

This 'finding a way in' has been especially important for Hughes's Australian work: to the European eye, the landscape *down under* can come as a bit of a shock. Fairly at odds with the conventional Western idea of what 'the land' should look like, the Australian bush is often described as sunburnt and unruly, dishevelled, scraggly or scruffy. The relative harshness of the Australian climate and of the light itself – which can throw the mid-day into a pared-down (almost binary) spectrum of contrasting black and bright – in tandem with the sheer scale and seemingly unpopulated nature of most of the interior, stands in stark contrast to the softer and safer, more subdued nature of the English countryside of Hughes's homeland.

Hughes has been navigating these essential differences for much of his life, visiting Australia repeatedly and regularly over the last sixty years. As his son-in-law, I have had the good fortune to accompany him on several of his trips to more remote areas of the Outback and have always been struck by the clarity of his intention when he sets to work. Often in mid-sentence or stride, he will pause to look carefully at something and then will be as good as gone, opening his notebook – always to hand – and beginning to sketch almost immediately.

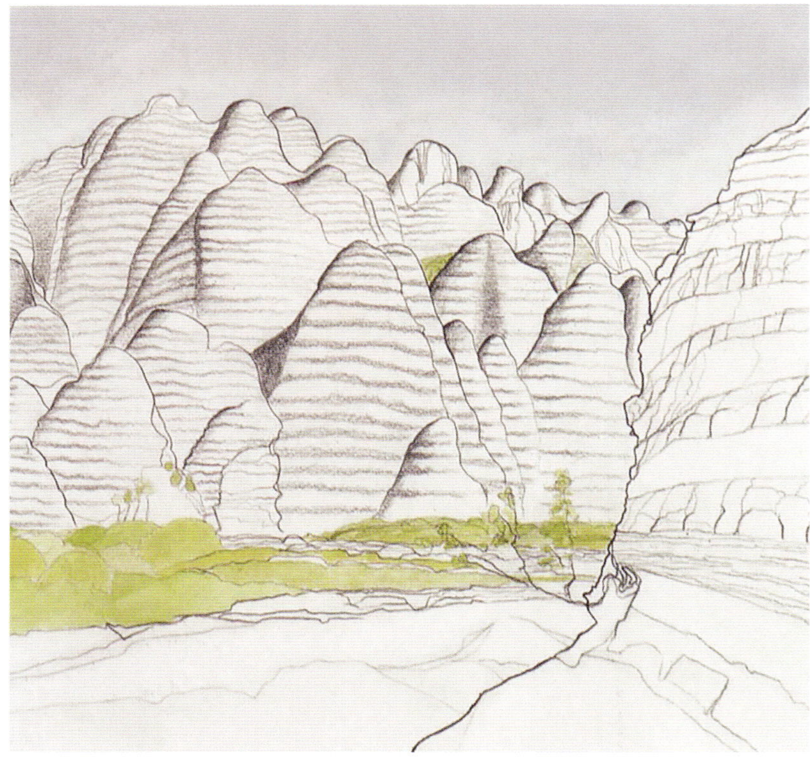

Luckily, these pauses (often lasting an hour or more) are inevitably located in the most compelling places one can imagine, and his family has learnt over the years to open our eyes and appreciate what we may well have missed had we been walking there without him.

He often uses the medium of distance itself to make evident the underlying structure of the land. While the visually simplified forms of crop fields or vineyards are conspicuous from almost any vantage point, it takes the bird's-eye clarity of the view down from an aircraft or peak to reveal the order of the desert or a flood plain, a fact made clear in Hughes's work from Central and Western Australia. That he managed to get his wife and constant companion Psiche into a helicopter (without doors!) to fly over and through the beehive domes and canyons of the Bungle Bungle Range is a minor miracle, and true testament to his determination.

But there is more to this fascination with the aerial. The urge to represent such vast, unbounded tracts of land signifies the importance of the sublime or the ineffable, inherent in and at the core of landscape art. As a subject, the sublime is problematic: for Hughes, something must be located, a datum taken, if one is to gain some sort of purchase in communicating the sense of how it feels to confront the boundless. The view down the spine of Lord Howe Island to the unbroken Pacific (page 157) leaves the viewer with a heightened sense that beyond the edge of the canvas, the horizon is endless.

The fear (and allure) of the sublime, of the infinite and intangible, of never being able to 'get there', has traditionally been fought off (and courted) by the geographer or cartographer. With maps, trails blazed, we are assured that someone has gone before us; someone else has reached there from here. Hughes has spent much of his life getting to many, many 'theres' from many 'heres', and it can be said that the *walk* has occupied a central position in his work from the very beginning. He has walked the Inca Trail in Peru, the pilgrim route to Santiago de Compostela through France and Spain, along the length of England's Ridgeway, across the breadth of Scotland's Rannoch Moor; he has taken a twenty-one-day trek to the kingdom of Zanskar in the Himalayas and rambled the rolling contours of the Sussex South Downs what must now be nearing a thousand times. In South Australia, he has followed the tragic trail of Burke and Wills from Innamincka along Cooper Creek, sadly reminded on this journey that some 'theres' are never reached. From daily sketched diaries to large abstract depictions of the paint-splashed rocks that mark the hiking trails in rural France, he has continually sought to represent the serial experience of the walk in his work.

In some of his more recent work, Hughes explores a particular walk or place by producing an extended series of related pieces rather than providing a single or definitive view that attempts to distil its character. In addition, these series are made up of studies conducted at many scales at once, telescoping from aerial view to minute detail, constantly shuttling between extremes. Maps or fragments of maps, many of them historical or geological, have found their way into these composites and offer both factual and visual counterpoint to the austere simplicity of his line.

This stylistic shift is indicative of the confidence that has gradually arisen in Hughes's mature work. He has progressed beyond the desire to solely depict, to present the object/image of a place. It is now a concern to relay the sense of immersion he has felt while moving through a landscape. Yet this is not a cinematic desire; the movement per se is not the issue. This could not be video, with its latent predication on the roving eye of the viewer. To the contrary, the works convey a composite repose and stillness: many things are seen at once, yet there is coalescence. Painted strips of abstracted trees are interspersed with bold stripes of pure colour (see pages 134–5), views are fragmented, shafts of light and shade deny the possibility of a single reading, and yet there is no mistaking the singular character of the forest.

This stillness also suggests a duration or perseverance beyond the artist's involvement: the land will outlive us. In his work from the colossal iron-ore mine of Mount Tom Price (pages 2–9), we witness a brutish embodiment of our culture's insatiable demand for mineral extraction, but somehow the implied cacophony of the trucks and machinery is quieted by the incorporation and importance of the backdrop of the rolling topography of the Pilbara into the picture, as it continues on beyond. The huge open pits and terraced scars will no doubt eventually be slowly swallowed up and repossessed by the land, once again dwarfed by genuine vastness when our rapaciousness has moved elsewhere – the remembered noise of the mine and the mute horizon in harmony, the ebb and flow of nature and industry seemingly at rest, a still point on the great curve of our progress.

Some recurring themes are clear: Hughes seeks out what for him makes a landscape readable. His methodologies and techniques are as varied as the places he has visited, and yet his pictures display a rigorous consistency. He has always shown a tendency to gentle abstraction; whether on the scale of an impact crater or the polished face of an opal in the hand, there is almost always a visual paring down of an image into simple flat fields of colour. This simplification or evening-out of Hughes's landscapes also hints at an equalising of subject matter. The work is democratic in the best possible sense of the word: culture and nature have equal validity within the picture plane. The cultivated and the wild, the geometric and the organic, never have to jockey for position, but coexist often within the same work, as they do in our lives.

NOTES

1   Parts of this text have been reworked from my introduction to the exhibition catalogue for *Philip Hughes: A Survey Exhibition*, which opened at the Drill Hall Gallery in Canberra, ACT, on 22 October 1998.

2   The Australian landscape has regularly and incorrectly been presented as a kind of tabula rasa, a wilderness only ever sparingly shaped or influenced by its 'nomadic' Indigenous cultures. This portrayal is finally being debunked through the research and writings of Bill Gammage, Bruce Pascoe and others.

**ABOVE**
*Piccaninny Creek*, 1996

# PAINTING THE ANCIENT LAND

# Mount Tom Price mine,
# Western Australia

**22°45'57.0"S 117°46'15.0"E**
**-22.765833, 117.770833**

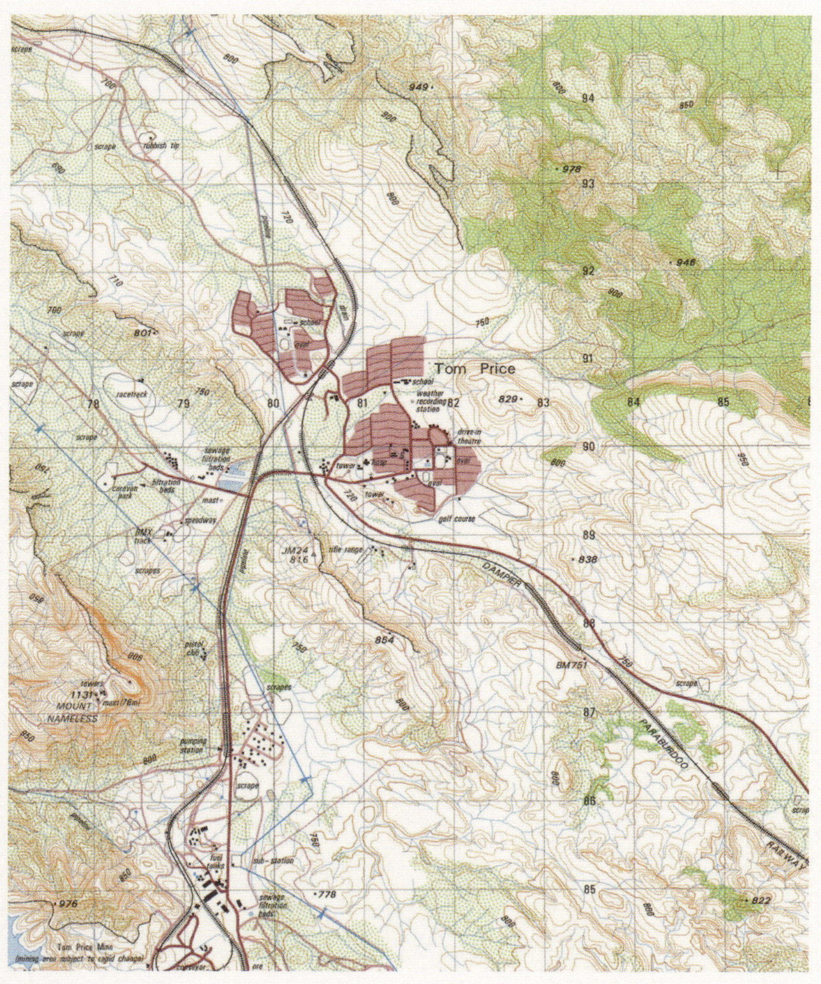

The Mount Tom Price iron-ore mine, in the Pilbara region of Western Australia, is immense. Nothing can prepare you for the sheer scale of the open pit. It is a series of terraces, going down and down, and in some ways I found them reminiscent of Inca terraces in Peru. The Mount Tom Price terraces are in fact much deeper, but viewed from the edge of the mine, this is not apparent. This is a scale deception, because the trucks in the pit below, carrying the iron ore, are huge. When you go down the mine and stand by one of these trucks, they tower above you. The tyres alone dwarf you.

I wanted to go to the mine at Mount Tom Price and the surrounding Hamersley Range after seeing, in London, a suite of large paintings of the mine by Fred Williams, which greatly impressed me, particularly the representation of the intense deep red of the Pilbara landscape. I approached the mine's owners, Rio Tinto, and they kindly agreed to my visit, giving me full access as I worked and providing accommodation for my wife, Psiche, and myself. That in itself was quite an adventure – meeting the mine workers in the dining rooms and bar and staying in the housing used by the workers.

A railway has been built specifically to take the iron ore from the mine to the port of Dampier, from where it is shipped – mainly to China. I watched the trains slowly crossing the open land: wagon after wagon, seemingly without end, being pulled by a number of huge locomotives. Just as the mine pit was the largest I had ever seen, these trains were the longest. Everything about the mine and its operation is on a huge scale.

Experiencing the scale of Tom Price gave me pause to think about the impacts of mining in Australia particularly. There is an inevitable clash of interests between mining, which is so important to the economy of Australia, and conserving the unique landscapes and ecology. Further, there is a cultural clash between the economic imperatives of mining and the preservation of vital Aboriginal sites. This came into sharp focus in 2020 with a number of mining companies expanding their operations in the Pilbara, in the process destroying sites of great cultural and archaeological importance, such as the Juukan Gorge caves.

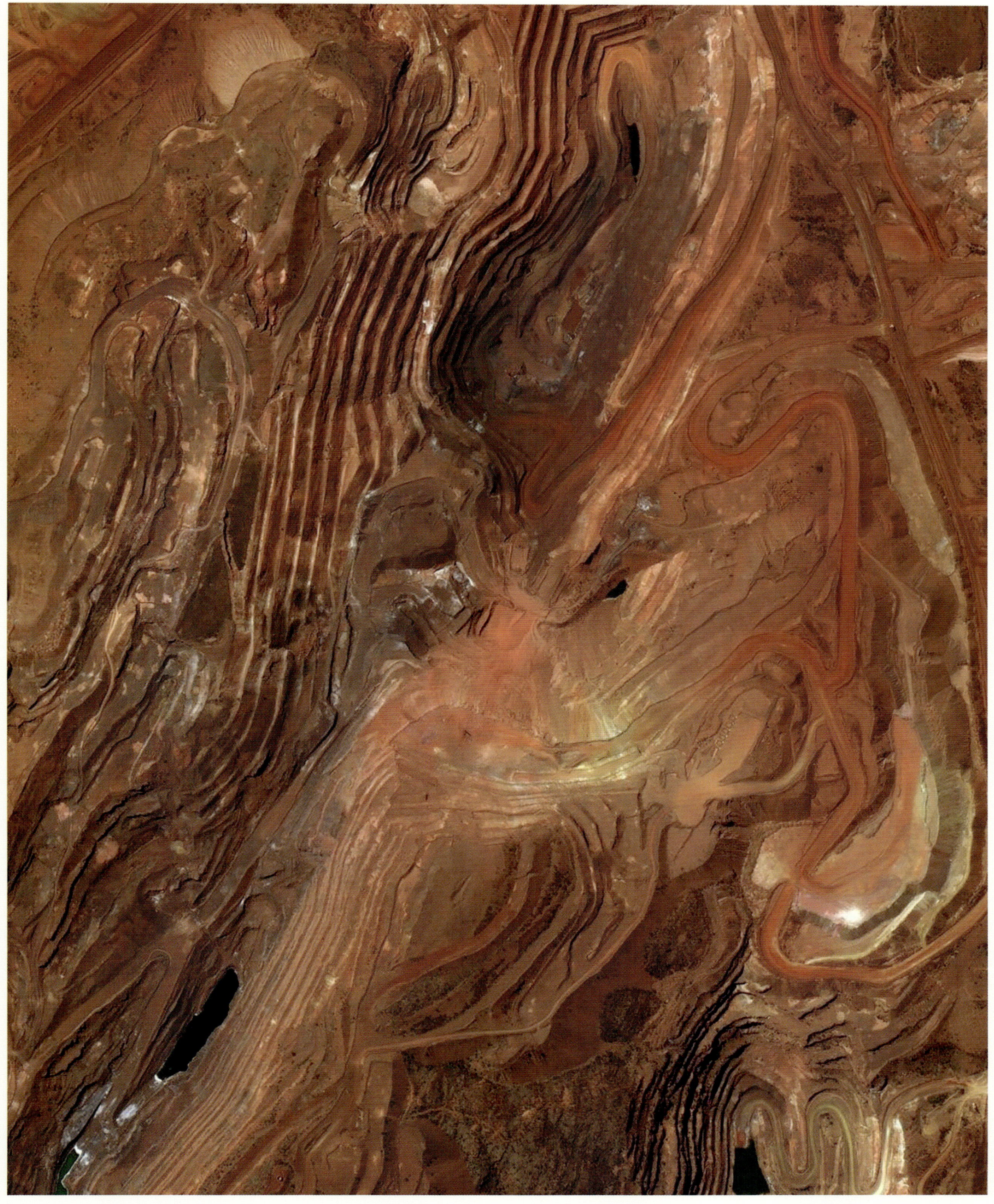

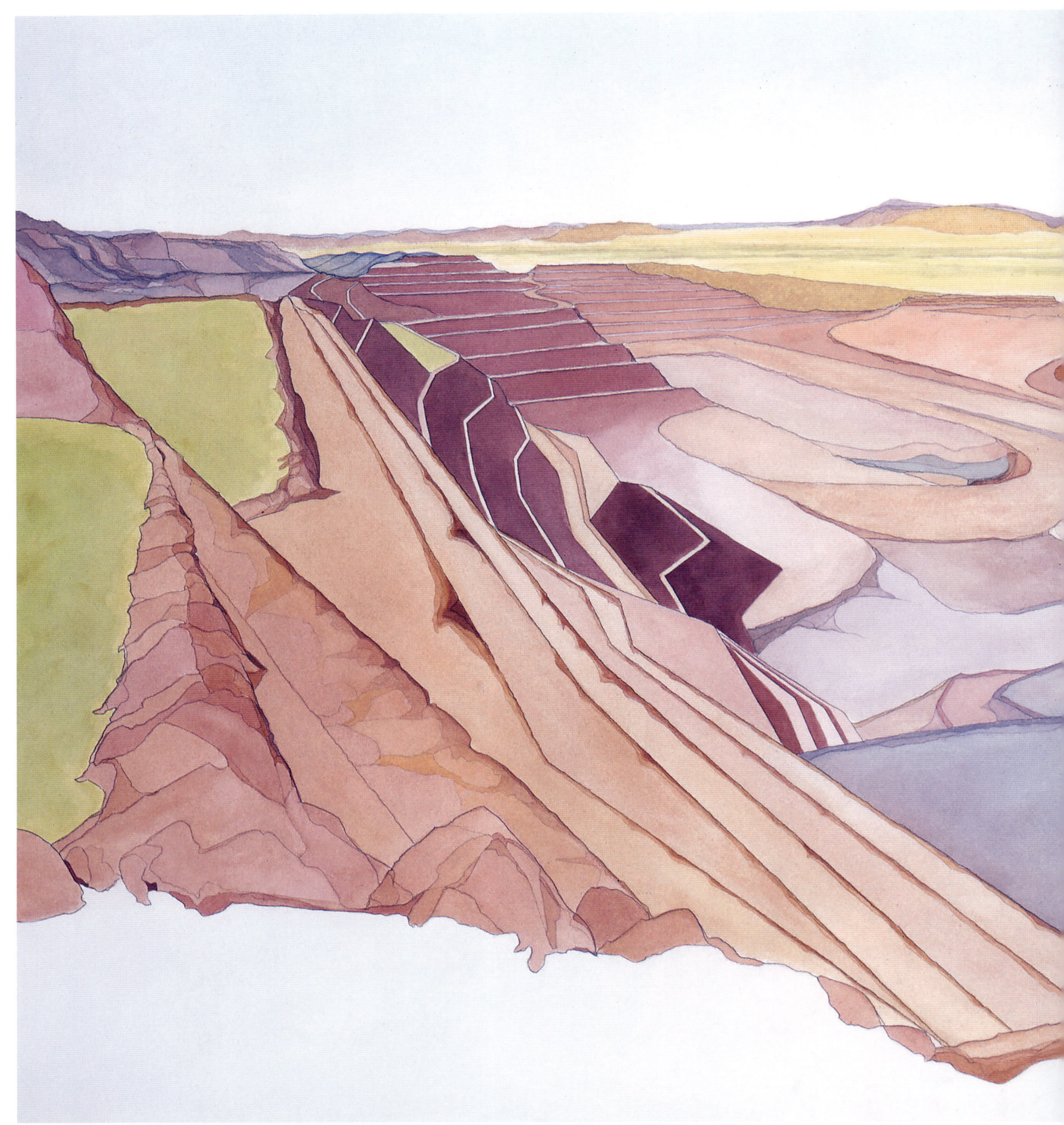

*The Terraces of Tom Price Mine,*
2005

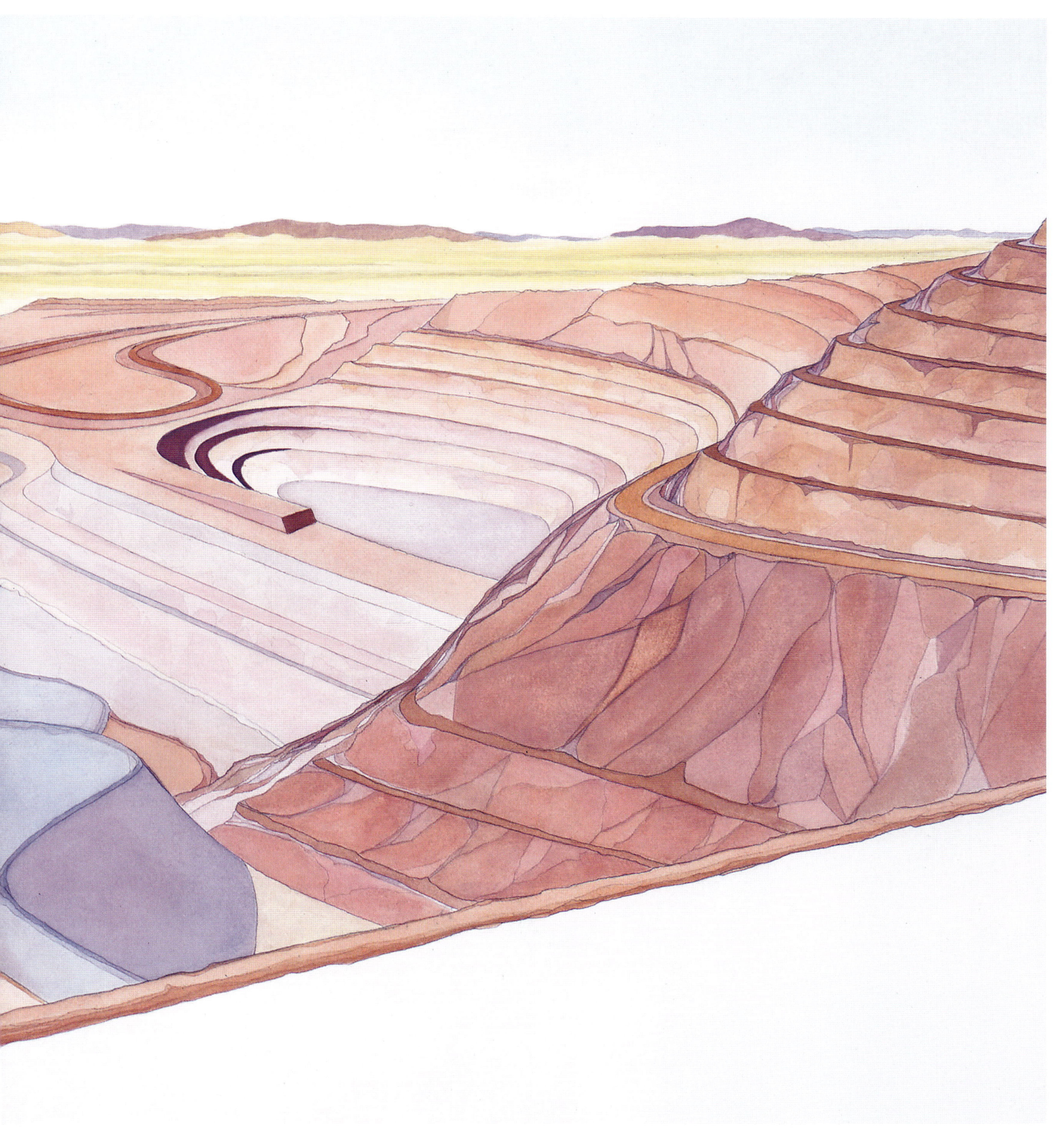

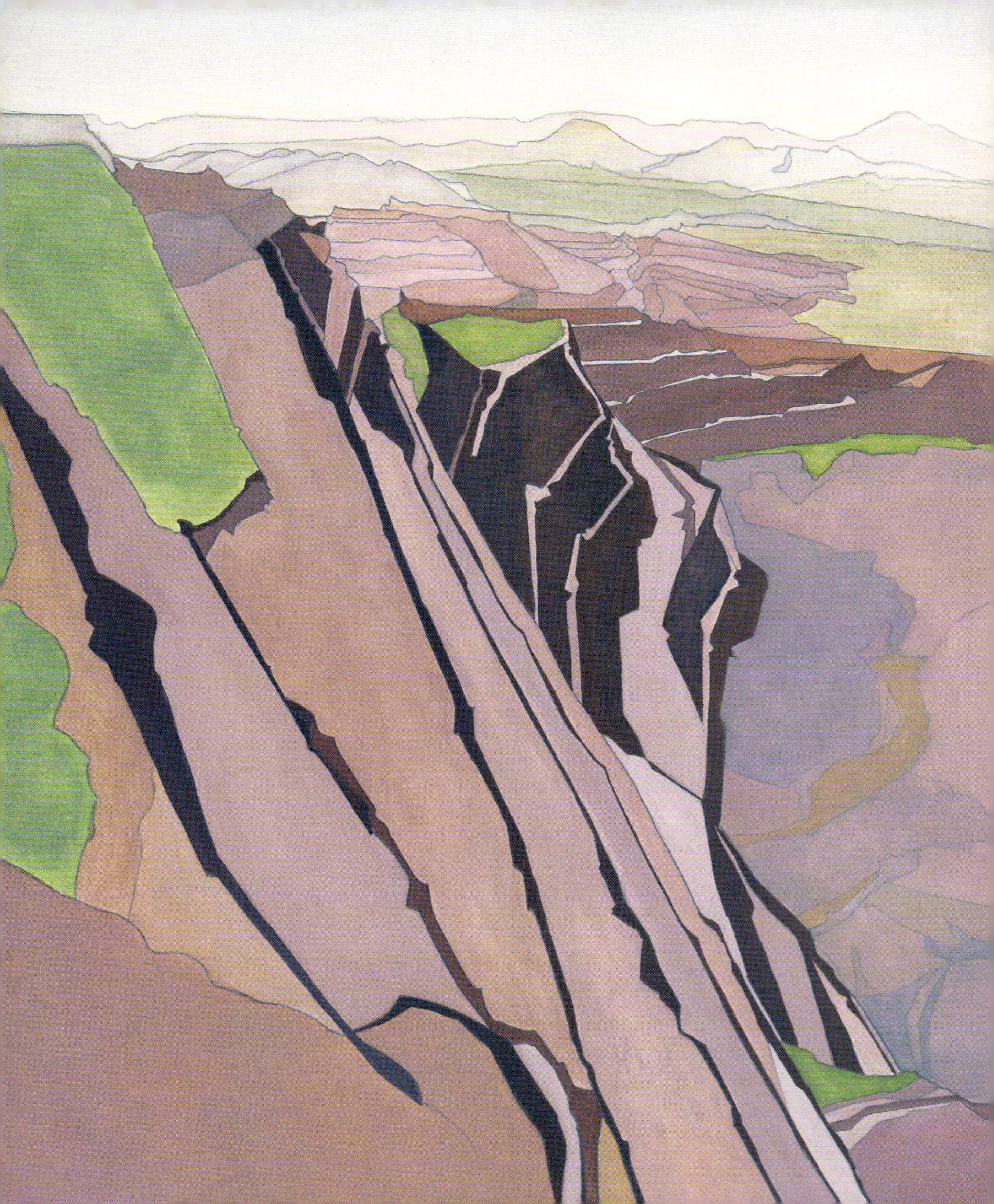

I watched the trains slowly crossing the open land: wagon after wagon, seemingly without end, being pulled by a number of huge locomotives. Just as the mine pit was the largest I had ever seen, these trains were the longest. Everything about the mine and its operation is on a huge scale.

*Tom Price Mine IV, Pilbara, 2005*

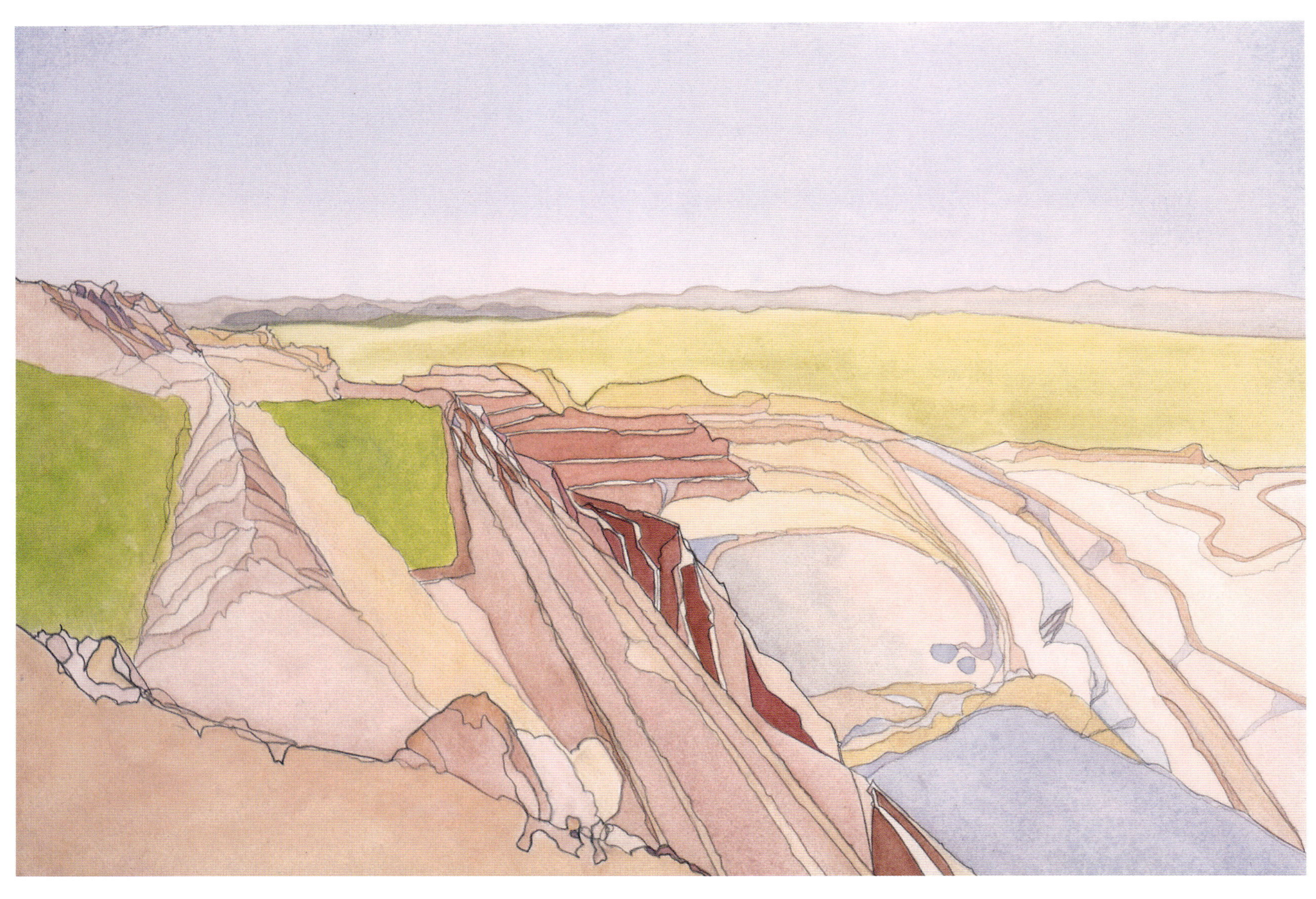

**ABOVE**
*Tom Price Mine I*, 2005

**RIGHT**
*Tom Price Mine II*, 2005

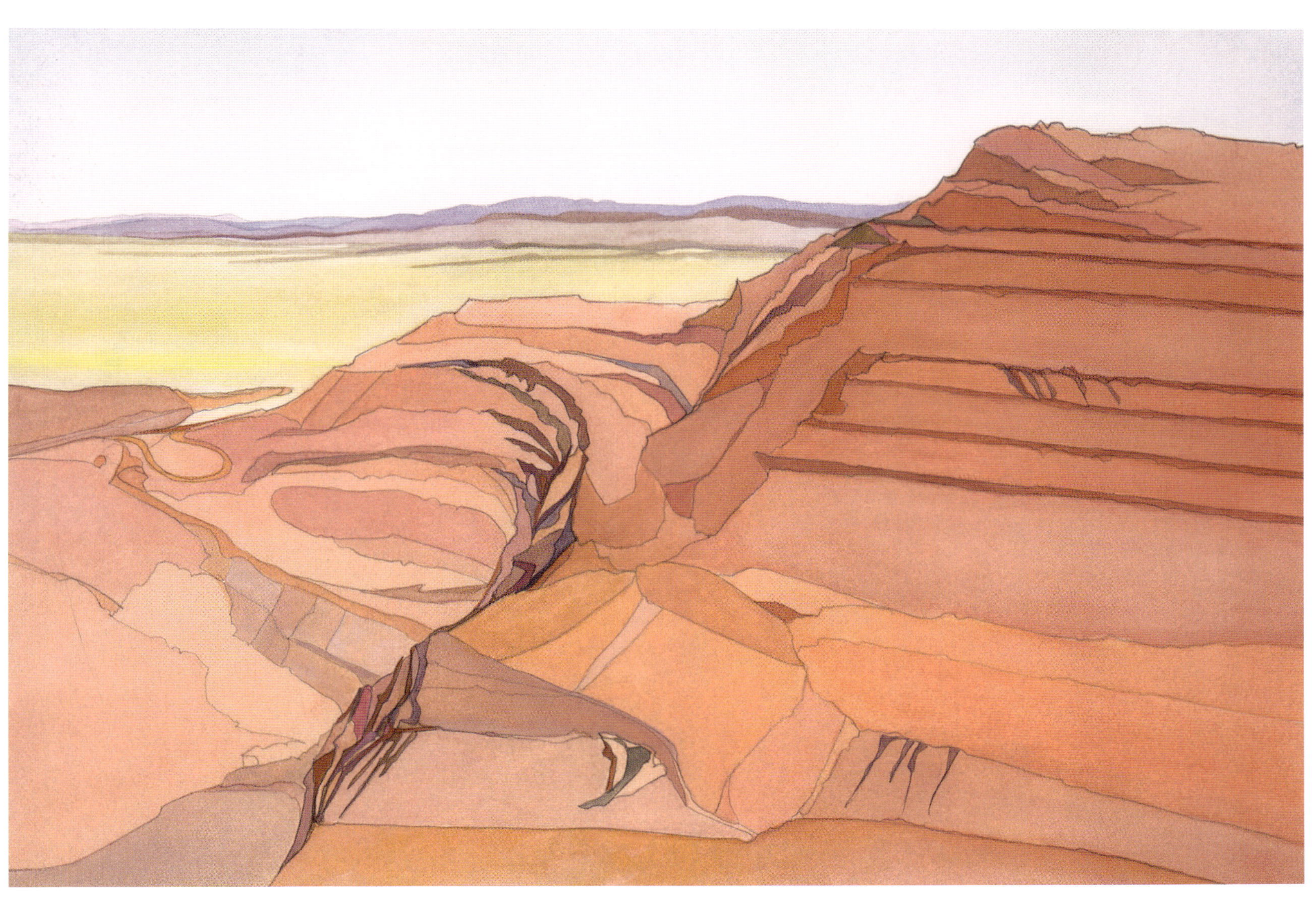

# Karijini National Park, Western Australia

22°23'24.7"S 118°16'08.0"E
-22.390200, 118.268900

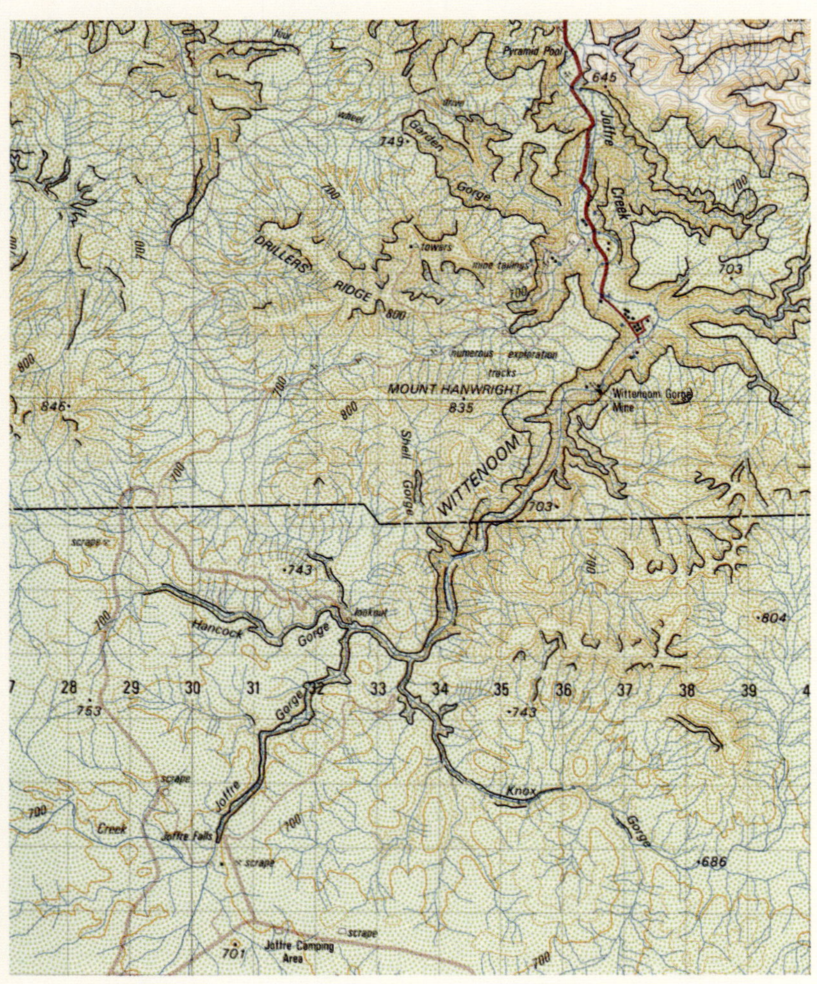

This is one of Australia's largest national parks. Located to the east of the mining town of Tom Price, it lies within the extensive region of the Pilbara. The rocks of the Pilbara are the oldest and best-preserved sedimentary rocks on Earth, more than three billion years old. They have within them traces of organic matter, the oldest evidence of life on Earth.

While we were visiting the Mount Tom Price mine, our hosts lent us a four-wheel drive vehicle to explore remote areas of the national park, which included Mount Bruce and the surrounding hills, and then, further east, Joffre, Weano and Kalamina gorges. All these deep gorges very clearly show the strata in the rock. When we were there – in May – water was flowing through the gorges, but not very strongly. The signs of erosion all around showed that at times these flows are greatly expanded, fierce and fast.

Rocks beside a creek we passed near the road on the way to the gorges had figures and a series of circles marked on them, which are shown on page 12. They are said to date from 15,000 years ago.

Included here are two works incorporating maps. I have used this combination of painting and map for artworks from other parts of the world. I have always been fascinated by maps. Psiche said once when we were camping: 'You read maps like others read books.' Good detailed maps are the real definition of a landscape. As well as providing the representation of surface – and in the case of geological maps, the sub-surface – they are beautiful graphics in their own right. When I incorporate maps into works, I have a dual intent – descriptive and graphic. I adjust the painting to match the map and vice versa, changing colours in the map to suit the painting.

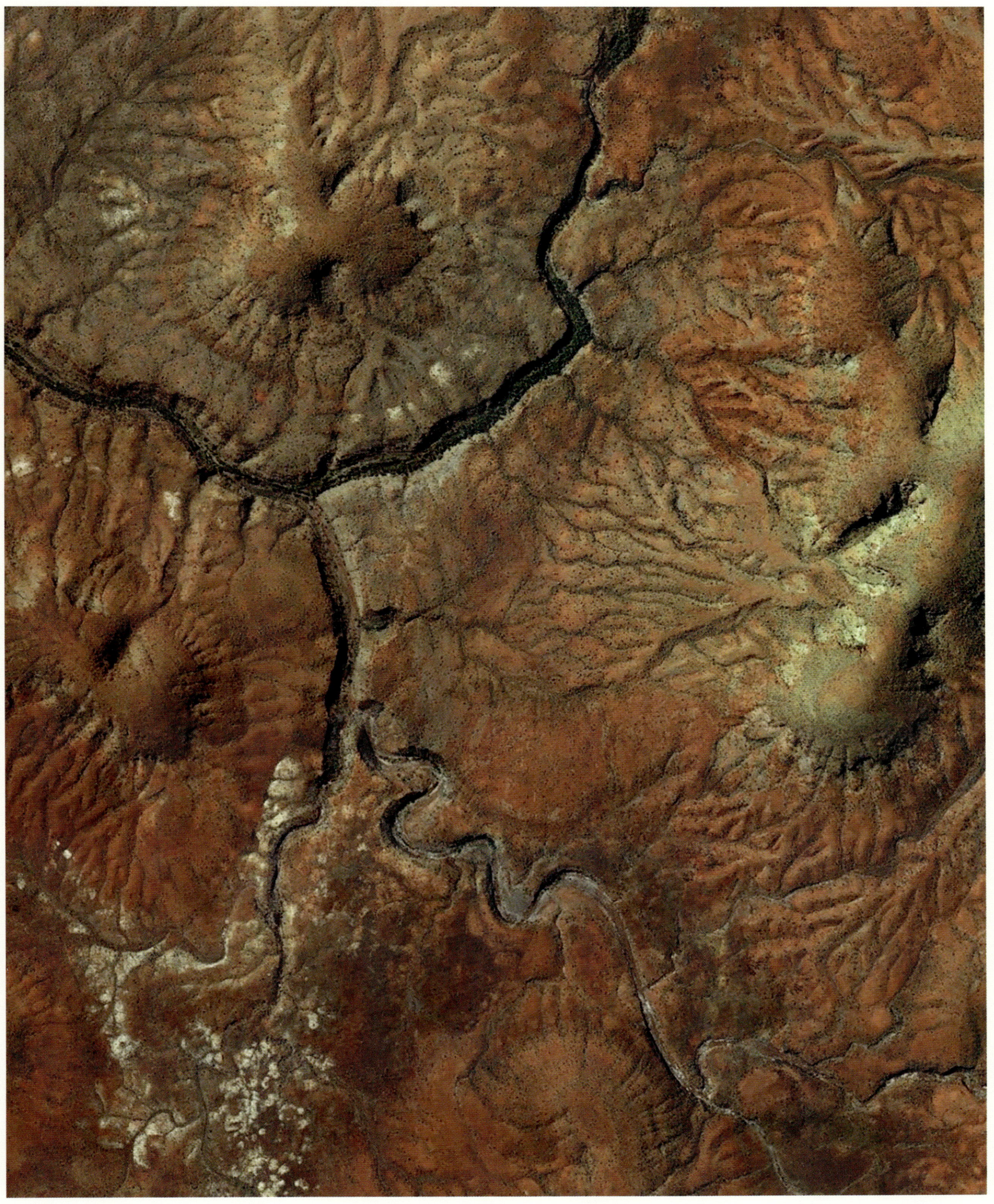

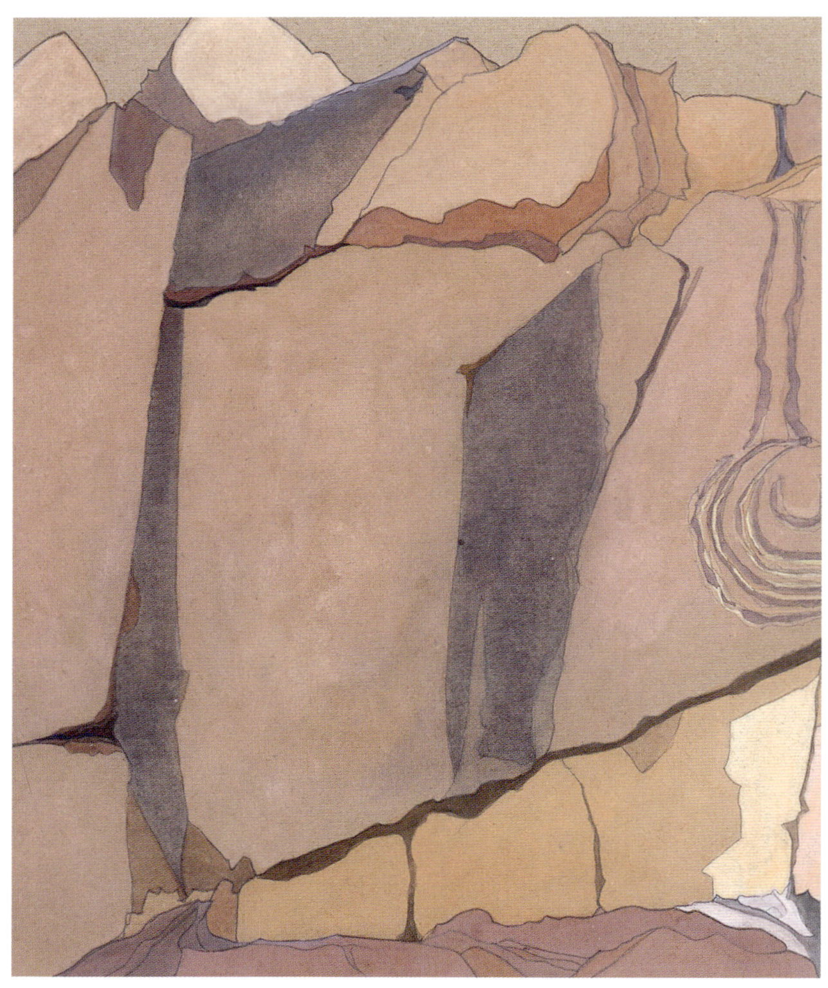
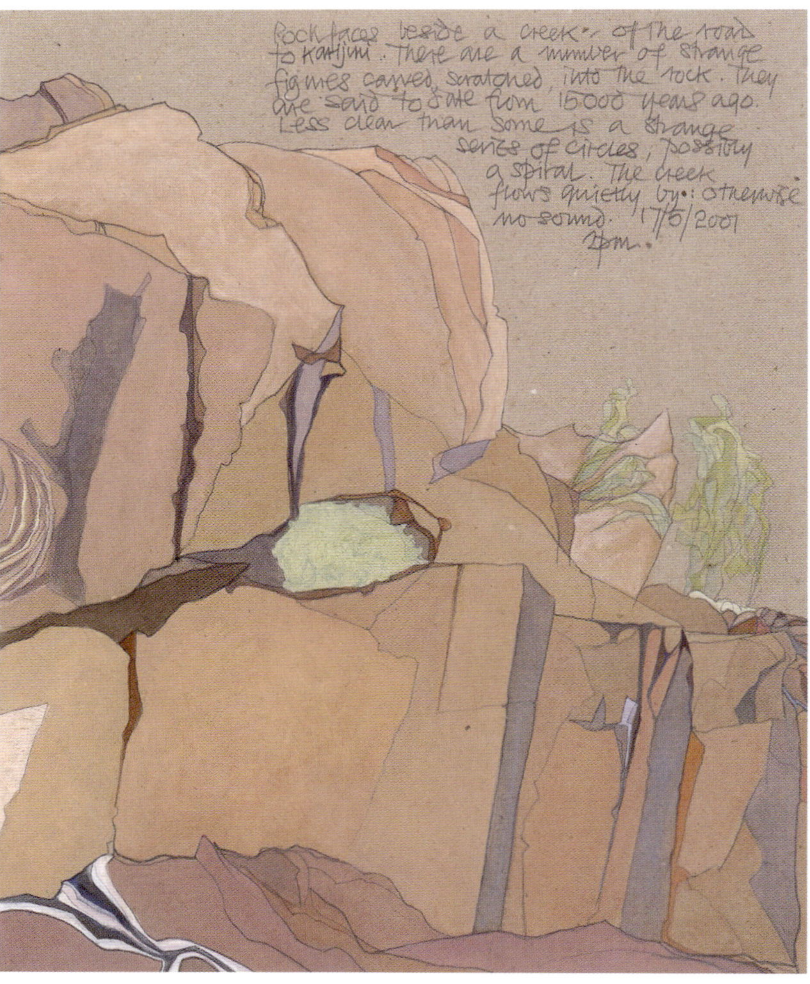
Rock faces beside a creek: of the road
to Karijini. There are a number of strange
figures carved, scratched, into the rock. They
are said to date from 15000 years ago.
Less clear than some is a strange
series of circles, possibly
a spiral. The creek
flows quietly by: otherwise
no sound. 17/5/2001
2pm.

ABOVE
*Road to Karijini, Pilbara,* 2005

RIGHT
*Spa Pool, Hamersley Gorge,* 2004

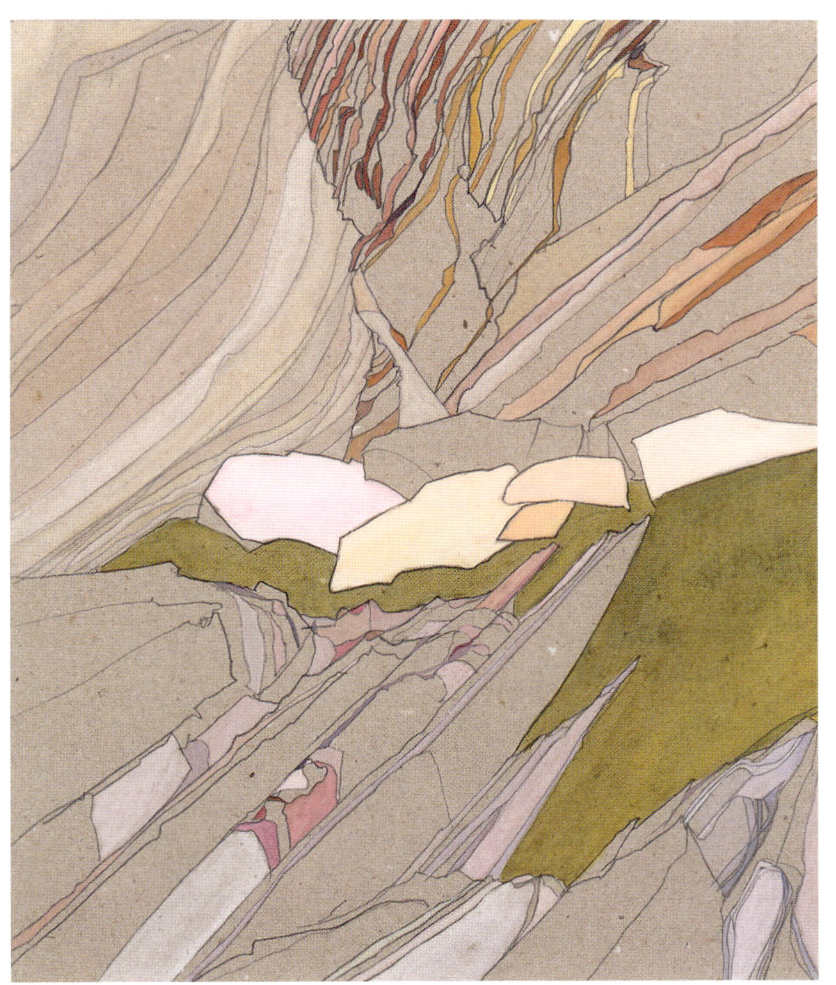
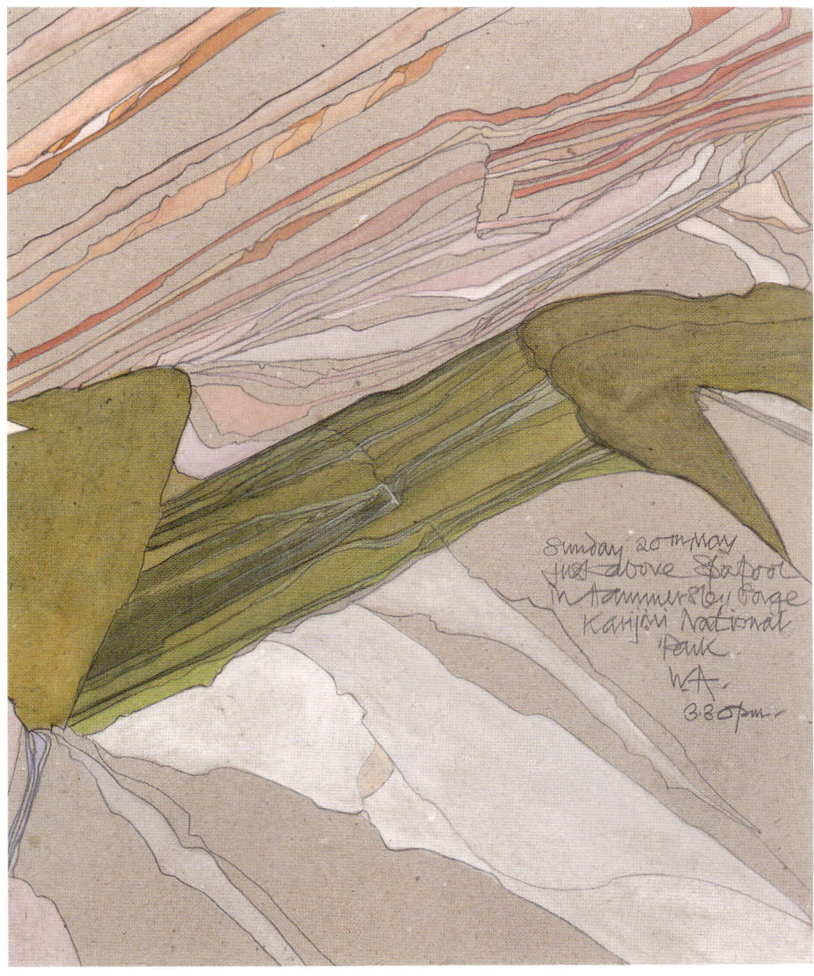
Sunday 20th May
just above Spapool
in Hamersley Gorge
Karijini National
Park.
W.A.
3.30pm

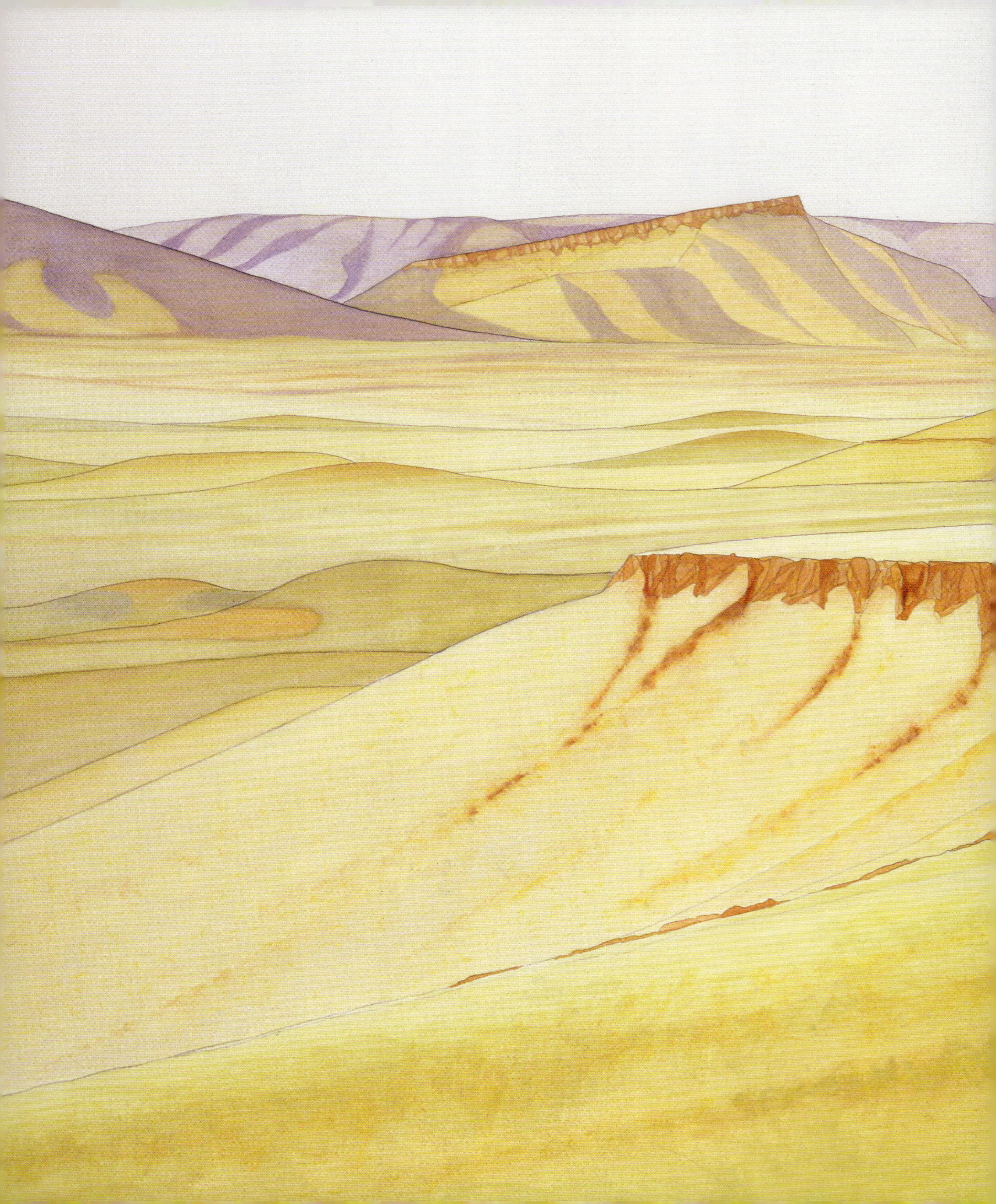

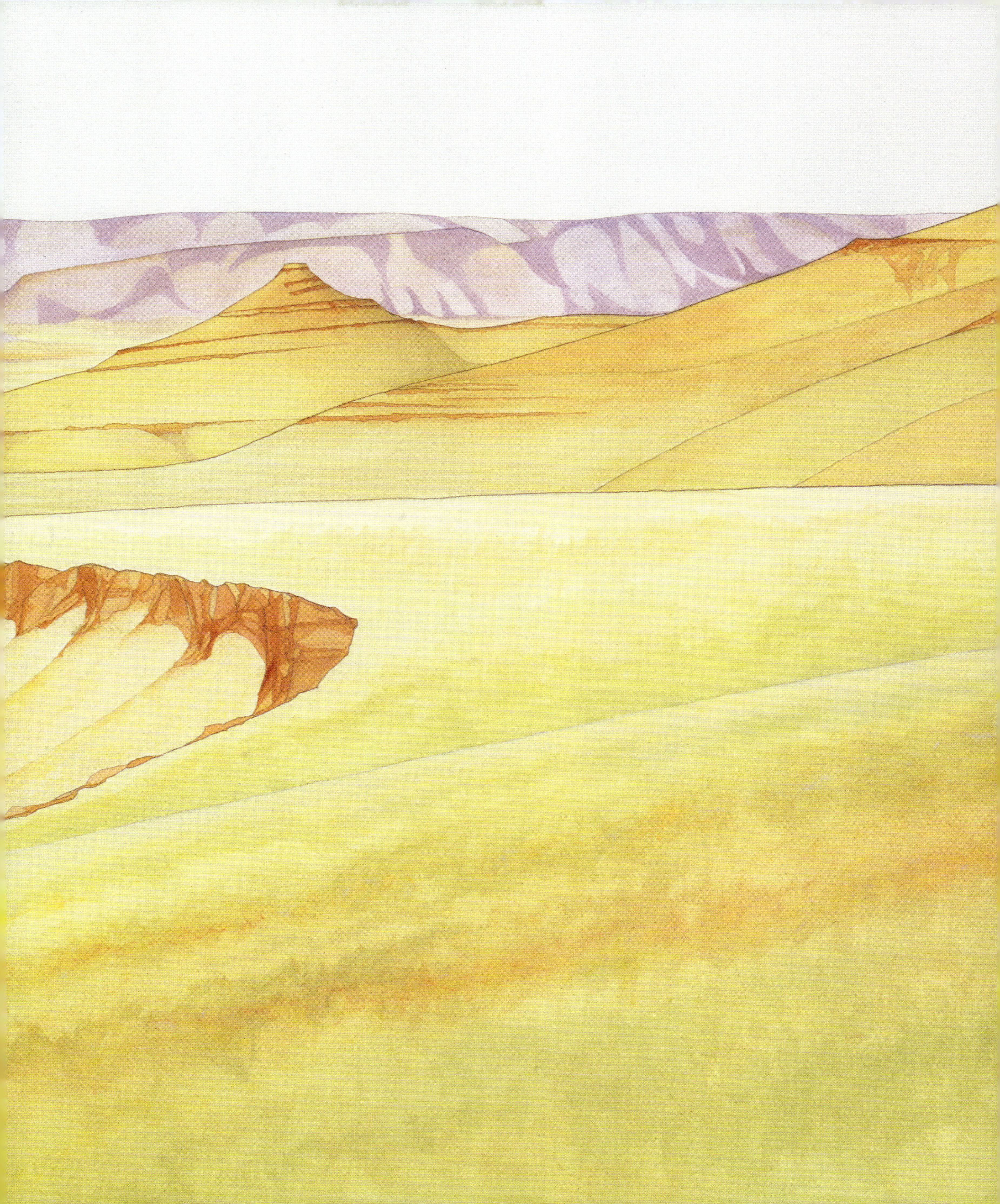

As well as providing the representation of
surface – and in the case of geological maps,
the sub-surface – [maps] are beautiful graphics
in their own right. When I incorporate maps
into works, I have a dual intent – descriptive
and graphic. I adjust the painting to match
the map and vice versa, changing colour
in the map to suit the painting.

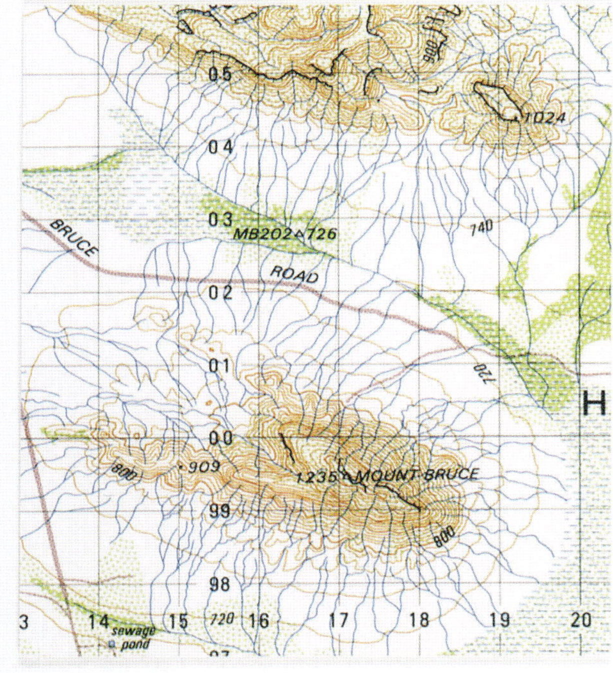

05
04
03
BRUCE
MB202 726
740
ROAD
02
01
720
H
00
800
909
1235 MOUNT BRUCE
800
99
98
3
14 sewage pond
15
720
16
17
18
19
20


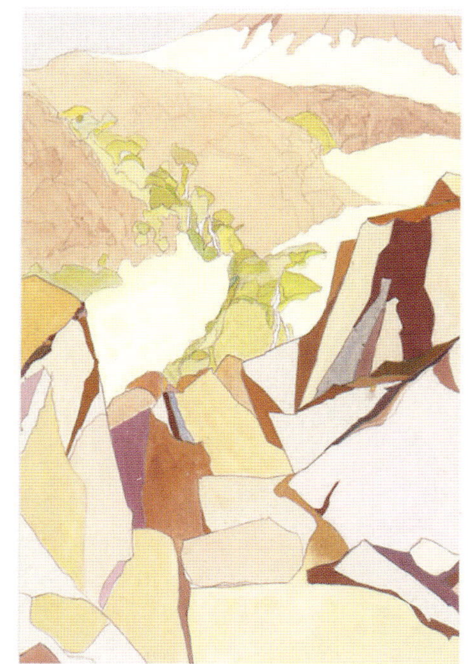

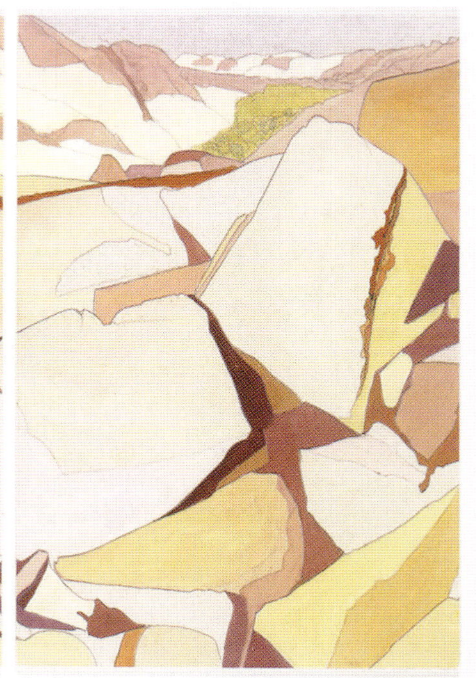

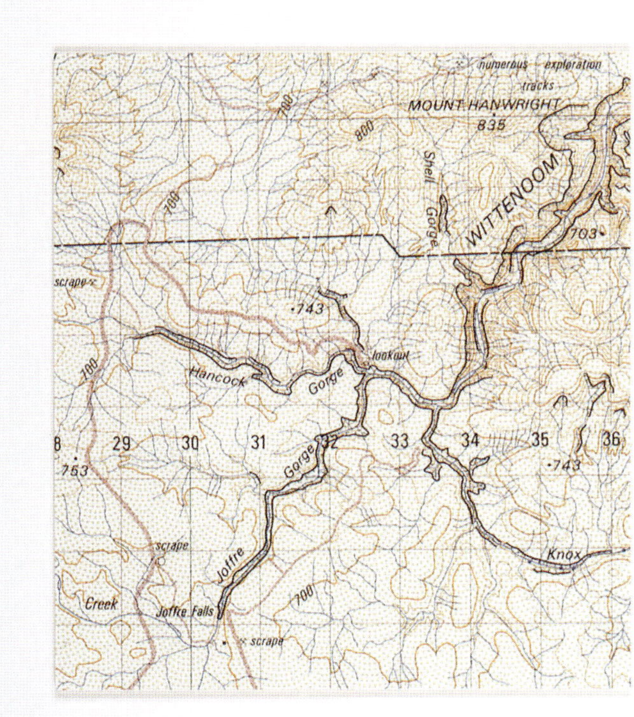

numerous exploration tracks
MOUNT HANWRIGHT
835
700
800
Shell Gorge
WITTENOOM
700
703
scrape
743
Hancock
lookout
Gorge
B
29
30
31
32
33
34
35
36
753
Gorge
743
scrape
Joffre
Knox
Creek
Joffre Falls
700
scrape


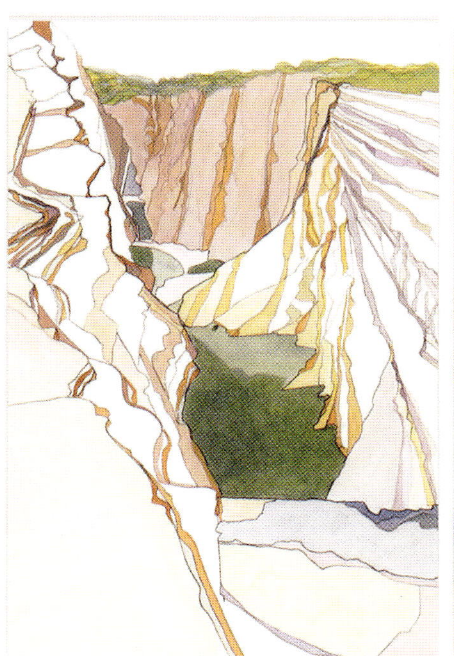

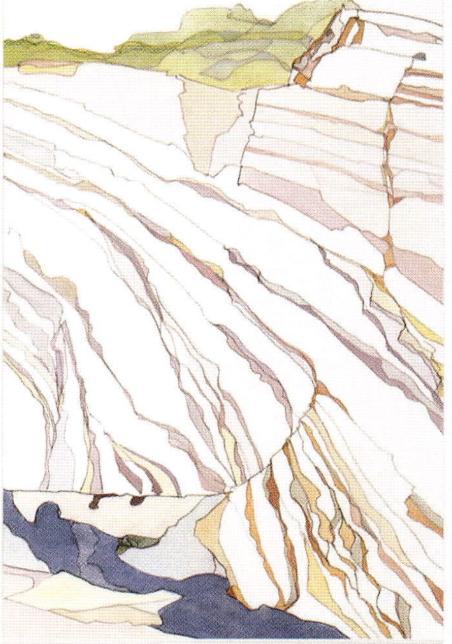

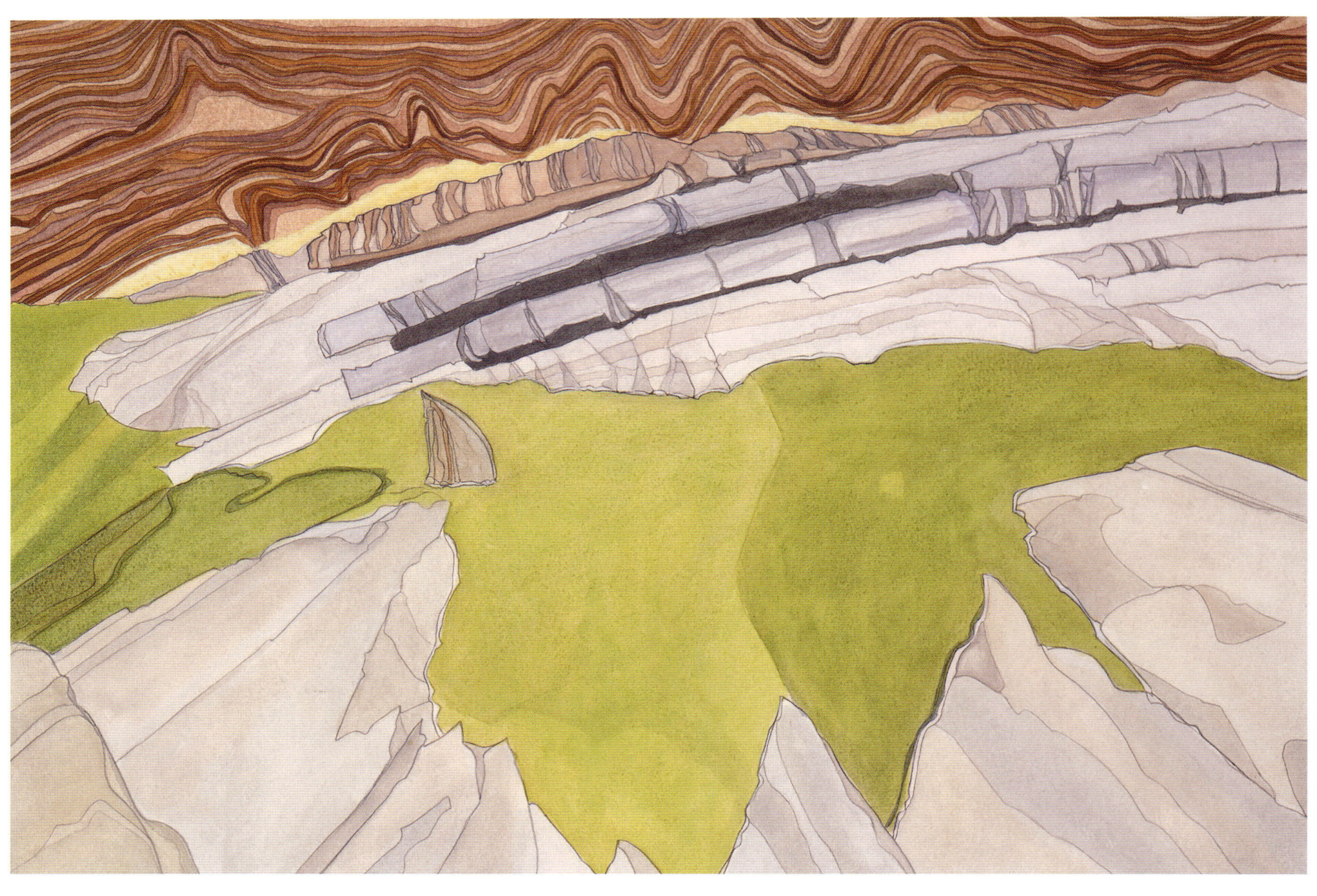

ABOVE
*Weano Gorge, 2005*

RIGHT
*Joffre Gorge, 2001*

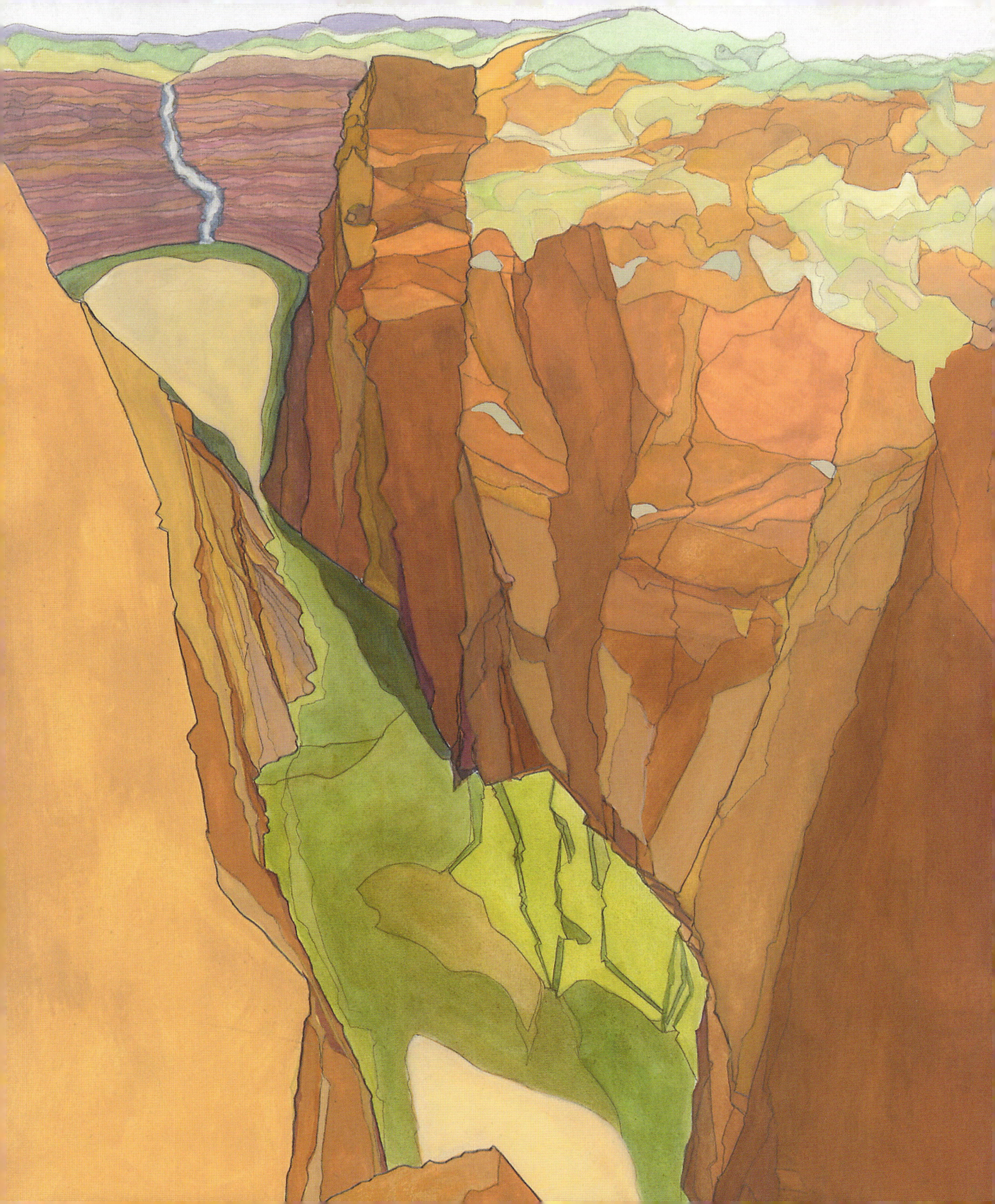

# Cabbage Tree Creek,
# Western Australia

16°19'40.8"S 128°22'39.7"E
-16.328000, 128.377700

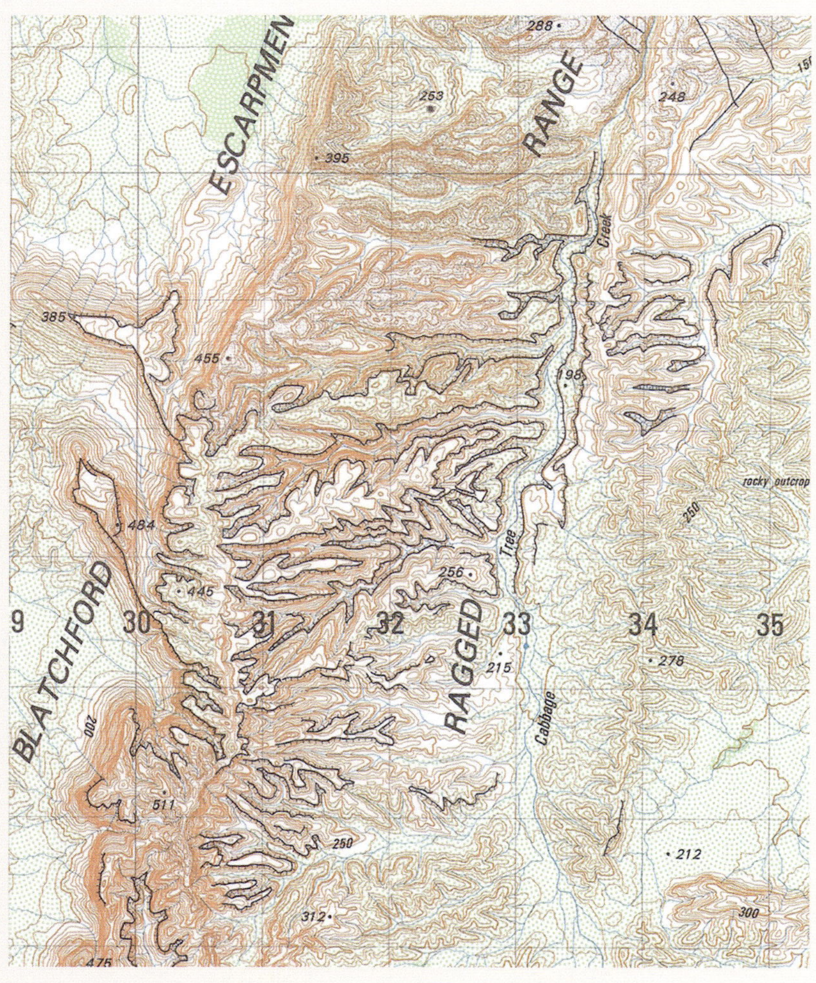

Cabbage Tree Creek, in the Kimberley, is a tributary of the larger Dunham River. We were told about it after we contacted a tourist agency in Halls Creek asking about access to the nearby Bungle Bungle Range. They said this could be organised, and added that they were making arrangements for a group of artists to camp beside a creek close to the Bungle Bungles. The location was remote, but they could arrange our travel, tent, etc. It seemed a good idea, so we said yes.

Thus we found ourselves on the banks of Cabbage Tree Creek with a group of amateur artists, wonderful company. This remote camping trip gave me time to spend quietly beside the creek – and indeed *on* the creek, in a small inflatable – and I could focus on capturing this location over a number of days. From this came a series of works in one of the notebooks that I was then using. These were made by a paper mill in southern France, from recycled paper that gave a particular background to the works. A selection from these notebooks was published as *Patterns in the Landscape* by Thames & Hudson in 1998, the format being the same size as the notebooks – like a facsimile.

I developed these notebook image works in two directions. First, I had tapestries made in Edinburgh by Dovecot Studios. This workshop is the leading maker of tapestries and hand-tufted carpets in the UK. One of these tapestries is illustrated here, on page 26. The second direction was to produce a four-panel screen (see page 23), which was derived entirely from a collage of scans and enlargements from the notebooks. In these, I repeat the image many times to construct an overall effect that emphasises the pictures as an abstract pattern of colour and shape.

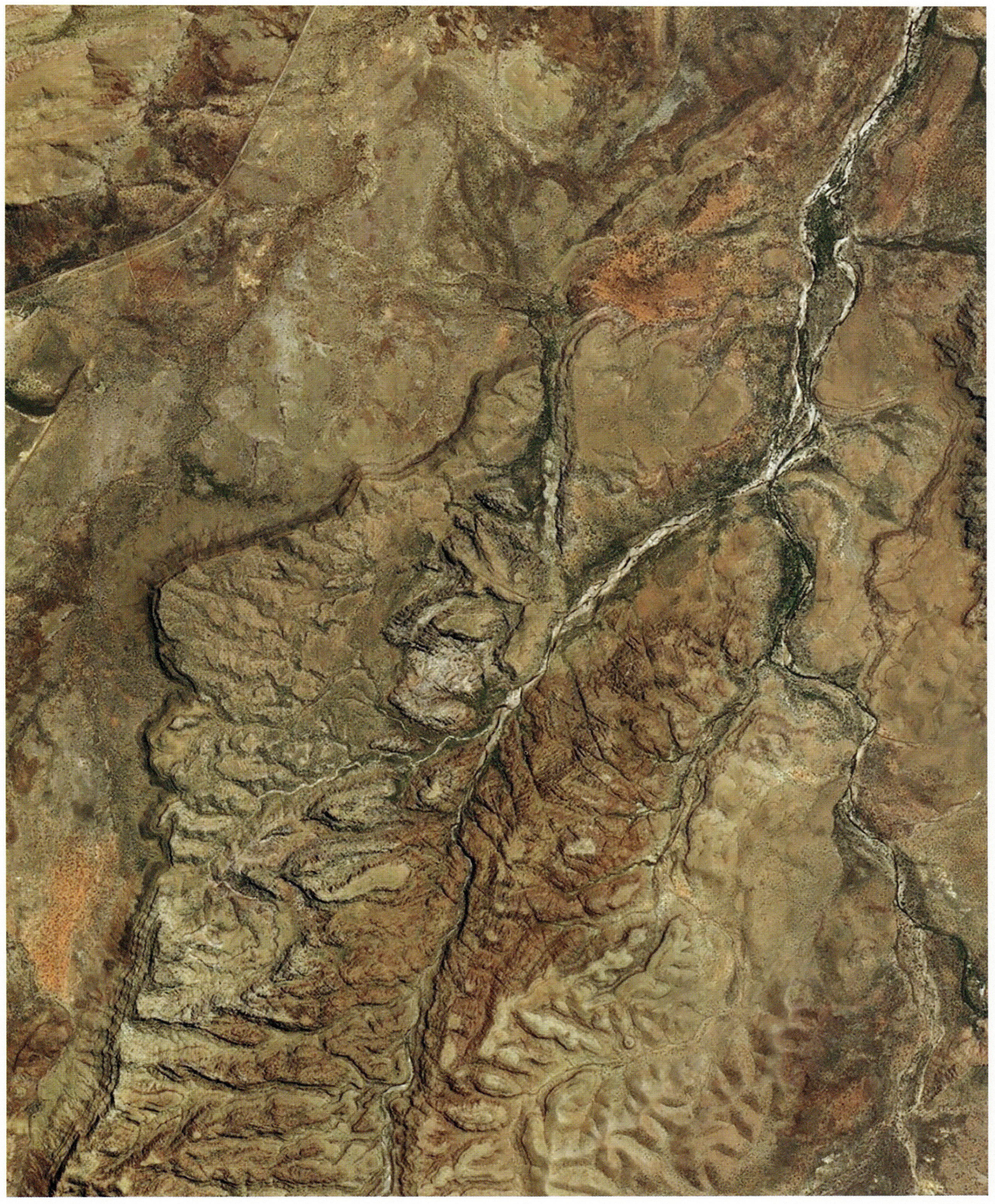

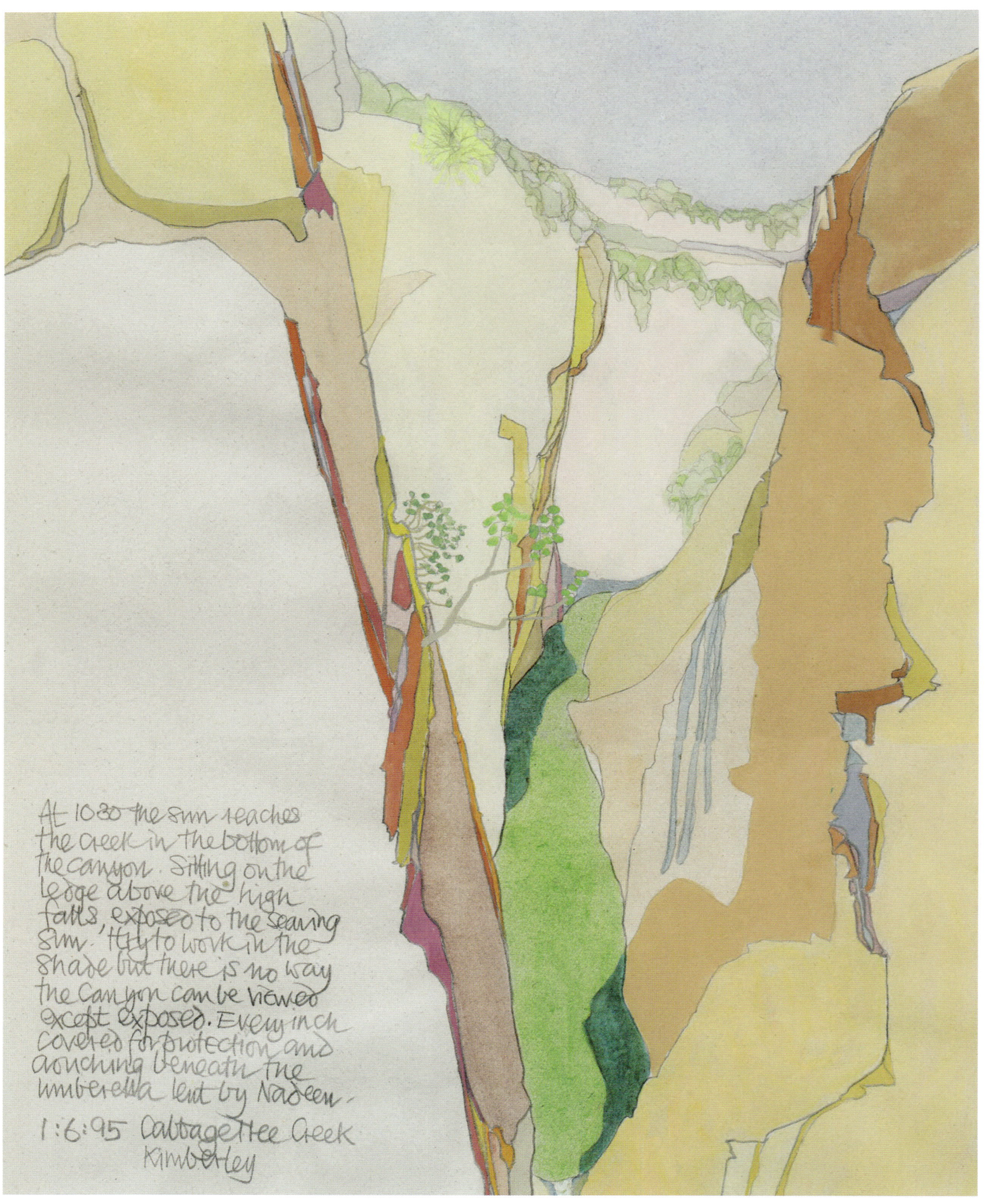

At 10.30 the sun reaches
the creek in the bottom of
the canyon. Sitting on the
ledge above the high
falls, exposed to the searing
sun. I try to work in the
shade but there is no way
the canyon can be viewed
except exposed. Every inch
covered for protection and
crouching beneath the
umberella lent by Nadeen.
1:6:95 Cabbage Tree Creek
Kimberley

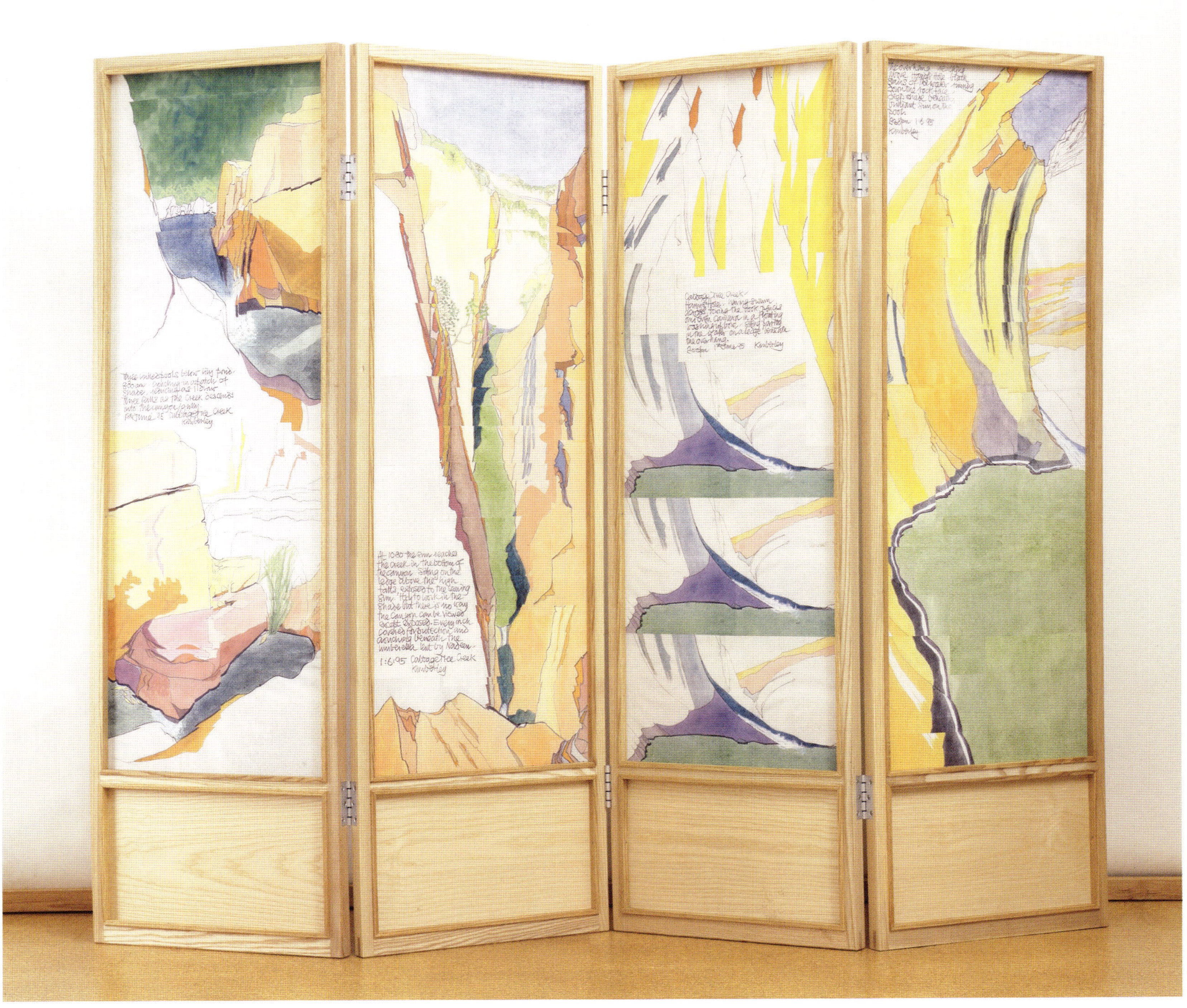



LEFT
*Cabbage Tree Creek,*
1 June 1995

ABOVE
*Four Days at Cabbage Tree Creek,*
1995

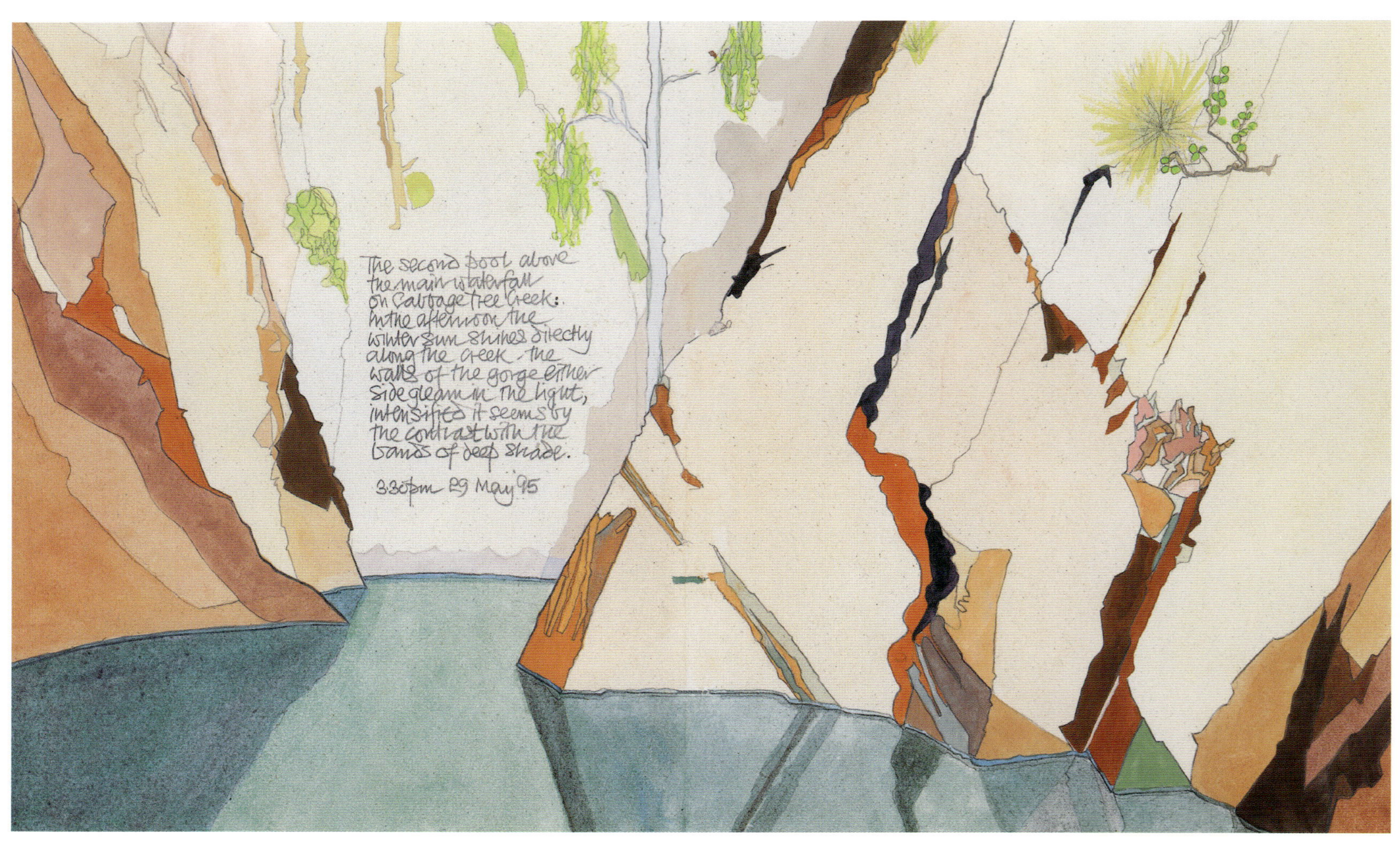


**ABOVE**
*Cabbage Tree Creek,*
29 May 1995

**RIGHT**
*Cabbage Tree Creek,*
2 May 1995

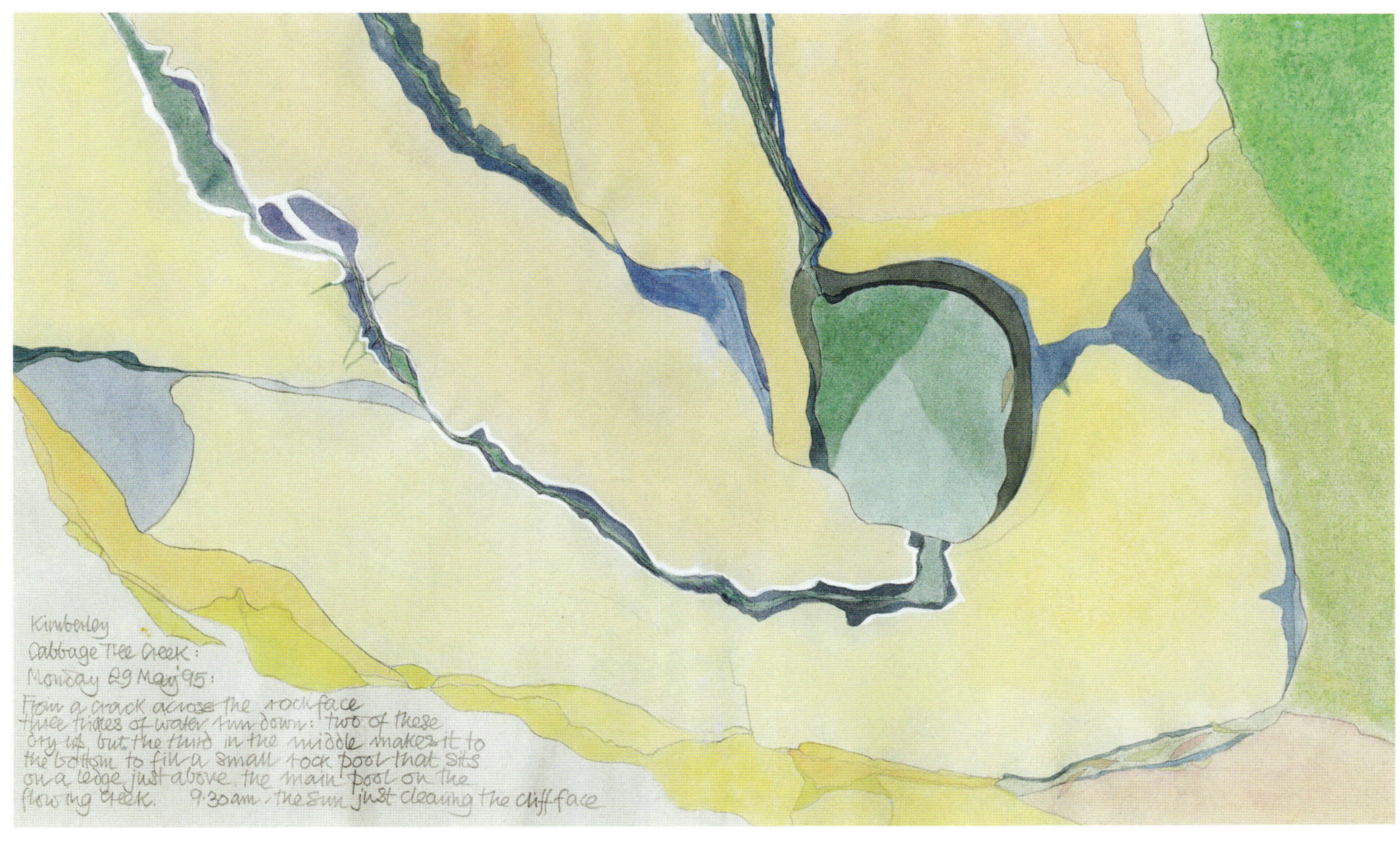

Kimberley
Cabbage Tree Creek:
Monday 29 May '95:
From a crack across the rockface
three trickles of water run down: two of these
dry up, but the third in the middle makes it to
the bottom to fill a small rock pool that sits
on a ledge just above the main pool on the
flowing creek.    9.30am. the sun just clearing the cliff-face

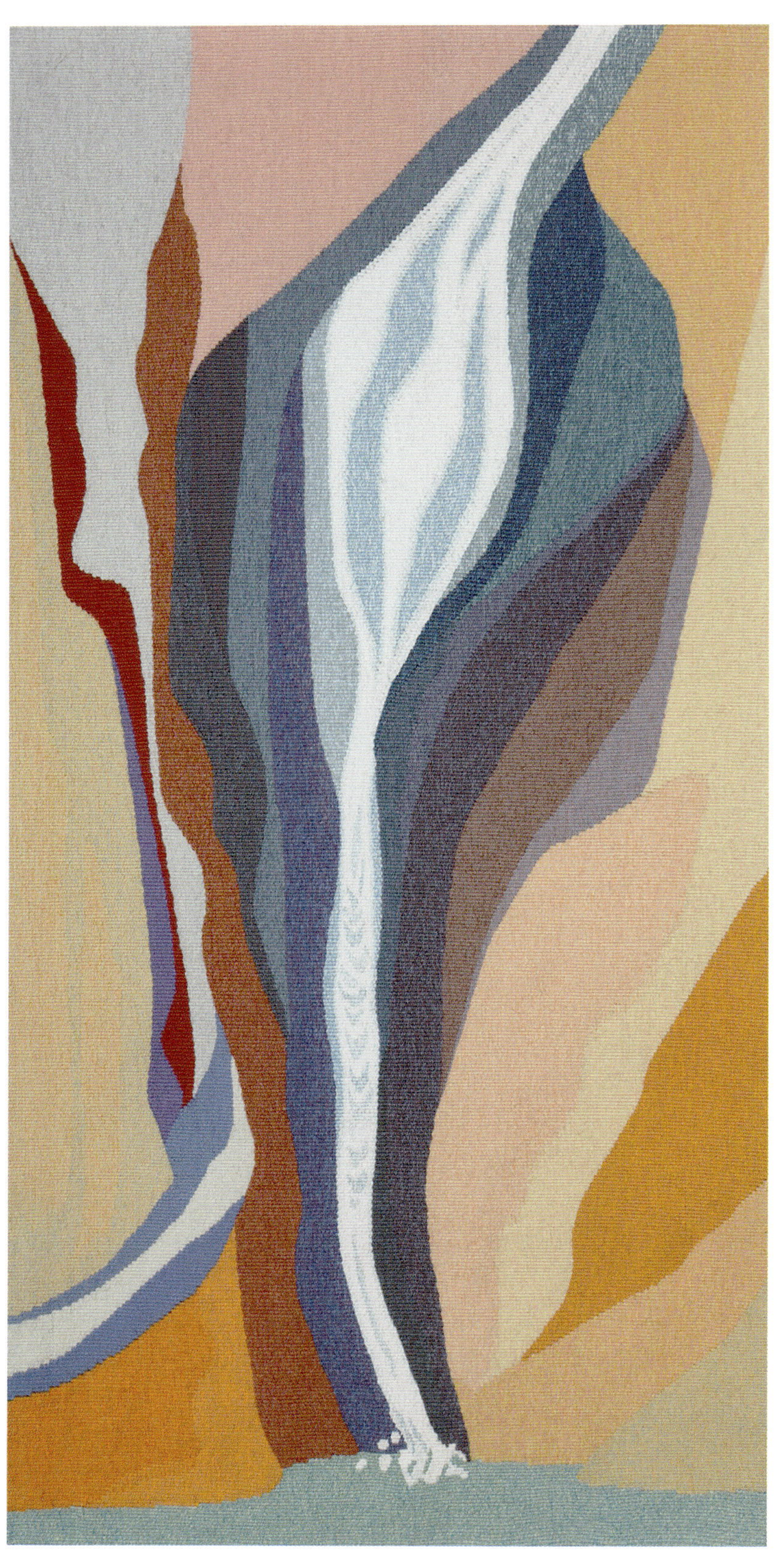

ABOVE
*Cabbage Tree Creek I*, 1995

RIGHT
*Mid Pool on Cabbage Tree Creek,*
1996

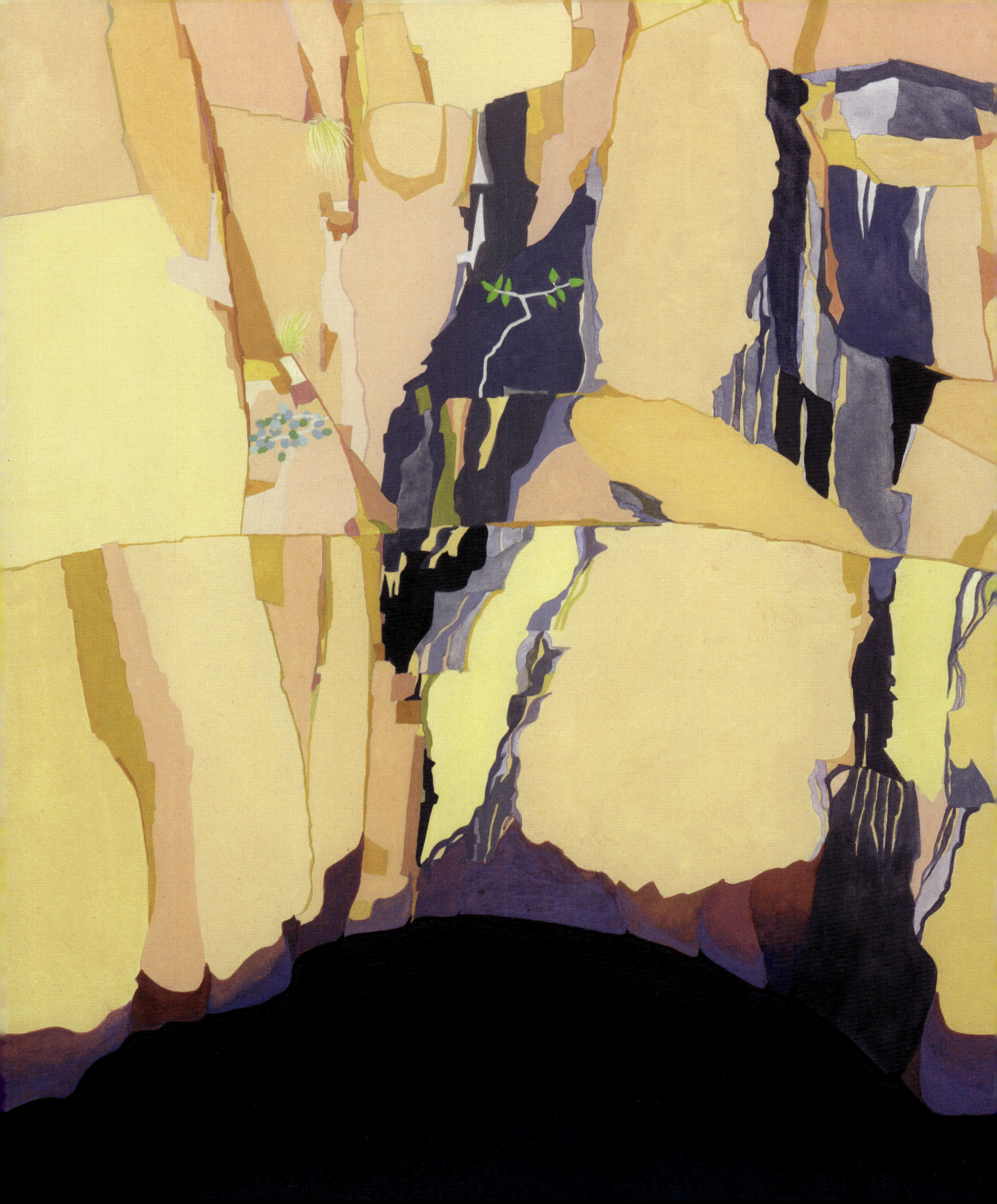

# Bungle Bungle Range / Billingjal, Western Australia

17°22'53.0"S 128°25'20.2"E
-17.381388, 128.422274

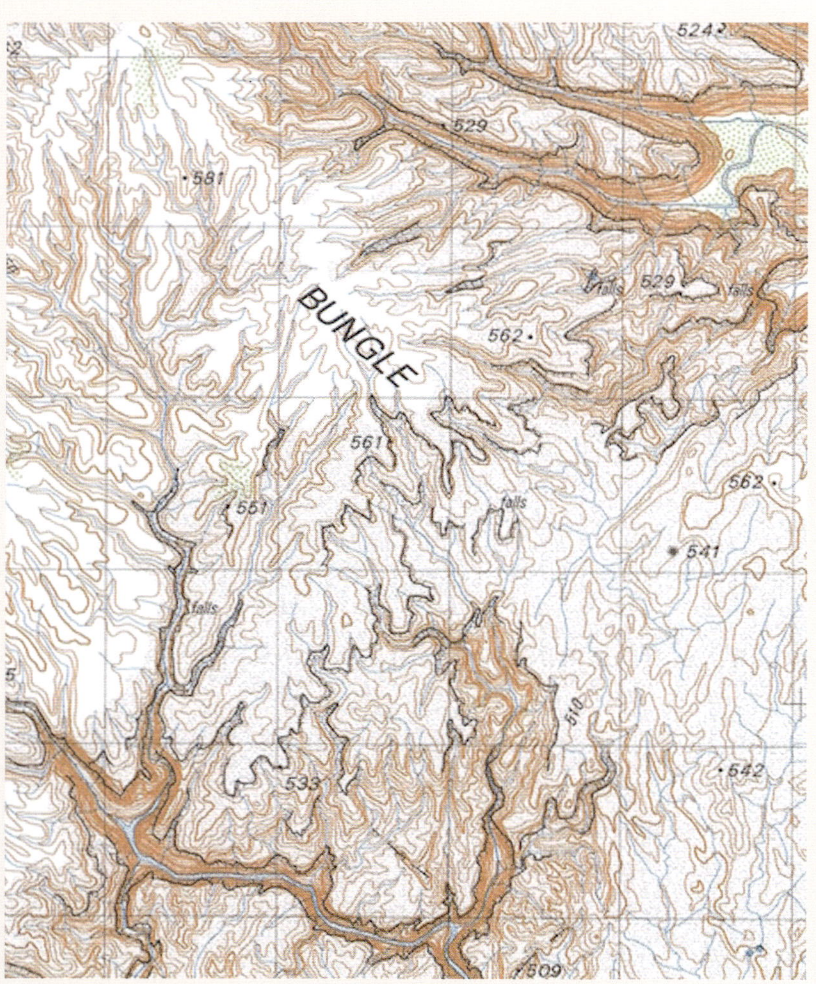


For years I had wanted to visit the Bungle Bungles, in the Kimberley region's Purnululu National Park. It looked spectacular in photographs, and indeed it is, to my mind only matched in Australia by Uluru and Kata Tjuta in the Northern Territory. Purnululu is a transliteration of the Djaru word for the area, Bullmanlulu. The region's Traditional Custodians, the Karjaganujaru, call the Bungle Bungle formation Billingjal, which roughly translates as 'sand falling away'. Access is difficult. I managed this visit in the winter of 1995, connected to our camping on Cabbage Tree Creek (page 20). We arranged to get to the park by four-wheel drive vehicle, and from there to be met by a helicopter to fly over the formations.

The magic of the Bungle Bungles comes both from the unique grouping of the dome-shaped rocks and from the striped appearance of the geological strata, the result of alternating layers of clay-rich and iron-rich sandstone. The high moisture content of the clay-rich layers supports the growth of cyanobacteria – single-cell organisms that give these bands a grey hue. Sandstone layers that are too dry for the bacteria to survive are coloured red by their coating of iron oxide. What results is a striped effect of grey and red bands on the rock face.

I show this in a large pastel that is based on a photograph I took while on the helicopter flight, shown on page 32. We flew without doors to get the clearest views. Scary. The banding of the rock strangely reminded me of limestone strata at the other end of the world, in Assynt in the far north-west of Scotland. Near the rocks are a series of baobab trees, each standing in isolation.

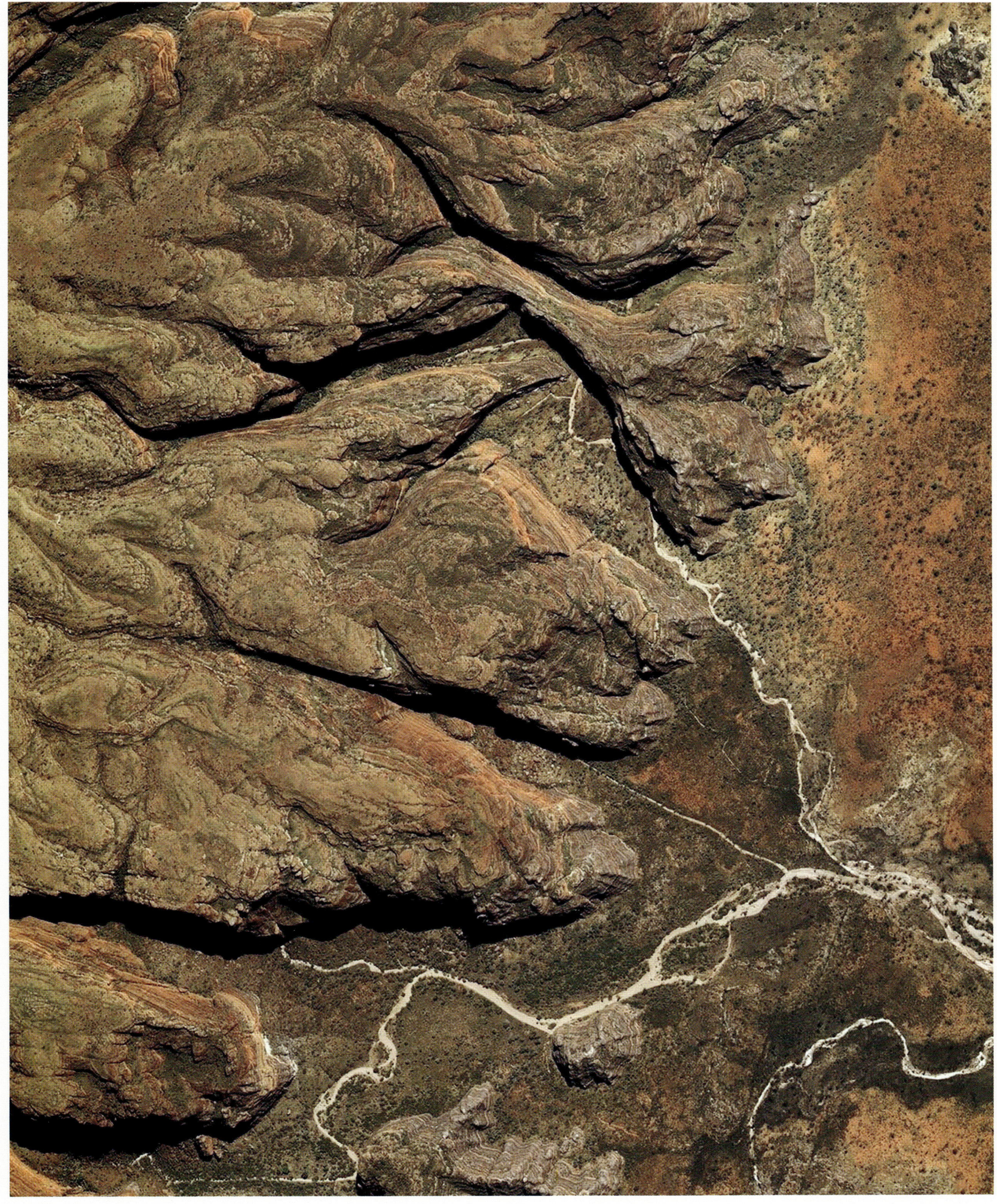

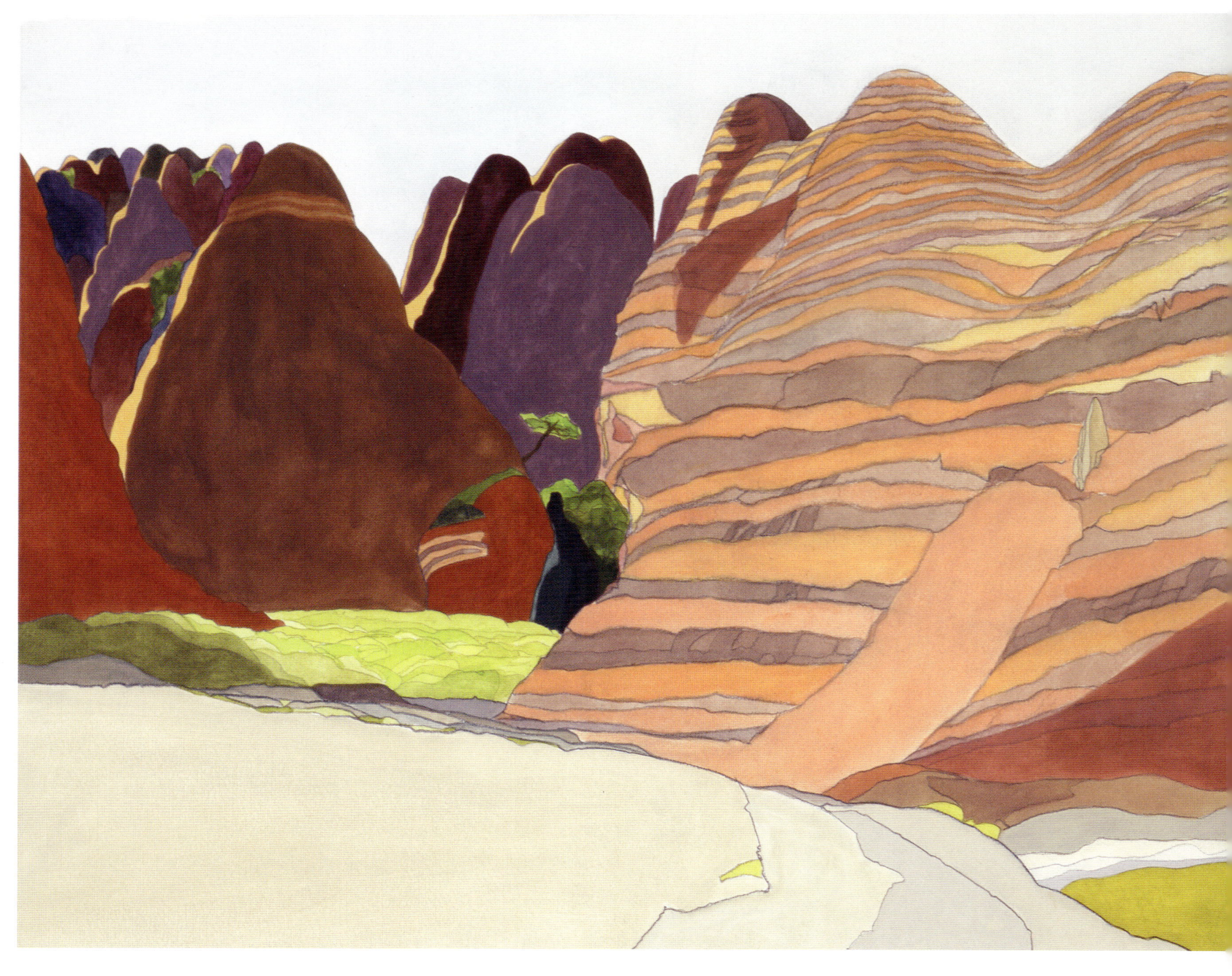

*Entrance to Cathedral Gorge,*
*Bungle Bungle,* 1996

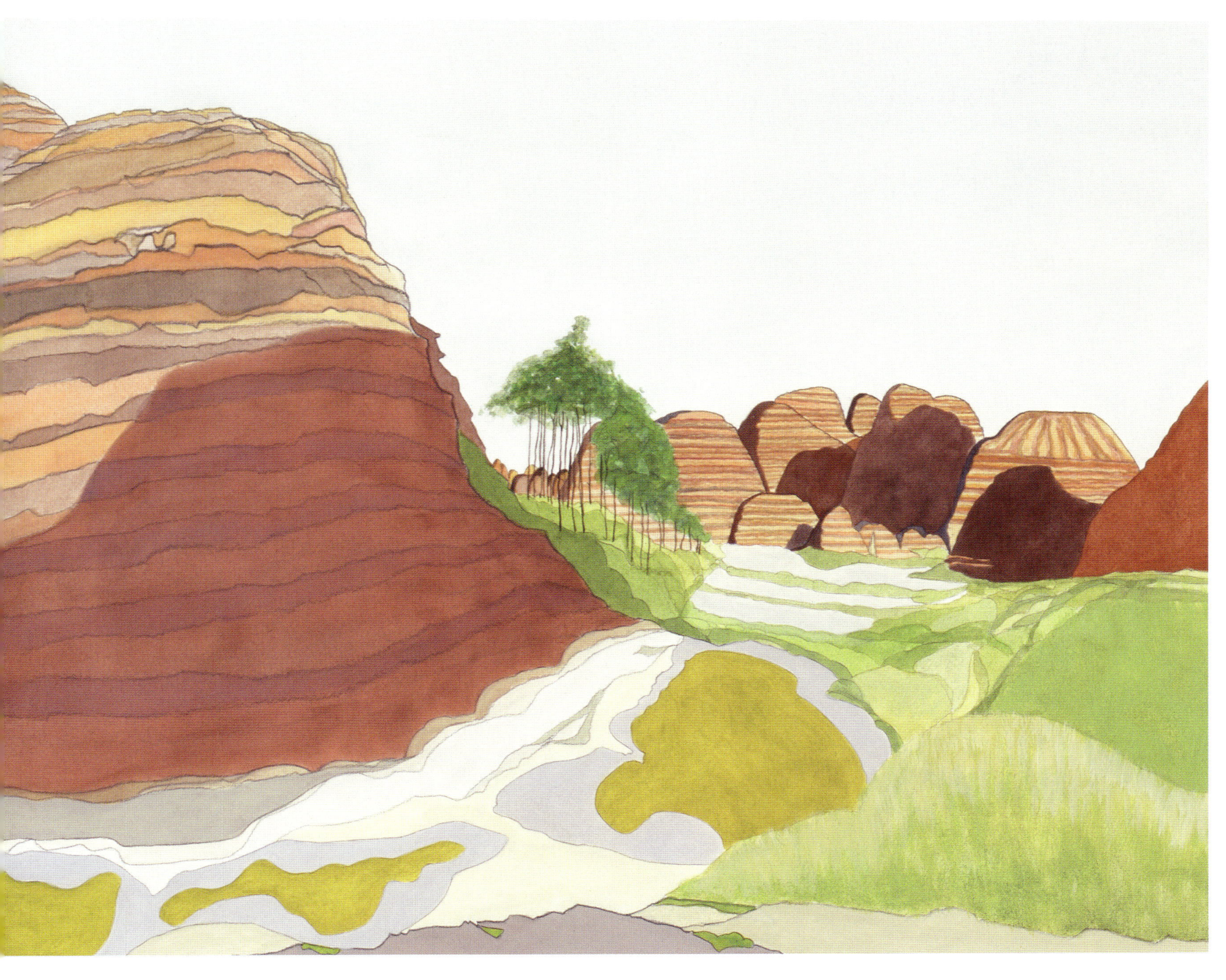

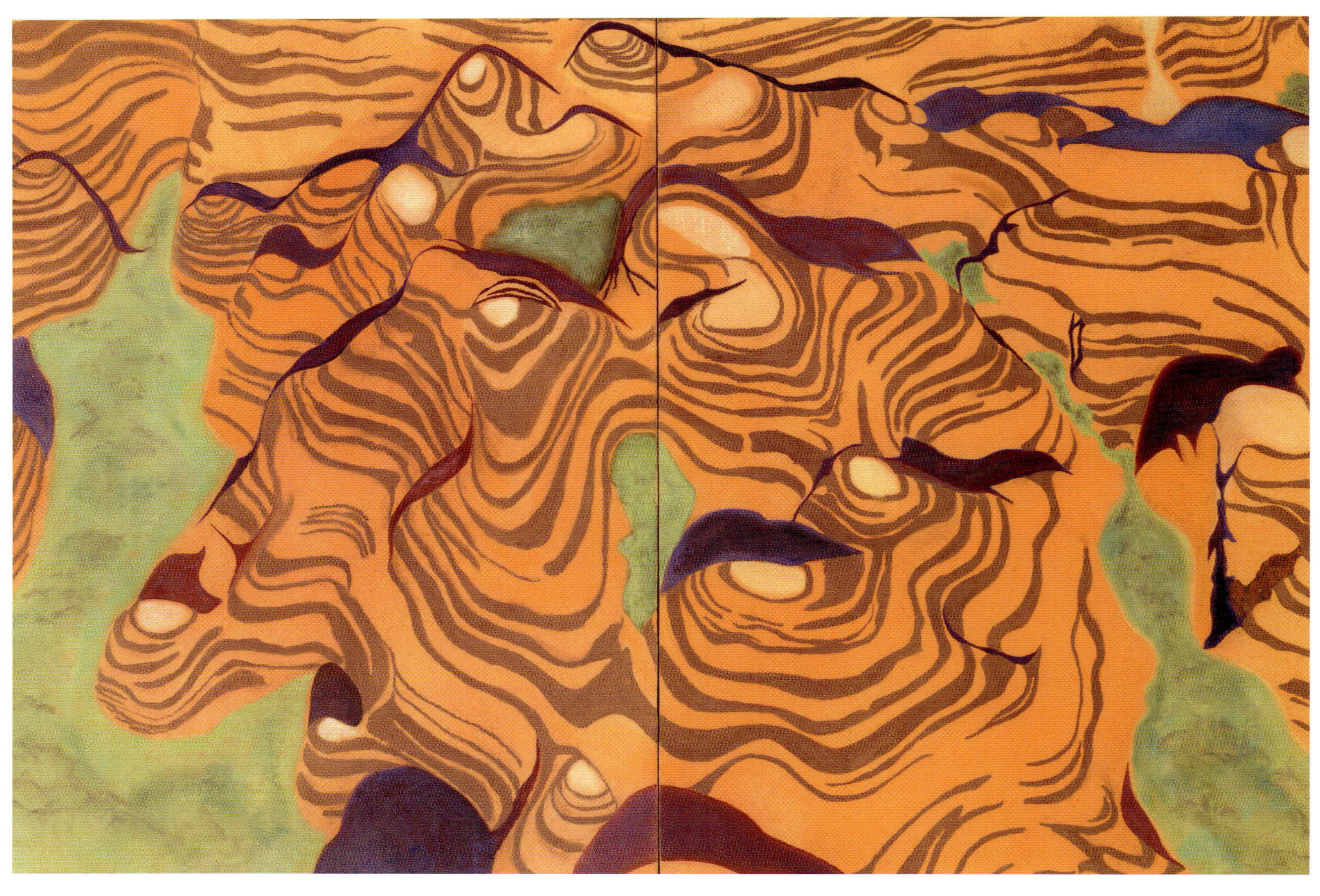

**ABOVE**
*Bungle Bungle*, 1995

**RIGHT**
*Piccaninny Creek*, 1996

**FOLLOWING SPREAD**
*Bungle Bungle*, 5 June 1995

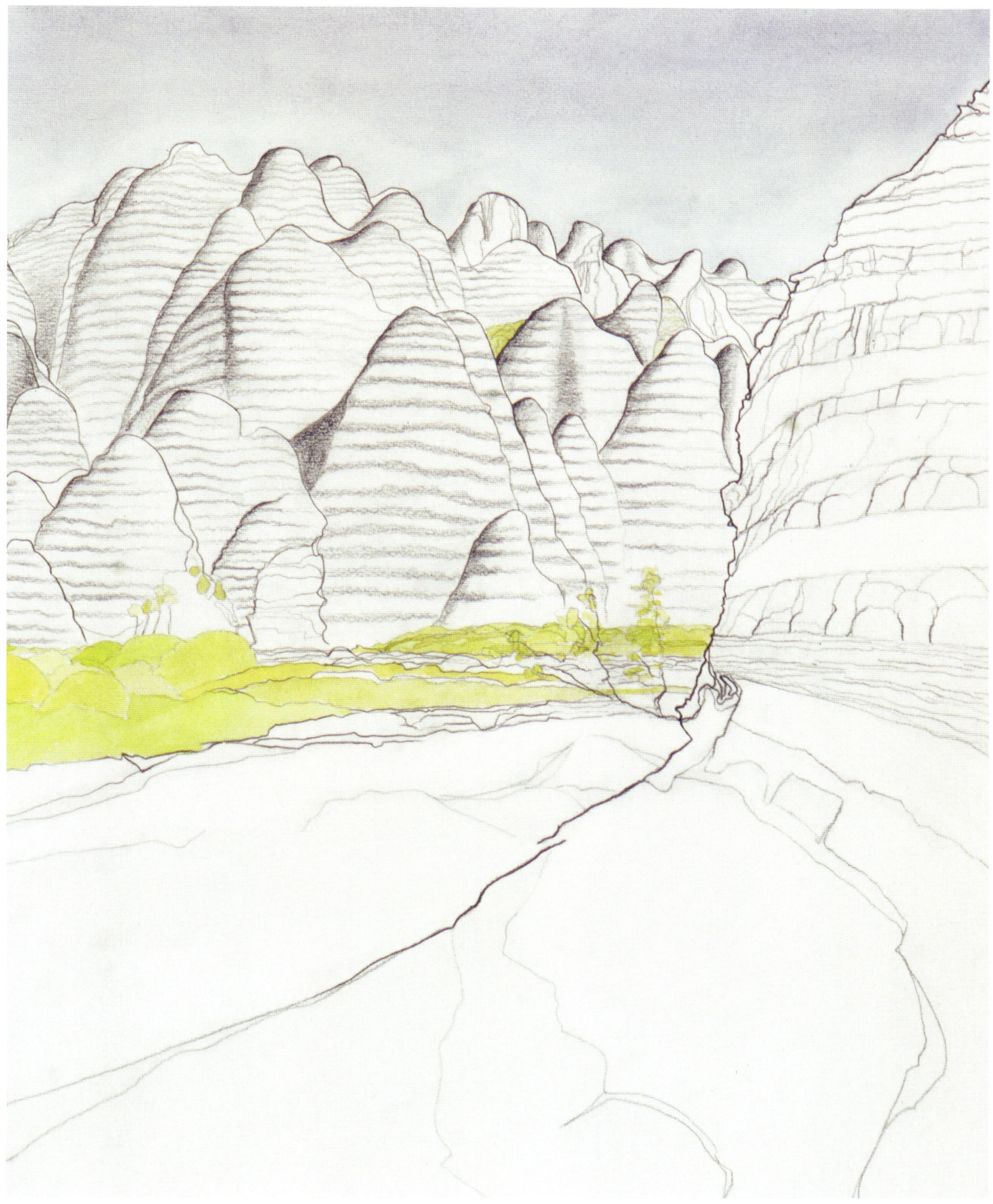

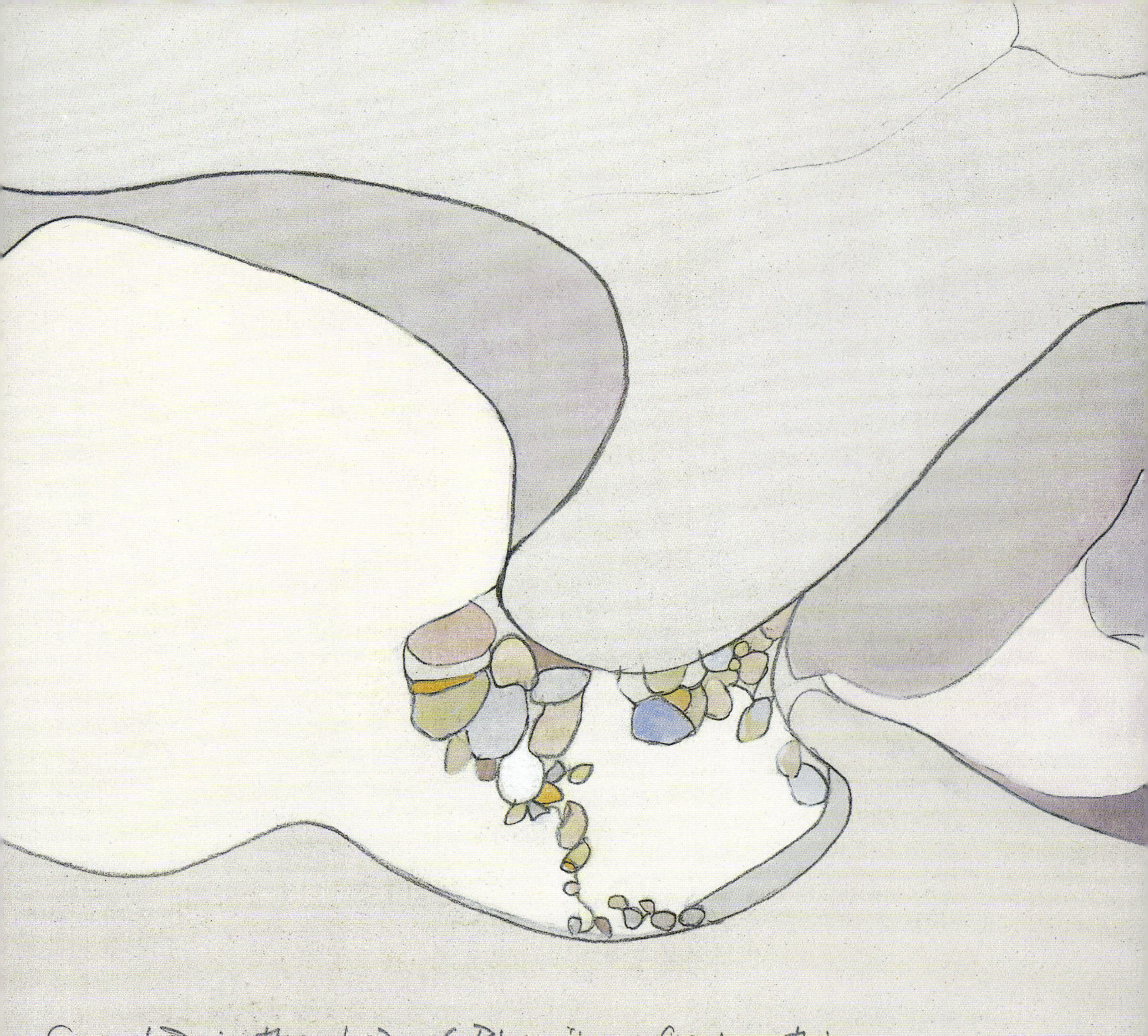

Crouched in the bed of Piccaninny Creek – this
provides partial shade from the midday sun but no
relief against the blowing dust and THE FLIES –
the creek bed is a giant sculpture of sand stone, pale
against the contrasting ochre and purple grey of the
beehive domes. The pebbles have been washed down
from the north of the massif where the rock is a
conglomorate,
Noon : 5th June '95                    Bungle Bungle                    Kimberley

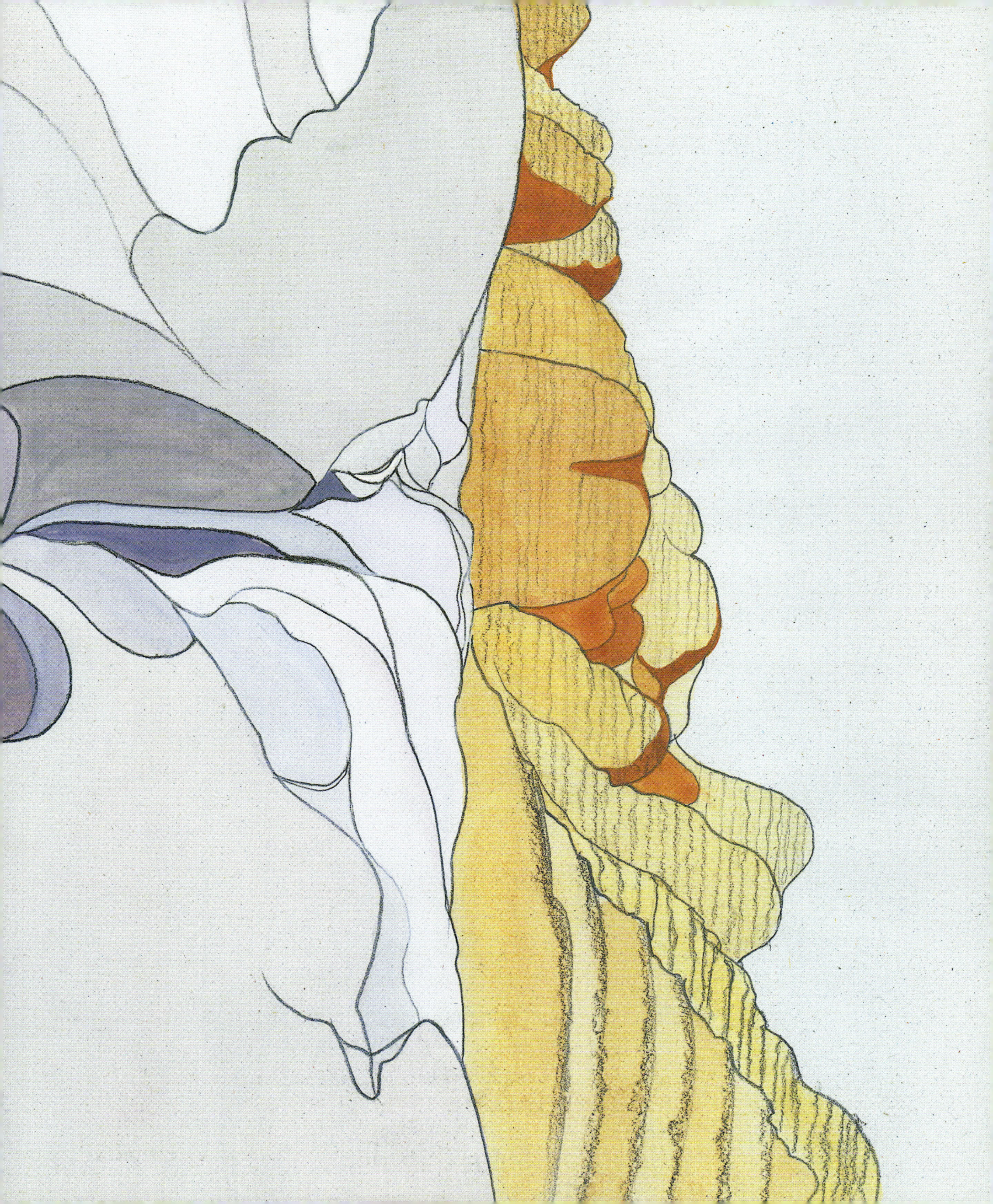

# Train across the Nullarbor Plain, South Australia to Western Australia

**30°36'49.7"S 130°24'46.7"E**
**-30.613800, 130.412969**

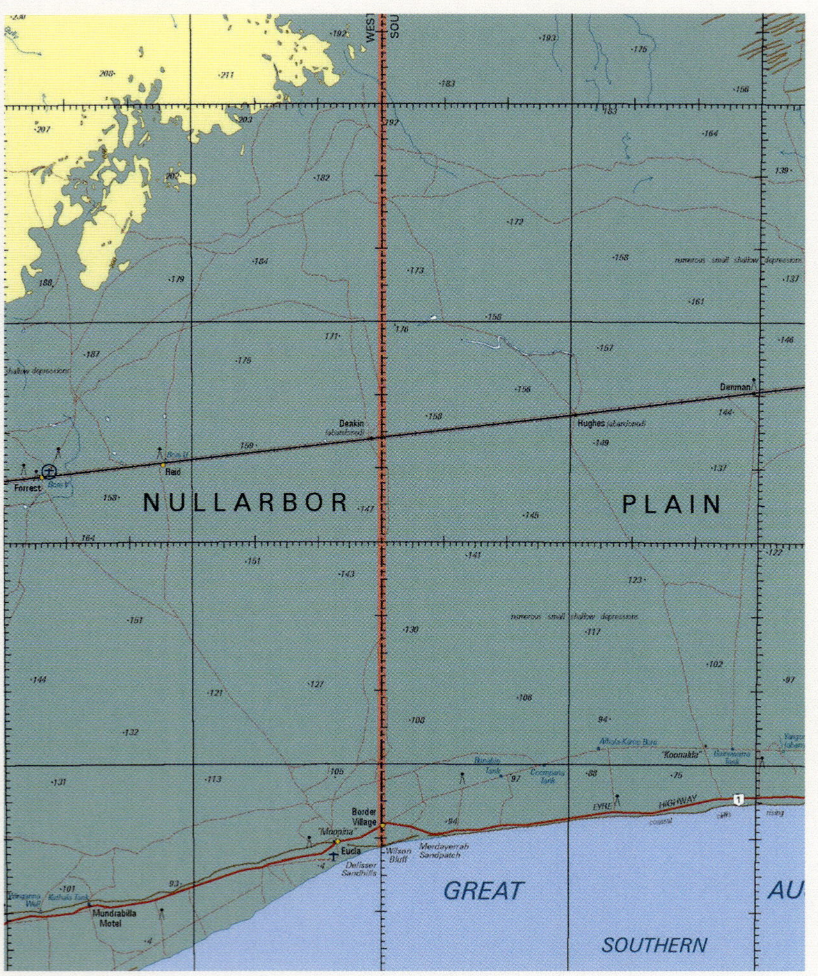

In 2014, Psiche and I took the Indian Pacific train from Adelaide to Perth. We left Adelaide at 6.40 pm on 9 January and arrived in Perth on 11 January at 9.10 am – two nights and one day of travel. Confusingly, during the journey the train passes through different time zones. In summer, Perth is two-and-a-half hours behind Adelaide. Instead of changing clocks as we crossed zones, we all operated on 'train time' throughout, which was set an hour after Adelaide time.

I stayed up much of the first night watching the landscape in the moonlight from my cabin window. Looking out at some stage, I saw a bright light in the night. But there was no sign of human habitation. What was it? Only later did I realise that it was the headlights of the huge engines pulling us, visible because of the curve in the track. At dawn we still had trees around us, but we soon reached the start of the empty Nullarbor Plain. All day I watched as we crossed the plain. The railway line is dead straight for hundreds of kilometres, the longest straight stretch in the world. You pass vestiges of past settlements built only for the construction of the railway and largely deserted afterwards. Finally, at the other side of the plain, trees reappear. When we arrived in Perth the following morning, the temperature was well over 40 °C, a shock after the air conditioning of the train.

All the works from this train journey were made in my notebook. Clearly, they had to be done very quickly, probably in much less than a minute each. As usual in my way of working, the paint was added back in the studio. I hope that showing a group of these notebook works in the same format as the originals gives a sense of a log of the travel.

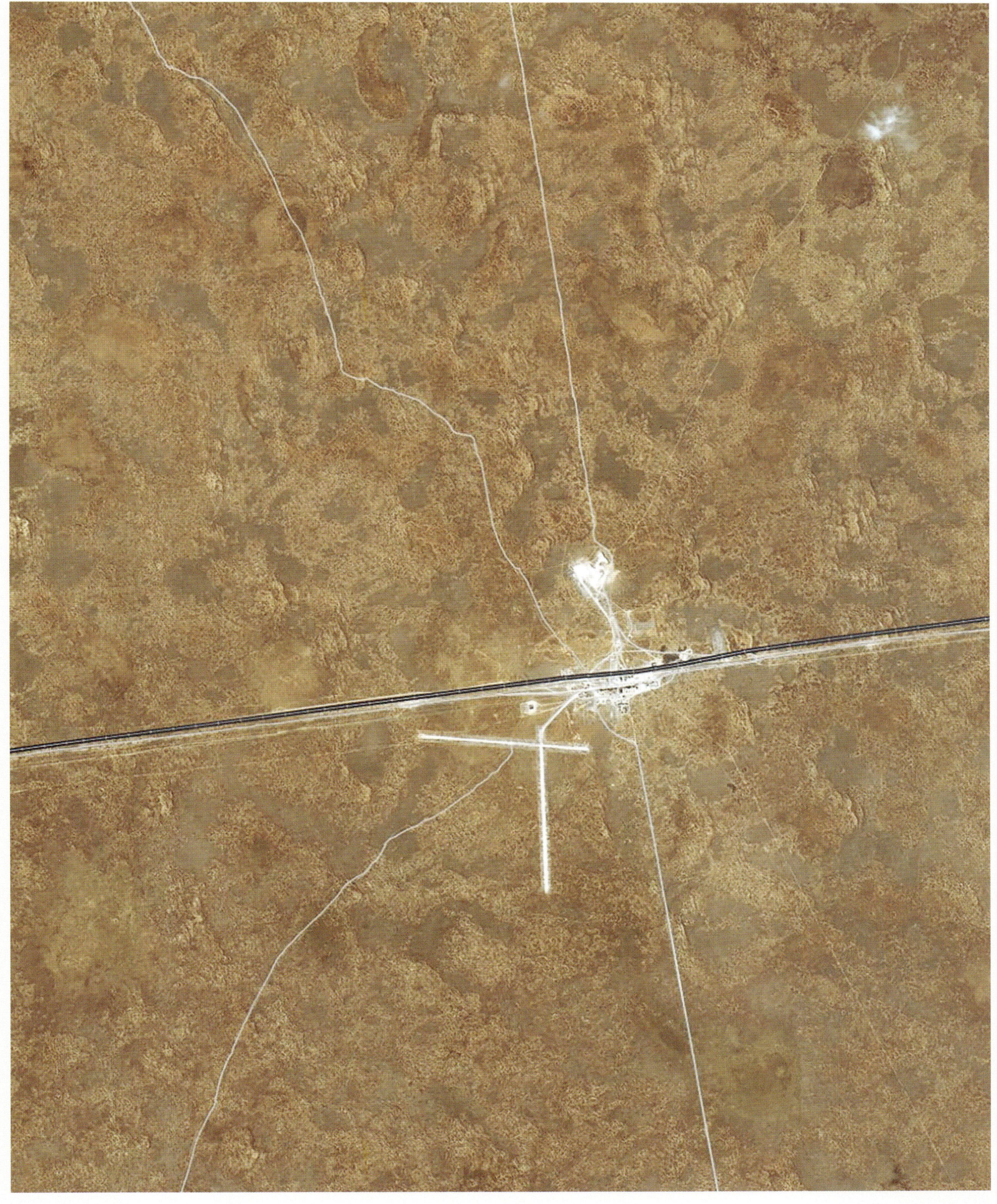

Thursday 9th Jan 2014
We set off on the train from Adelaide to Perth. Leave at 6.40pm.

During the night. I awoke and watched the 3/4 moon as it set. It seemed to dance from side to side of the panoramic window as the train progresses. We must have been going on quite steep curves.

At one stage I saw moving lights. At first I thought they we cars. But later I realised that it was the front of the train as we went on a curve. I saw the beam of the engines lights.

The moon dance became up and down as well as side to side as it approached the horizon. Sometimes dipping out of sight then re appearing. This went on for what seemed a long time

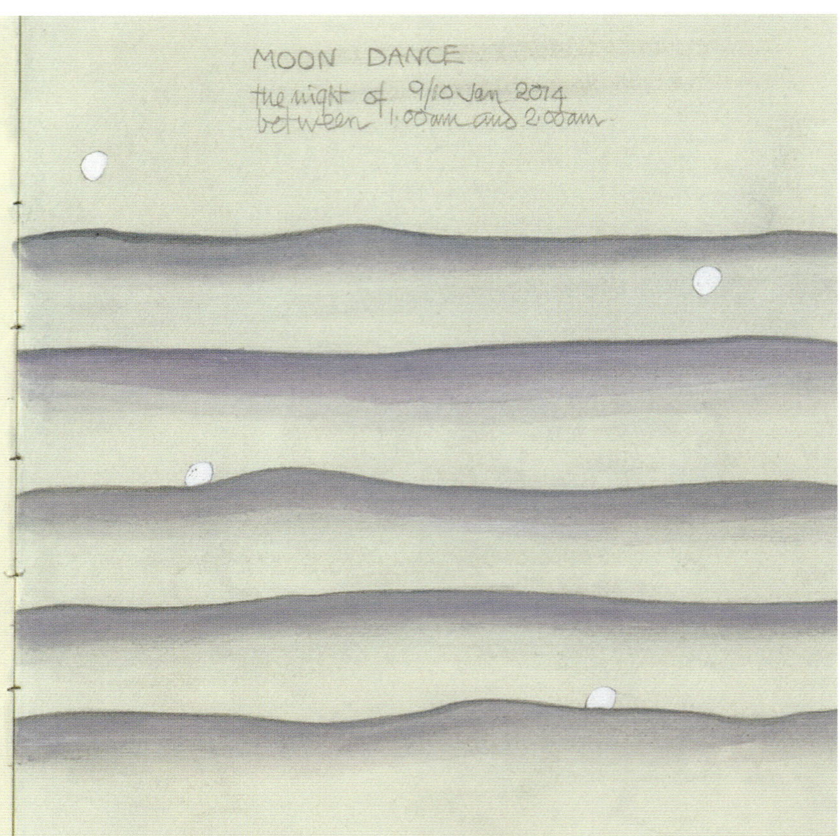


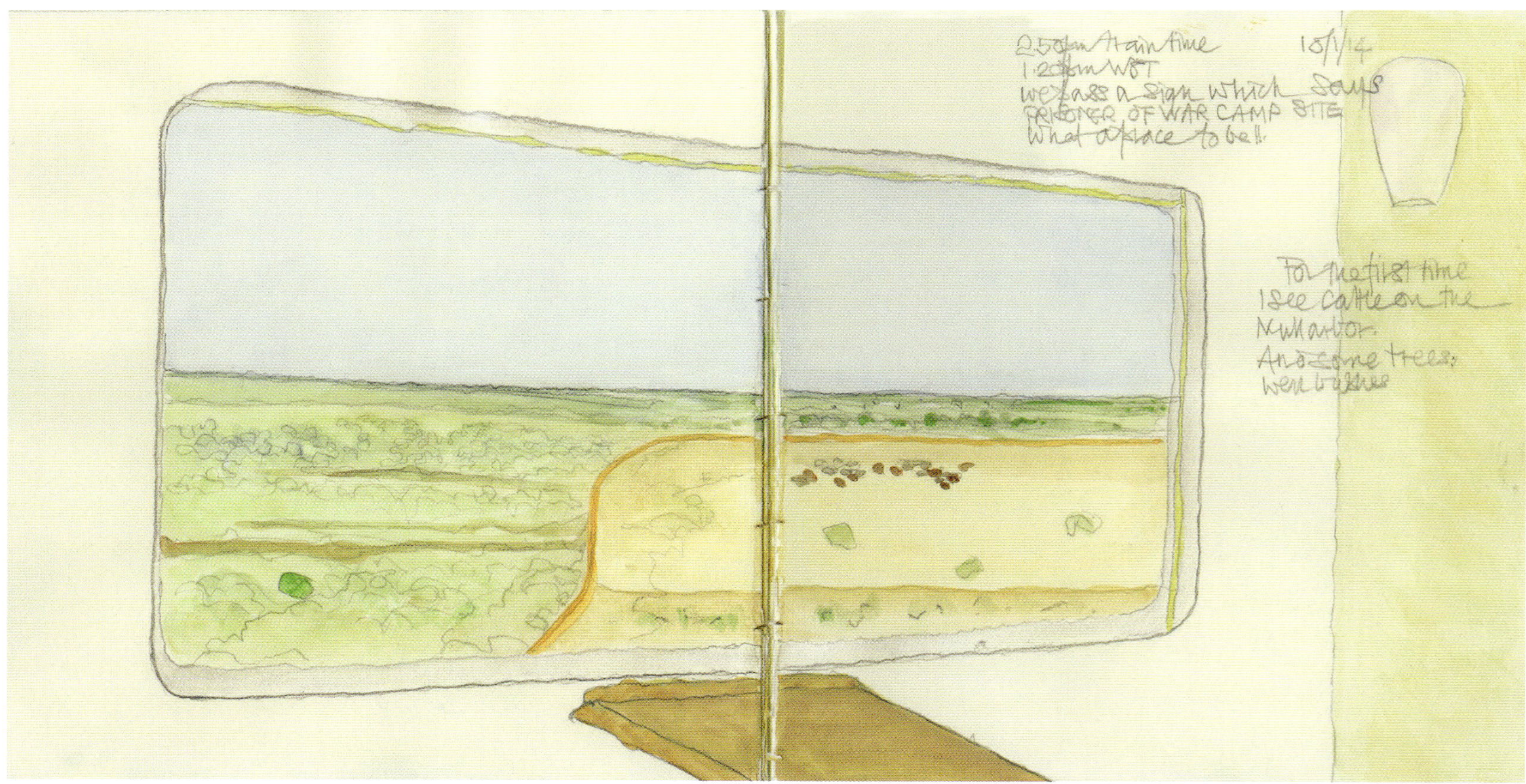


*Crossing the Nullarbor, 1.00–2.00 am,*
9–10 January 2014

*Crossing the Nullarbor, 11.30 am,*
10 January 2014

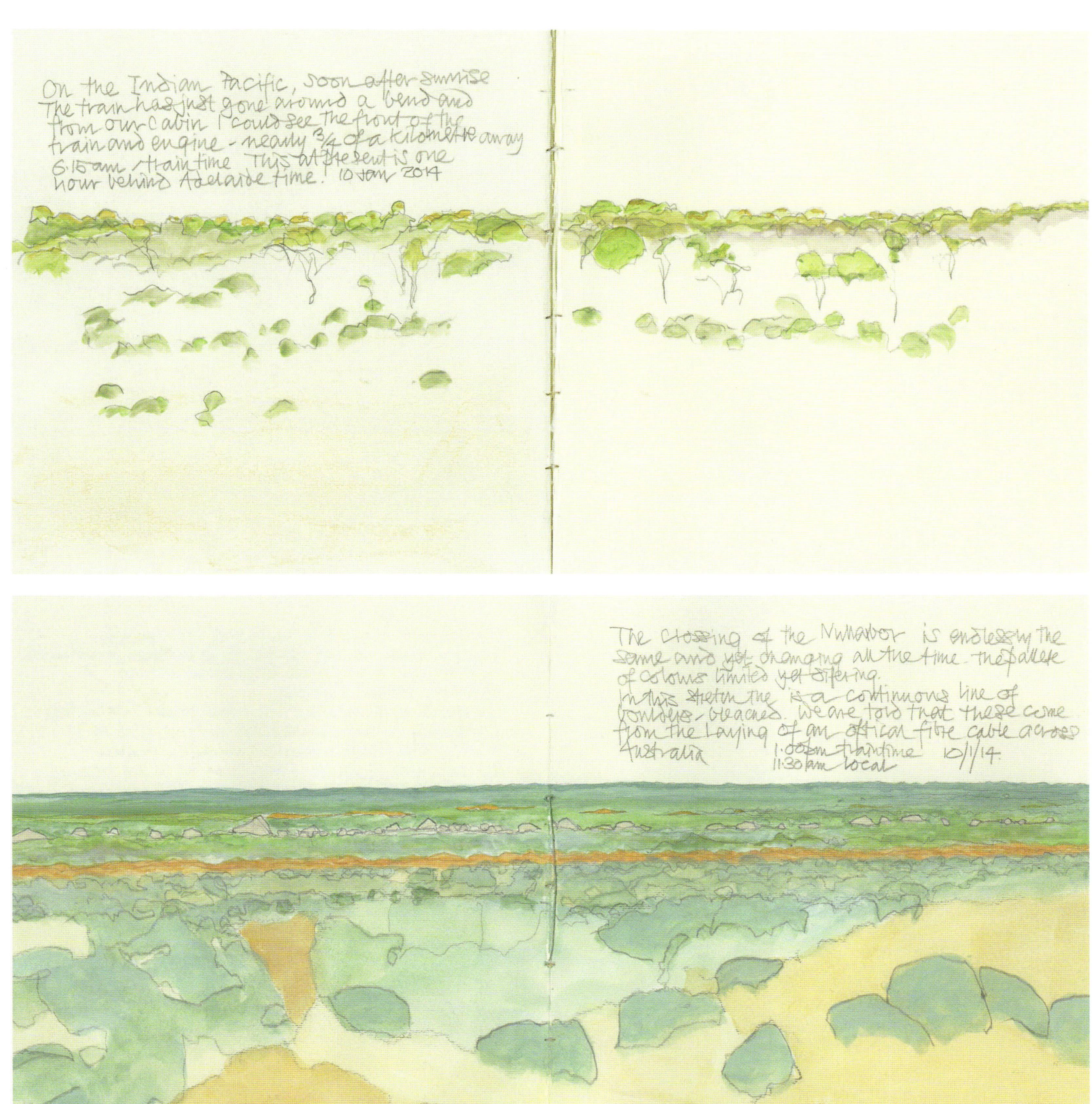


*Crossing the Nullarbor, 6.15 am,*
10 January 2014

*Crossing the Nullarbor, 1.00 pm,*
10 January 2014

All day I watched as we crossed the
plain. The railway line is dead straight
for hundreds of kilometres, the longest
straight stretch in the world. You pass
vestiges of past settlements built only for
the construction of the railway and largely
deserted afterwards. Finally, at the other
side of the plain, trees reappear.

*Crossing the Nullarbor, 2.50 pm,*
10 January 2014

*Crossing the Nullarbor, 5.35 pm,*
10 January 2014

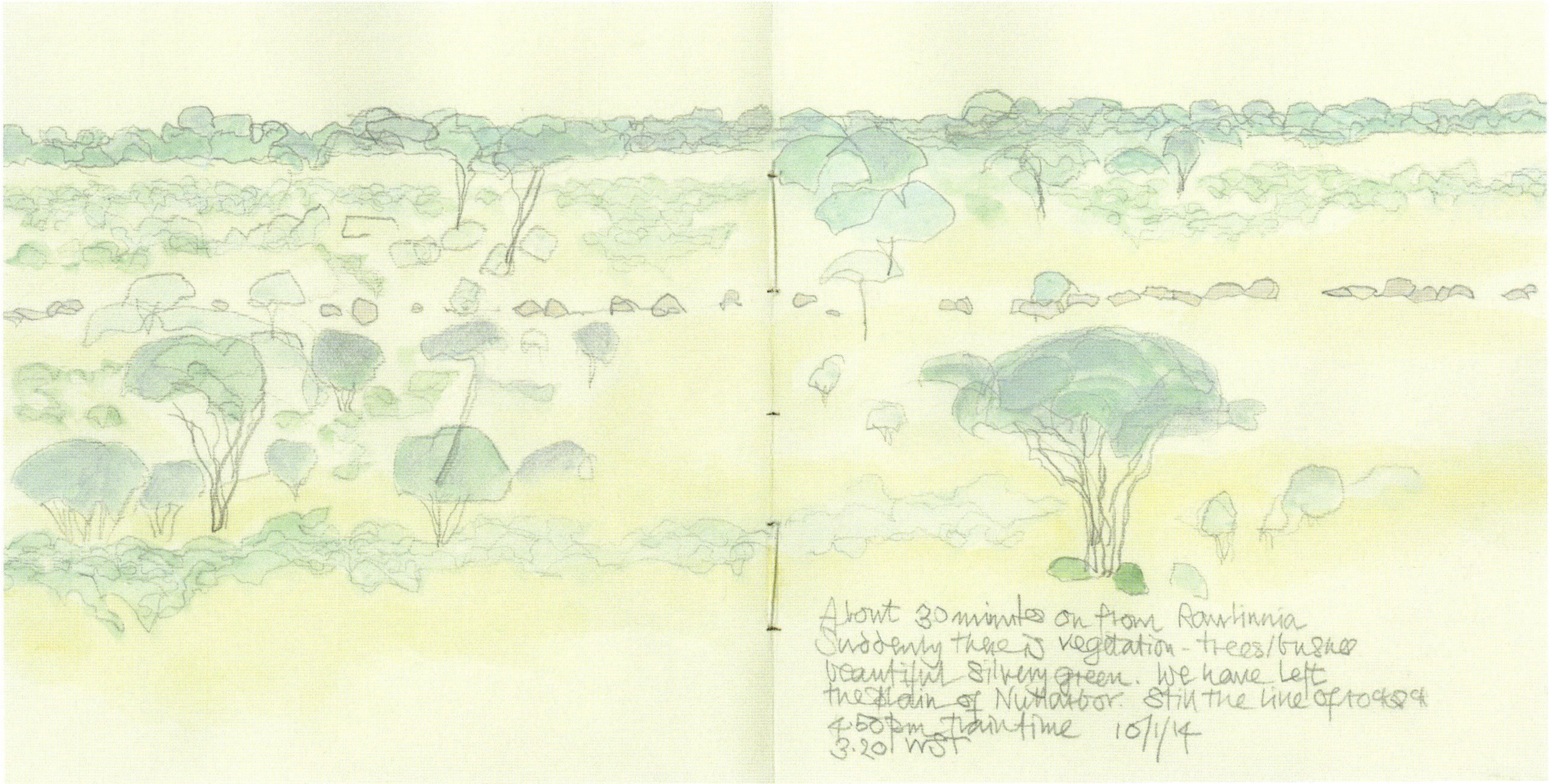

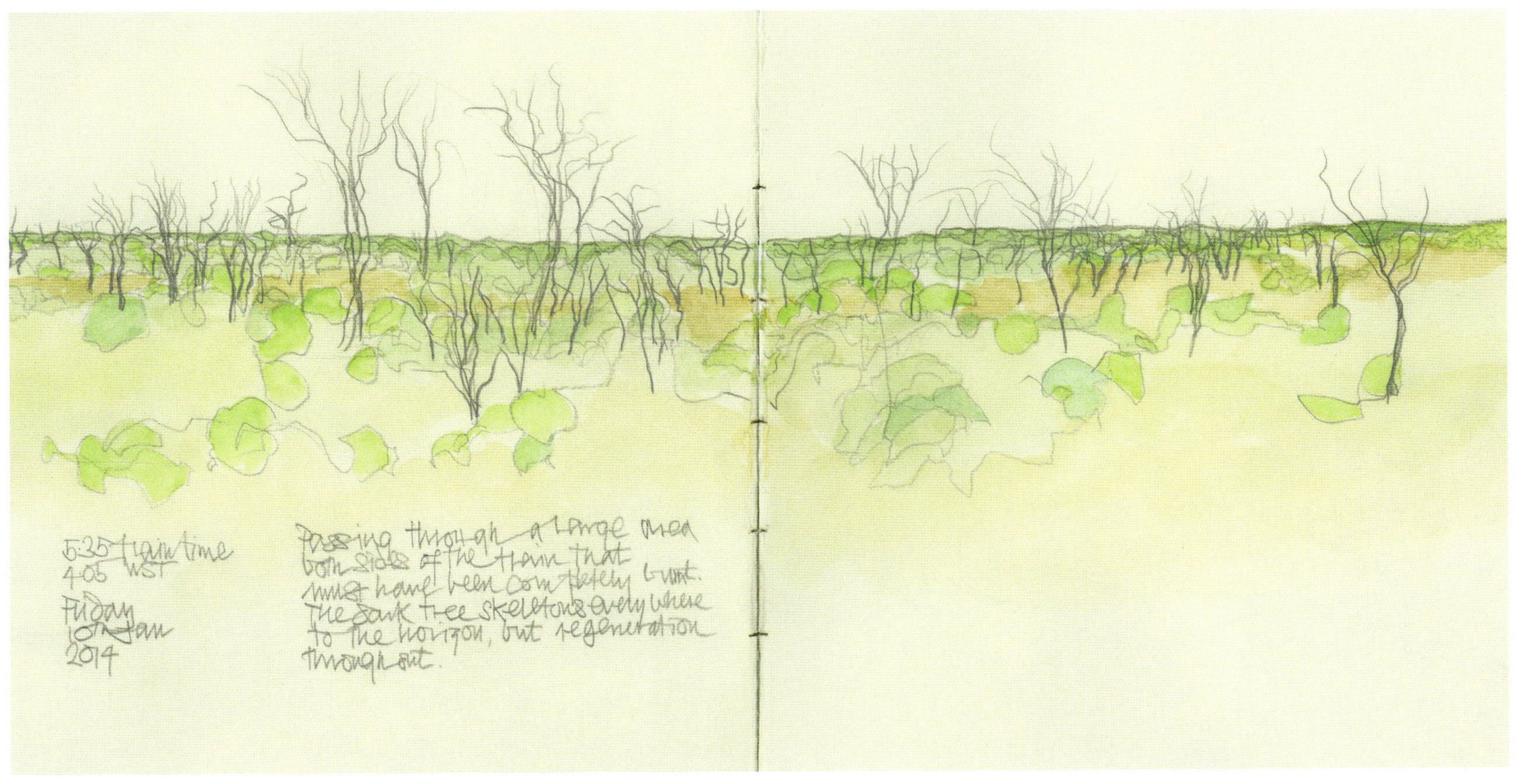

About 30 minutes on from Rawlinnia
Suddenly there is vegetation - trees/bushes
beautiful silvery green. We have left
the plain of Nullarbor. Still the line of trees at
4.50pm train time    10/1/14
3.20 WST

5.35 train time
4.05 WST
Friday
10th Jan
2014

Passing through a large area
both sides of the train that
must have been completely burnt.
The dark tree skeletons everywhere
to the horizon, but regeneration
throughout.

# Kata Tjuta / the Olgas,
# Northern Territory

25°18'00.3"S 130°43'46.2"E
-25.300095, 130.729508

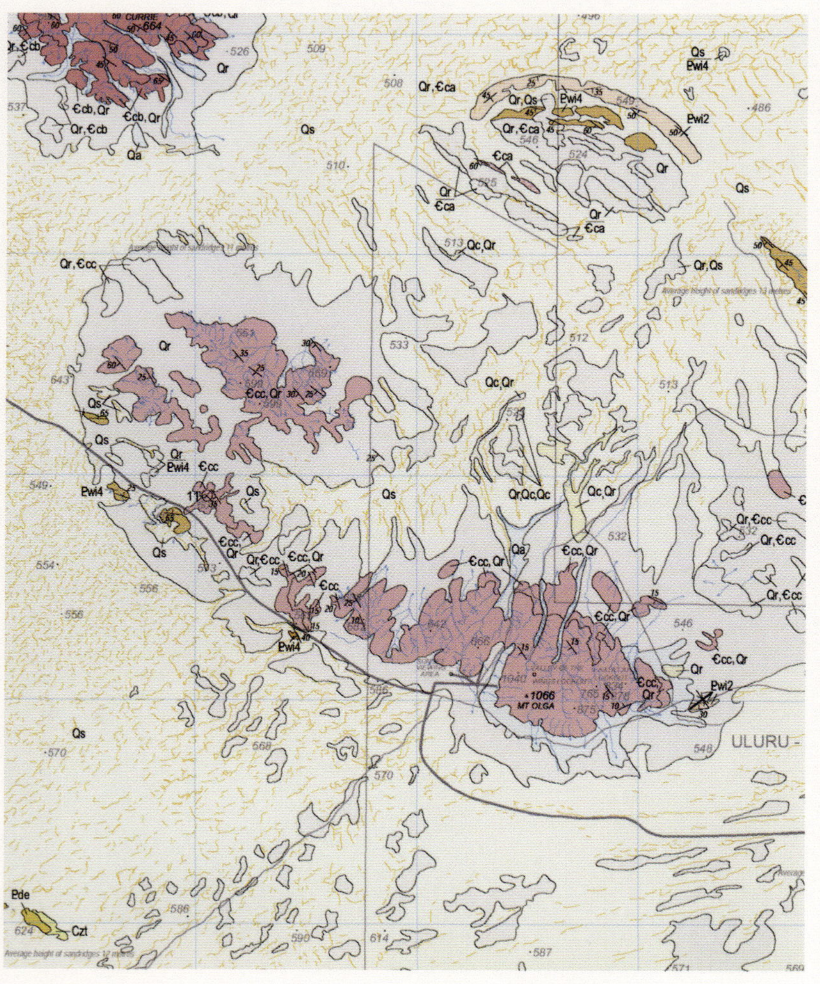

Kata Tjuta, also known as the Olgas, is just 25 kilometres from Uluru. One is clearly visible from the other. They are like brother and sister – close but strikingly different. This relationship is shown in my painting of Kata Tjuta from the summit of Uluru (page 44). As I say in the piece on Uluru (page 48), this viewing point rightly can no longer be visited.

Uluru is a single formation, unlike Kata Tjuta, which is made up of multiple domes – over twenty of them. Between the domes of Kata Tjuta, there are valleys that you can walk through. When you are within them, the steeply curved rock faces tower above you. The valleys are covered by vegetation, the greens contrasting with the deep red of the rock.

Kata Tjuta seems a different red from Uluru, deeper, almost tending to blue-grey in places. Indeed, the rock underneath the surface coating is exactly that colour. The red is a patina of oxidation, a kind of rust. But the most striking feature of the rock of Kata Tjuta is that it is a conglomerate, and very arrestingly so. It is a gigantic amalgam of pebbles, rocks, cobbles and even boulders, all mixed up and set in the surrounding rock. This is quite distinct from the rock of Uluru. Conglomerates exist widely around the world, but none I have seen is as impressive as Kata Tjuta.

It is the contrast offered by Kata Tjuta that is most compelling after working at the edges of Uluru. There is an intimacy about being able to wander between the domes. You can seek the shade, and sit to draw with green all around you. When I went, I was alone, for it is considered – I think wrongly – rather the poor relative. The crowds all go to Uluru. You were in peace at Kata Tjuta if you sought out the remoter canyons.

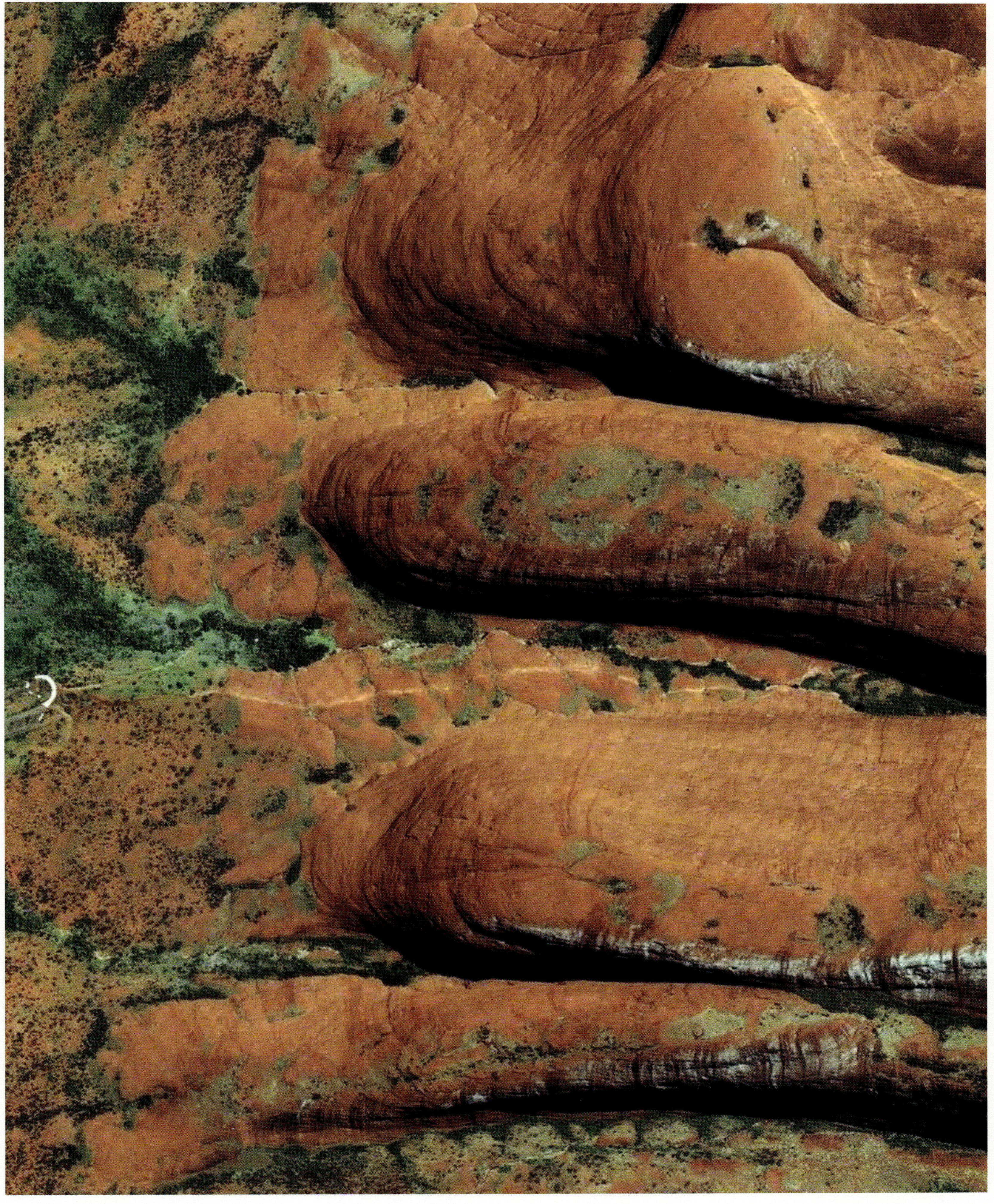

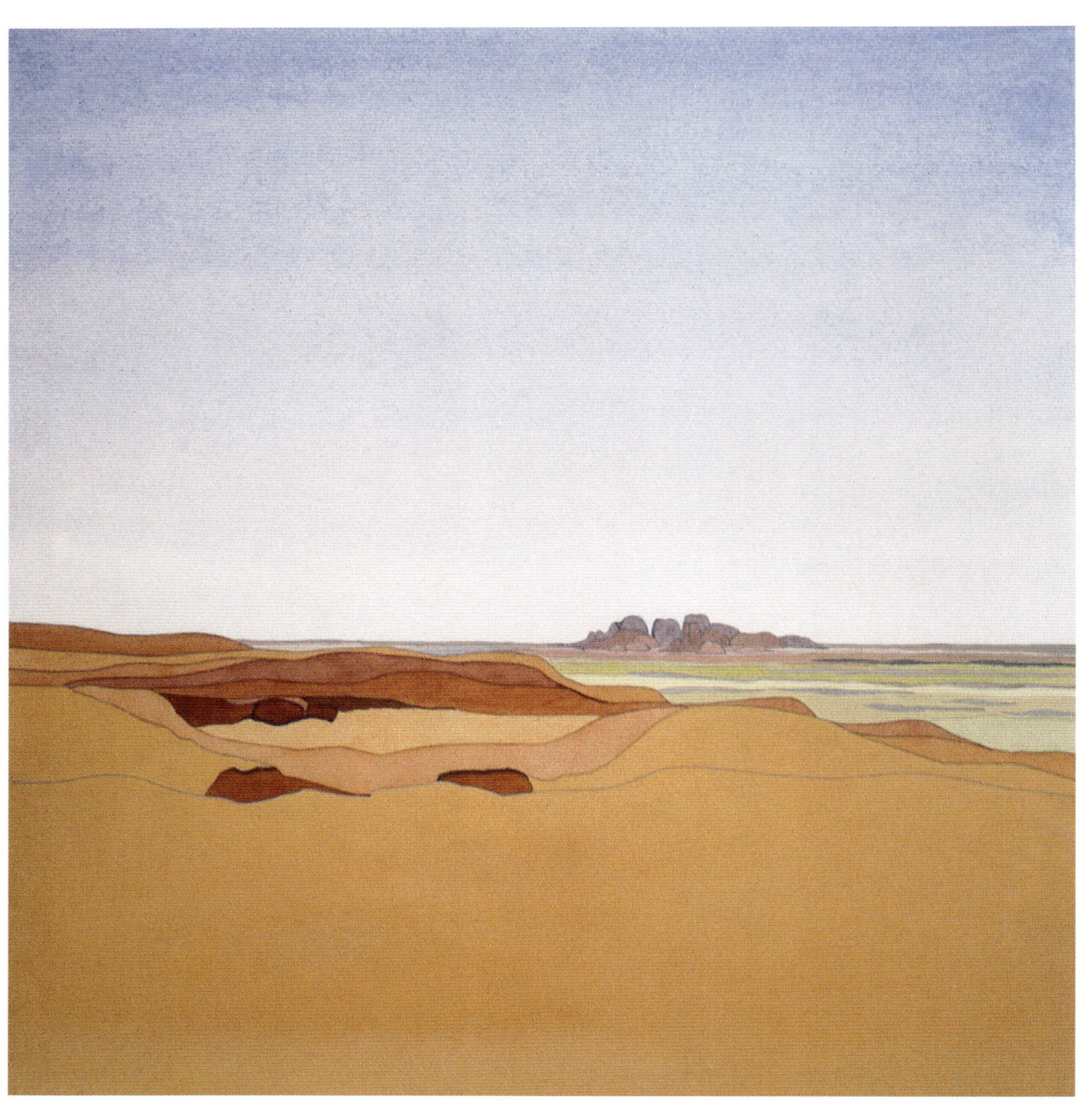

ABOVE
*The Olgas from Summit of Uluru,*
1981

RIGHT
*Olga Gorge,* 1999

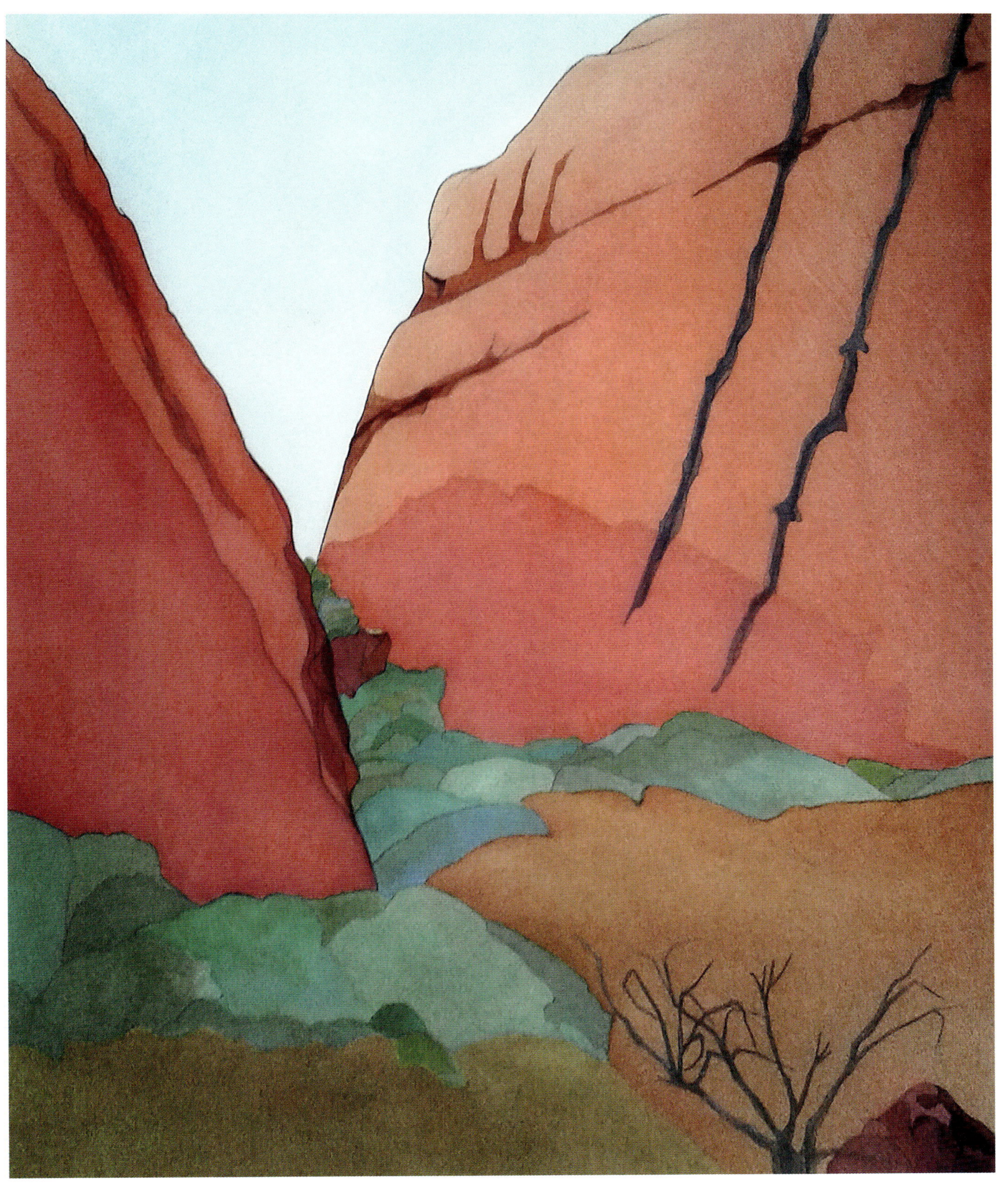

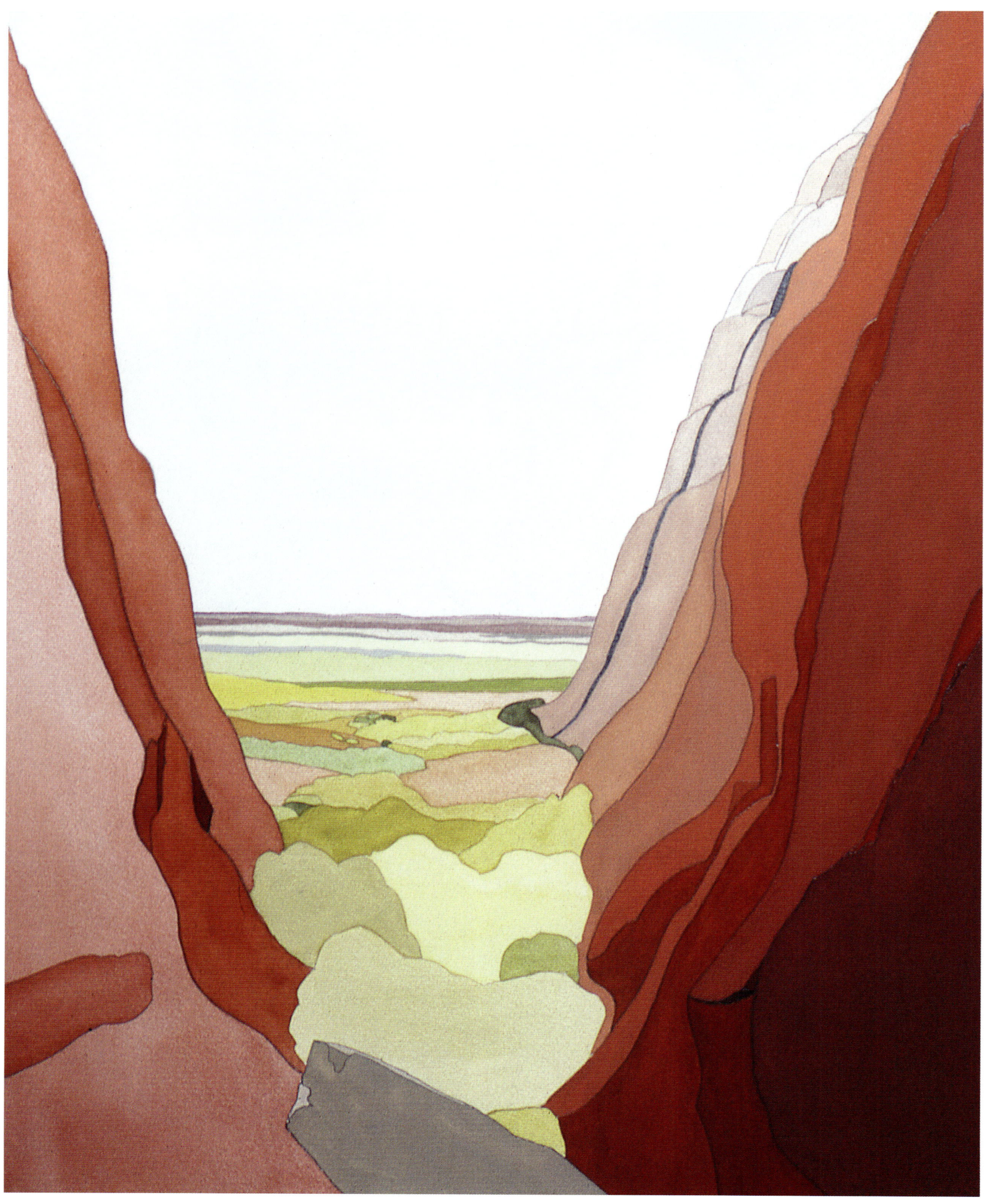

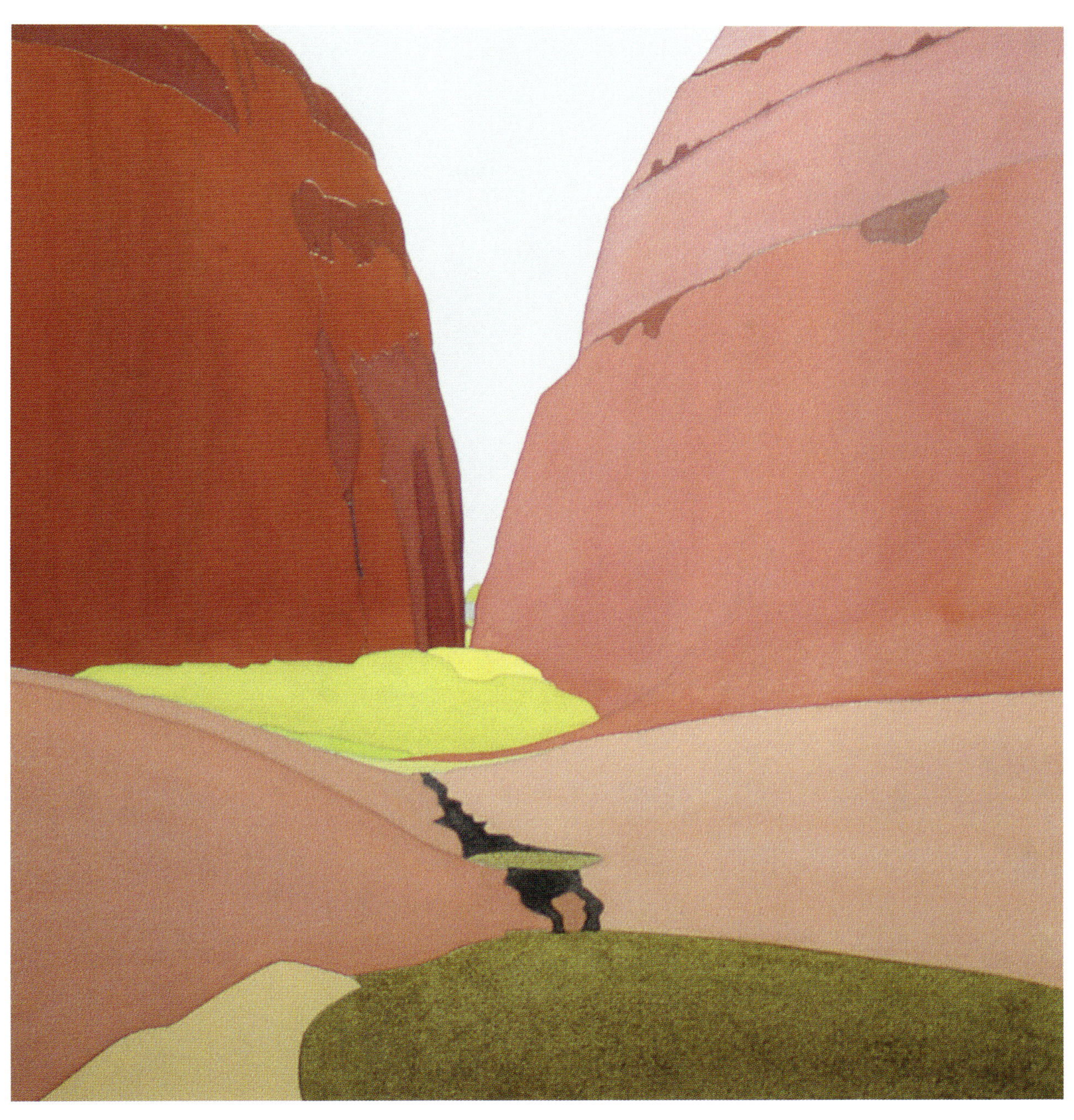

LEFT
*Looking out from Olga Gorge,*
1981

ABOVE
*Olga Gorge,* 1981

# Uluru / Ayers Rock, Northern Territory



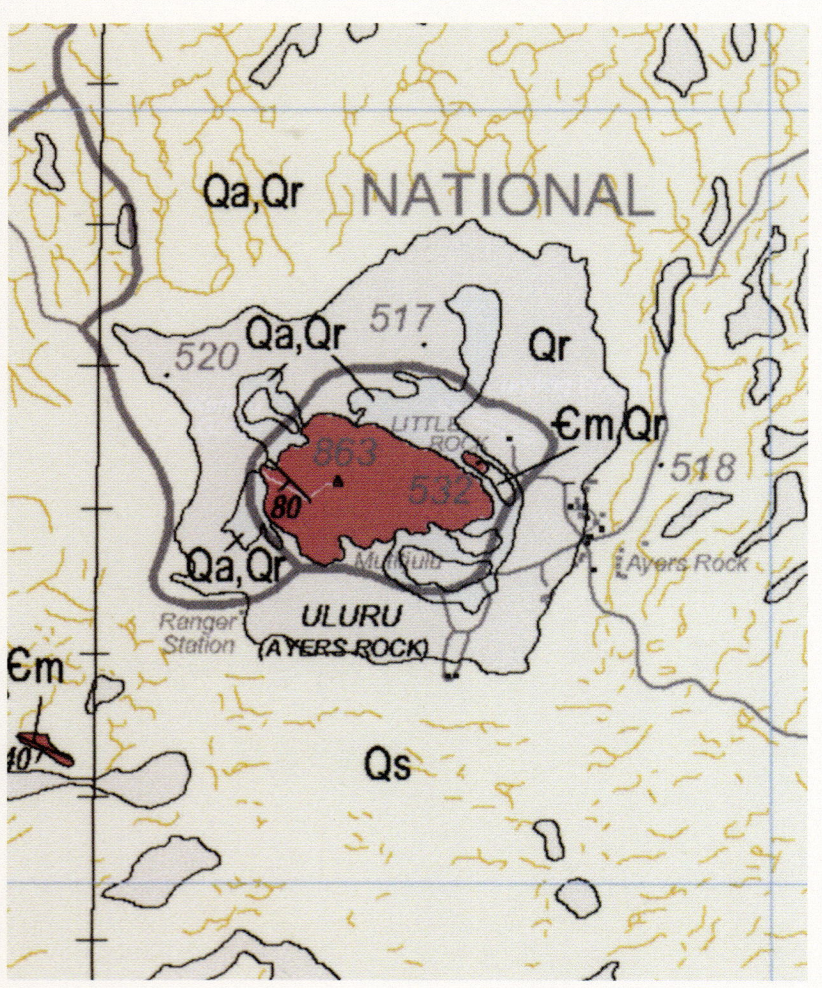


My longest and most intensive visit to Uluru, when I did the majority of the work shown here, seems like a different era. It was called Ayers Rock back then. Beside it was just one small motel. No airstrip. No visitor centre, nor the resort complex of today.

Staying in that motel, you were right up against the rock. You had its presence just there, especially on a moonlit night. People regularly climbed the rock then, and I did too, making my drawings from a vantage point that is quite rightly now no longer accessible to visitors. I have debated whether to include some of these drawings, but feel that I can because of what was accepted then. In that sense, many of the works here are 'historical'.

Uluru is such an iconic place to visit. It lives up to all expectations – indeed, far exceeds what you expect from the many reproductions. But given all the photographs and paintings, it is a test to add anything 'new'. So I concentrated on the rock close up rather than seen from afar. I made just one work from a distance (on page 53). Included here is an aerial photograph, which shows a very different aspect of the structure.

I was particularly struck by the blue-grey stains left by the cascading waters of the infrequent rains, built up over thousands of years. These cascades have fed a number of ponds that remain even in the dry seasons. It is magical to sit beside these pools in such surrounds.

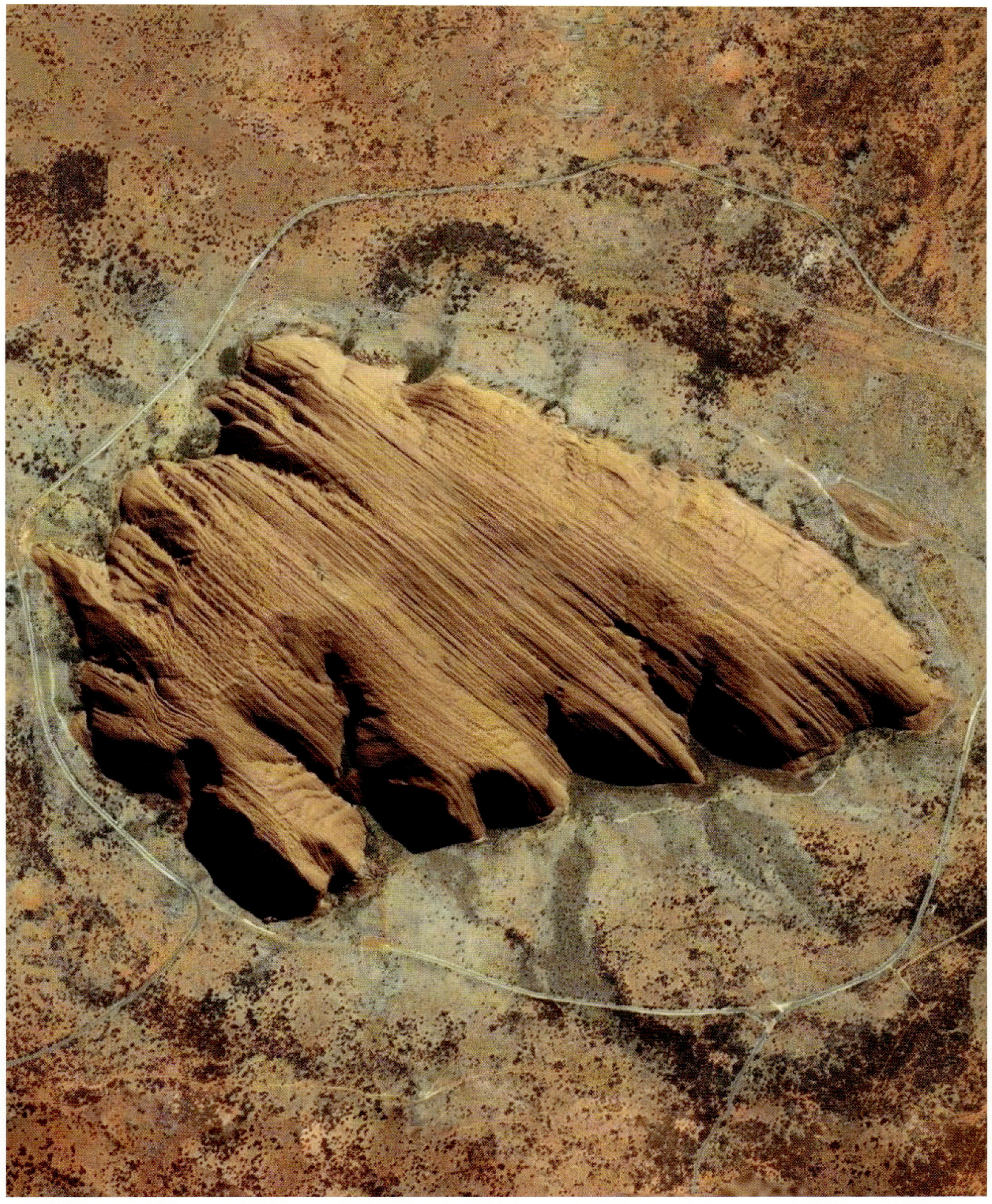

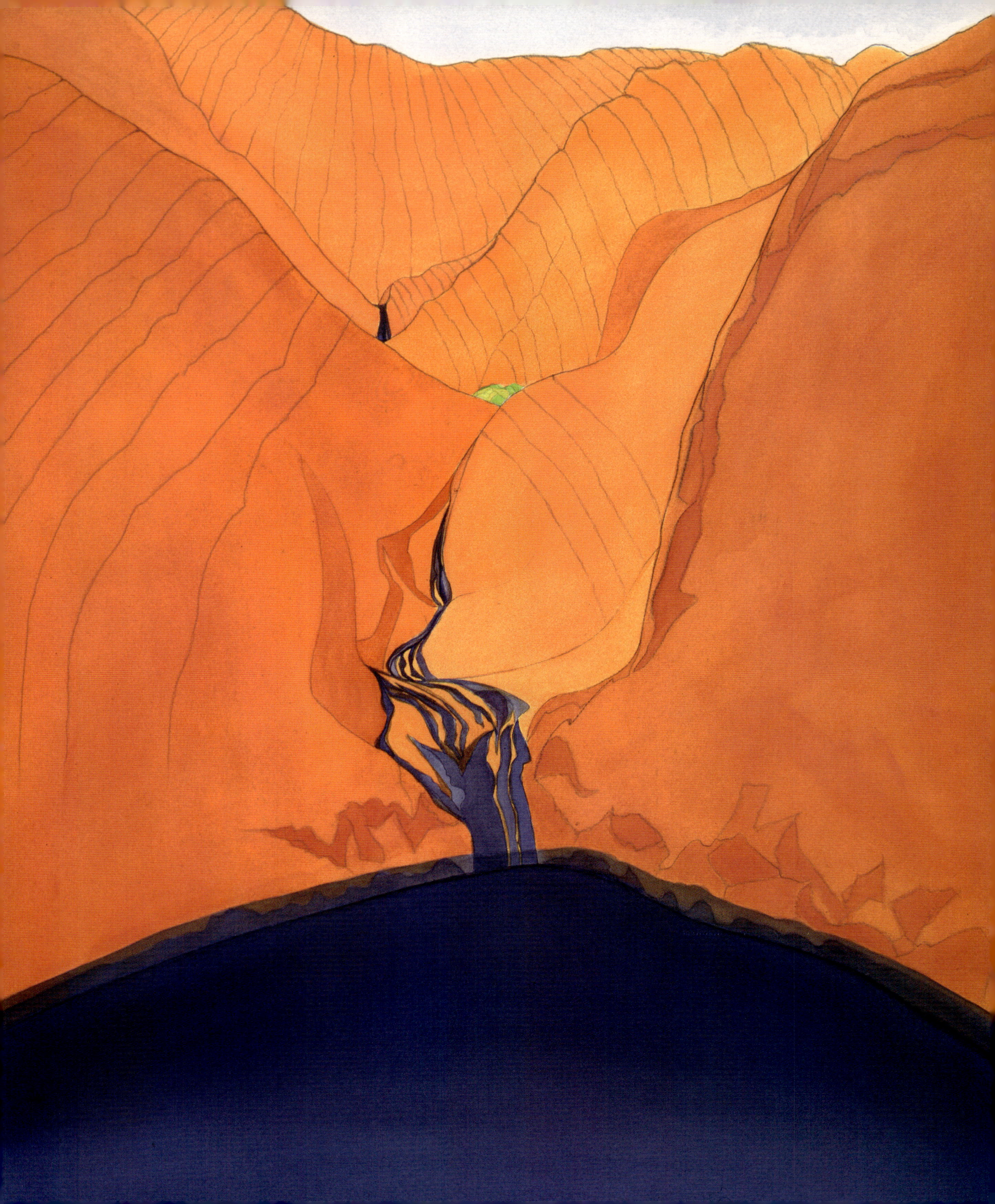

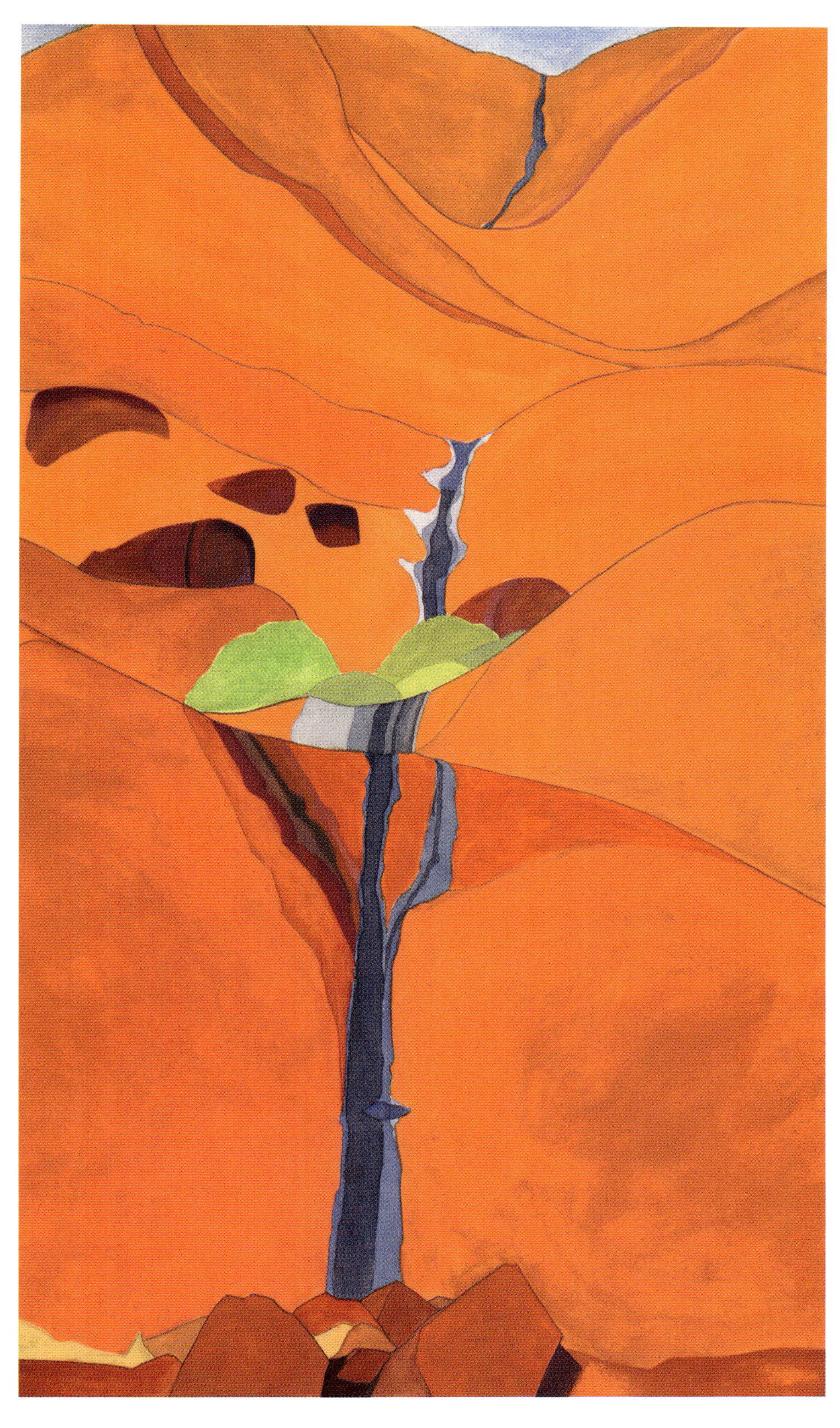

LEFT
*Evening at Mutitjulu*, 1999

ABOVE
*North Face*, 1999

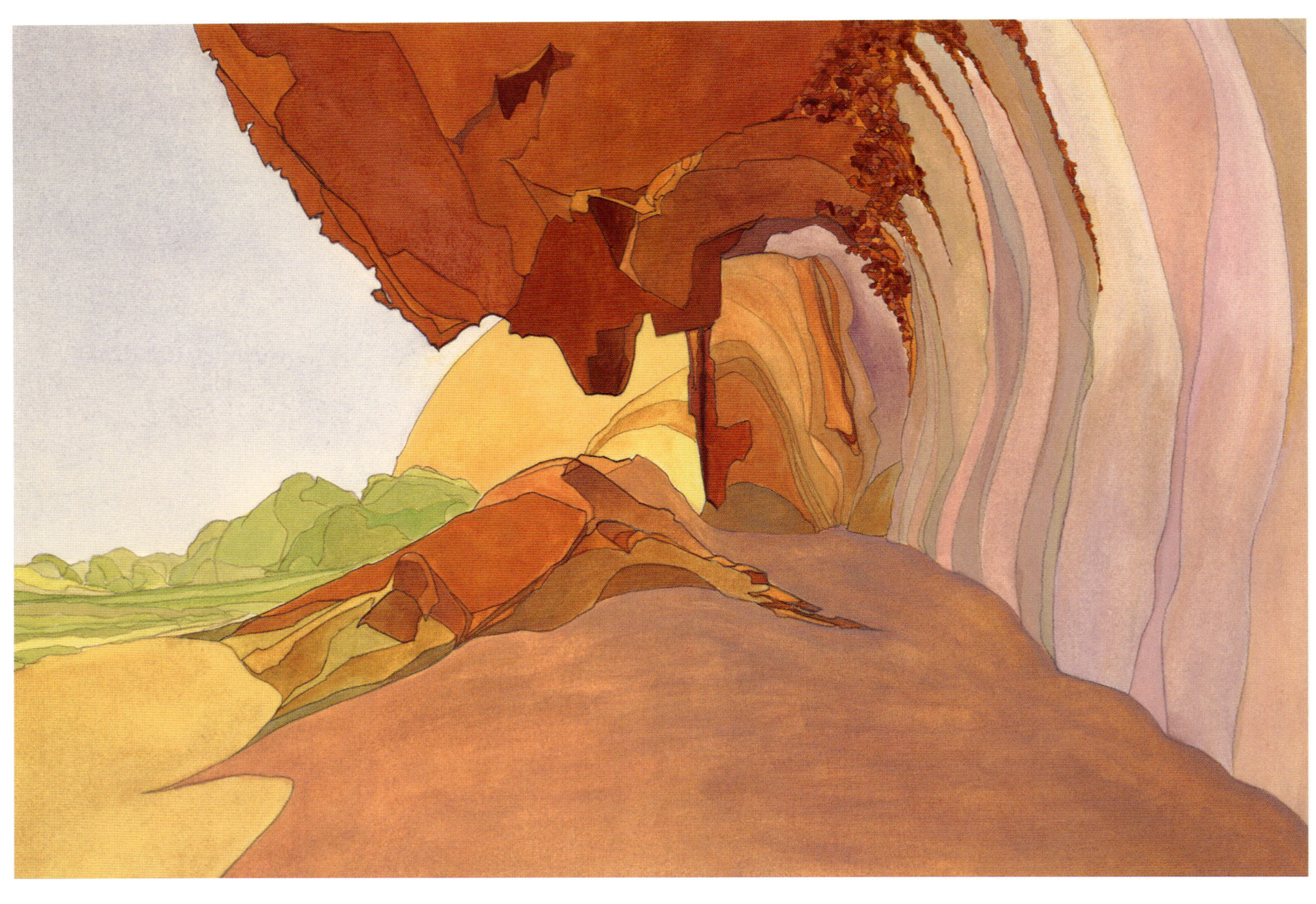

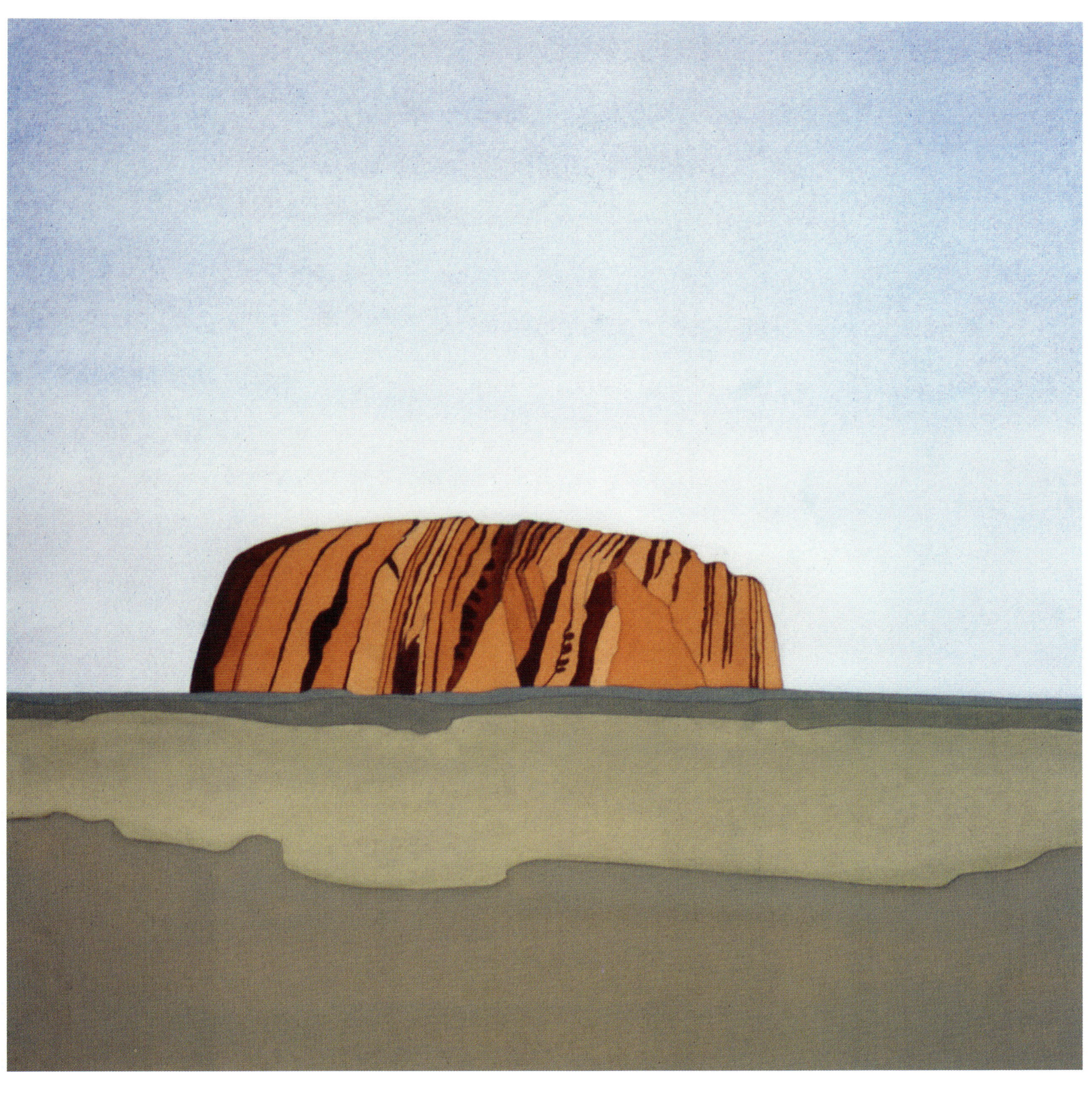

I was particularly struck by the blue-grey
stains left by the cascading waters of the
infrequent rains, built up over thousands
of years. These cascades have fed a
number of ponds that remain even in
the dry seasons. It is magical to sit beside
these pools in such surrounds.

*Above Mutitjulu*, 1982

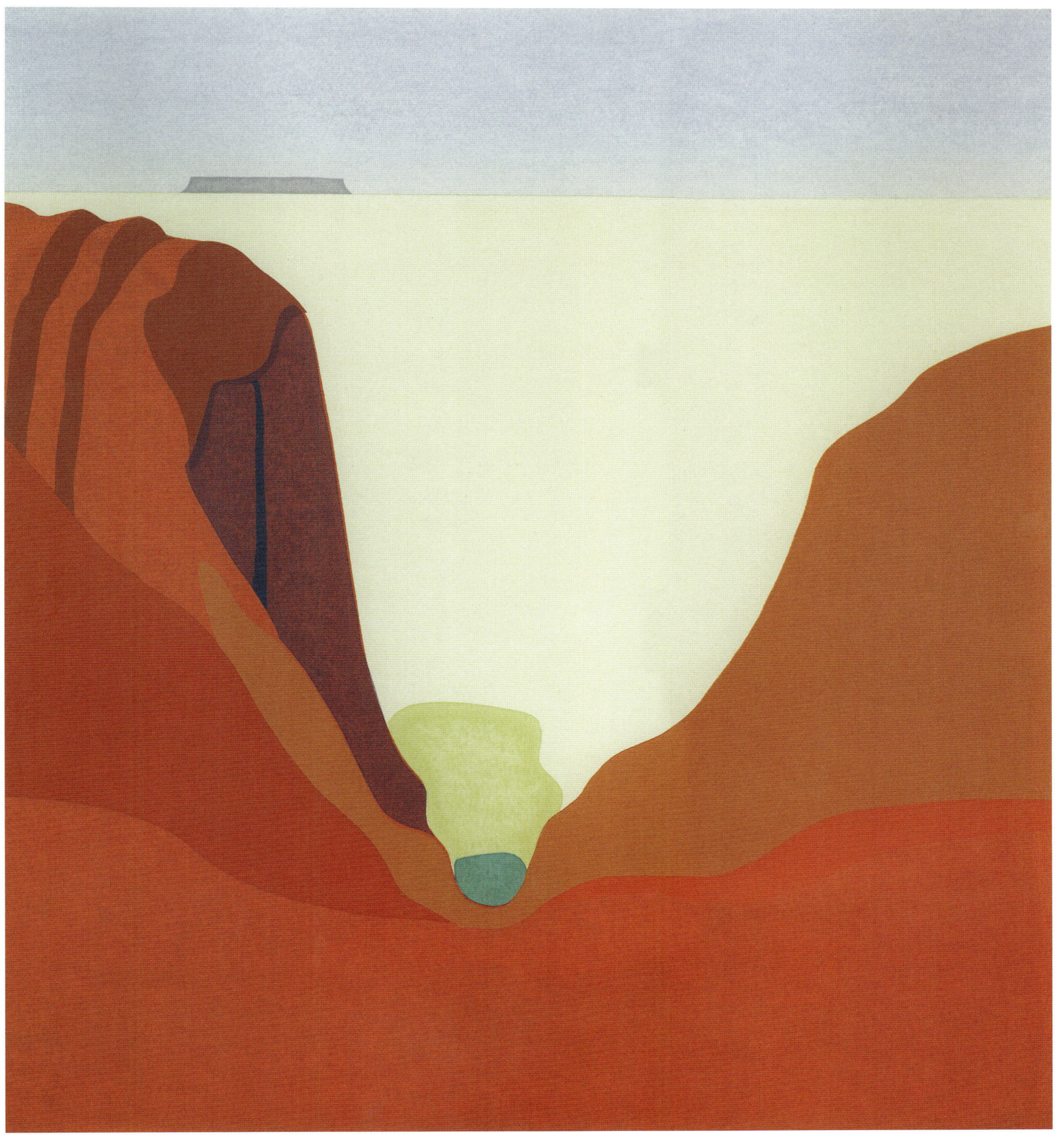

# Tnorala / Gosse Bluff, Northern Territory

**23°49'09.1"S 132°18'25.9"E**
**-23.819189, 132.307198**

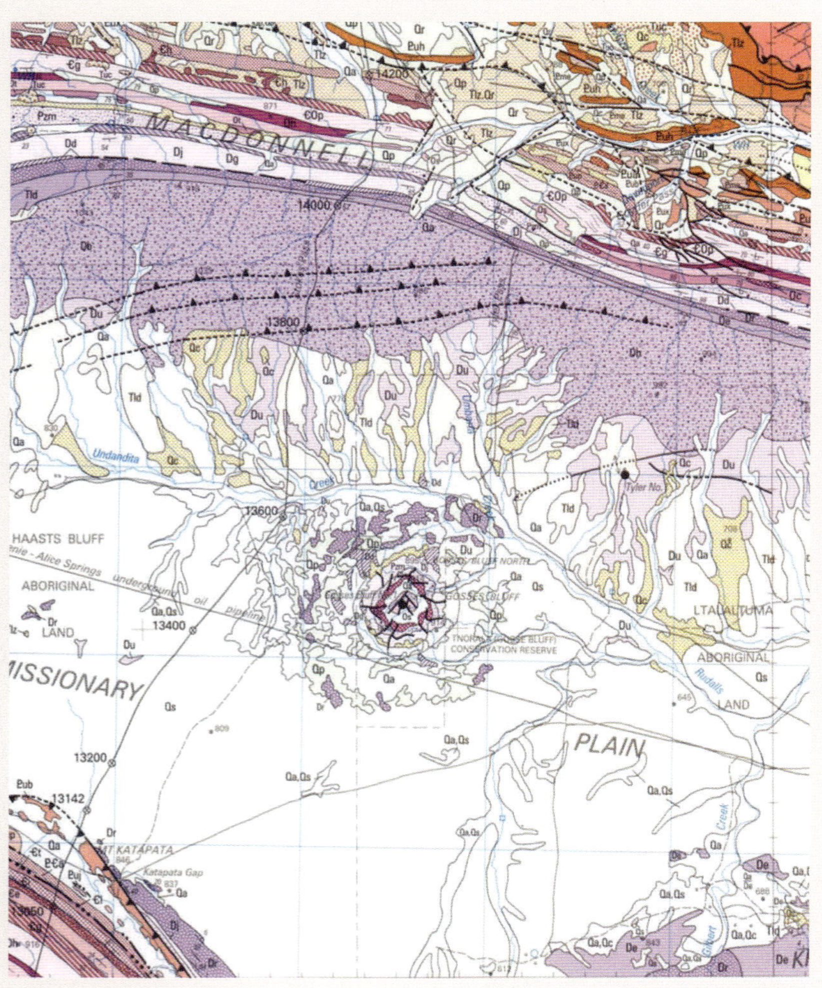

Tnorala, also known as Gosse Bluff, is a giant meteorite crater set in the Missionary Plain to the south of the MacDonnell Ranges. It lies about 175 kilometres to the west of Alice Springs. Access is by a deviation along a dirt road off Namatjira Drive. Tnorala is a sacred place for the Western Arrernte people, who attribute the crater's formation to cosmic impact. Their origin Dreaming story tells of how a group of celestial women were dancing, when one grew tired and placed her baby in a basket made of stars (the constellation Corona Australis). The baby slipped from the basket and fell to Earth, and its impact made the crater.

As you drive over the plain towards it, the crater's rim is seen clearly, looking like a range of hills. These 'hills' are on average just under 200 metres high. At this stage, you have no idea that you are approaching a crater. This becomes clear when you find and enter the single gap. There before you is the complete arena, about 5 kilometres in diameter.

The date of the impact has been fairly closely fixed at about 142 million years ago. It is believed that the meteorite involved in the impact was about a kilometre in diameter. The original crater was some 20 kilometres in diameter and has been eroded down to what we now see. And it is still dramatic. We were there inside the crater alone, a wonderful experience. The images here show Tnorala as seen from above and the ring of hills seen as you approach. This I have coupled with an aerial photograph of the whole crater.

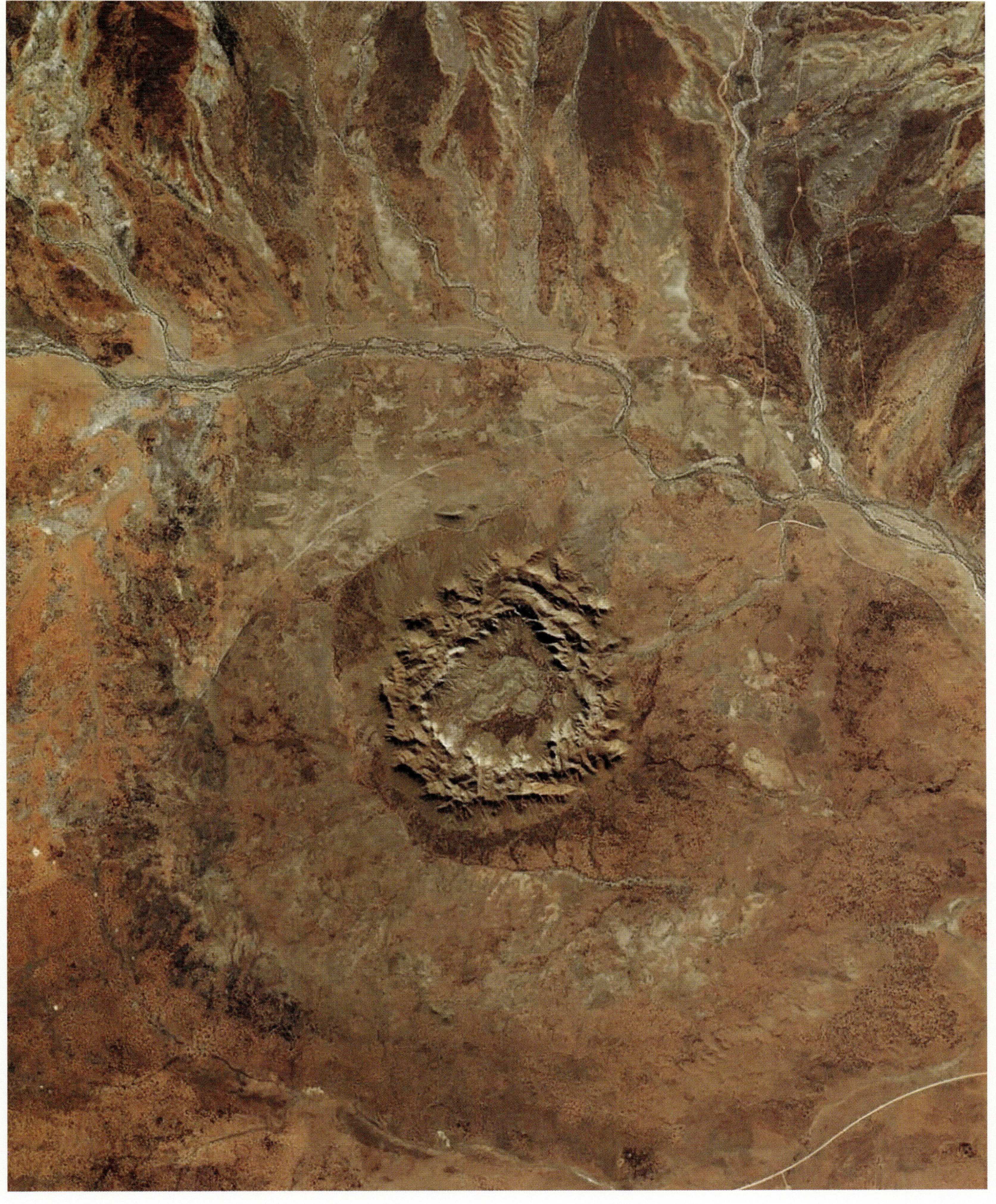

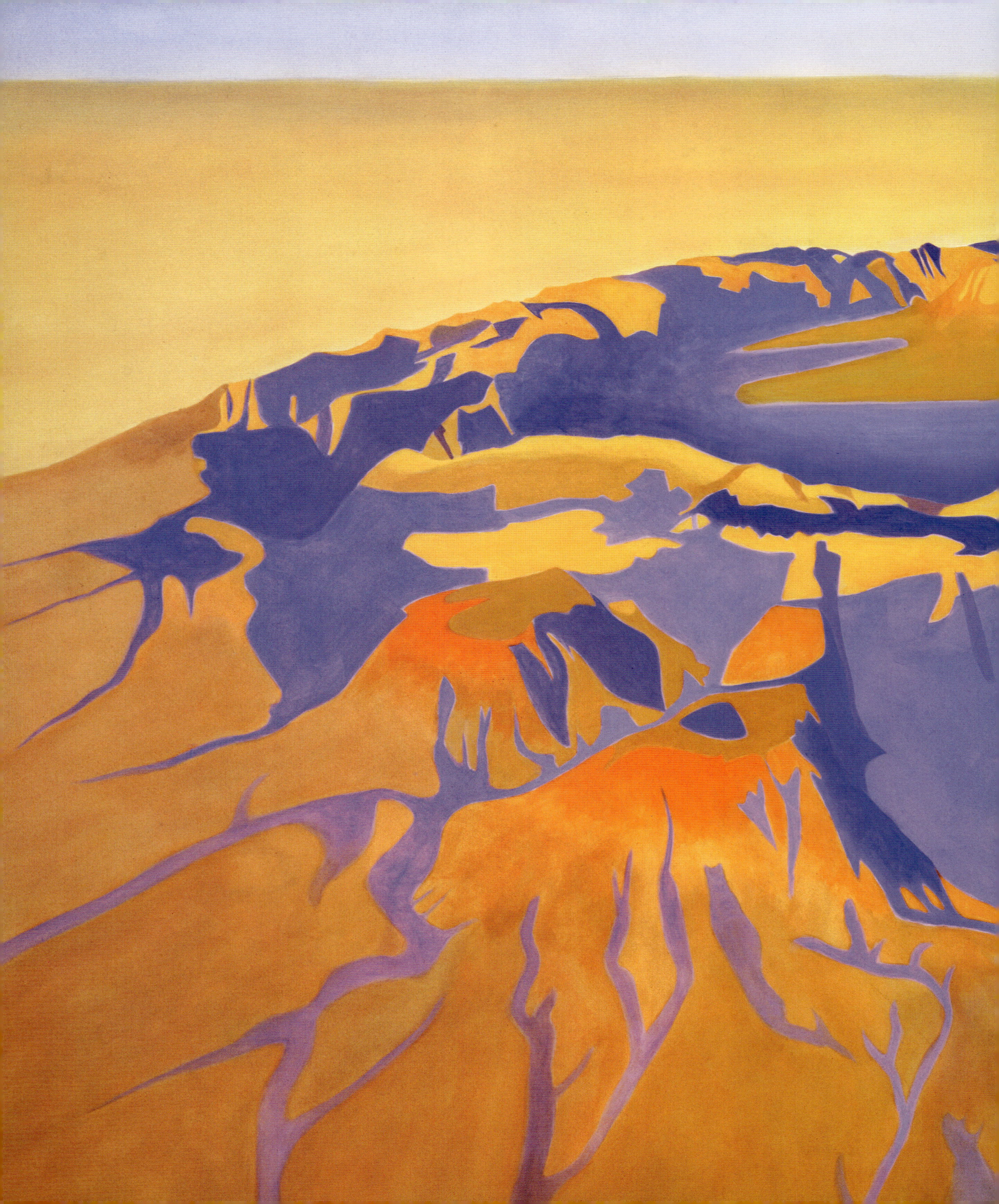

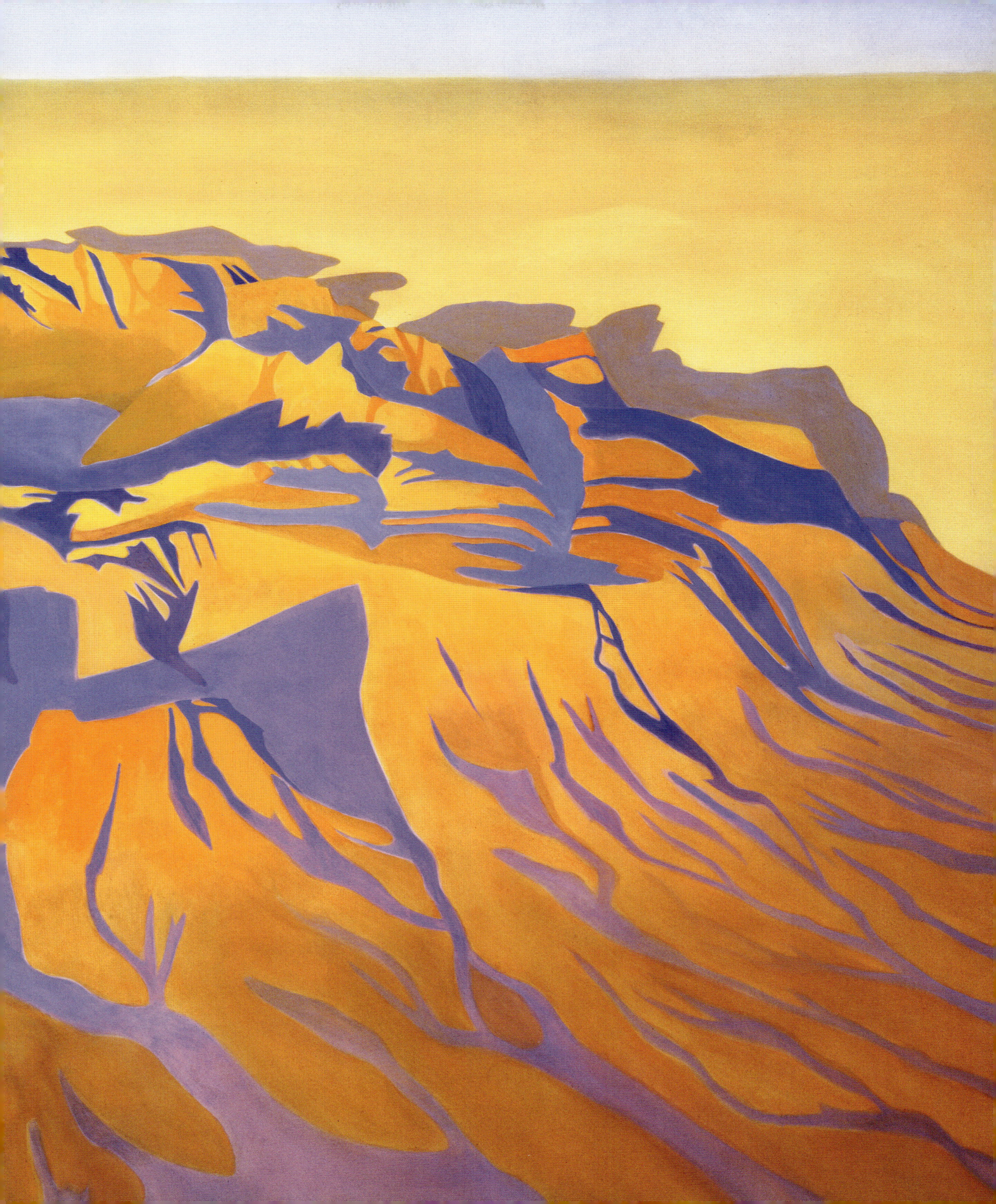

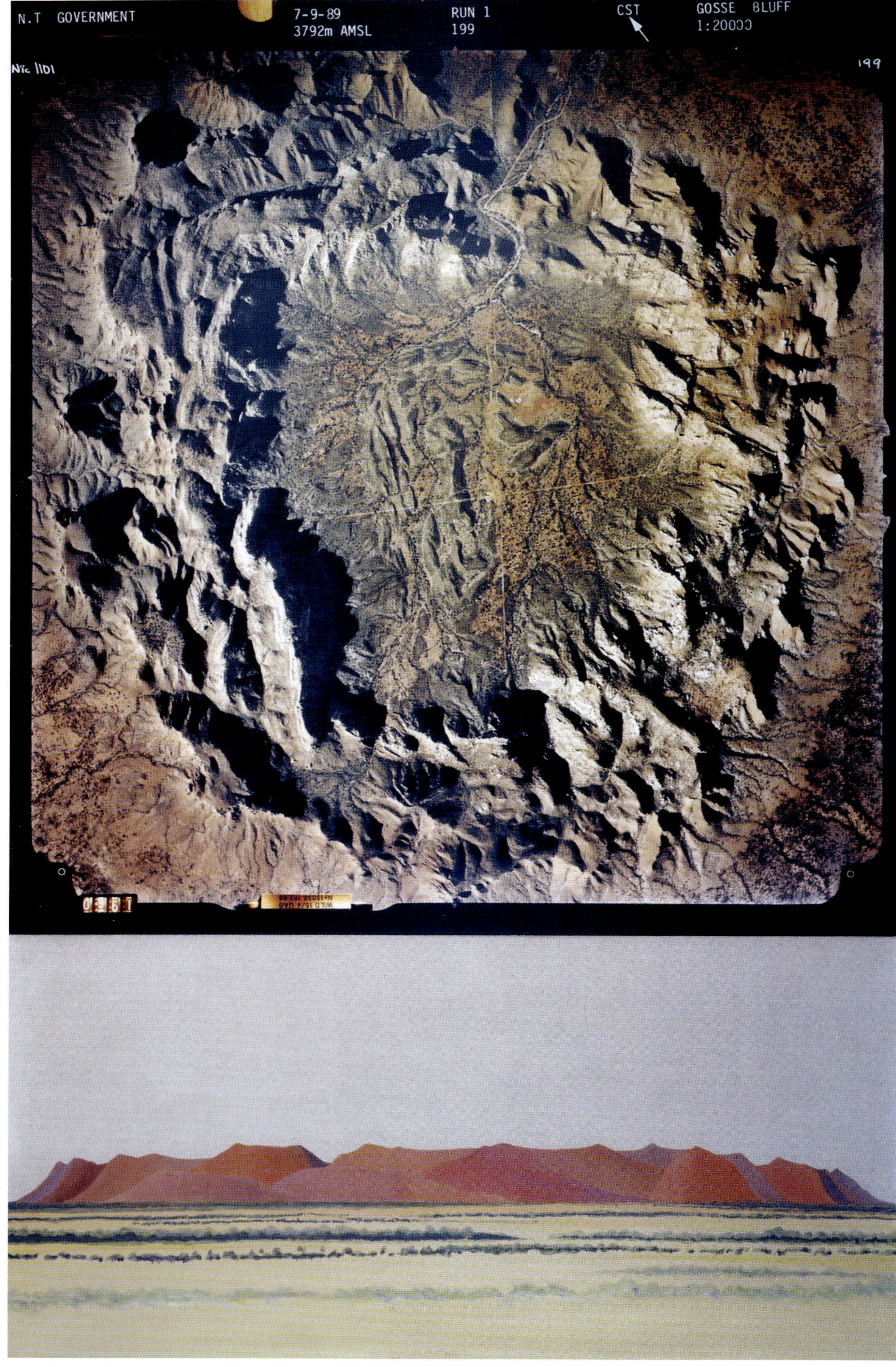
N.T GOVERNMENT
7-9-89
3792m AMSL
RUN 1
199
CST
GOSSE BLUFF
1:20000
Nic 1101
199

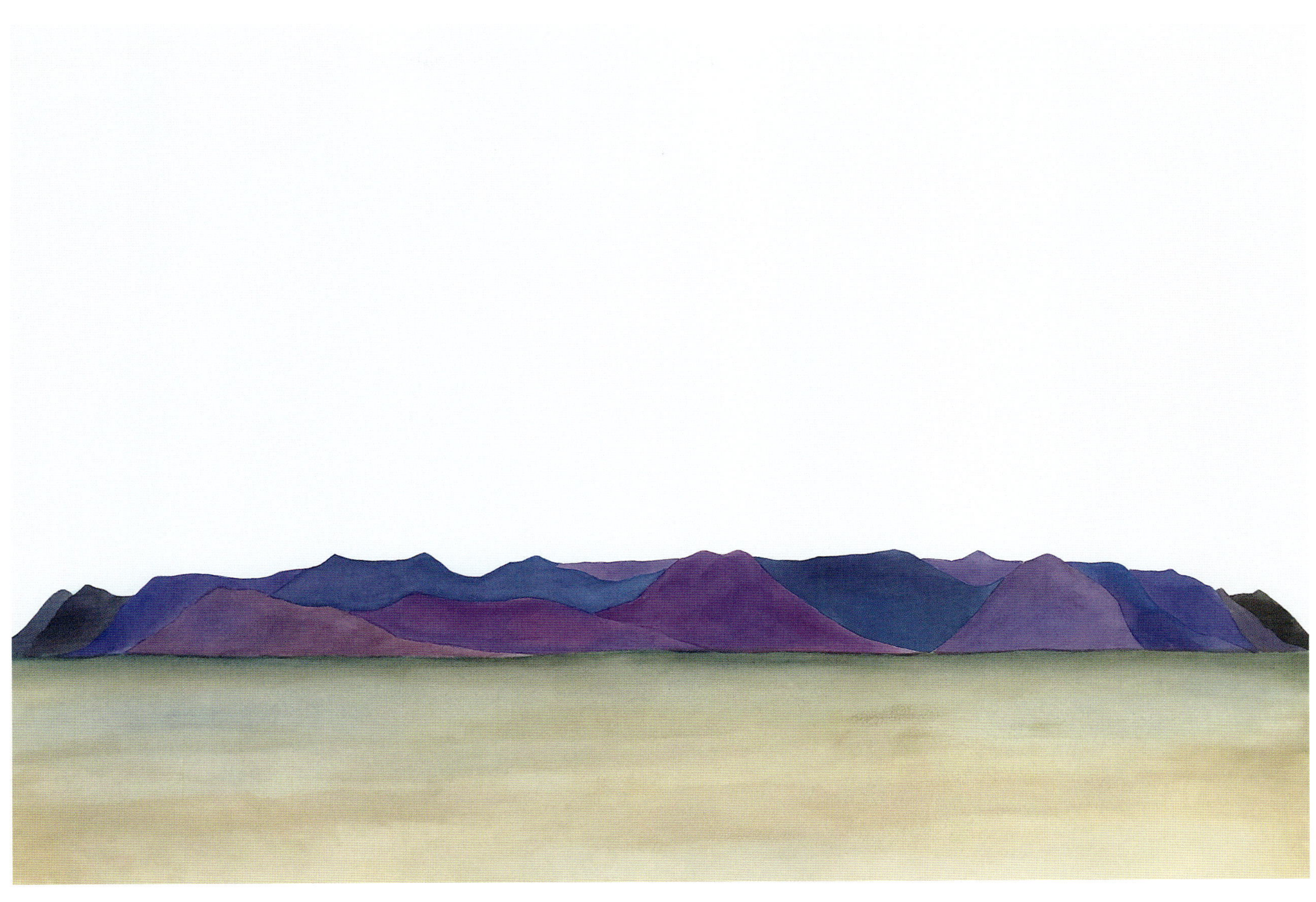


*Gosse Bluff: Evening*, 1998


*Gosse Bluff*, 1998


*Gosse Bluff*, 1998

# Kakadu, Northern Territory

12°24′41.0″S 132°57′26.1″E
-12.411378, 132.957255

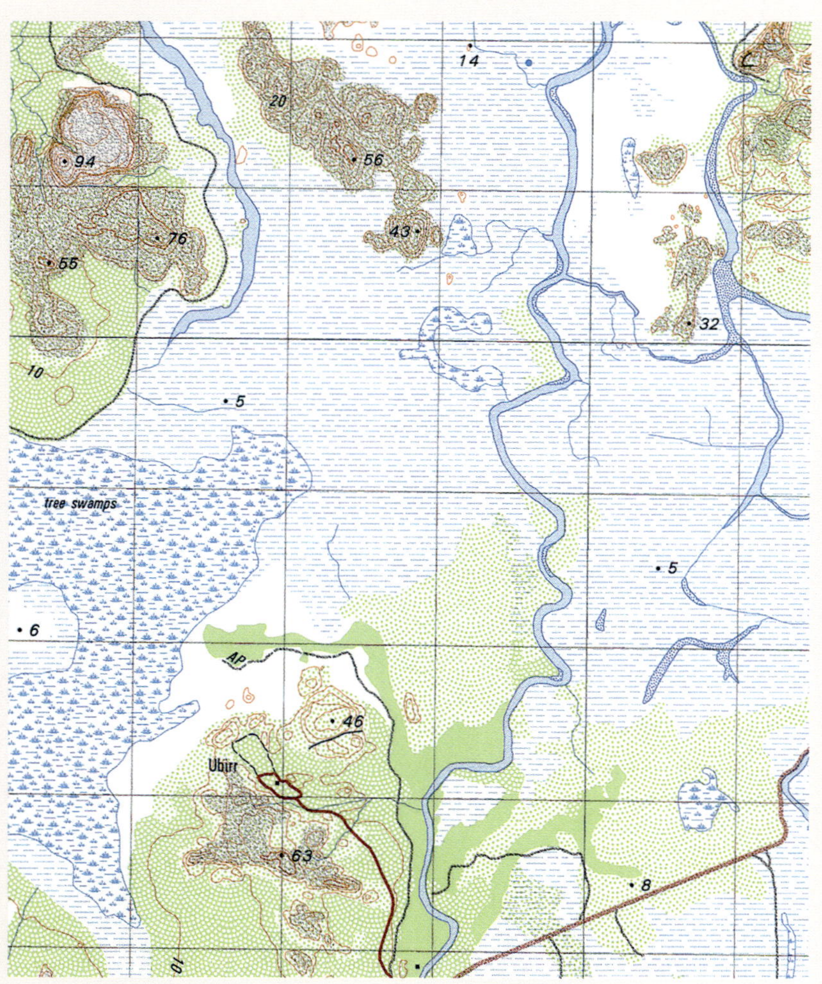


Kakadu National Park lies about 170 kilometres south-east of Darwin. There is easy road access. The park is huge, about 20,000 square kilometres, its topography presenting a contrast between rock outcrops and escarpments and large flood plains. My prime interest in visiting was to view the Aboriginal rock paintings, but it was also striking to see the flood plains below the rock outcrops, stretching far into the distance. They are neither land nor water, but rather a mixture, with vegetation so thick upon the water that you cannot tell the two elements apart.

There is evidence for at least 60,000 years of continuous Aboriginal habitation. The rock paintings here, some in excellent condition, are up to 20,000 years old. They are outstanding, and make a deep impression, enhanced by the location of the painting sites in overhangs on the rock outcrops overlooking the flood plains.

The paintings and drawings that I did (see pages 66–7) were perhaps foolhardy. These rock paintings should just be looked at, absorbed on site, rather than inspiring attempts at copying. But nevertheless, that is what I did. In doing so, I was trying to show their visual link to the surrounding rocks and to the wider setting.

My visit was a long time ago. At both the Ubirr and Burrunggui (Nourlangie) sites, I had the place to myself. I could quietly study the works, following the sinuous lines of the bodies and the use of line and colours combined in the animals – especially the great painting of a fish. The colours are still very definite and clear. Perhaps they have been repainted, restored, many times. But surely the designs are just as they were made so long ago. One is struck by the sophistication. This is such a contrast to the simple artist images found in northern Europe – and those date from only 5000 years ago.

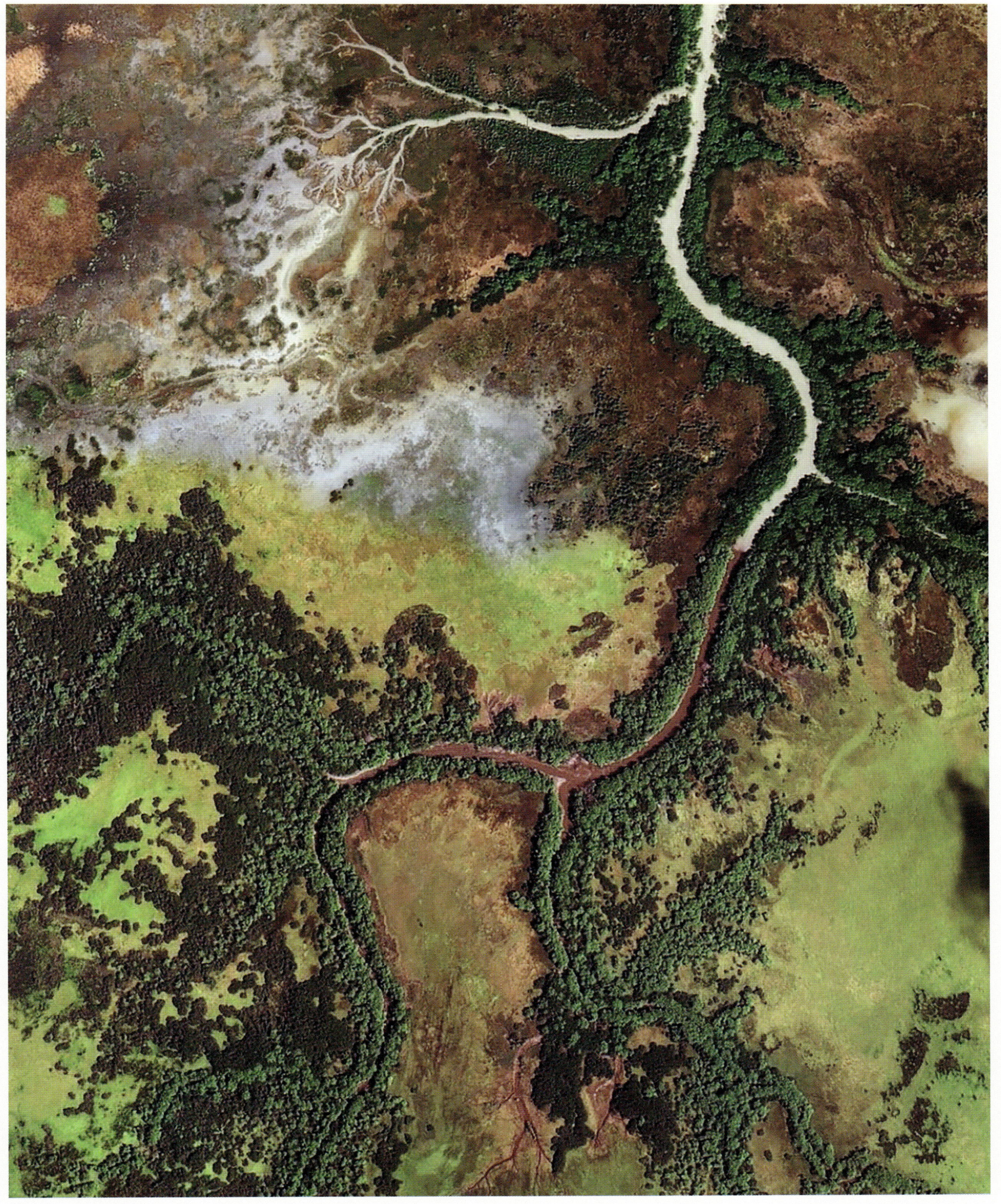

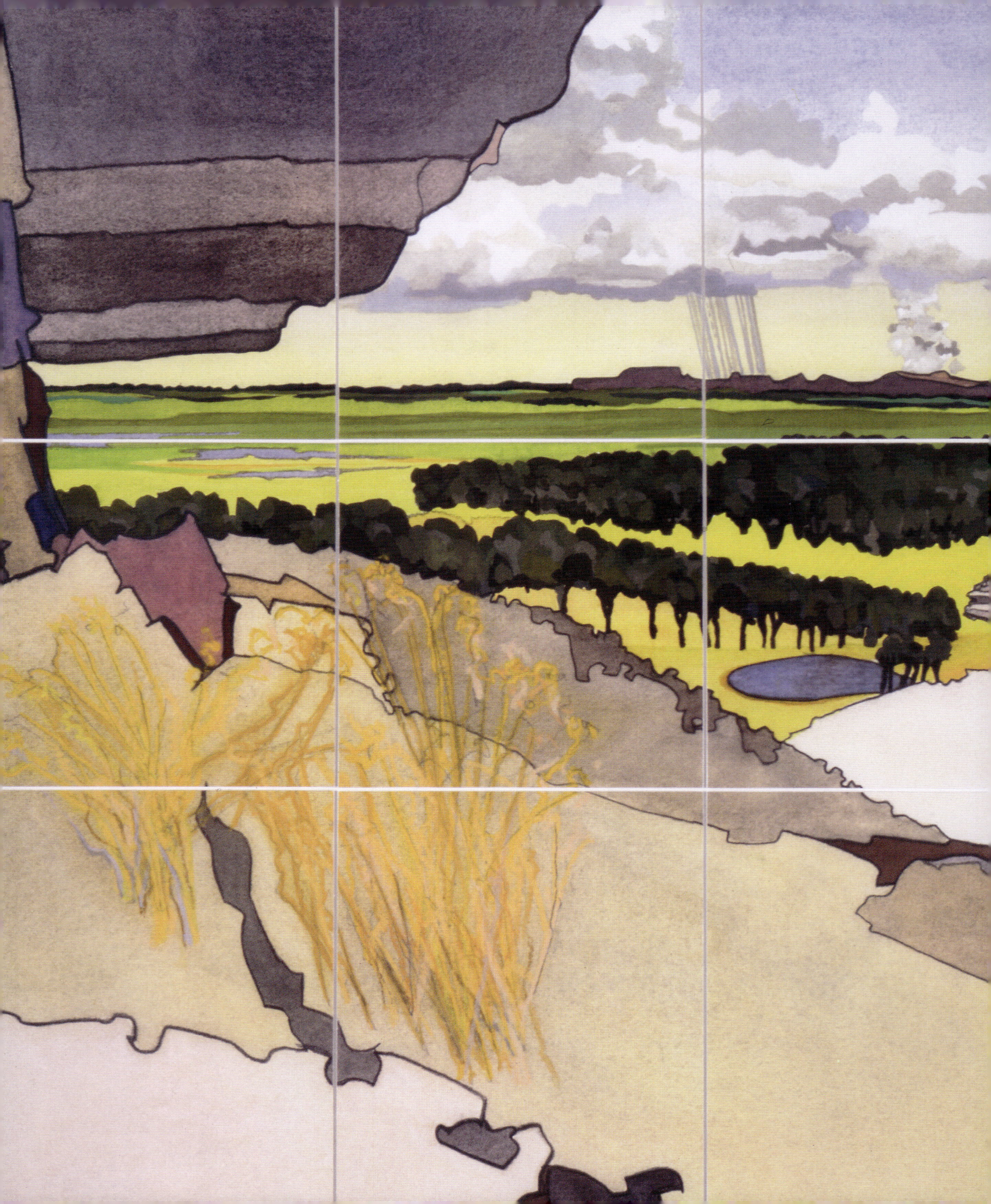

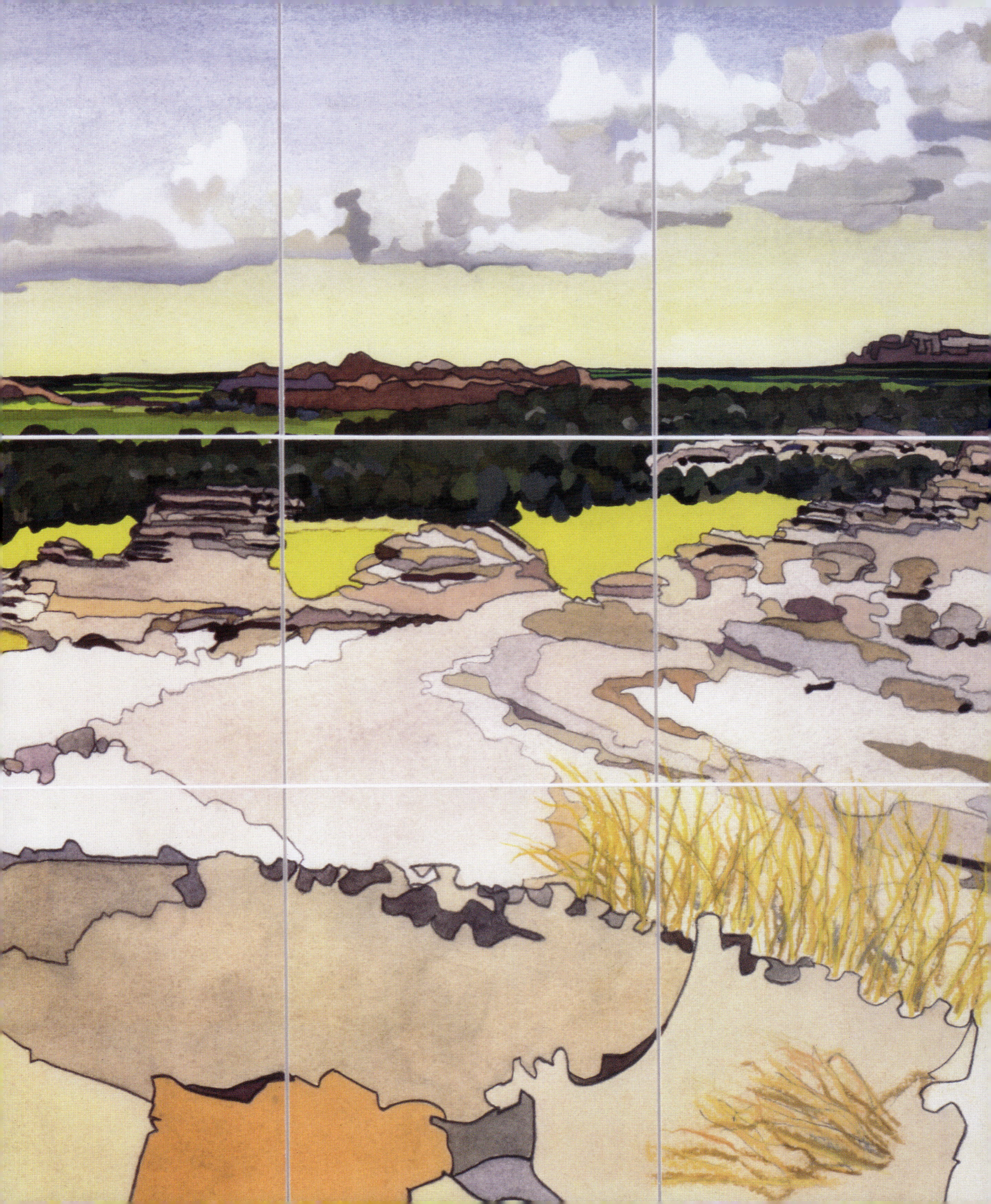

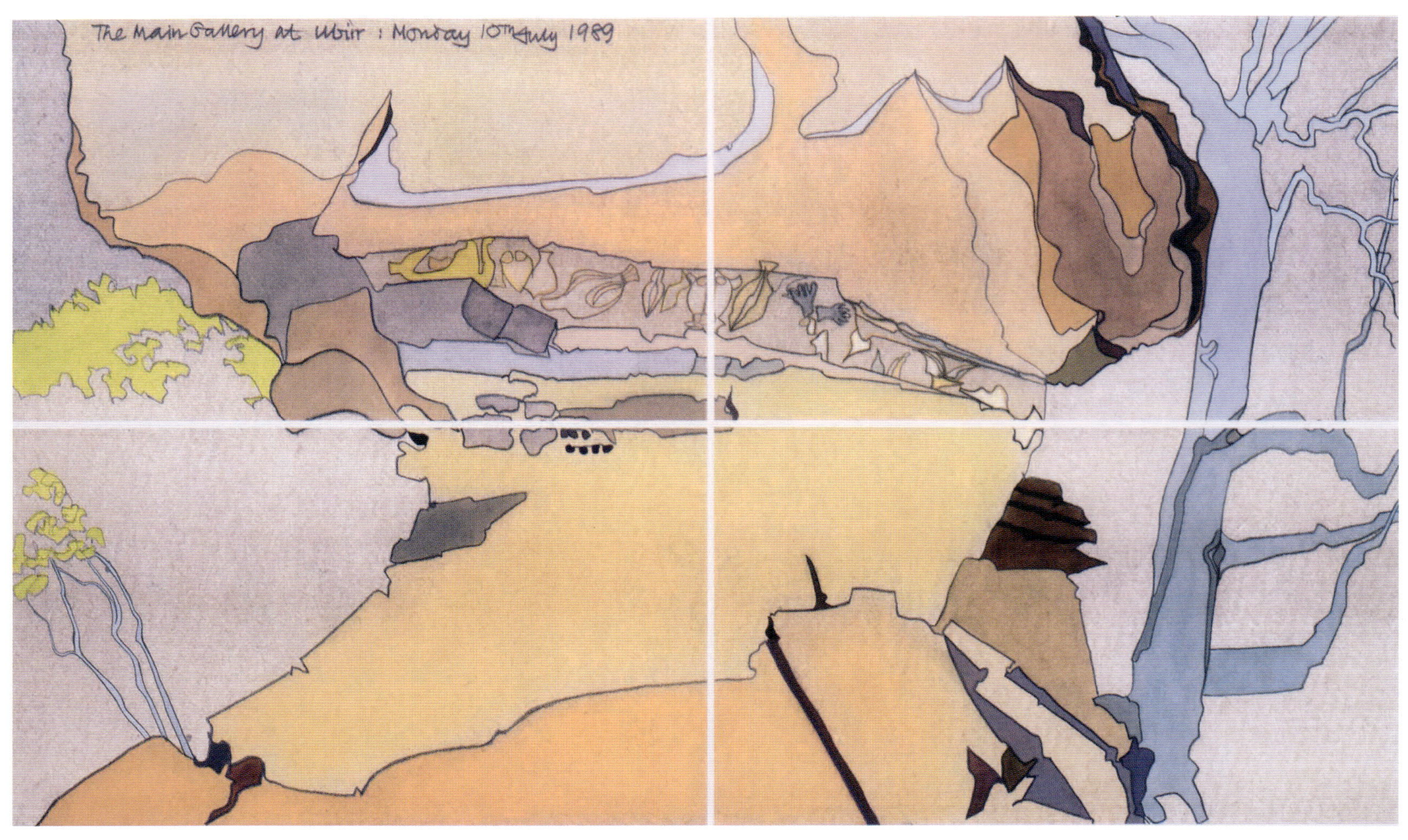
The Main Gallery at Ubirr : Monday 10th July 1989

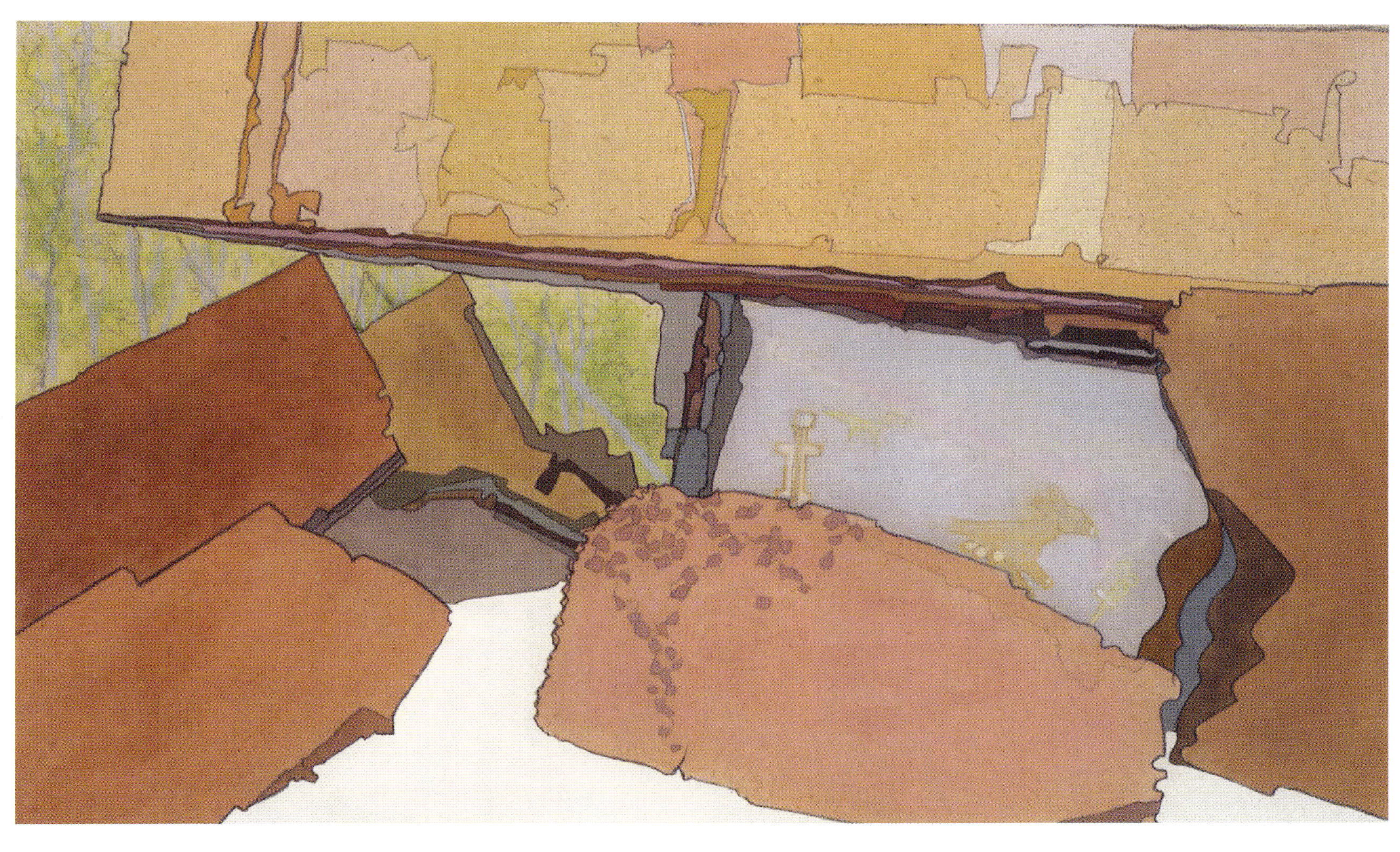

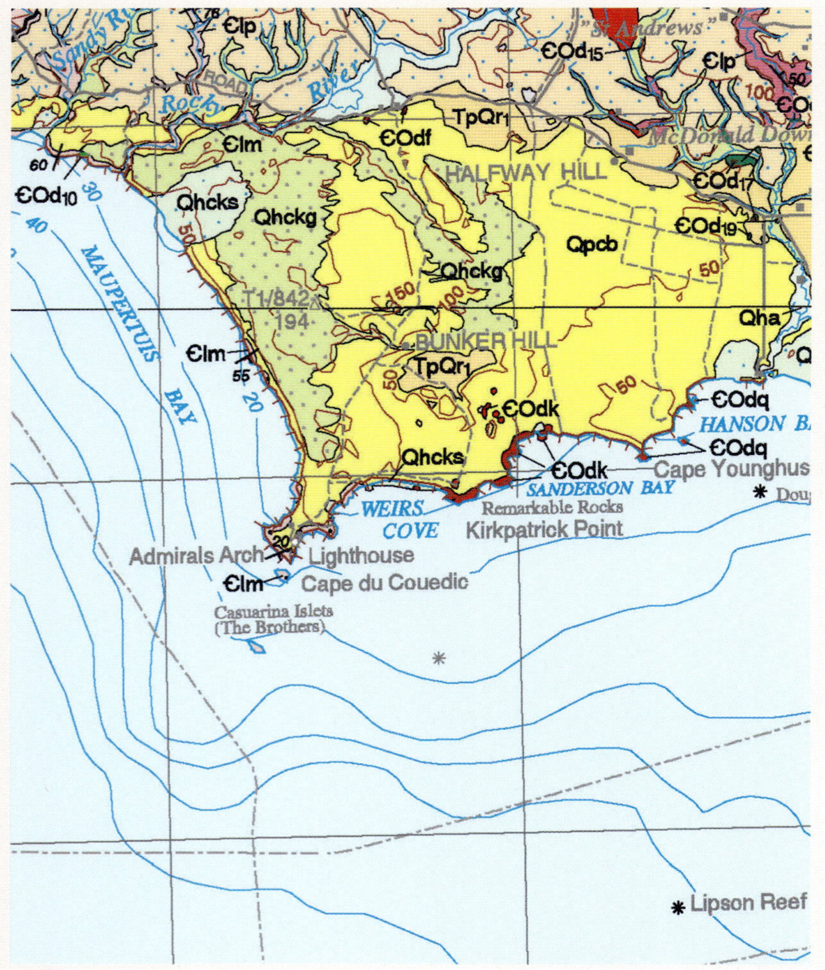


# Kangaroo Island, South Australia

36°02'54.0"S 136°45'26.1"E
-36.048333, 136.757262

Kangaroo Island lies less than 15 kilometres off the coast of South Australia. During our visit, we concentrated on the western end, where the Flinders Chase National Park is located. While the main part of the island – Australia's third largest – is cultivated, the west is all wild.

My visit to Kangaroo Island was specifically aimed at seeing Remarkable Rocks in the south-west of the island. The name is apt: they are remarkable. The works shown here are all of these rocks, which are perched 60 metres above the sea. Remarkable Rocks are composed of granite – mostly comprising black mica, blue quartz and pink feldspar – and fierce westerly winds crossing the Great Australian Bight have eroded them into dramatic shapes, beautifully curved. They are topped with intensely coloured orange lichen.

The rocks sit on a dome of granite, like a carefully carved giant sculpture set on a pedestal. What is particularly striking about these sculpted rocks are the different curves that intersect in complex forms. The top of the rocks loom far above you as you stand on the dome. There, the curves are broad, smooth, large, and there are small cavities within the rocks with complex networks of curves.

I have always loved curved, weathered rocks and have sought them out around the world, from Colombia to the UK. In England, the most striking granite outcrops are in Dartmoor and in the far west of Cornwall. I have recently visited these tors, as they are called, and painted large canvases of their forms. But of all such outcrops I have visited, I think that Remarkable Rocks are the most striking, in part because of their setting beside the wild Southern Ocean.

The fires of late 2019 and early 2020 in the east and south of Australia were the most catastrophic recorded since European arrival. A total area of 20 per cent of Australia's forests was burnt during the many months of fires, and Kangaroo Island was among the worst hit. About half the island was devastated, with a concentration of destruction in the remote western half where Remarkable Rocks are situated. These fires had a devastating effect on the special animal populations of the island. My paintings of Remarkable Rocks were done many years ago. I have now added a painting based on this fire damage, completed in 2020, on page 73.

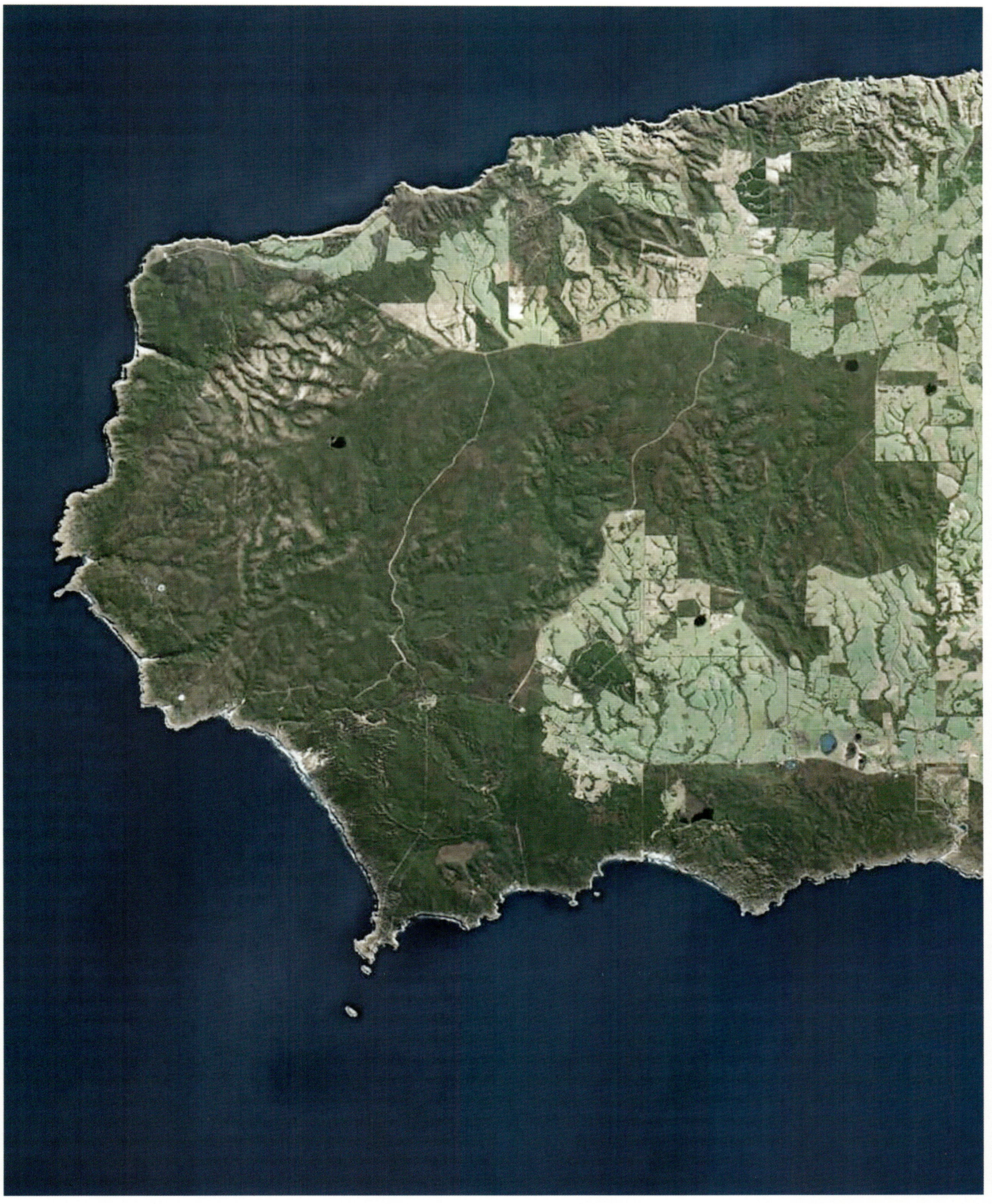

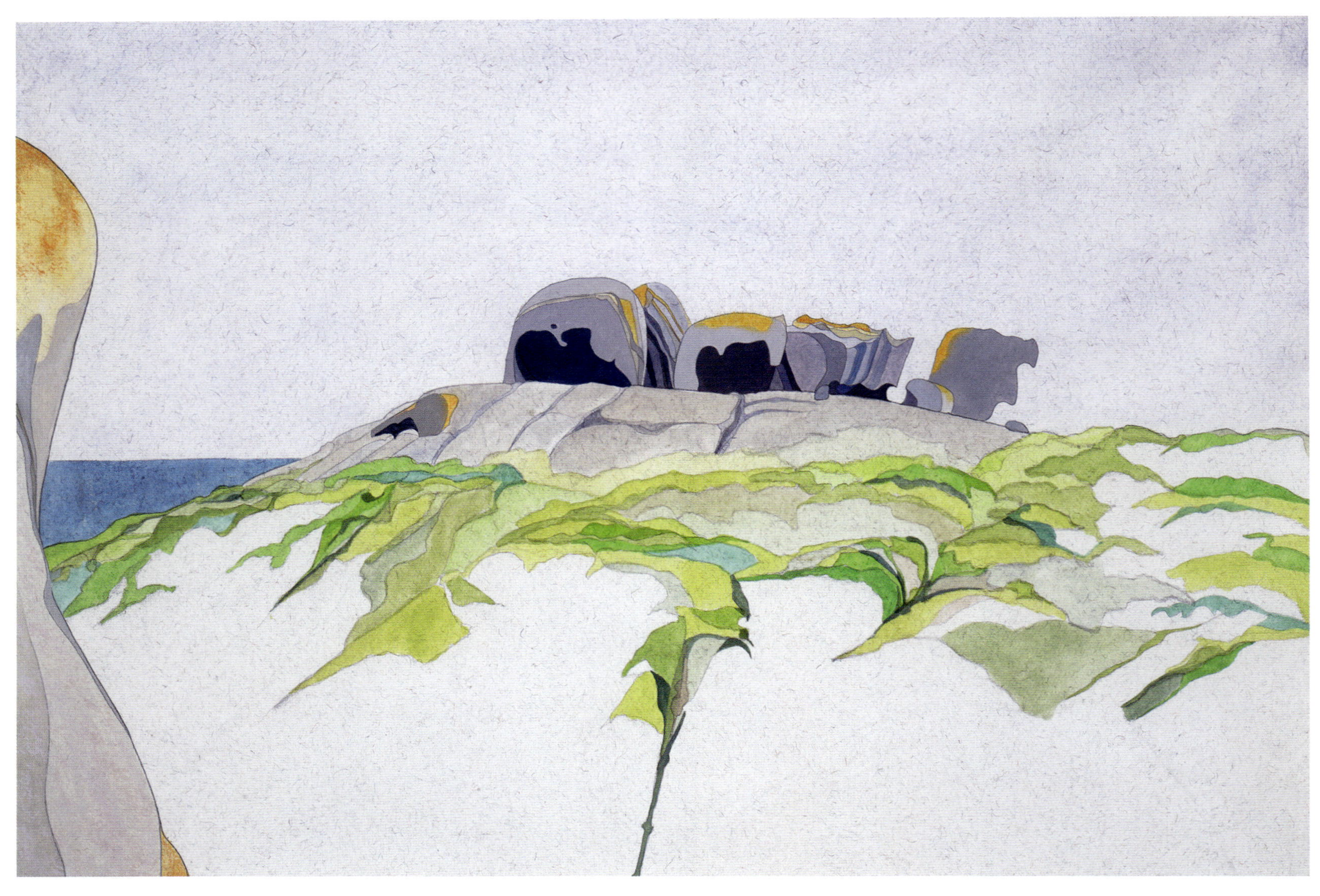

ABOVE
*Remarkable Rocks: the main complex*, 1994

RIGHT
*Remarkable Rocks: looking between the rocks*, 1994

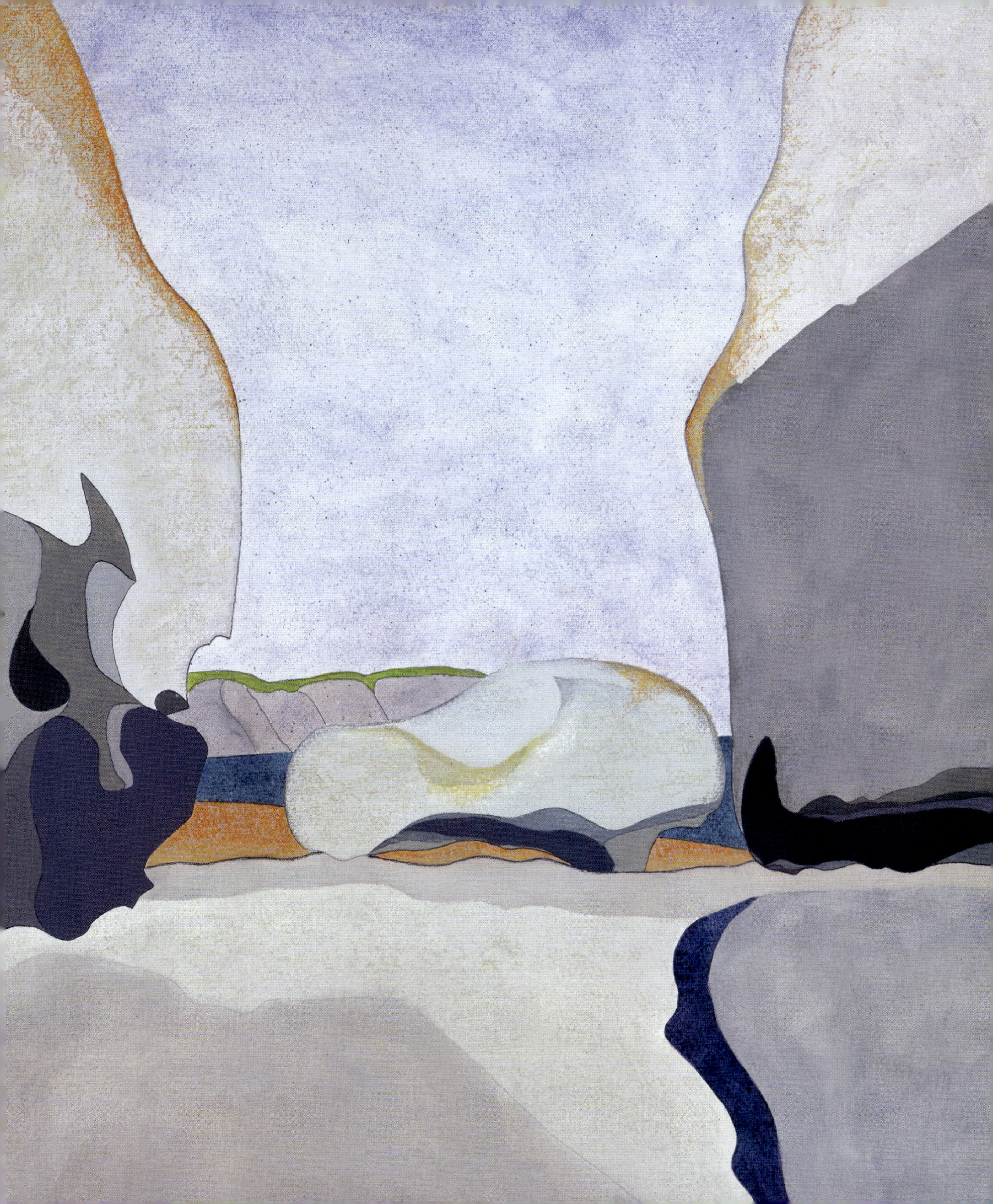

The fires of late 2019 and early 2020
in the east and south of Australia were
the most catastrophic recorded since
European arrival ... Kangaroo Island was
among the worst hit. About half the island
was devastated, with a concentration of
destruction in the wild western half where
Remarkable Rocks are situated.

*Fire: Kangaroo Island, 2020*

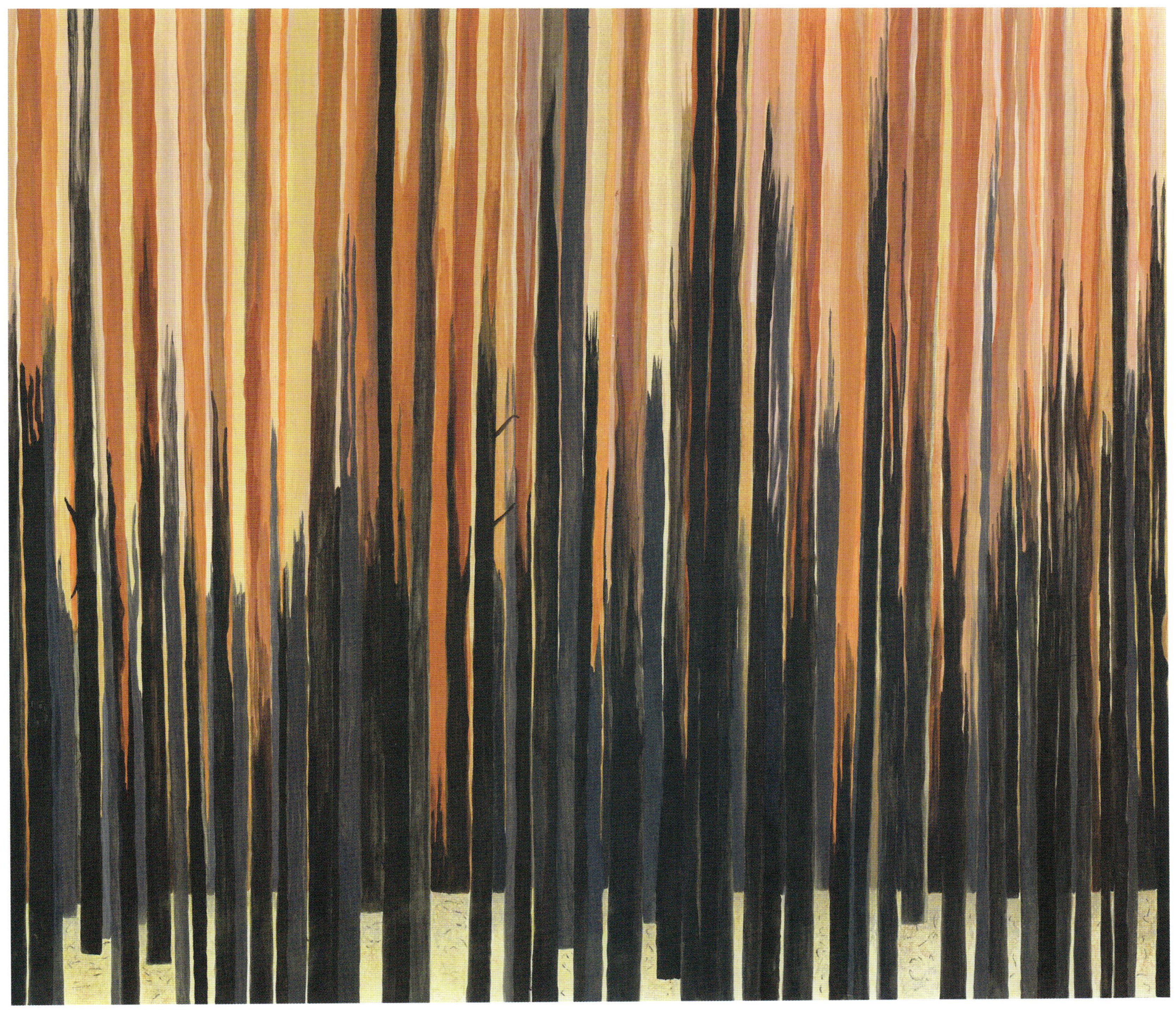

# Flight from Alice Springs, Northern Territory, to Kalamurina, South Australia

FROM
23°48'18.0"S 133°54'11.8"E
-23.805001, 133.903275

TO
27°42'44.1"S 138°19'40.5"E
-27.712247, 138.327926

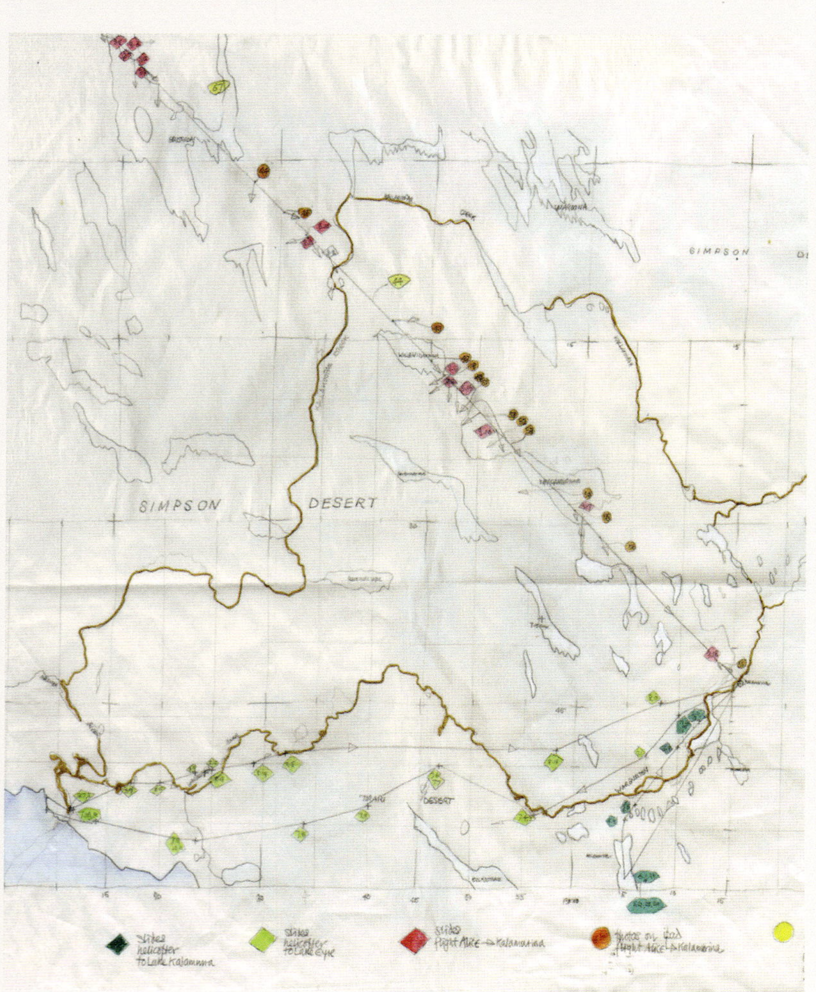

To get to Kalamurina, we had to fly in, as overland access was cut off by the recent rains. So it meant going to Alice Springs and from there chartering a plane. This was expensive, but the plane took four of us: my wife, my sister Sally, a friend and myself. The plane was a twin-engine Cessna piloted by Tim Rossiter. He was so helpful, explaining both the details of the flight and how to interpret the instrument readings. We were strictly limited in the weight of our luggage. This was particularly testing, as we had to take all our provisions for three days. I remember shopping in the supermarket at Alice Springs and agonising over how best to use our allowance. For example, could we afford the weight of beer? No. A decision we regretted!

The flight took two hours, travelling south-east. I am enthralled by flying at low altitude, especially over Central Australia. The land is most striking seen from the air. The view from above is a major theme in my work in general, so this was a special opportunity to draw and photograph. I was able to track the exact location of each of the drawings by taking readings from the pilot's instruments. The drawings had to be done very quickly, in perhaps thirty to forty seconds at most. So that meant a roughness, which shows, but it did force me to concentrate on the essentials of the land below. Some of these drawings are shown here, as well as the paintings later derived from the notebook drawings and photographs.

The most striking features on the flight were the parallel ridges of the dunes in the Simpson Desert, and the lakes – strange shapes, mostly all white or pink salt, but some with water. From our altitude, 7500 feet, these marks on the desert stretched away into the far distance.

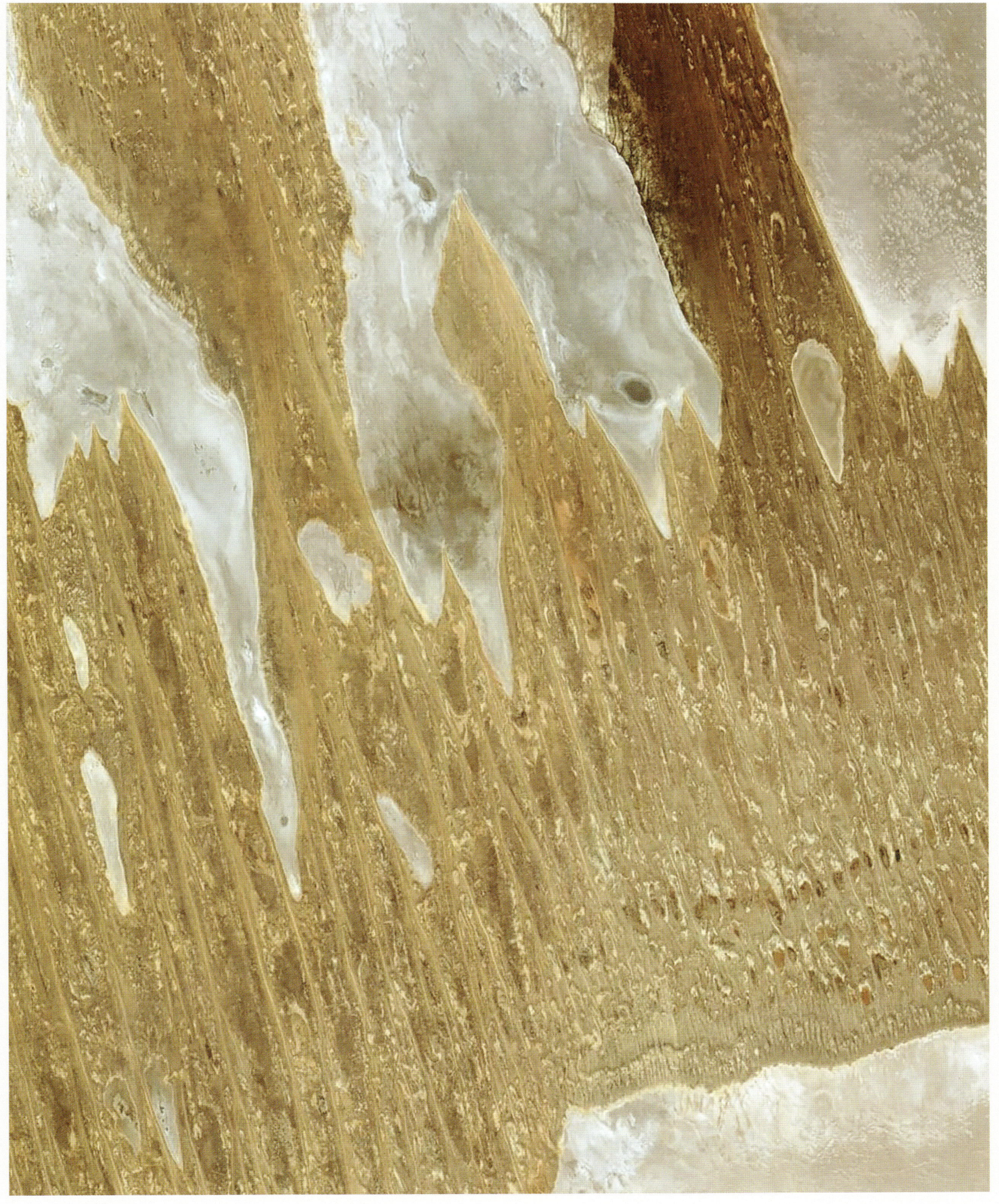

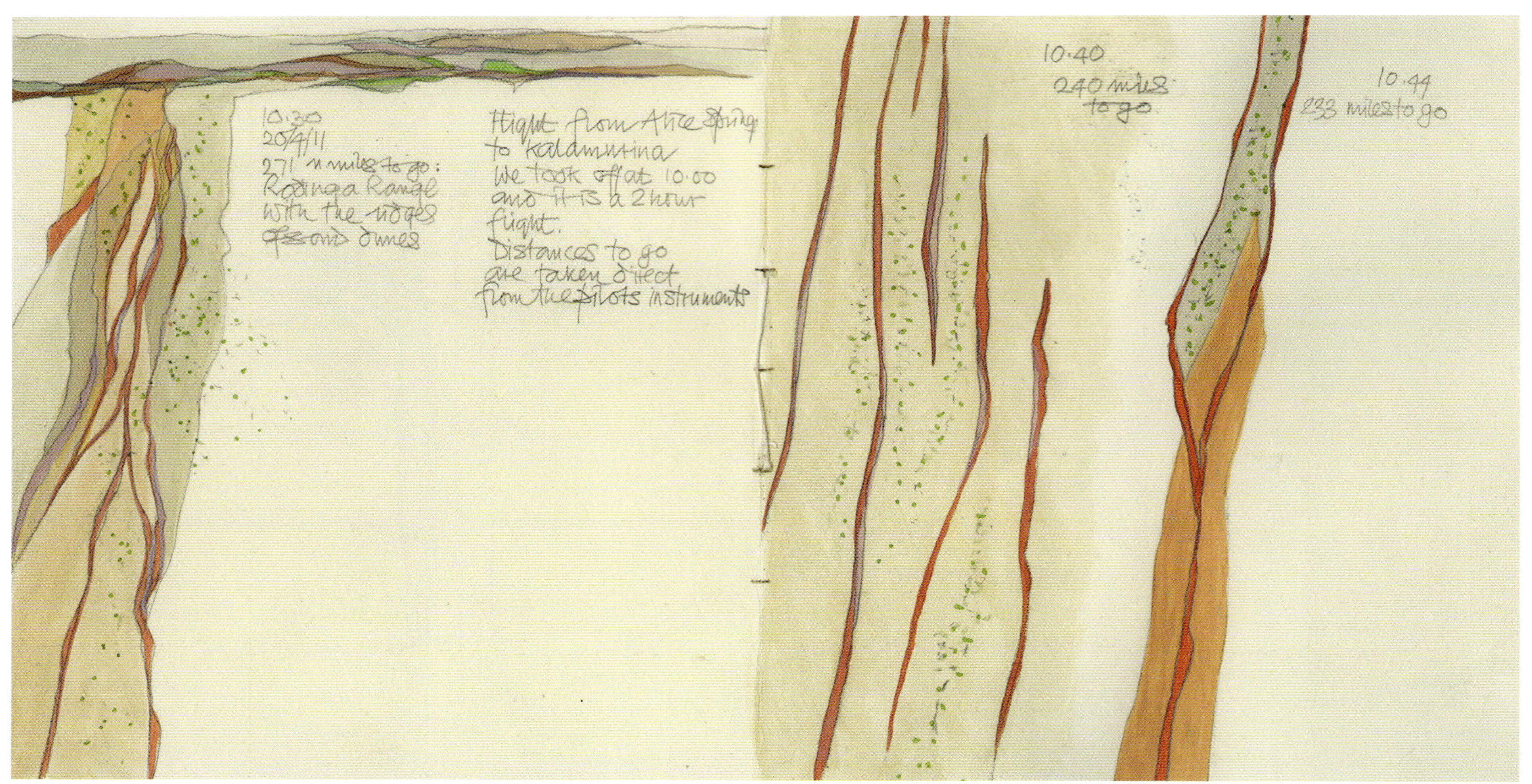


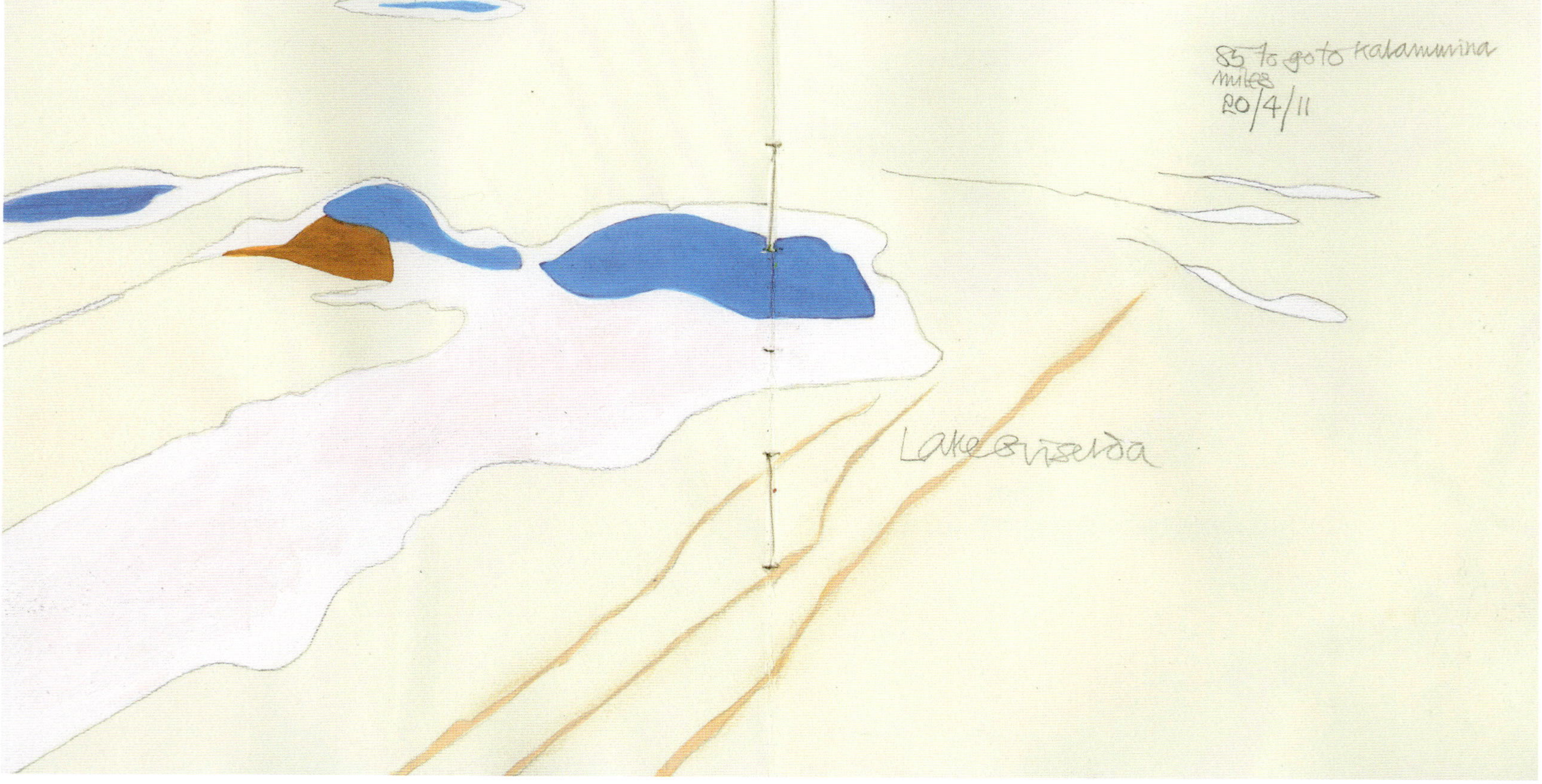


*271 and 240 miles to Kalamurina,*
20 April 2011

*85 miles to Lake Griselda,*
20 April 2011

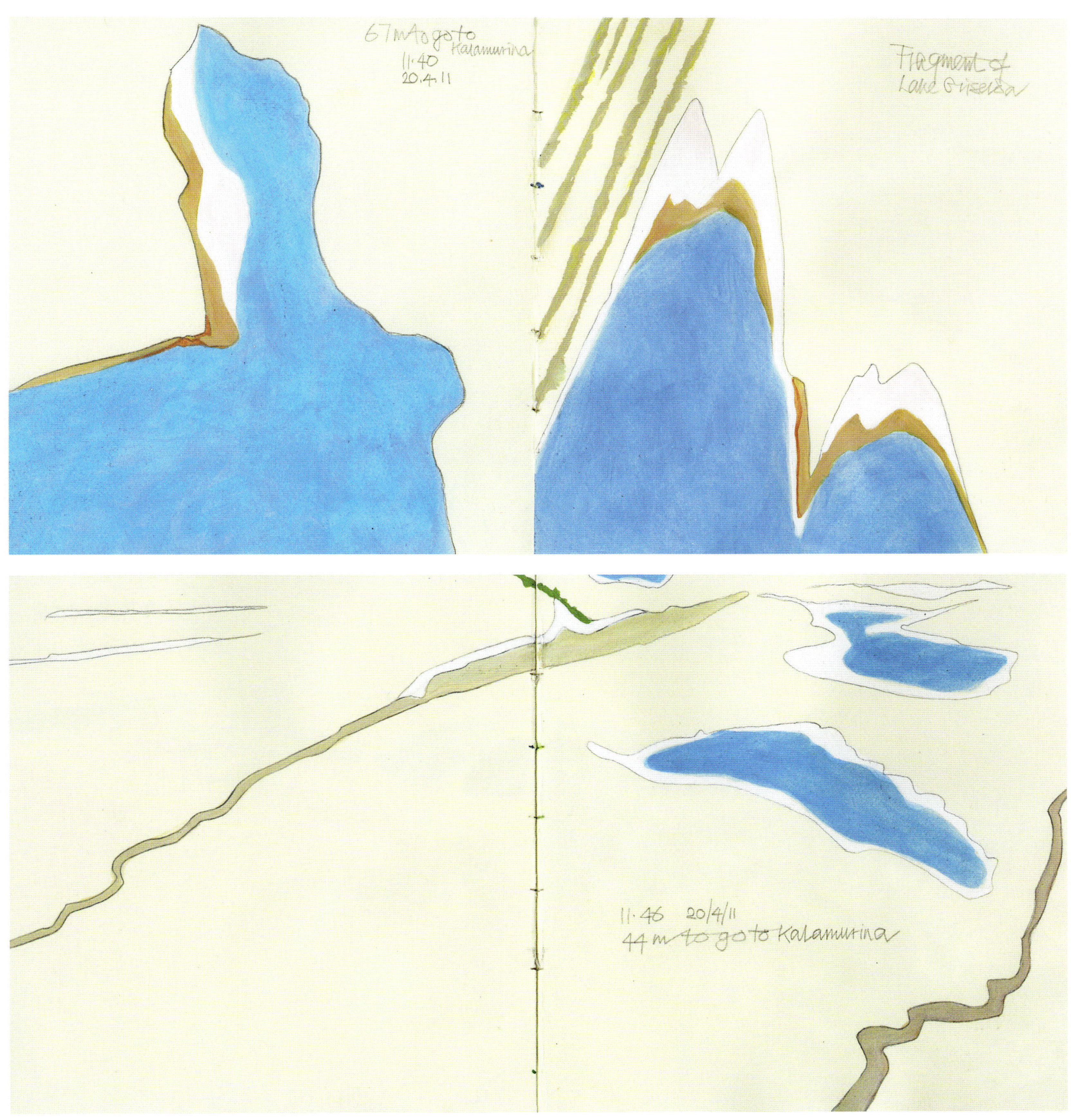


*67 miles to Kalamurina,*
20 April 2011

*44 miles to Kalamurina,*
20 April 2011

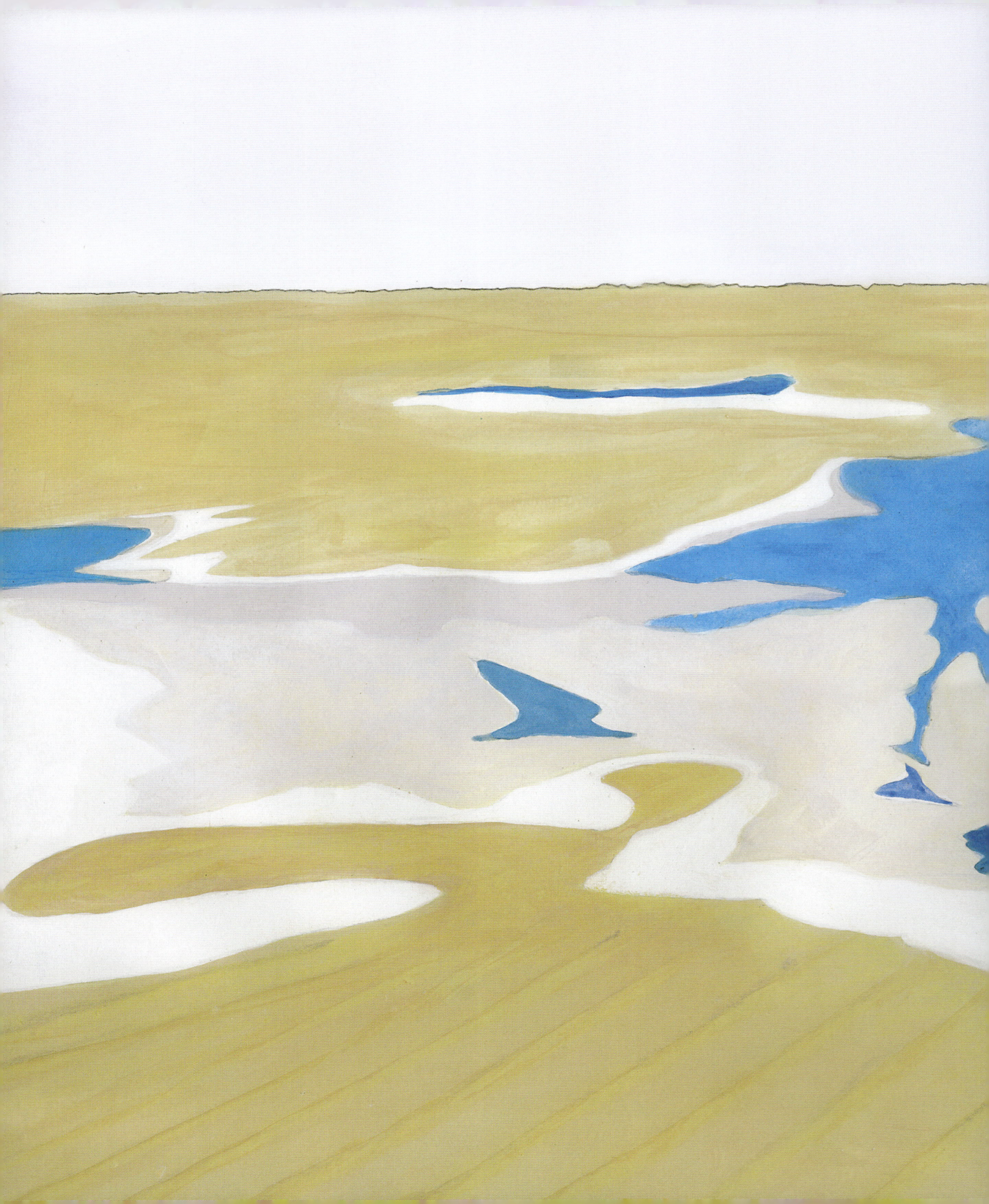

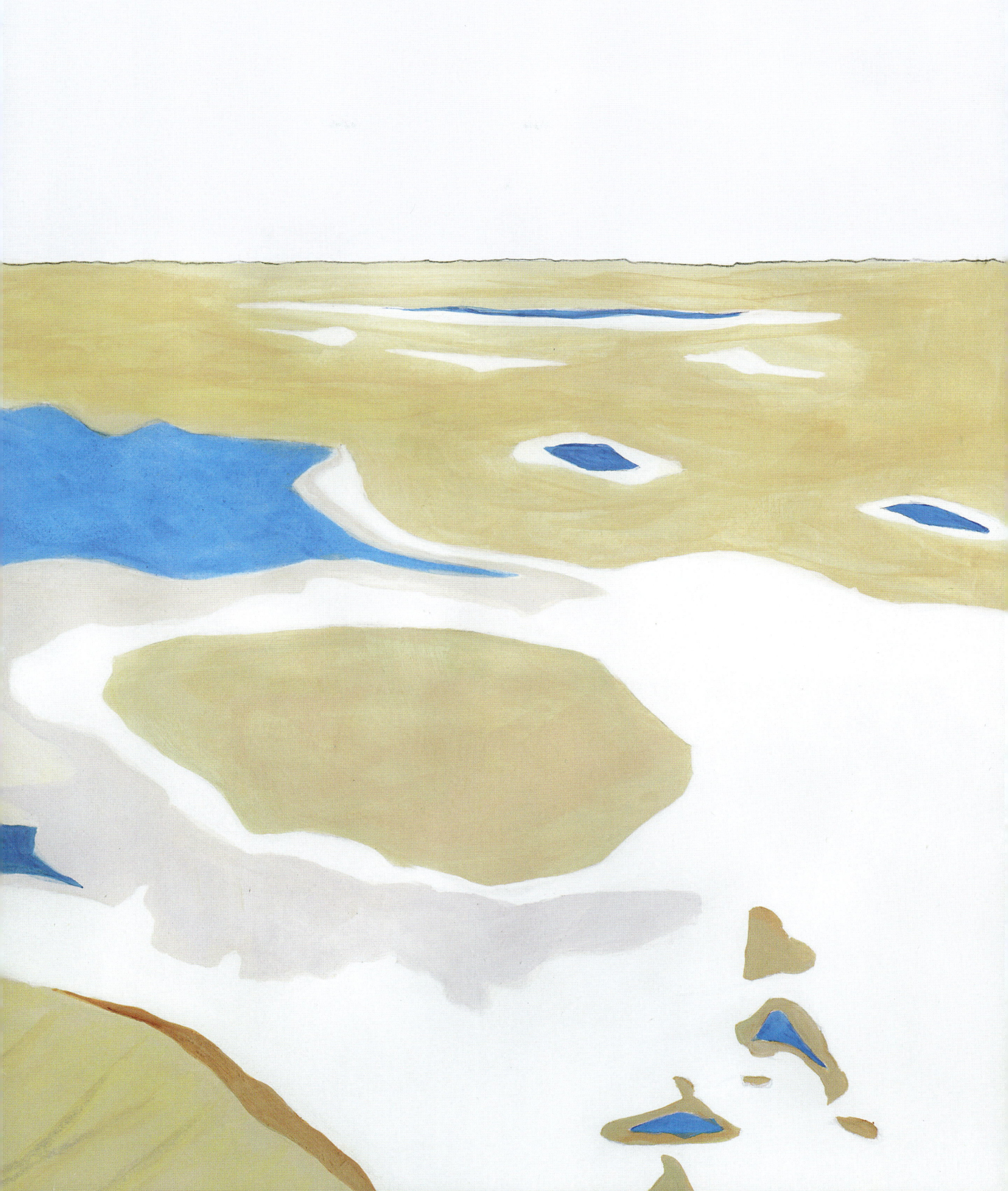

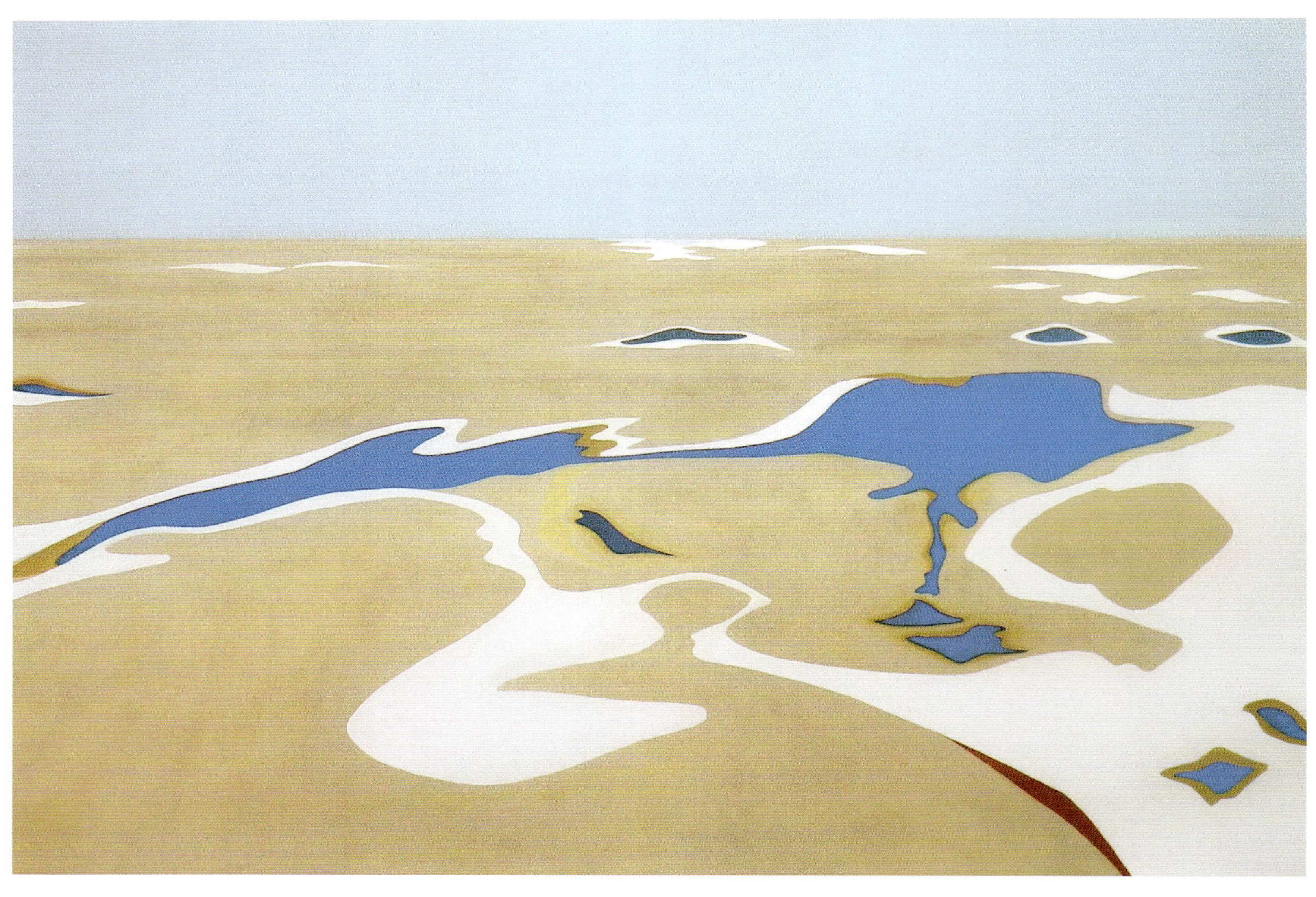

PREVIOUS SPREAD
*Lake Griselda II*, 2012

ABOVE
*Lake Griselda*, 2012

RIGHT
*Flight from Alice Springs to Kalamurina*,
2011

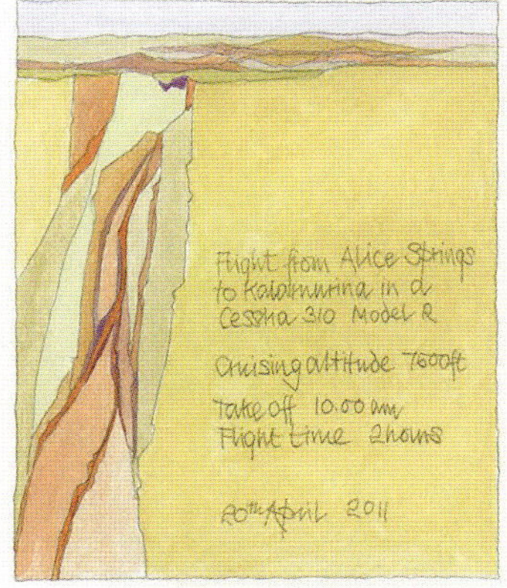
Flight from Alice Springs
to Kalotwinna in a
Cessna 310 Model R

Cruising altitude 7600ft

Take off 10.00 am
Flight time 2hours

20th April 2011
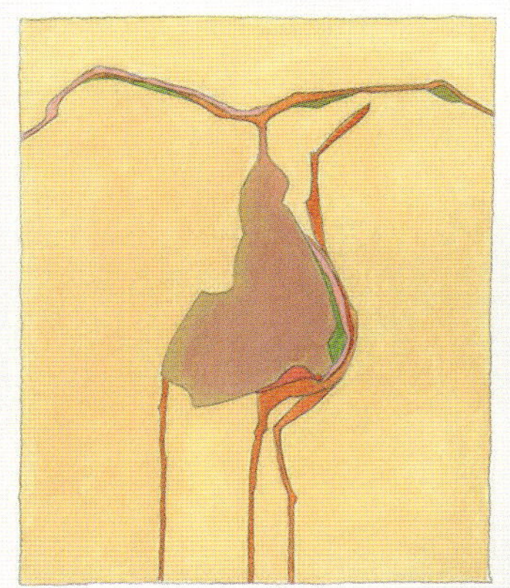
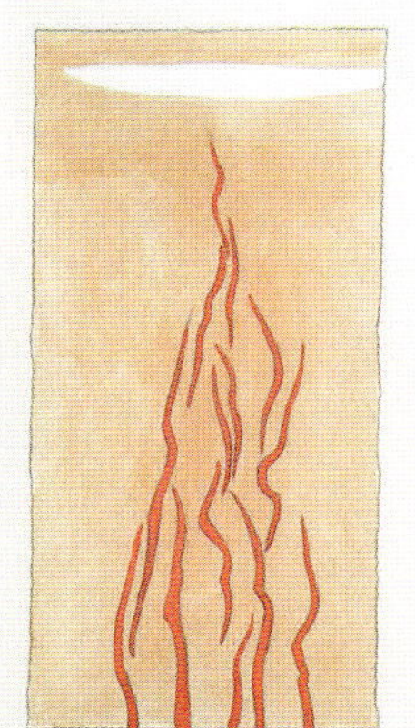
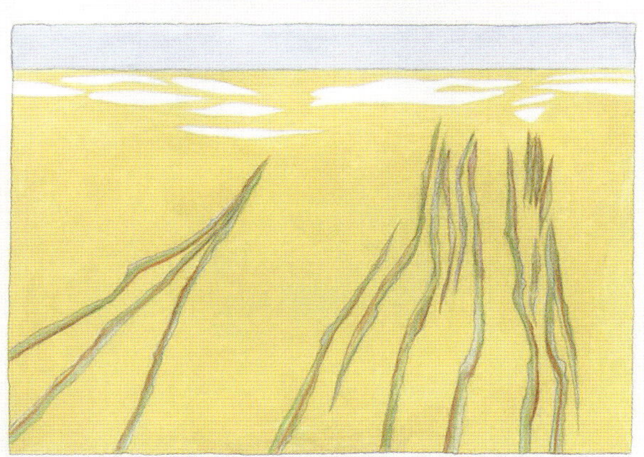
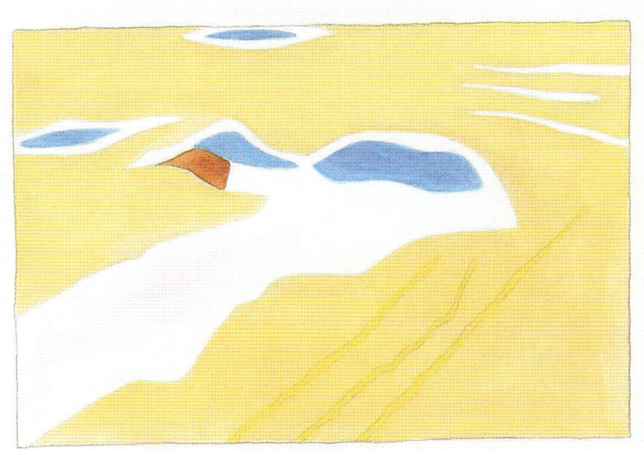
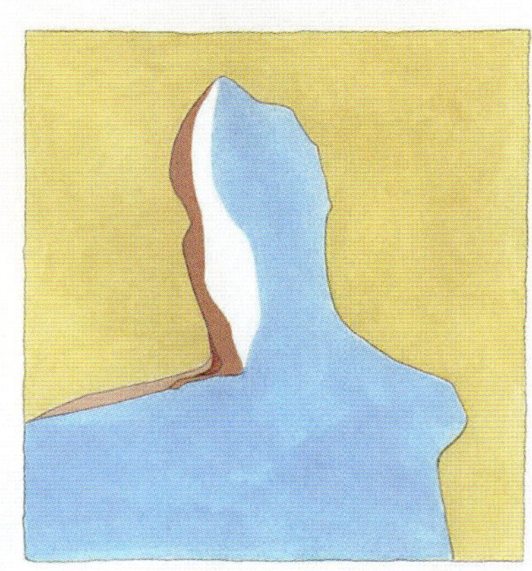
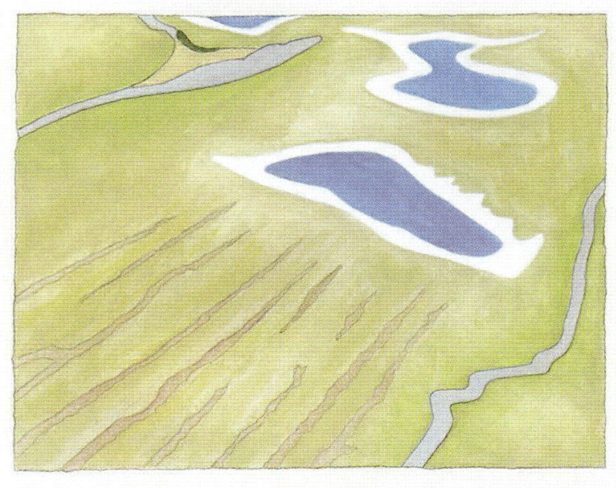

# Kalamurina Sanctuary, South Australia

27°43'13.1"S 138°15'10.3"E
-27.720301, 138.252846

The Australian Wildlife Conservancy (AWC) owns and maintains the sanctuary of Kalamurina, which lies to the north of Kati Thanda, also known as Lake Eyre. The main remit of the AWC is to protect the indigenous species of Australia and to help them flourish. This often means fencing off large areas to create protective zones, within which invader species such as feral cats are eliminated. Kalamurina is at the intersection of three of Central Australia's deserts: the Simpson Desert, the Tirari Desert and Sturt Stony Desert. The sanctuary is huge, almost 680,000 hectares, and 140 kilometres from east to west. To try to grasp its size, I sought to compare it to something more familiar to me. I calculated that it is about one-third of the size of Wales.

The AWC invited us to stay as guests at the only homestead on the reserve, which was built when the area was a huge cattle station. A couple in permanent residence at the homestead were the only people living at Kalamurina full-time. There was limited accommodation in the house, and then two or three outbuildings where those on working-site visits could stay. This provided accommodation for Tim Rossiter, the Cessna pilot, and for the pilot of the chartered helicopter, Bridgette Kies, who flew in from the Barossa Valley to the south.

The helicopter was essential. Only that way could we get to the remote northern shore of Kati Thanda. But it also allowed us to visit another lake, Lake Kalamurra – totally dry – and it gave us amazing views of the surrounding landscape from above. Drawing was easier than it had been from the Cessna. I had more time for photography too. Included here are a number of paintings derived from drawings and paintings of the surrounding dunes and lakes made from the helicopter. At Lake Kalamurra, where we landed and walked around, we saw the tracks of animals that had crossed the dry lake bed – camel, emu and dingo. I created photo works and paintings to illustrate these tracks.

When we visited Kalamurina, it was after a period of exceptional rains. Indeed, that is *why* we went then, so as to see Lake Eyre in flood. This meant that the bush, usually desert-like, was green and covered with plant life, including a proliferation of wildflowers. The Warburton, which flows close to the station and then right through the reserve into Lake Eyre, was full, instead of the usual trickle. The water was still rising as it continued to flow down from Queensland, the level being watched nervously as it approached the top of the creek's banks. Though riddled with disastrous potential, the life-bringing flow was a wonderful sight, especially from the helicopter.

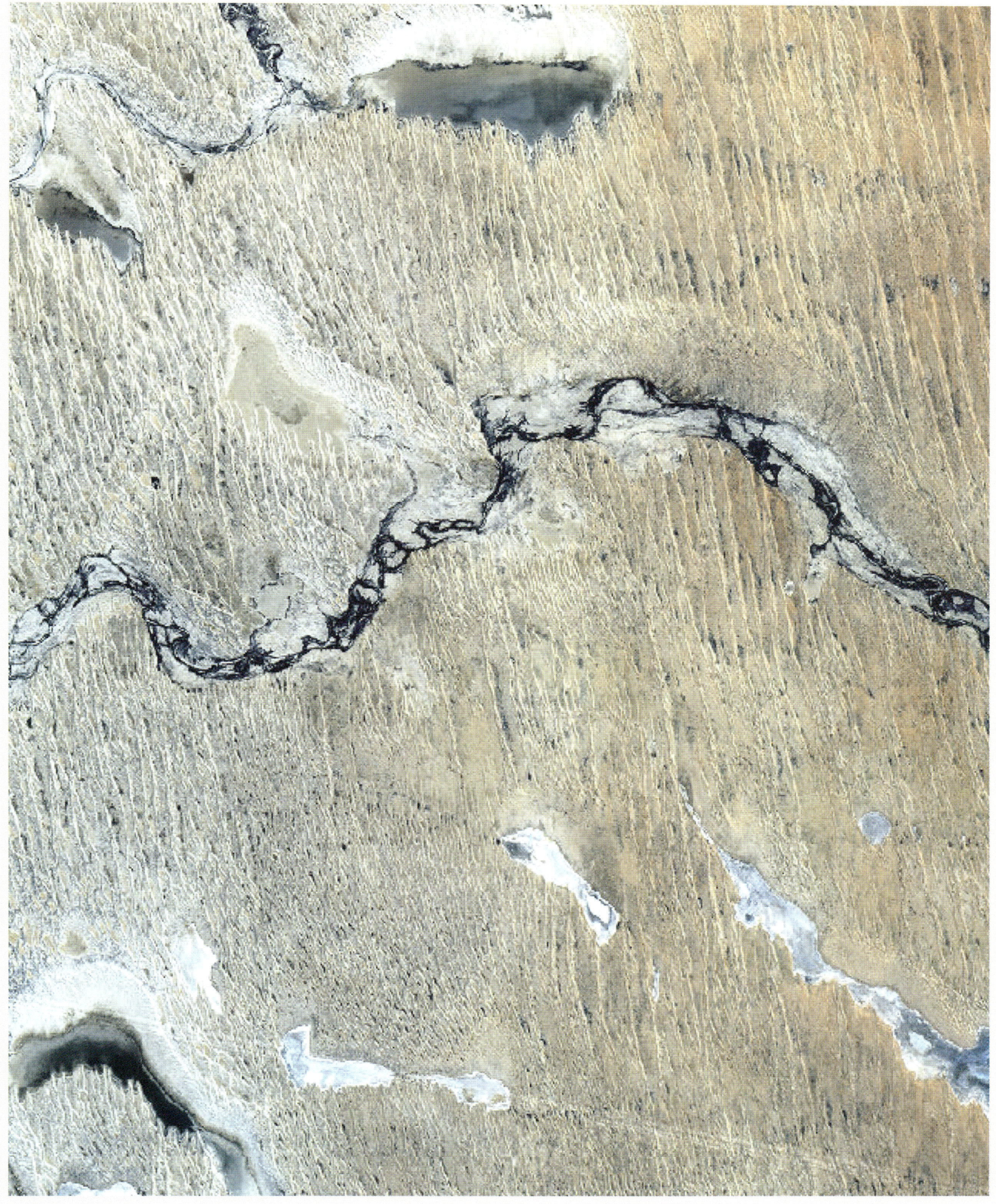

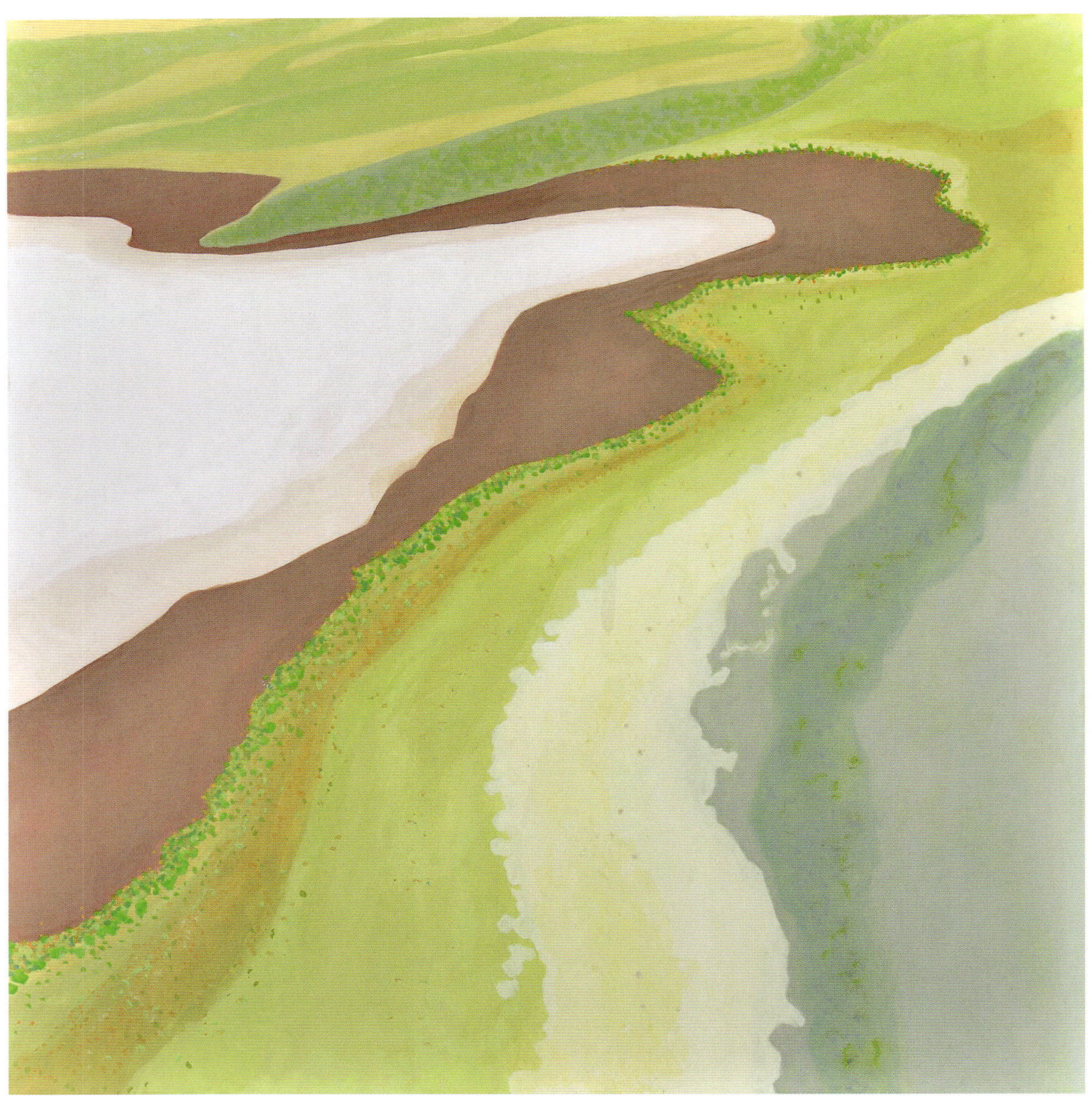

ABOVE
*Salt Lake en route to Kallakoopah,*
2012

RIGHT
*Lake and sand dune en route*
*to Kallakoopah, 2012*

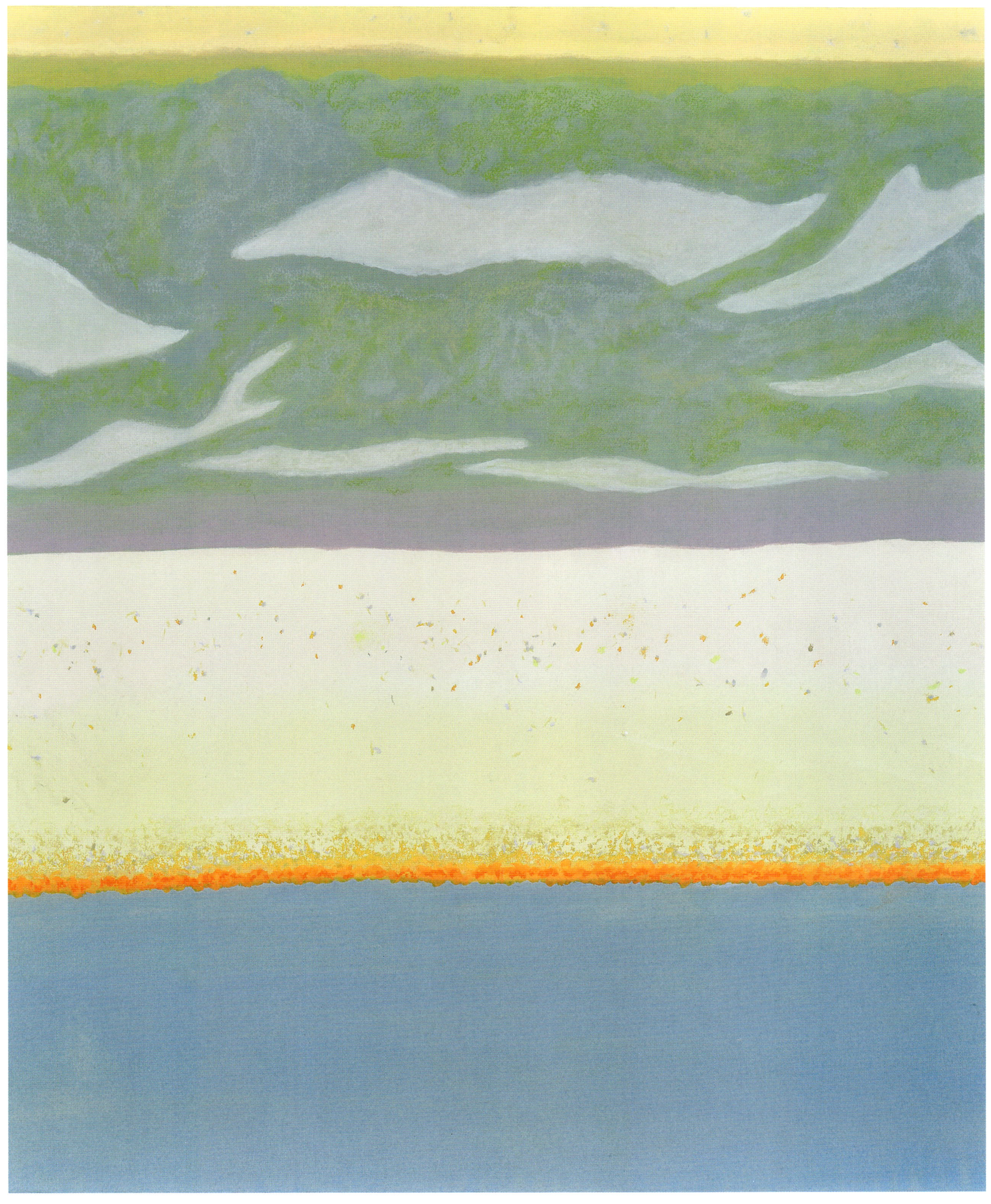

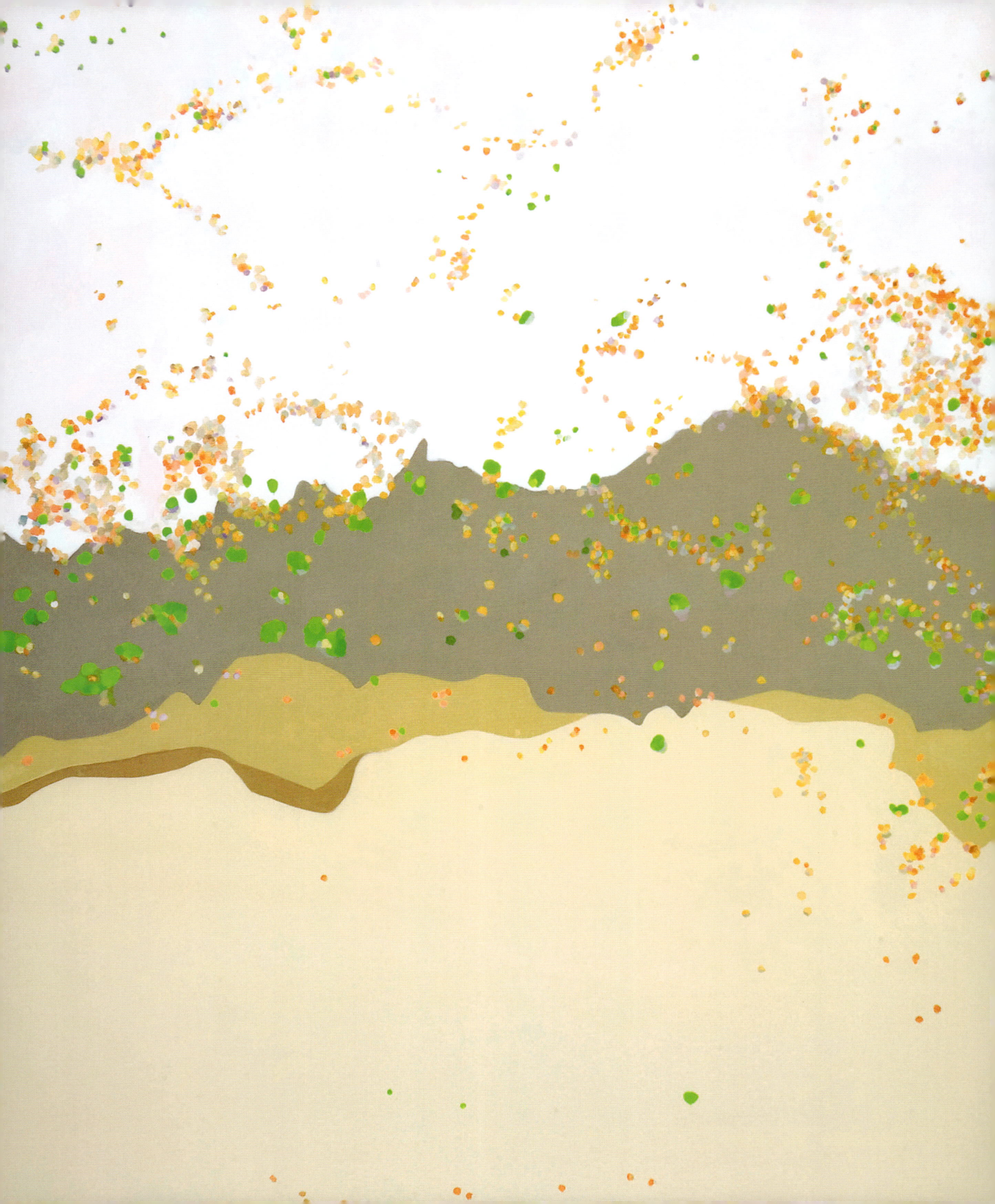

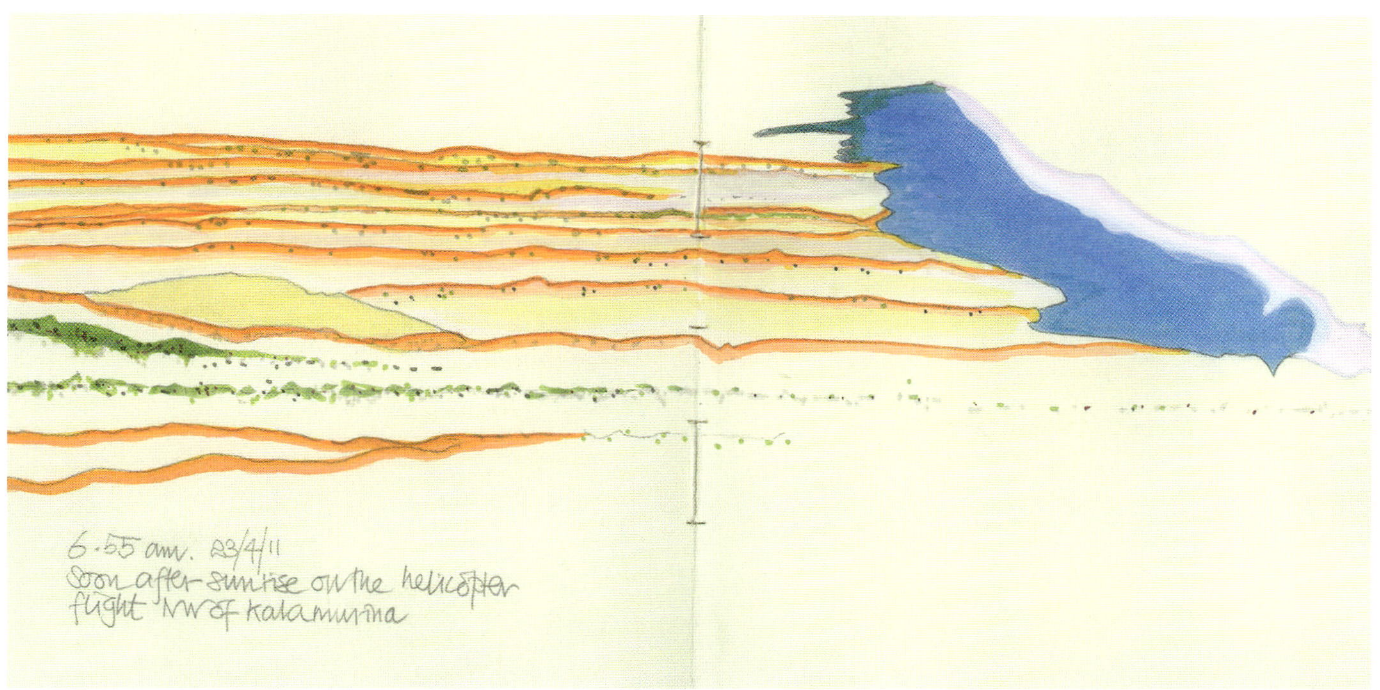

6.55 am. 23/4/11
Soon after sunrise on the helicopter
flight NW of Kalamurina


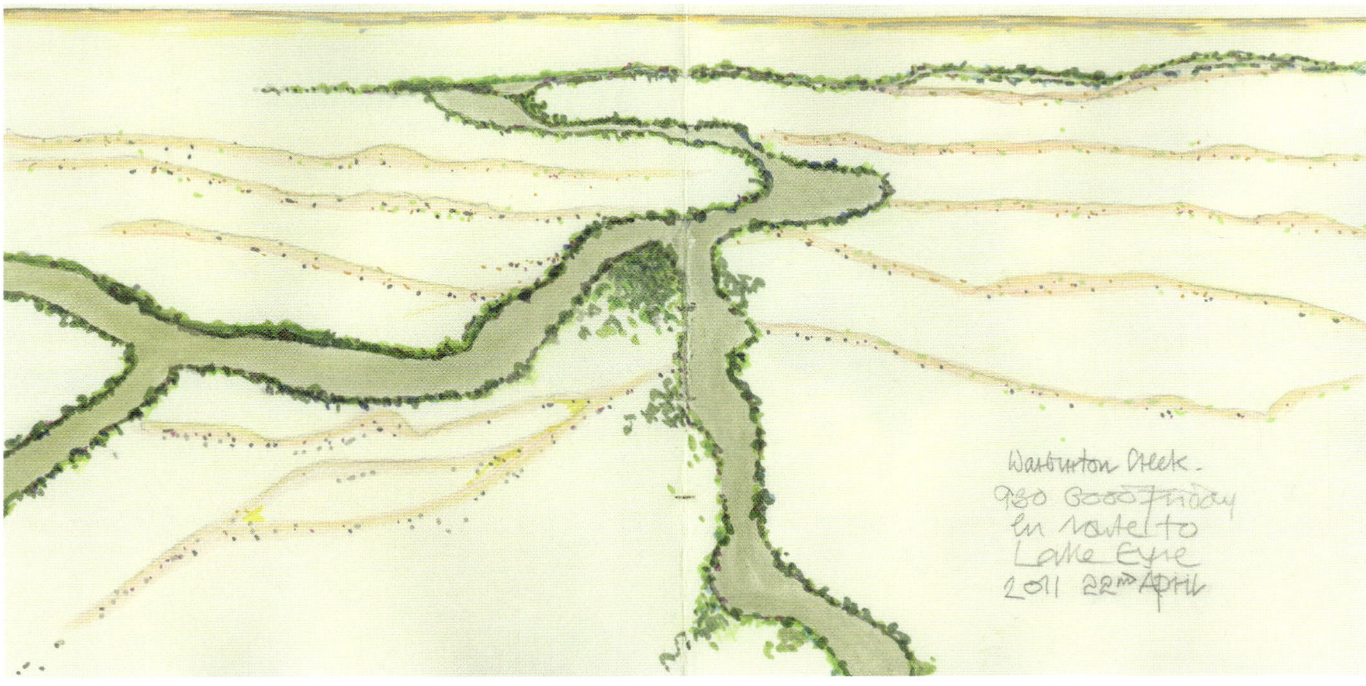

Warburton Creek.
9.30 Good Friday
en route to
Lake Eyre
2011 22nd April



**LEFT**
*Flight to Kallakoopah,* 2011

**ABOVE**
*Flight north-west of Kalamurina,*
23 April 2011

*Warbuton Creek en route to
Lake Eyre,* 22 April 2011

# Kati Thanda / Lake Eyre, South Australia

28°12'23.4"S 137°14'59.0"E
-28.206509, 137.249727

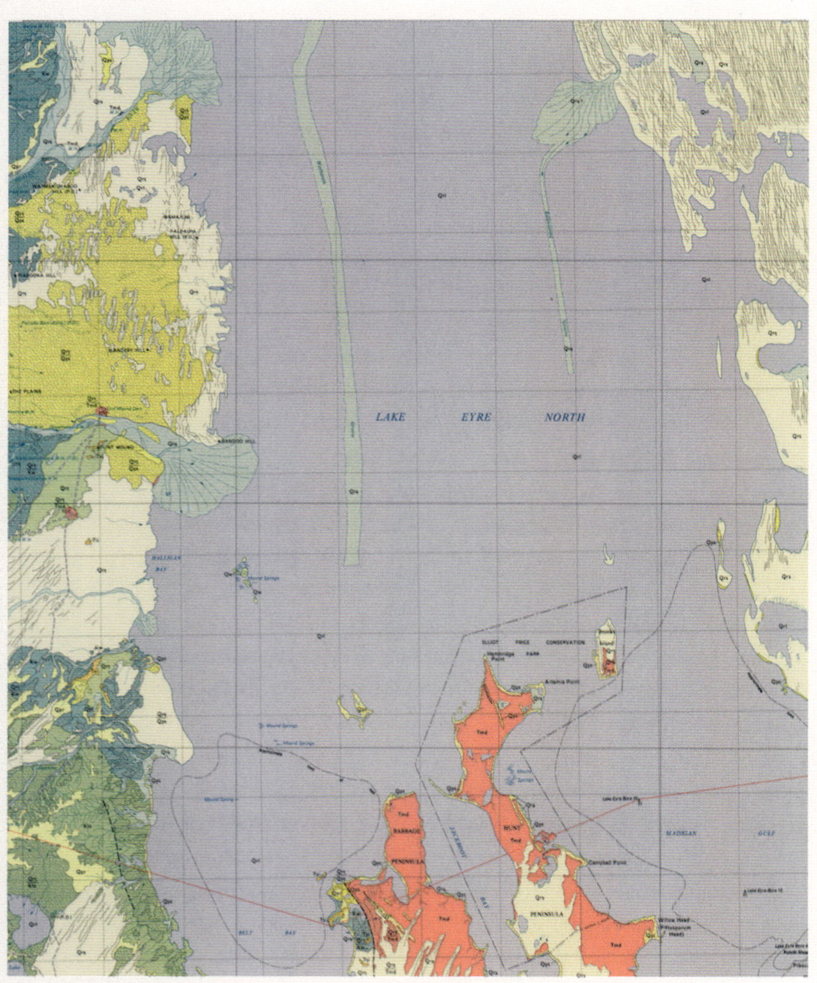

In 2011, Kati Thanda was flooded, which on average happens about every fifteen years. Over 65 per cent of the water that flows into Kati Thanda passes through Kalamurina, and the lake's major source is Warburton Creek, a catchment for water flowing down from Queensland. On our visit, we stayed just beside the Warburton, now full. The vegetation was green. The desert was in flower.

I had always wanted to see Kati Thanda flooded. The Australian Wildlife Conservancy made it possible to reach the northern shore of the lake. On Good Friday, we flew there by helicopter, following the Warburton. As we approached Kati Thanda, we passed the junction of the rivers feeding the lake. The vast area of water filling the flooded lake opened before us. This was our destination, the goal of the long journey starting in Sydney, leading to Alice Springs, Kalamurina Homestead and, finally, to the lake.

We landed on the shore. There was a real sense of achievement in having arrived at such a remote and inaccessible location. The expanse of the waters stretched to the horizon. Water and land seemed to intermingle, as if there was no real shoreline. I did a couple of drawings and Psiche took some photographs. As well as the lake, I drew the pelican tracks in the salt at the lake's edge. We had seen huge flocks of pelicans as we flew.

We left the next day by Cessna, flying right over the lake. Seen from this air-crossing, you realise just how big the lake is and how impressive when full of water. We had to make a deviation to William Creek in order to refuel for the long flight back to Alice Springs, and while the plane was being tended to, we went to the famous bar at the William Creek Hotel. This is a key stop for those bravely driving along the Oodnadatta Track. The walls are completely covered with what seems like thousands of business cards left over the years by those passing through.

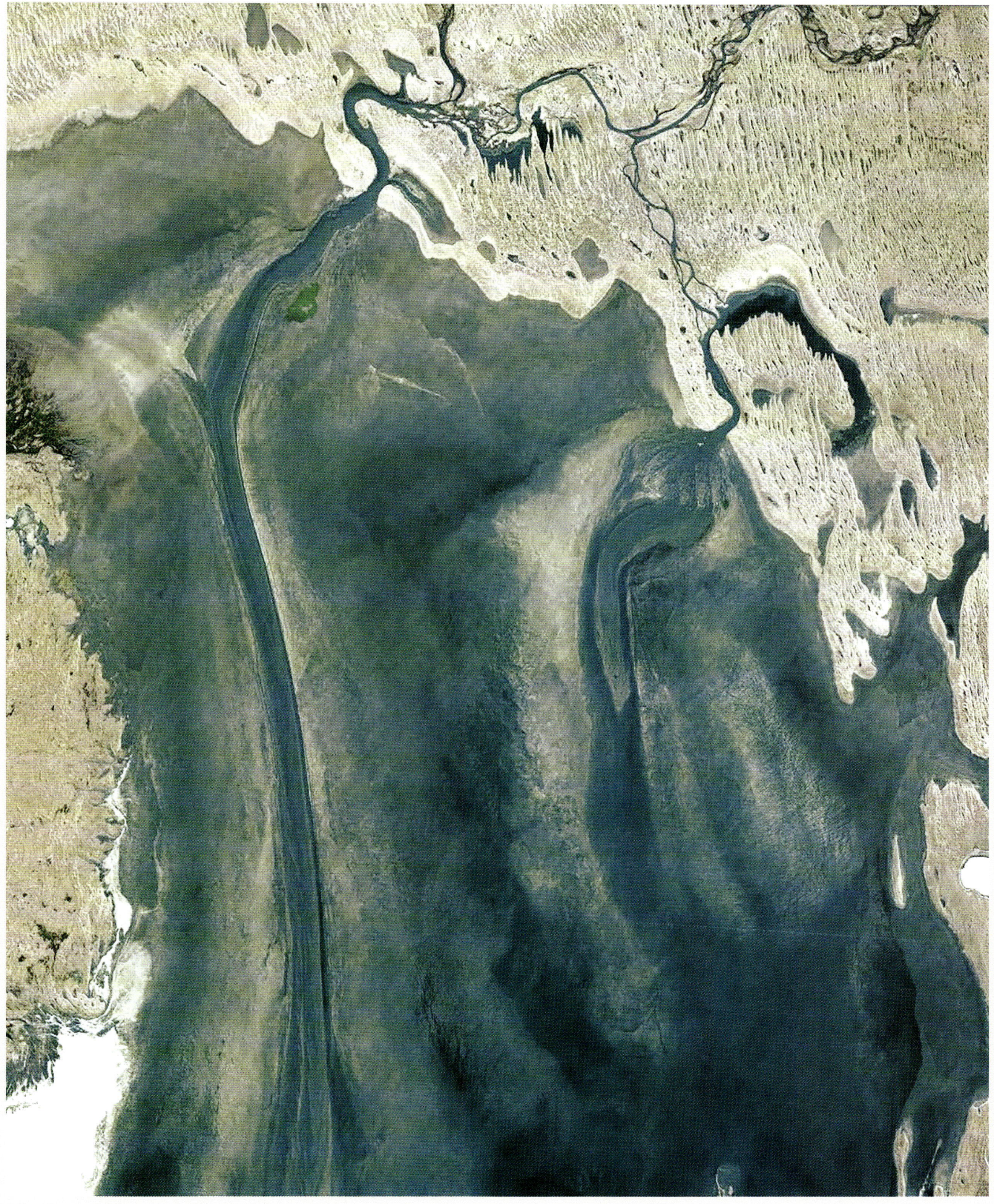

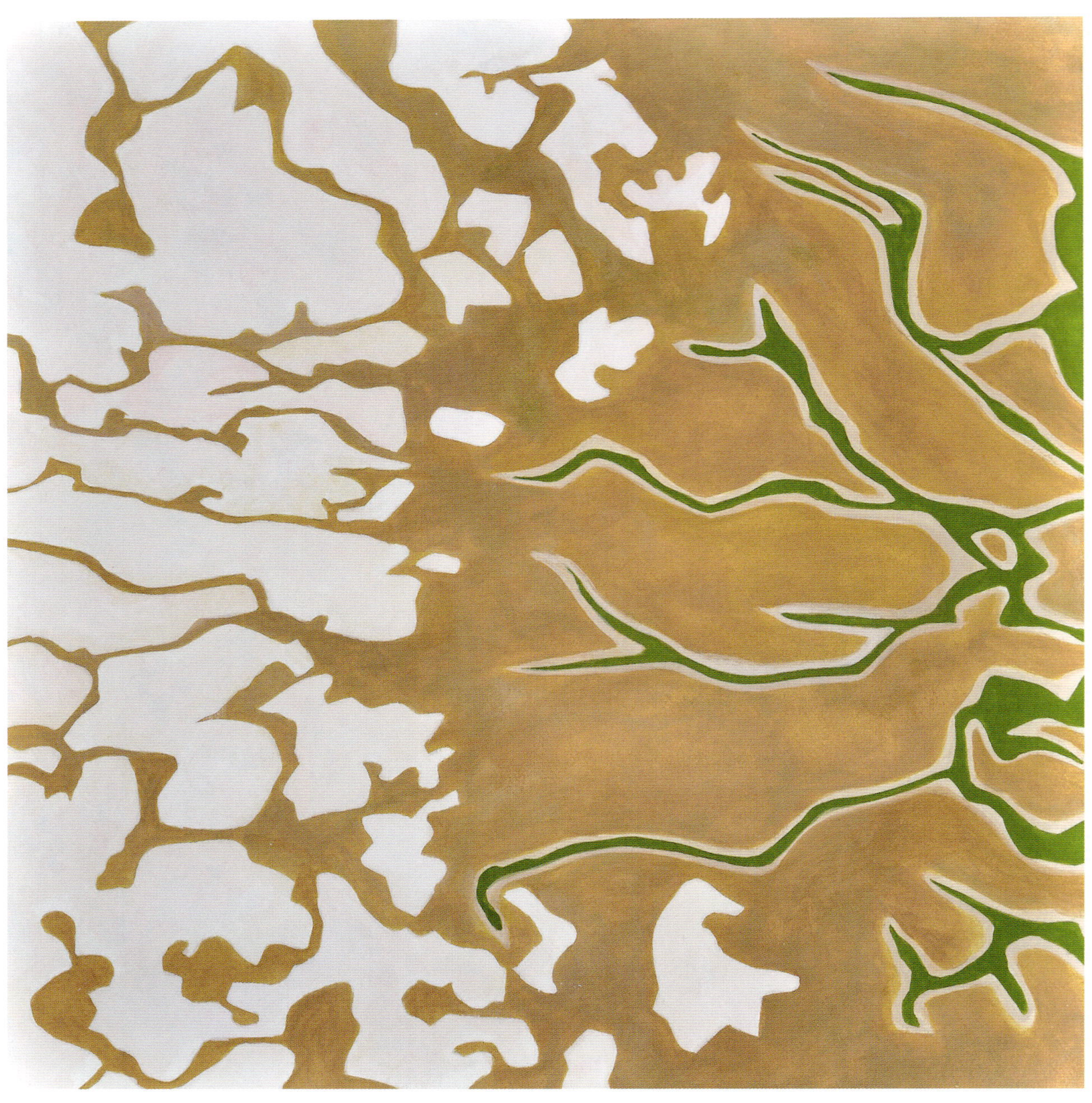

**ABOVE**
*Warburton Groove,* 2012

**RIGHT**
*Lake Eyre, Shore,* 2012

**FOLLOWING SPREAD**
*Edge of Lake Eyre,* 2012

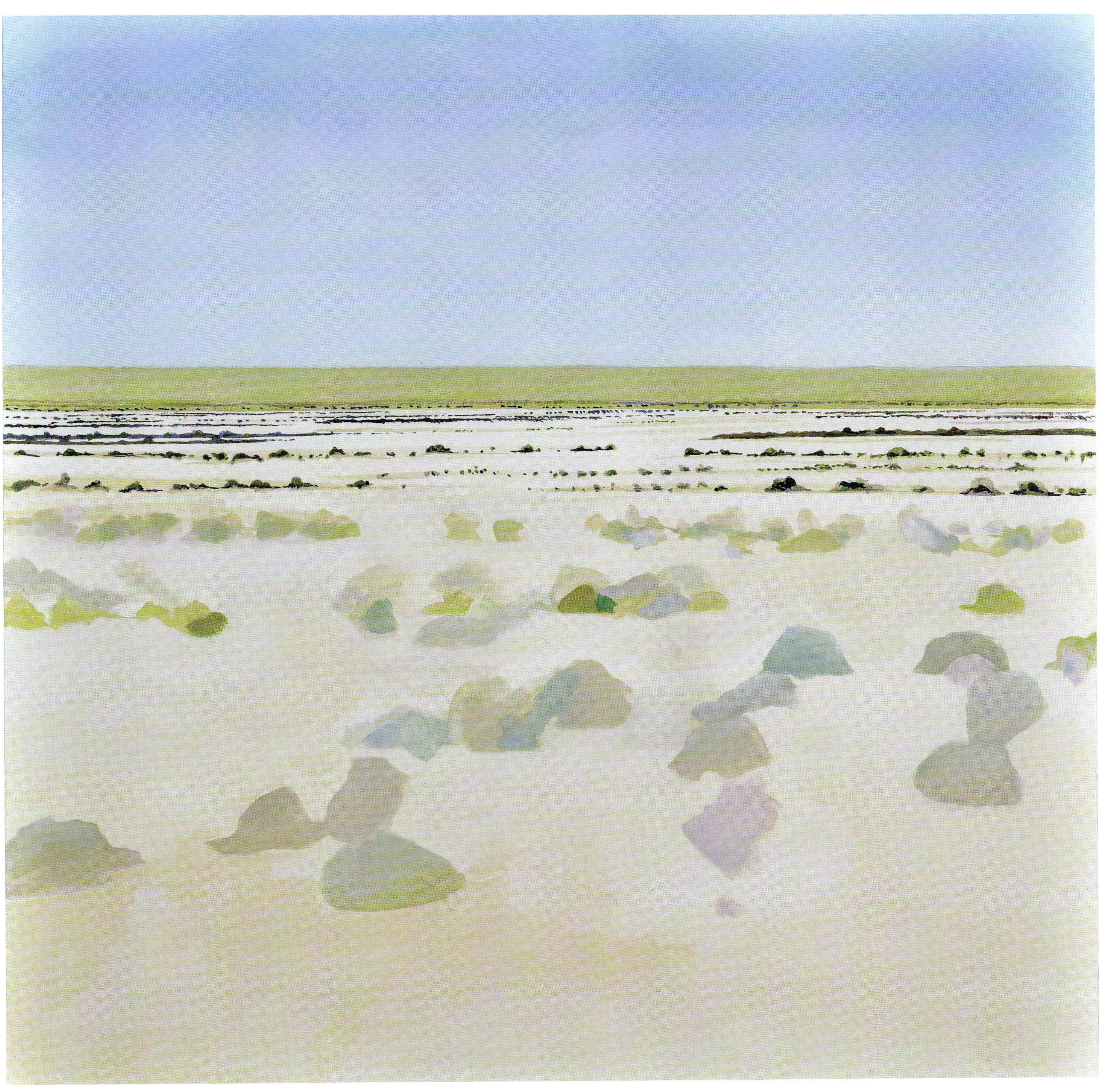

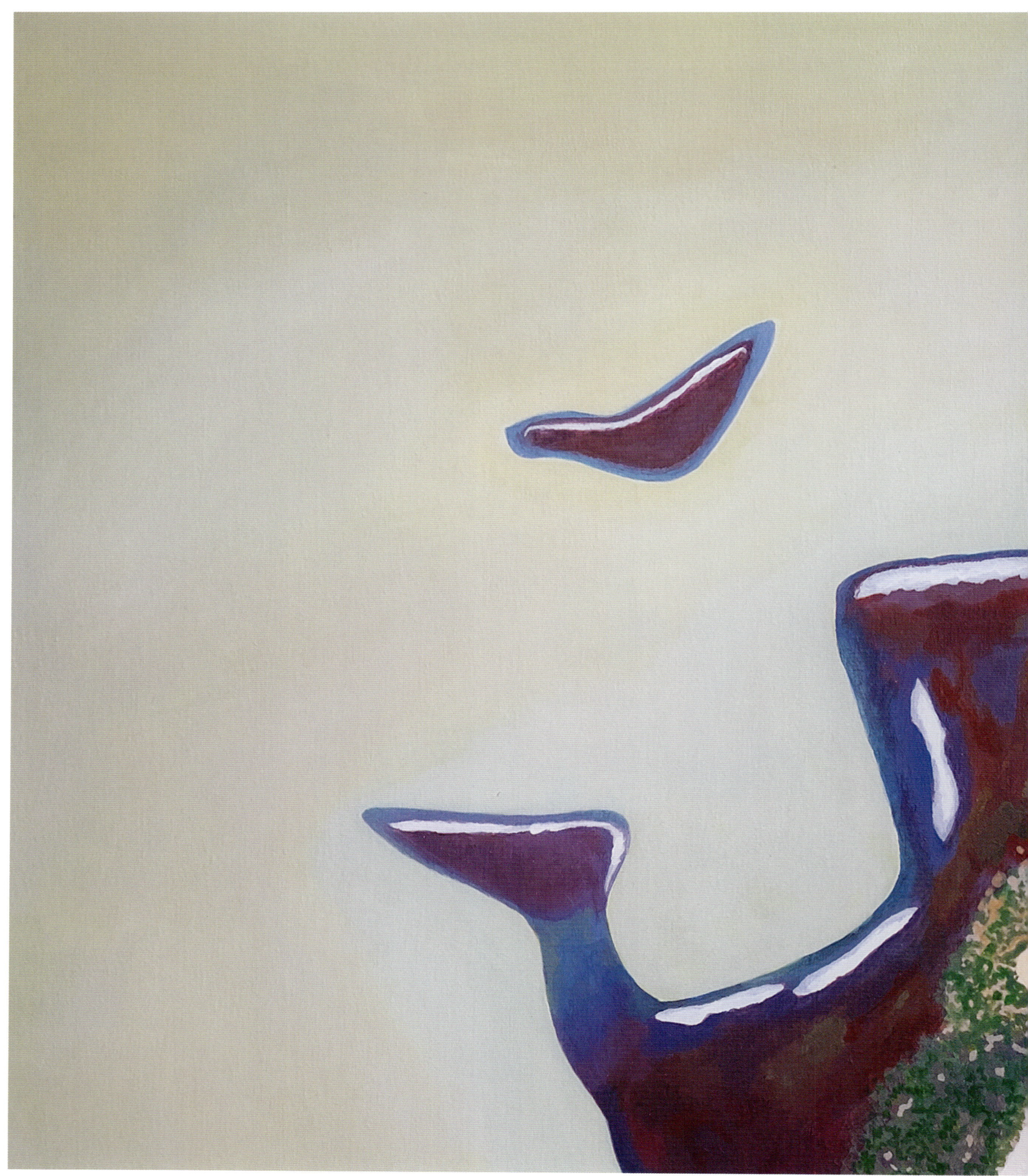

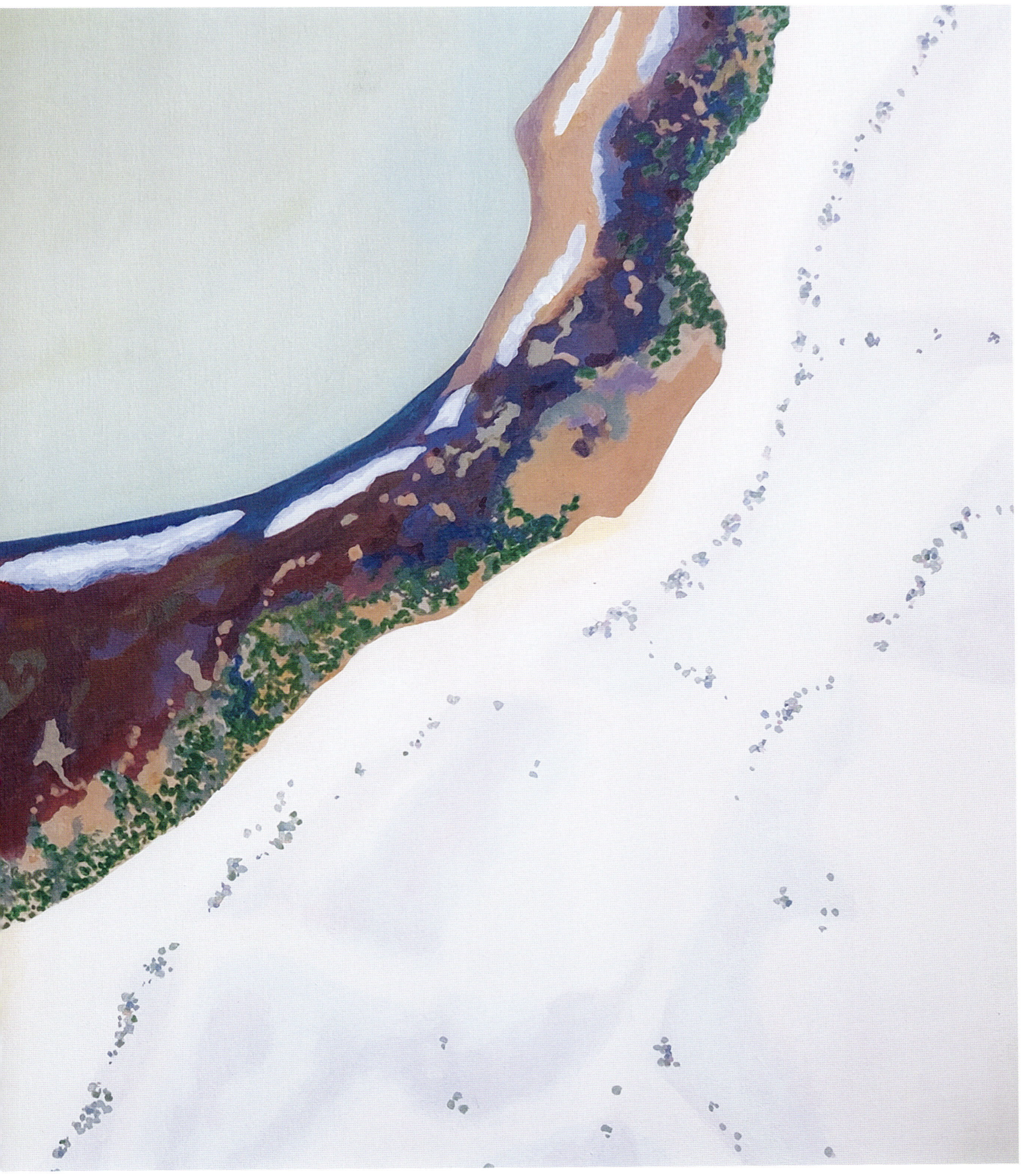

I had always wanted to see Kati Thanda
flooded … We landed on the shore.
There was a real sense of achievement
in having arrived at such a remote and
inaccessible location. The expanse
of the waters stretched to the horizon.
Water and land seemed to intermingle,
as if there was no real shoreline.

*Lake Eyre: First View, 9.55 am,*
22 April 2011

*Lake Eyre from above Warburton Gap,*
*11.57 am,* 22 April 2011

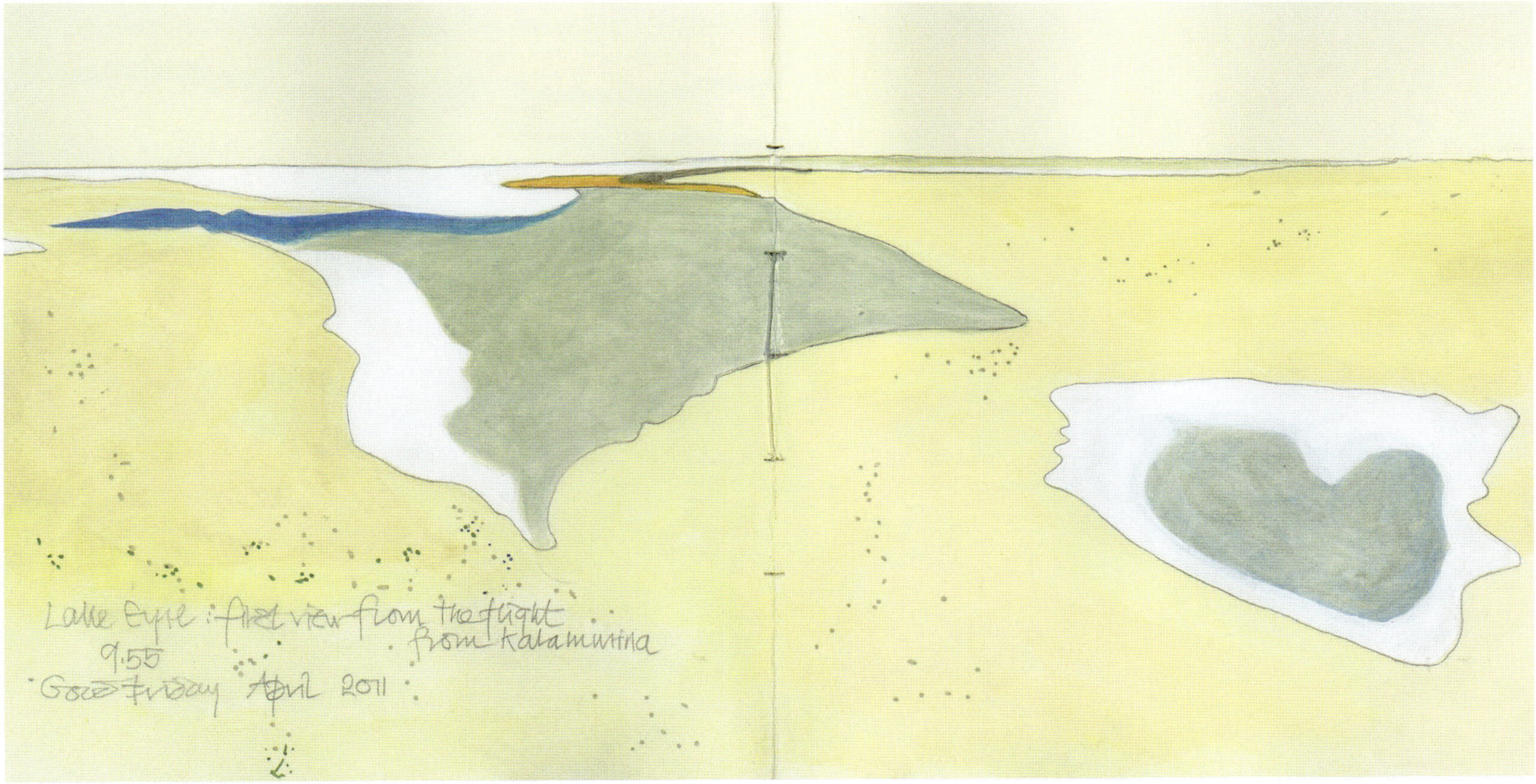

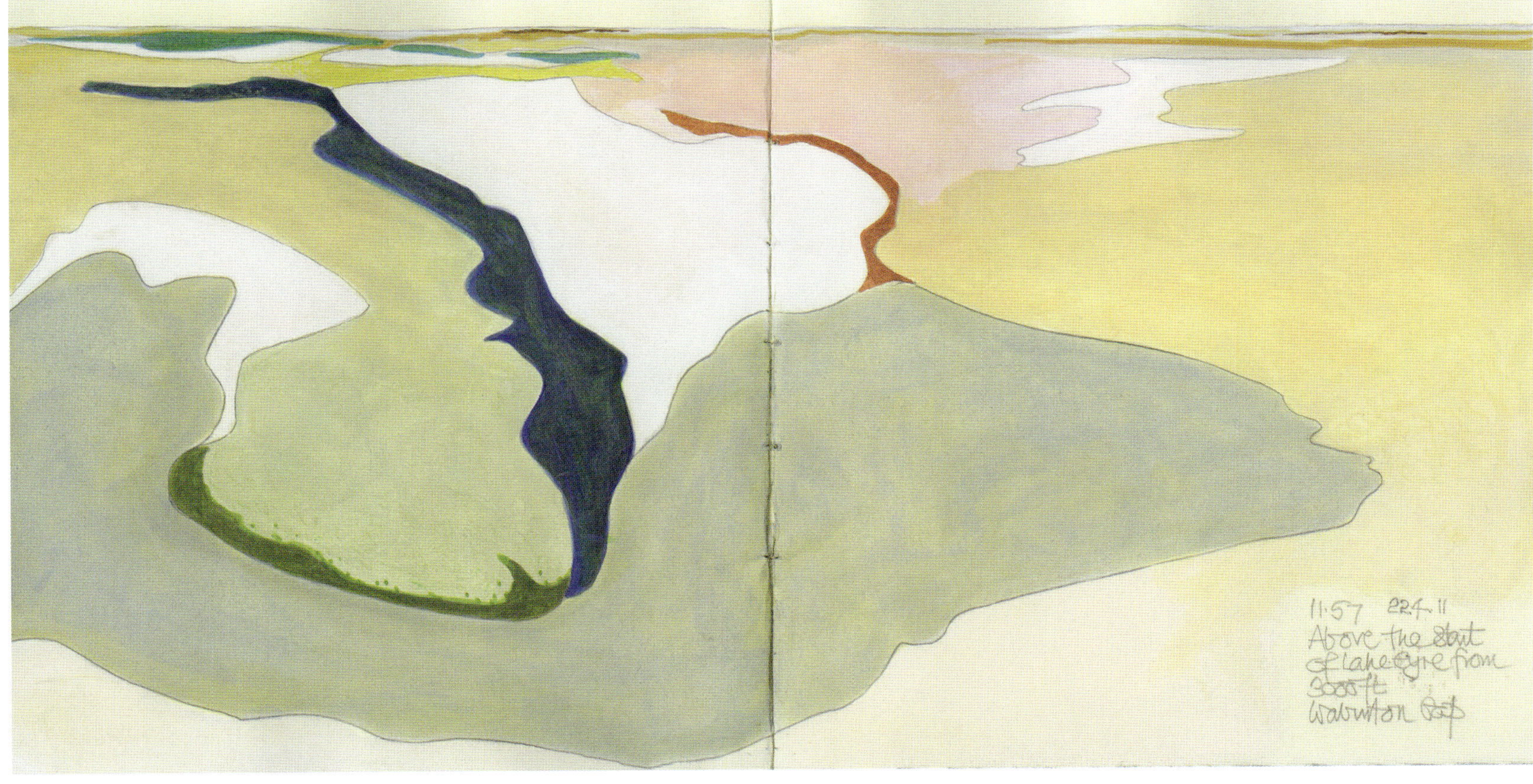


Lake Eyre : first view from the flight
from Kalamurina
9.55
Good Friday April 2011



11.57   22.4.11
Above the start
of Lake Eyre from
3000 ft
Warburton Bay

# Ikara / Wilpena Pound,
# South Australia

31°30'14.7"S 138°33'09.3"E
-31.504077, 138.552574

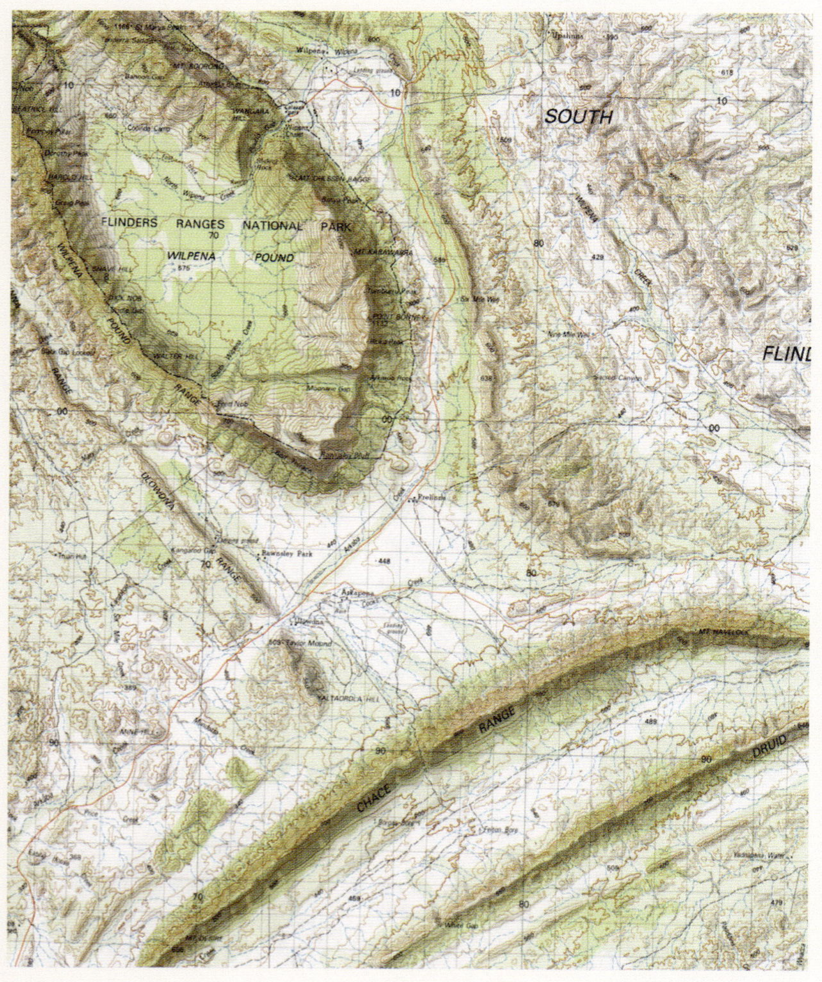

The centrepiece of the Flinders Ranges is Wilpena Pound – also known by its Adnyamathanha name, Ikara – a natural amphitheatre in the southern part of the ranges. This is easily reached by a good road from Port Augusta. I concentrated my visit on this area, and the paintings included show an outer view of Ikara, with its huge surrounding cliffs, and a view inside the amphitheatre, as seen from the summit of St Mary Peak (Ngarri Mudlanha). Also from the summit, looking to the north-west, you see in the distance the huge white salt expanse of Lake Torrens. I know few places where the Earth's structure is so evident in shaping the landscape. The twisting of the thick strata of the Adelaide Geosyncline has created the huge bowl shape of Ikara. This is extremely noticeable in aerial photographs and on maps. The inside of the bowl is green, in marked contrast to the dry vegetation outside the ring of mountains, I suppose because it acts to collect the scarce rainwater. This is clear when viewed from the rim.

Grass trees (*Xanthorrhoea* species) grow extensively on the outer slopes of Ikara. I had never seen these before and was fascinated by their twisted black shapes topped with crowns of thin green leaves. I developed drawings from my notebook into large paintings of this strange landscape, one of which is shown on pages 98–9. I think it was on this visit that I had my first sight of a large area of land affected by bushfire (I have seen many, many more since). I found the black, burnt trees striking, as if the view had been marked with scribbles of charcoal. I show both the grass trees and the burnt-out landscape (page 101) in the paintings here.

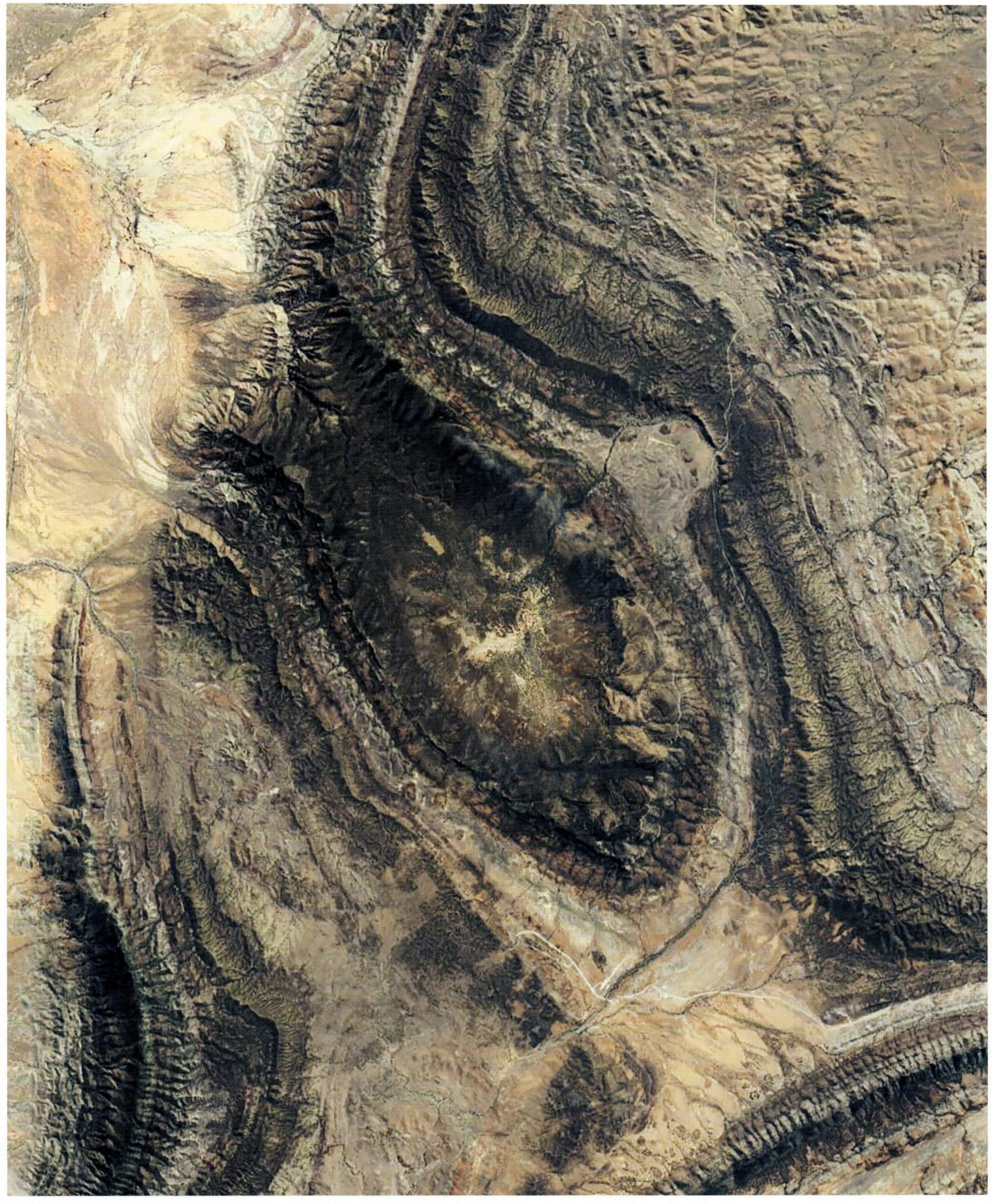

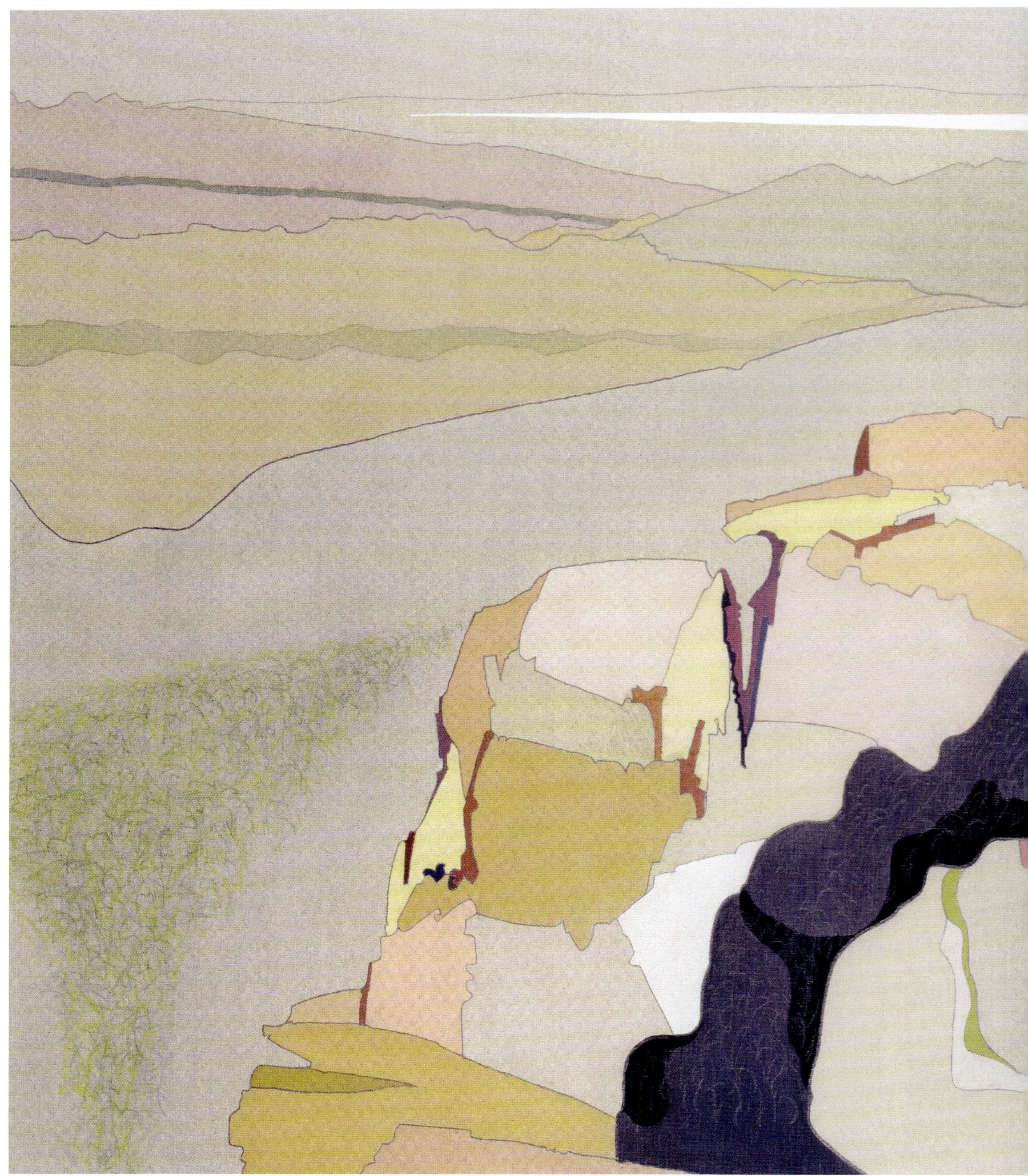

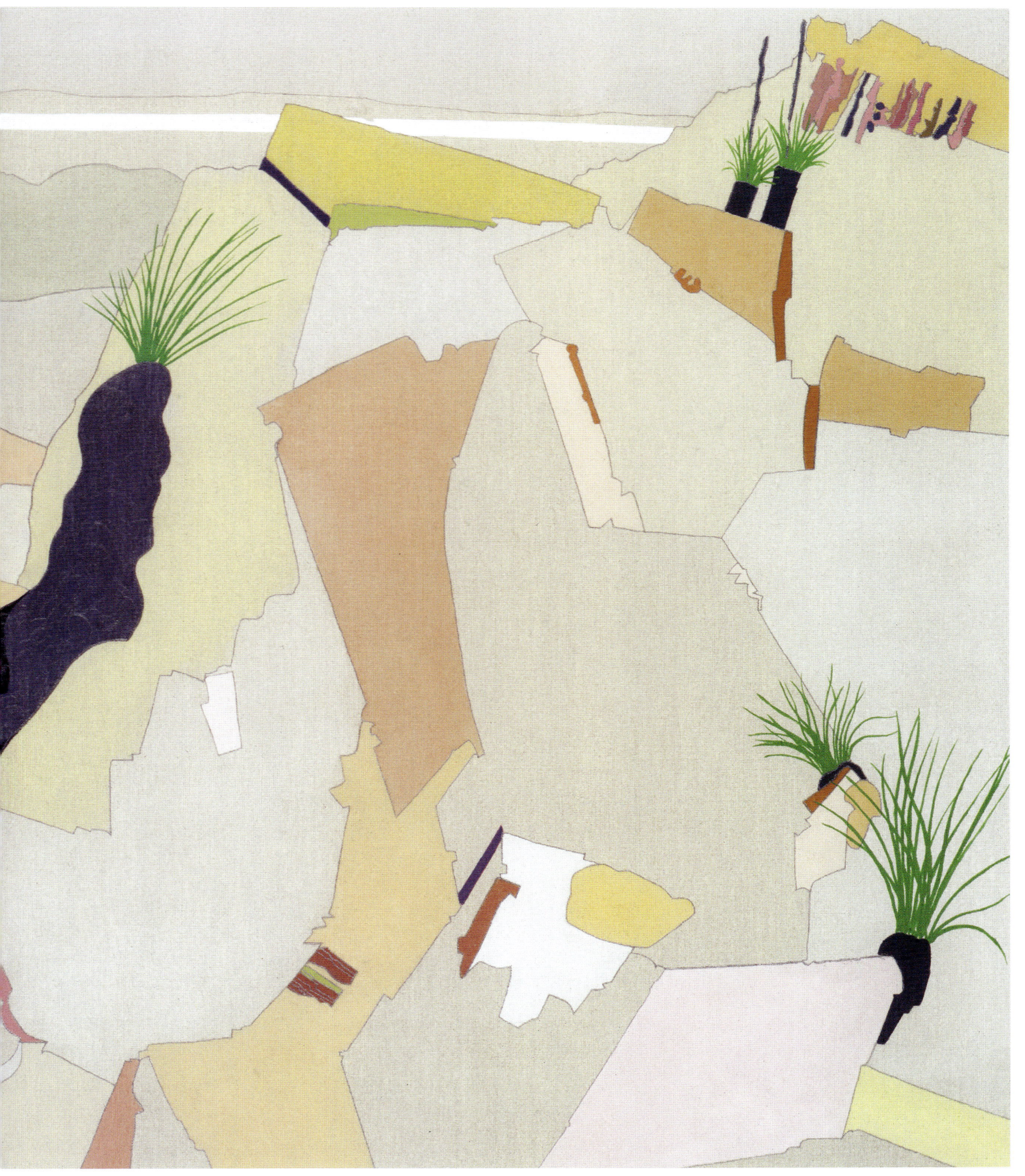

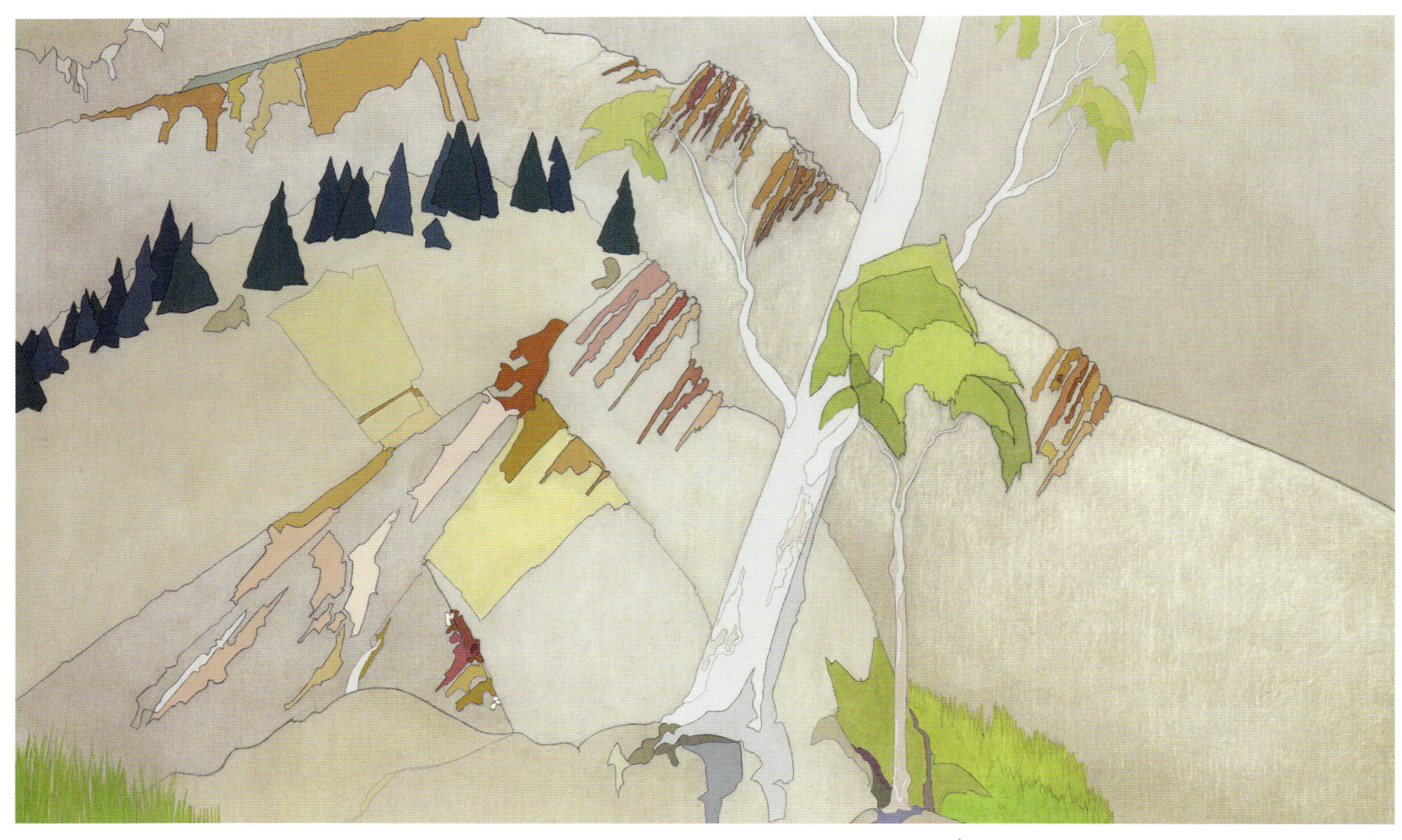

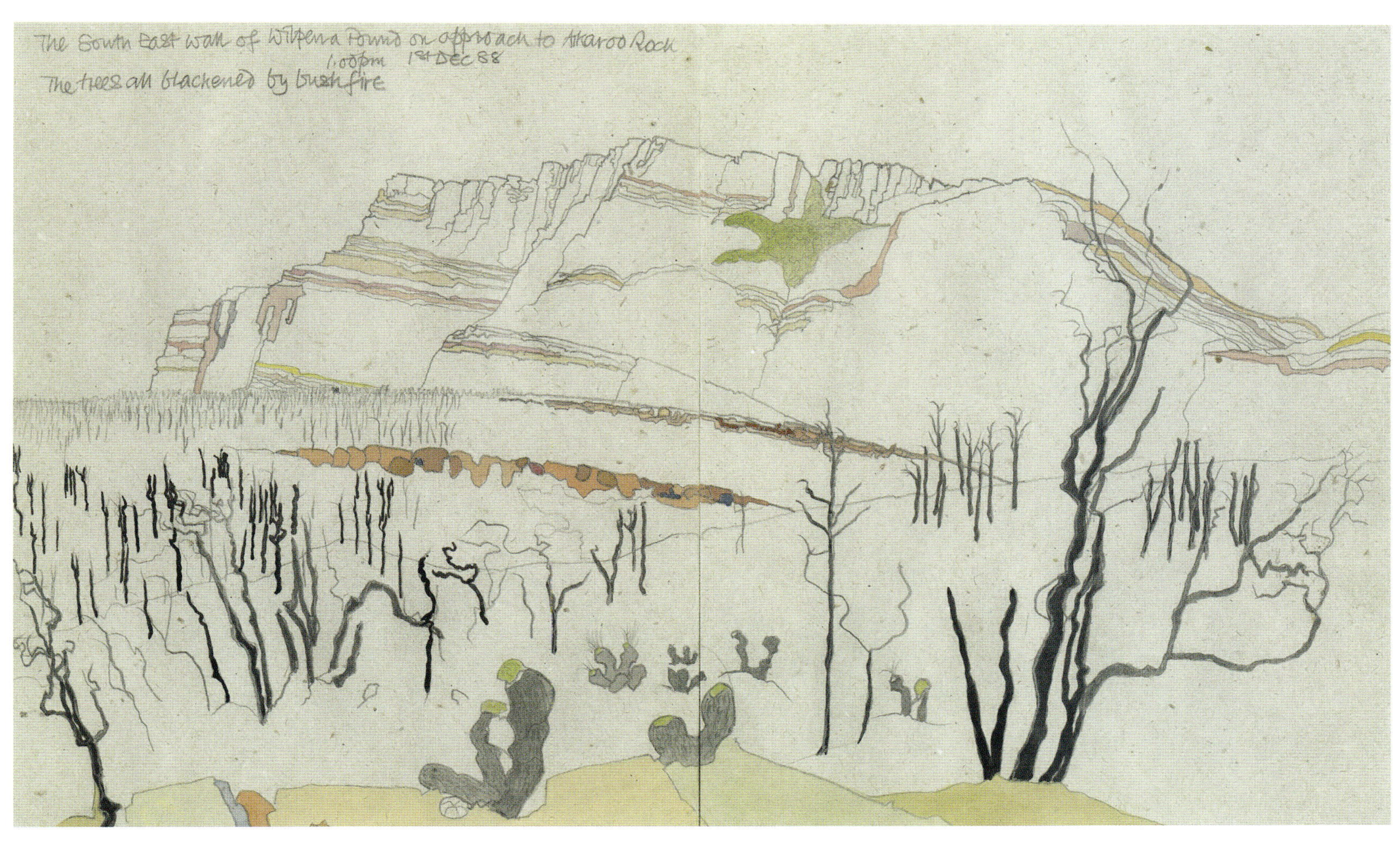

The South East wall of Wilpena Pound on approach to Akaroo Rock
1.00pm   1st Dec 88
The trees all blackened by bush fire

# Port Campbell and the Great Ocean Road, Victoria

38°38'47.8"S 143°04'13.3"E
-38.646615, 143.070354

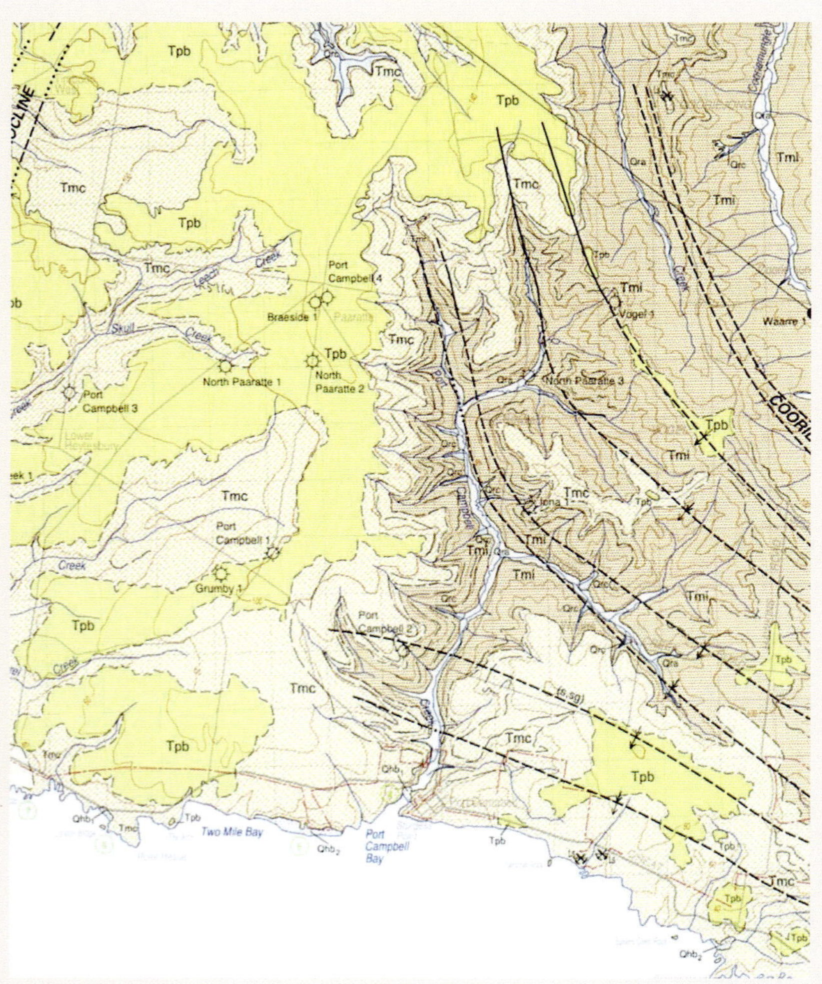

Port Campbell is about 220 kilometres south-west of Melbourne. It sits at the centre of the Great Ocean Road, which stretches some 12 kilometres each side of the town. The coast is composed of limestone, a relatively soft rock, which has been eroded by the wave power of the Southern Ocean, and the dramatic cliffs edging the water feature bands of colour, ranging from a deep coral pink to a sandy yellow. The erosion has created a series of rock pillars, rising up to 50 metres from the ocean, separated from the cliffs of the main coast. These are known as the Twelve Apostles.

I went right along the coast doing a series of drawings, some of which evolved into paintings. This is a standard example of the way I work. Nearly all the work I do is based on drawing in the landscape. These drawings are not usually done in great detail (the image of Loch Ard Gorge shown on page 106 is rather an exception); instead, at any location, my process of drawing is to simplify, seeking out the underlying. The drawings are usually done quite quickly, but it takes perhaps hours of walking, looking, to choose just what I want. I never paint outdoors. All that is done back in the studio. The colours used are based on brief notes made on the drawing itself. But I am not always concerned with the 'real' colour. For example, in the painting showing the Twelve Apostles (page 104), I have made the rock pillars much darker than they actually are to define their shapes against the cliffs.

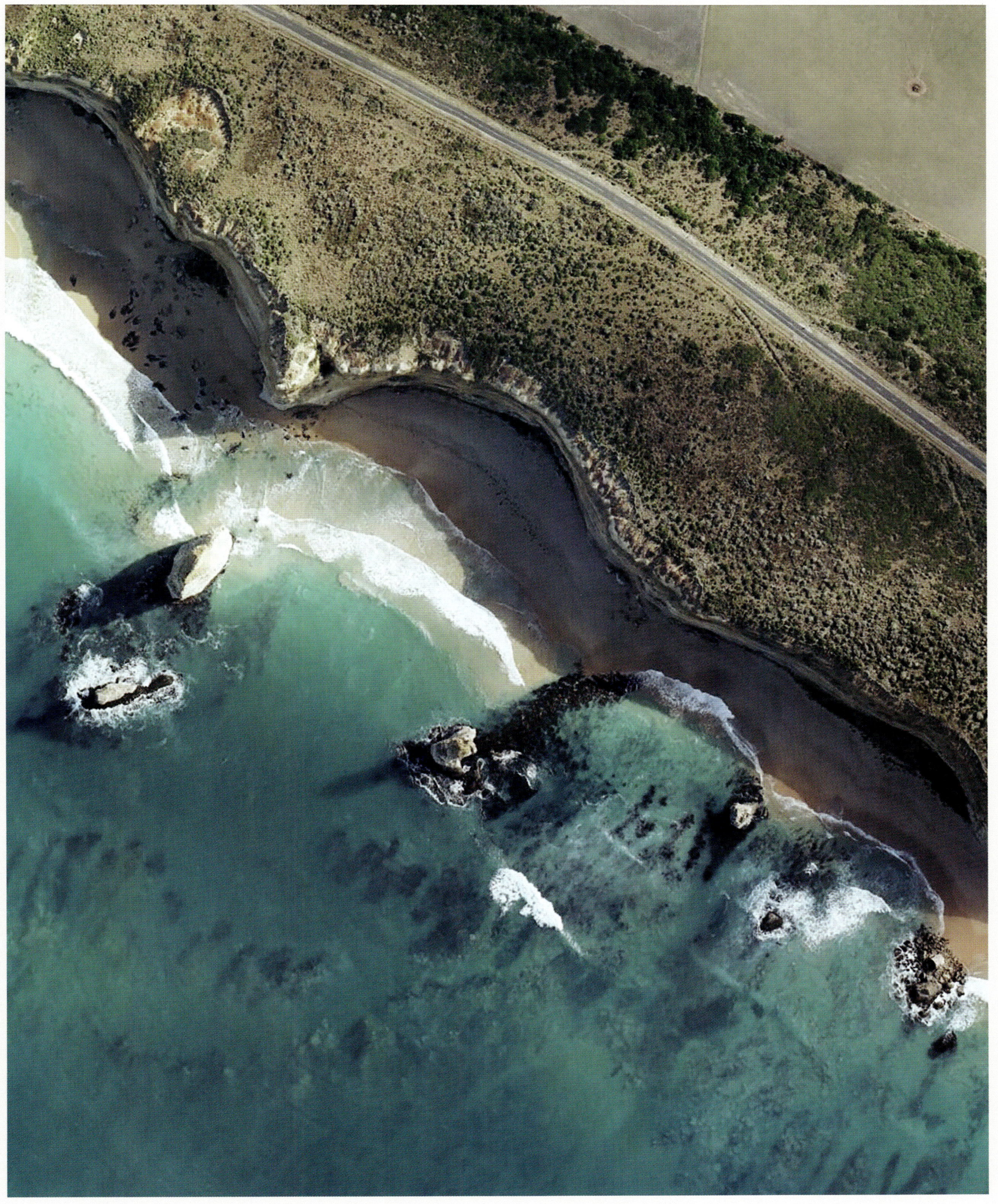

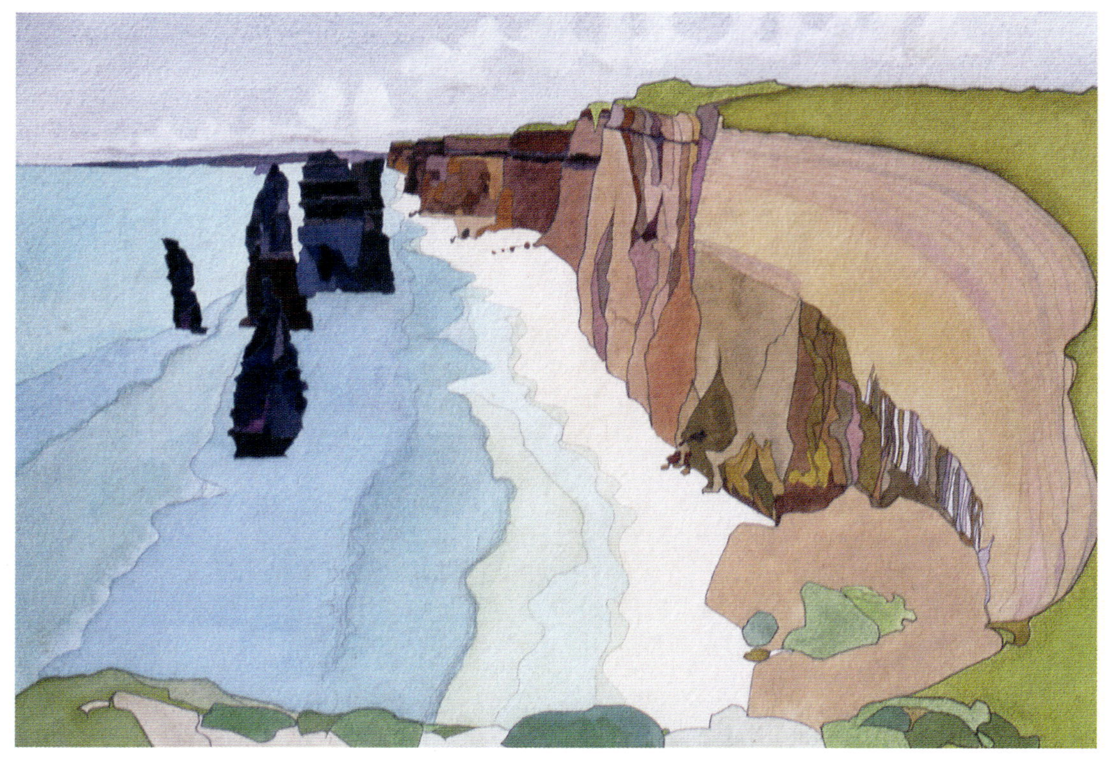

The coast is composed of limestone, a relatively soft rock, which has been eroded by the wave power of the Southern Ocean, and the dramatic cliffs edging the water feature bands of colour, ranging from a deep coral pink to a sandy yellow.

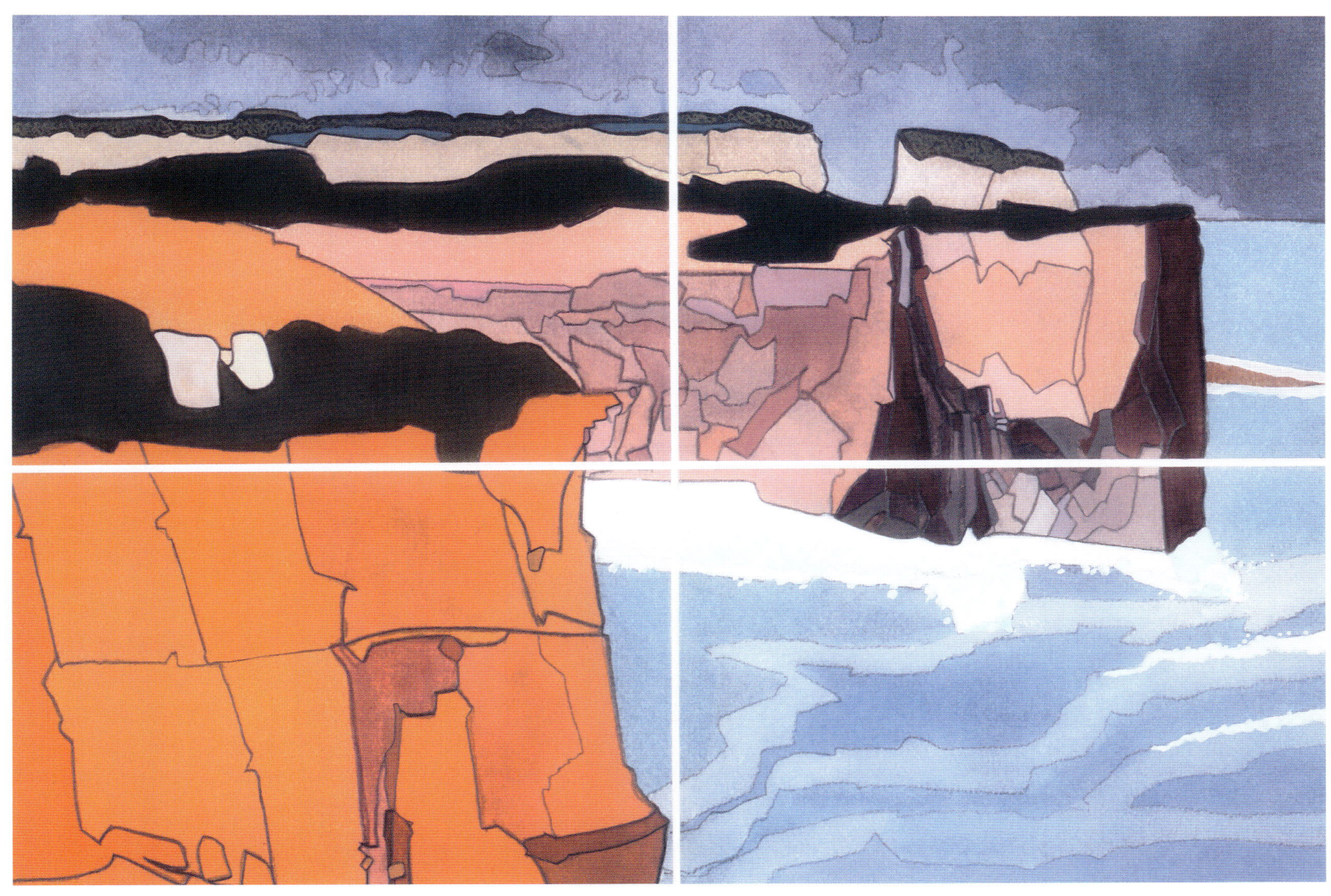

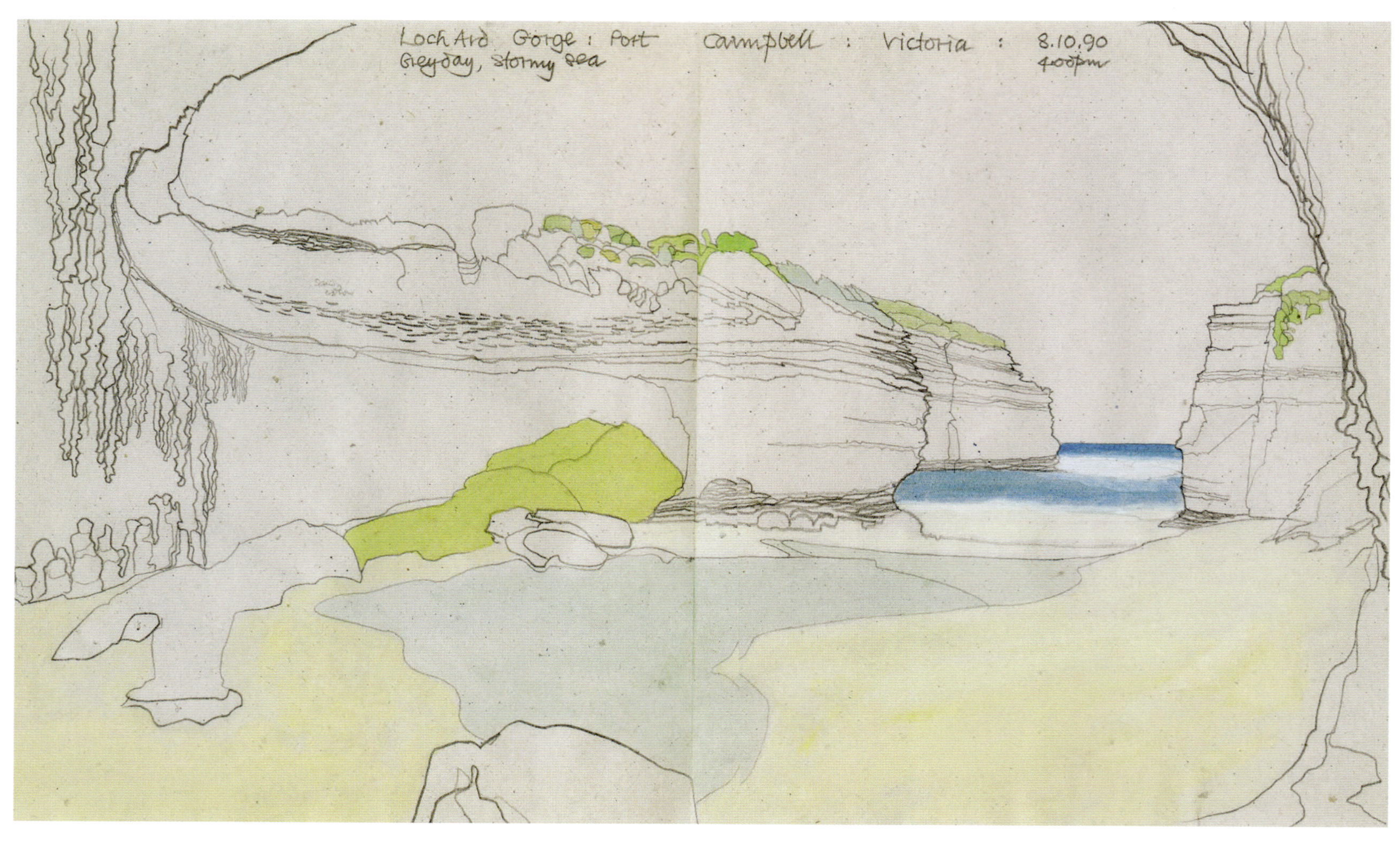




ABOVE
*Loch Ard Gorge, Port Campbell,*
8 October 1990

RIGHT
*The Grotto, Port Campbell,* 1991

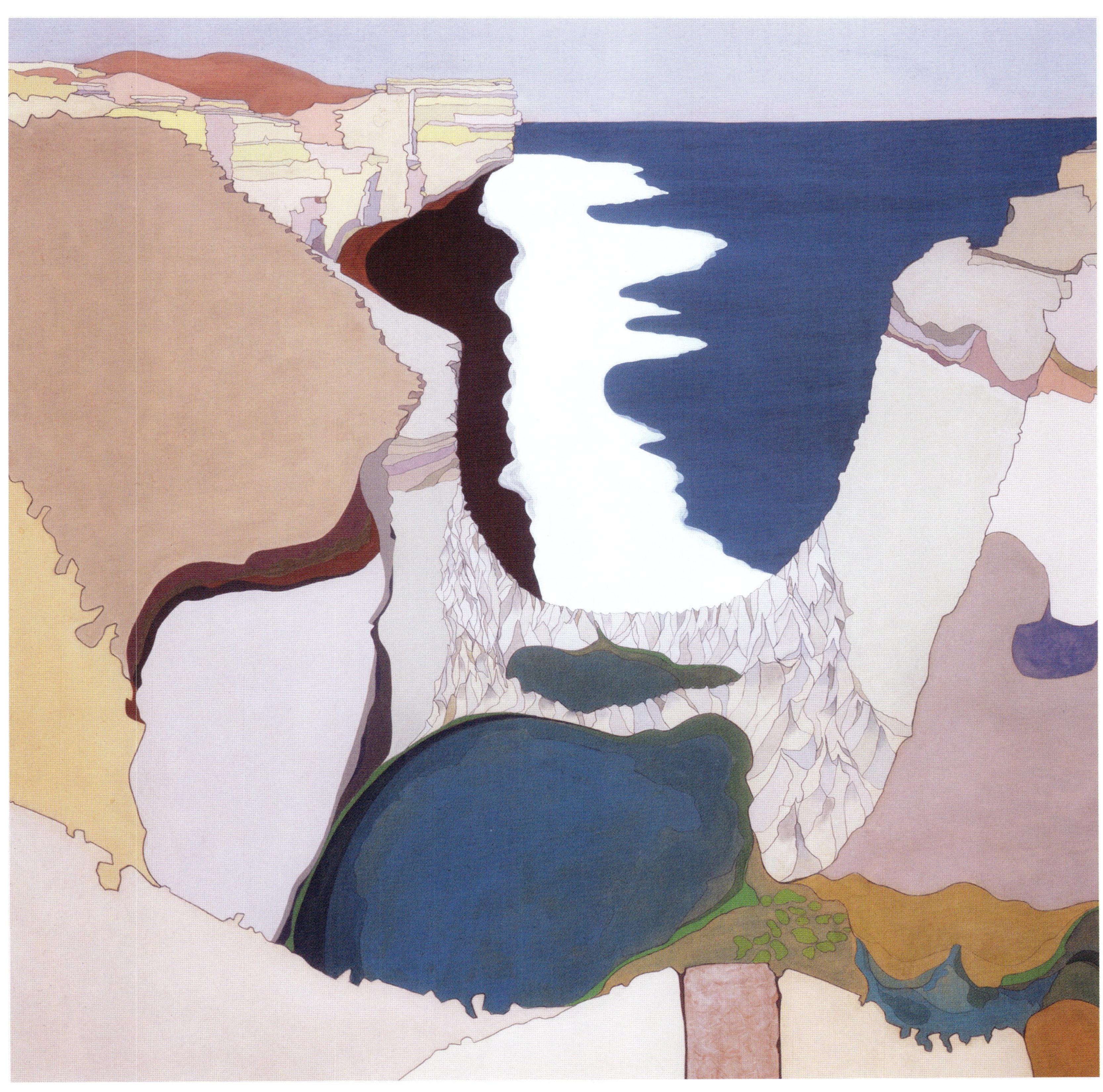

# Franklin and Gordon rivers, Tasmania

**42°35'22.2"S 145°44'22.6"E**
**-42.589488, 145.739617**

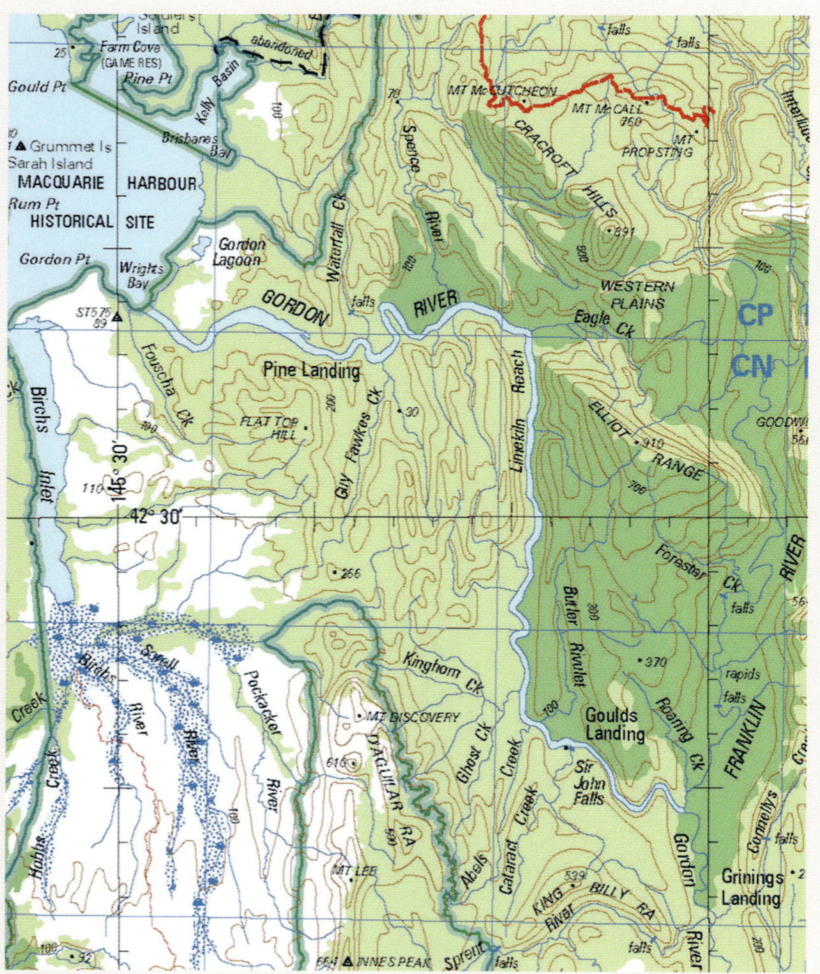

In early 1983, the protests against the proposed dam construction on the Franklin and Gordon rivers reached a crescendo, becoming one of Australia's most significant environmental campaigns. I went to take part.

The protestors' camp was exceptionally well organised. Those planning to go upstream to demonstrate at the dam site first had to undergo days of training at the town of Strahan. The environment in Strahan was hostile. The protests were not popular – potential jobs were at stake. The majority of locals wanted the dam project to succeed and were against the campaign. I went with the intention of doing drawings at the dam site and then developing paintings, to be exhibited in London, to further international support for the protest.

As my time was limited, I was taken upstream without going through training. I then camped at the site and was provided with facilities to work there. The river is quite extraordinarily beautiful. It has a stillness, a calmness, as it flows through the virgin forest. All of this would be destroyed if the dam went ahead. Indeed, one of my paintings (page 112) shows just the beginning of destruction as the bulldozers started work.

The protest movement was effective in raising awareness. It became a nationwide issue and was a factor in Bob Hawke's success in the federal elections in 1983. It became an issue of federal v. state as Tasmania carried on with construction. The rivers became part of a UNESCO World Heritage area, and that gave the federal government the right to intervene. A famous High Court ruling in 1983 found in favour of the federal government's case. The project was halted. The vast wilderness of south-west Tasmania remains almost entirely untouched.

I did exhibit paintings in London in 1984, even though publicity was no longer relevant. Some of those paintings are shown here.

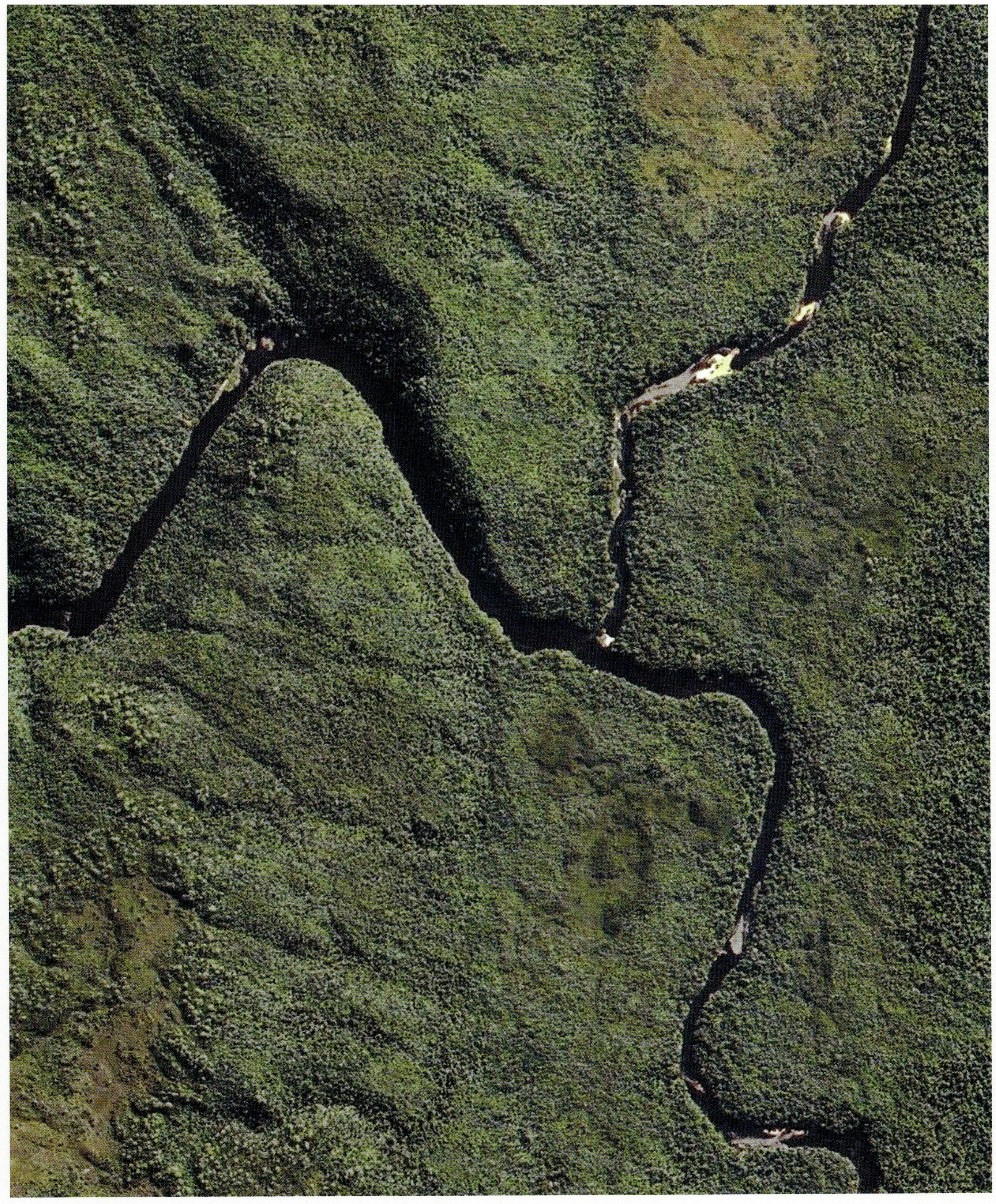

ABOVE
*Just Before the Site of the Dam,*
1983

RIGHT
*Beside Butler Island,* 1983

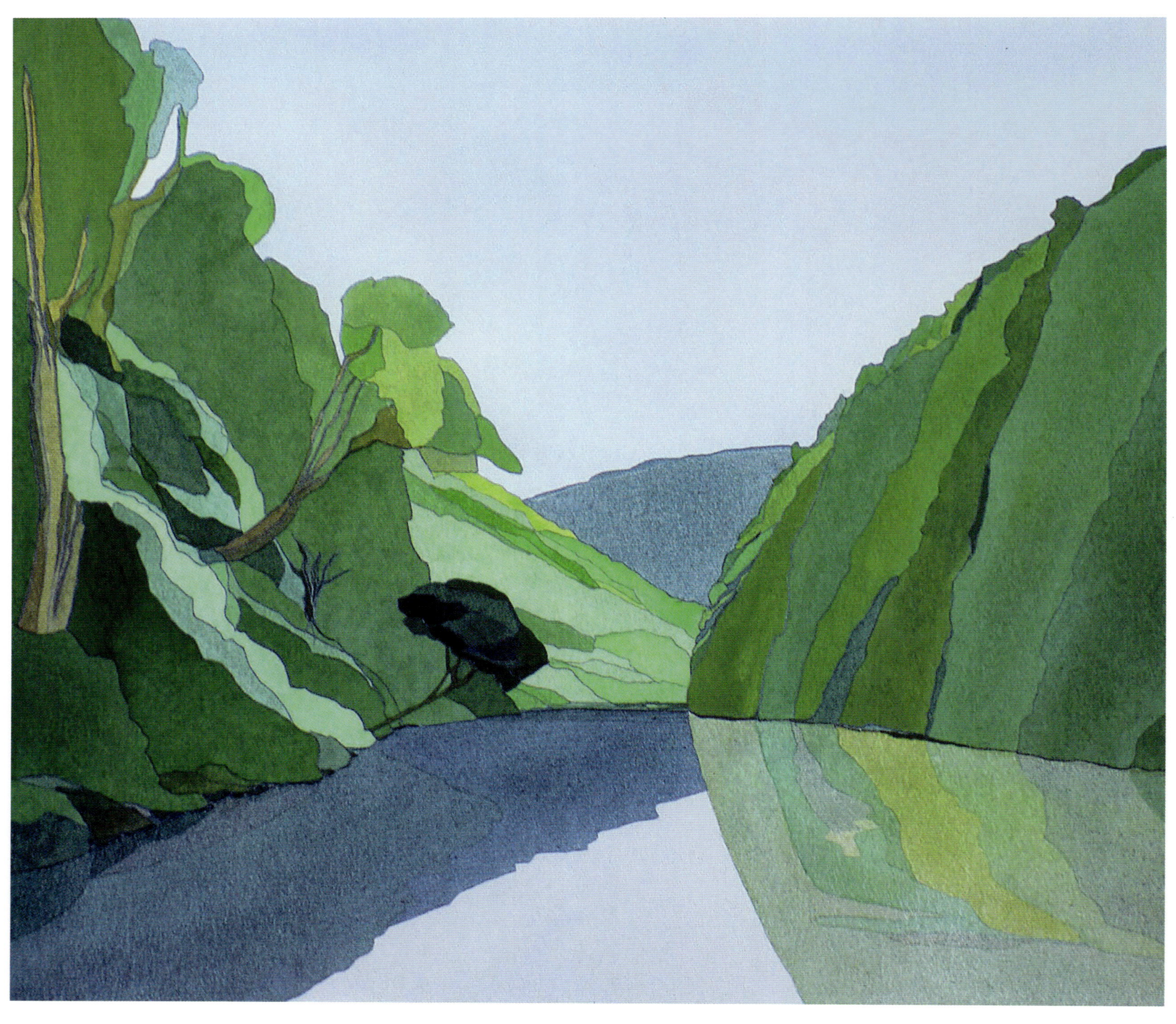

110

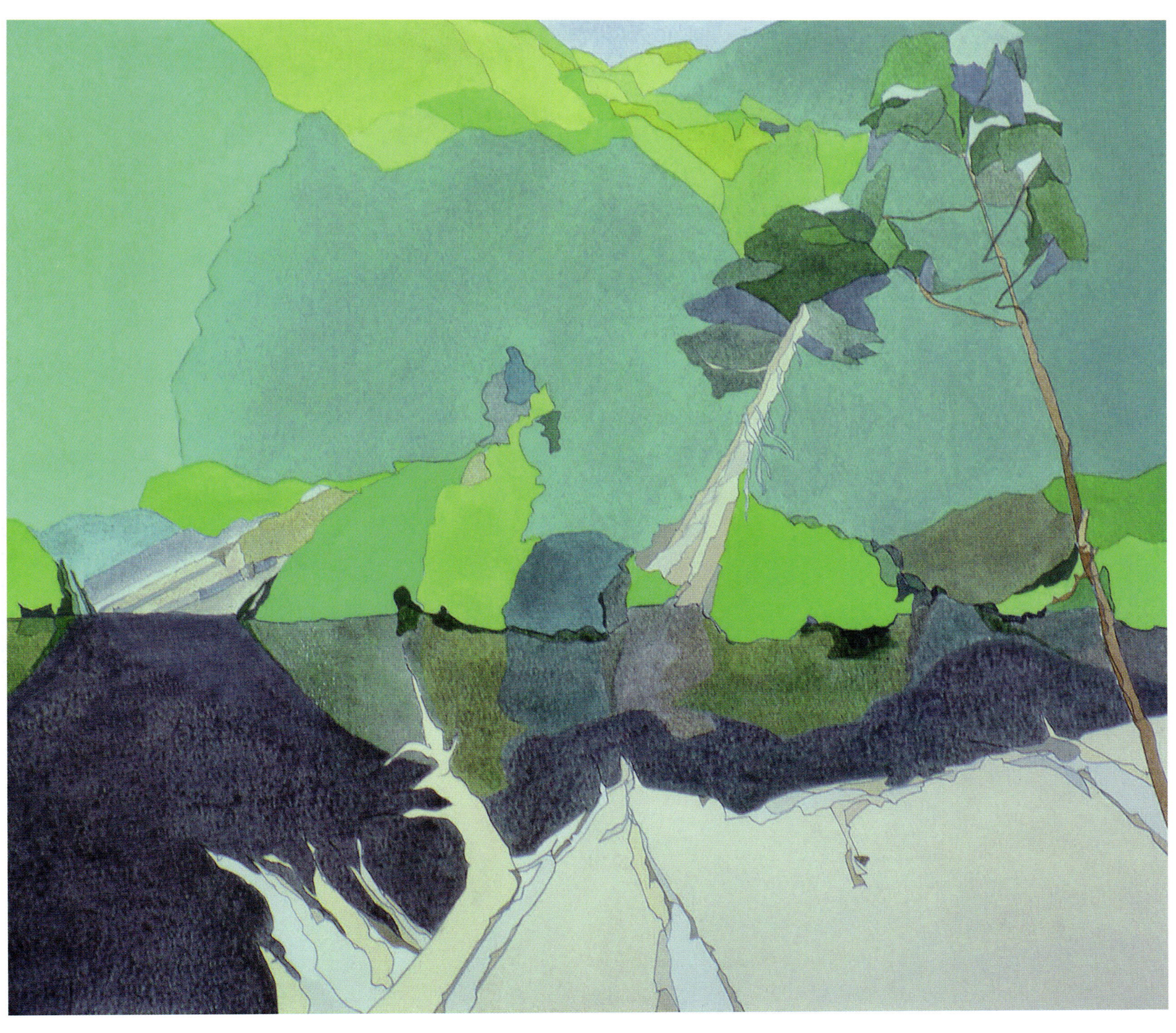

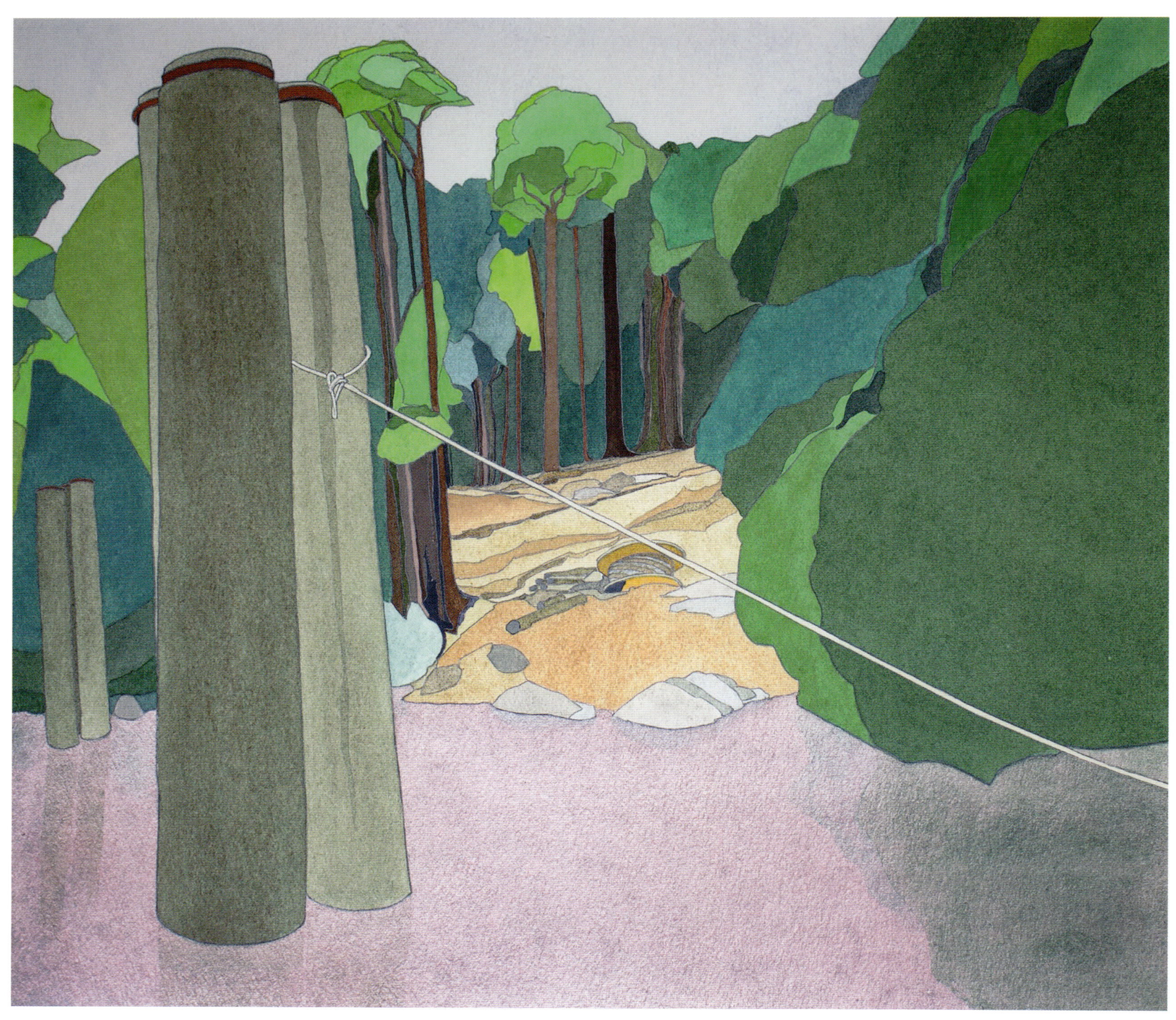

**ABOVE**
*Warners Landing, building the access
road,* 1983

**RIGHT**
*Meeting Tent in TWS Camp,* 1983

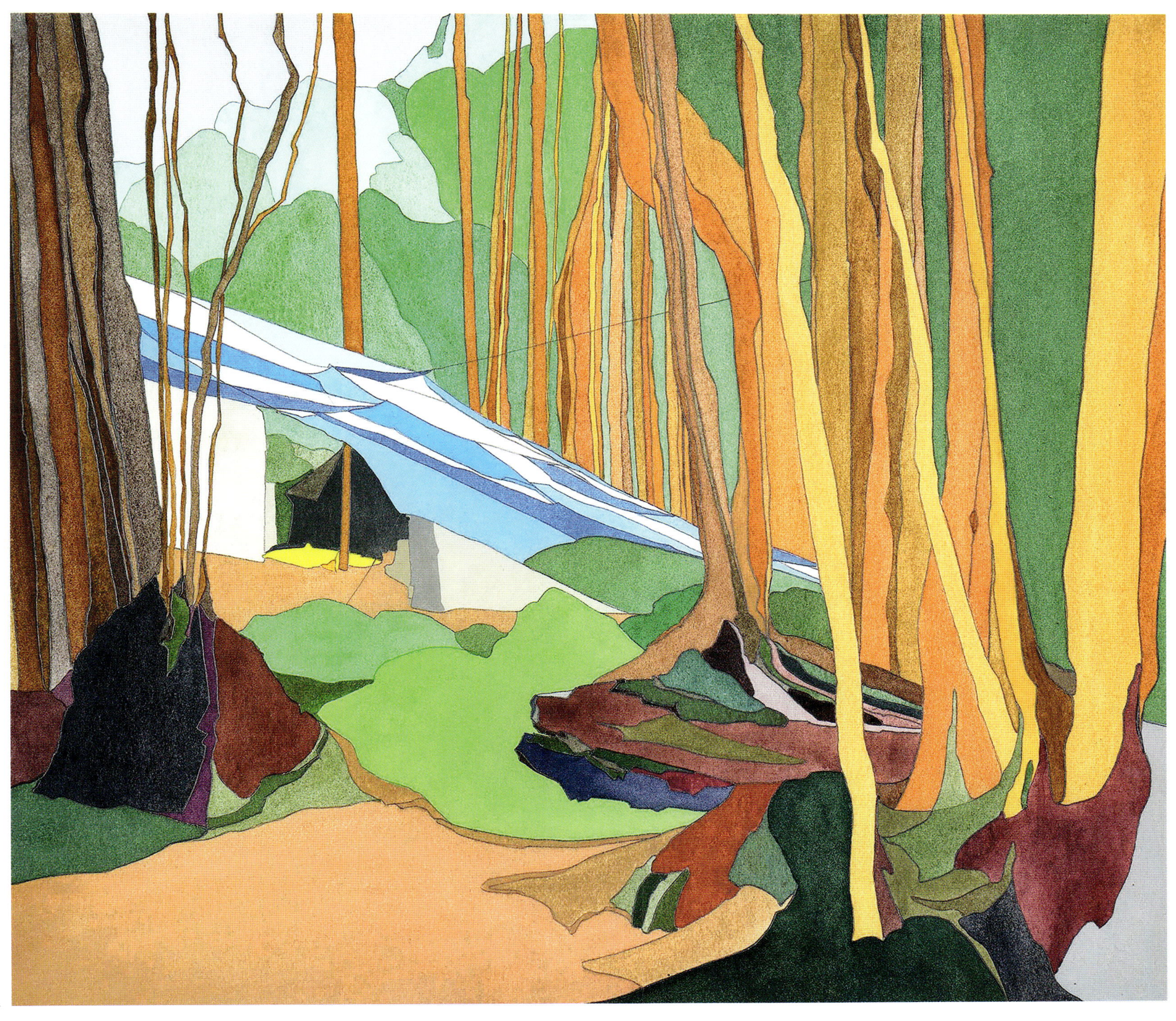

# South-west Tasmania

**43°25'06.8"S 146°10'00.5"E**
**-43.418544, 146.166801**

The whole of south-west Tasmania is a wilderness protected by national parks and by its World Heritage status. I visited the region in early 2019. Long before then, in 1983, I had been to the Franklin River (page 108) during the demonstrations to protect that area. Looking back, one can see the great moves that have been made to ensure protection of this extraordinary wilderness area of worldwide importance.

In revisiting, I went to two different areas. The first was the Hartz Mountains, which can be accessed by a road starting at Geeveston, near the Huon River. This road climbs from sea level to an altitude of about 1000 metres, passing through five completely different zones of vegetation. Partway up, there are huge swamp gums, *Eucalyptus regnans*. Indeed, close to the road is one that is reputed to be the third-tallest tree in the world, and the tallest flowering plant. Higher up, the vegetation changes, with completely different trees and extremely dense forest. Then it opens out to a subalpine tundra. This upper zone again has plants that are unique in the world. They are low to the ground and extremely colourful, like a series of cushions. Included is a painting of this terrain. I was told by David Attenborough that some of these cushion plants are many hundreds of years old, and that if these fragile plants are trodden on, their structure can be damaged, their ancient form destroyed. Recognising this, there are designated areas where walkways have been installed so that you can approach closely without risk of damage.

The second area I visited, by contrast, was extremely remote. I went with Jonathan Meyer, my son-in-law, to Melaleuca, in the far south-west. We were on a mission to try to see one of the rarest birds in the world – the orange-bellied parrot. This bird is a critically endangered species. In the wild, it breeds only in and around Melaleuca, and then migrates to southern Australia. There are about thirty breeding pairs. We managed to see the birds. Although I decided not to include the image here, I have made a painting of the parrot as it was so central to this journey. It is most unusual for me to do such a work. The only other time I made a bird painting, that I can recall, is when I illustrated an albatross from my working visit to Antarctica.

Melaleuca is accessible only by sea, air or foot. There is no road access. We flew in a small plane from Bruny Island, a thirty-minute flight. There is a meagre dirt airstrip left over from the time when a mine operated in the area. Now, there are just a few houses used by those working in the national park, watching over the parrot. The area's vegetation is striking low scrub, habitat for the bird. Nearby is a lagoon, where I did the drawing shown on page 117. The flight to Melaleuca passes over completely wild areas. The southern route follows a dramatic coastline; a painting from this is included. A more direct route goes over forest and mountains. There is not a single trace of human habitation, except for glimpses of the track that allows access after a five- to seven-day walk.

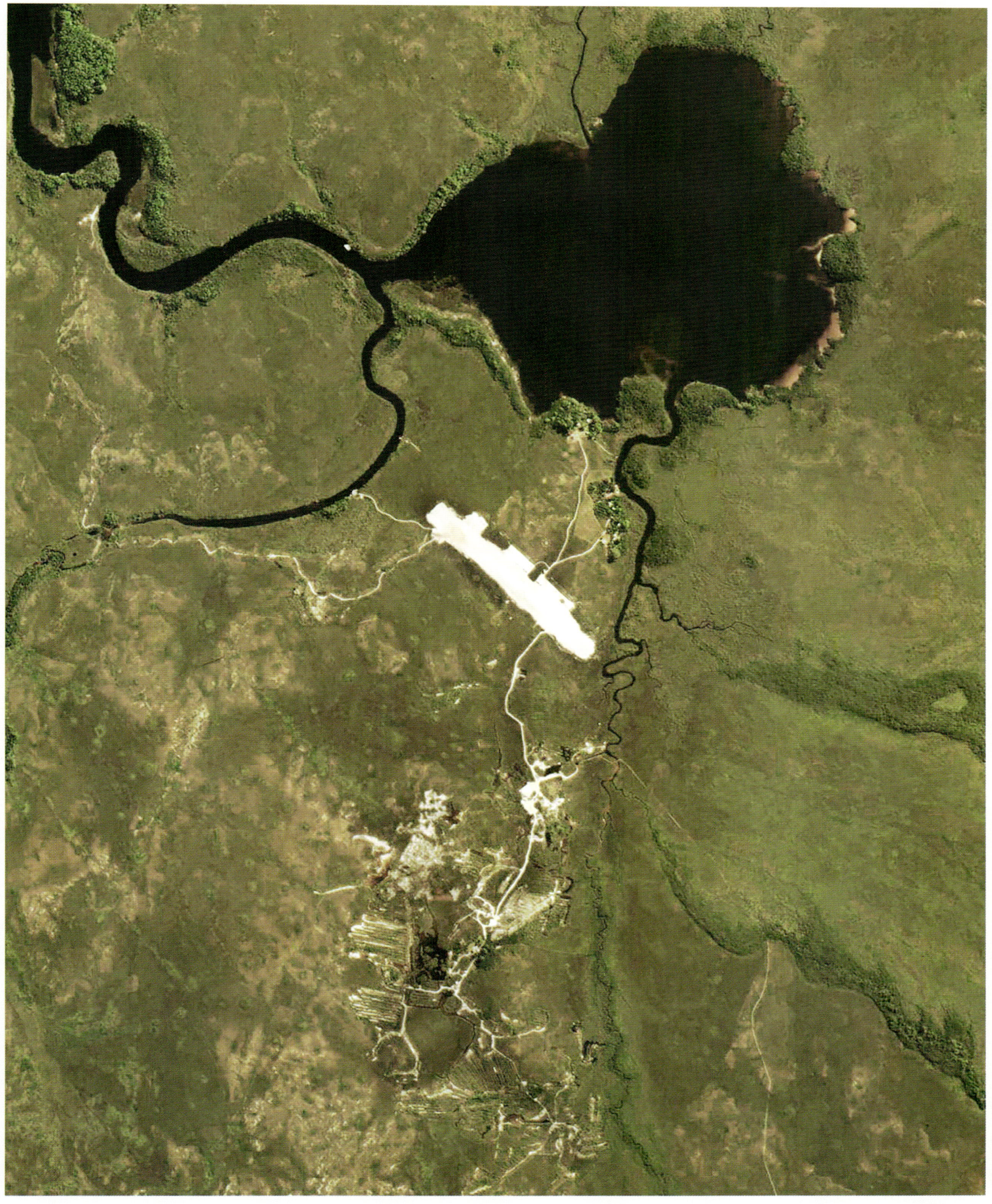

Melaleuca is accessible only by sea, air
or foot. There is no road access. We
flew in a small plane from Bruny Island ...
The flight ... passes over completely wild
areas. There is not a single trace of human
habitation, except for glimpses of the
track that allows access after a five- to
seven-day walk.

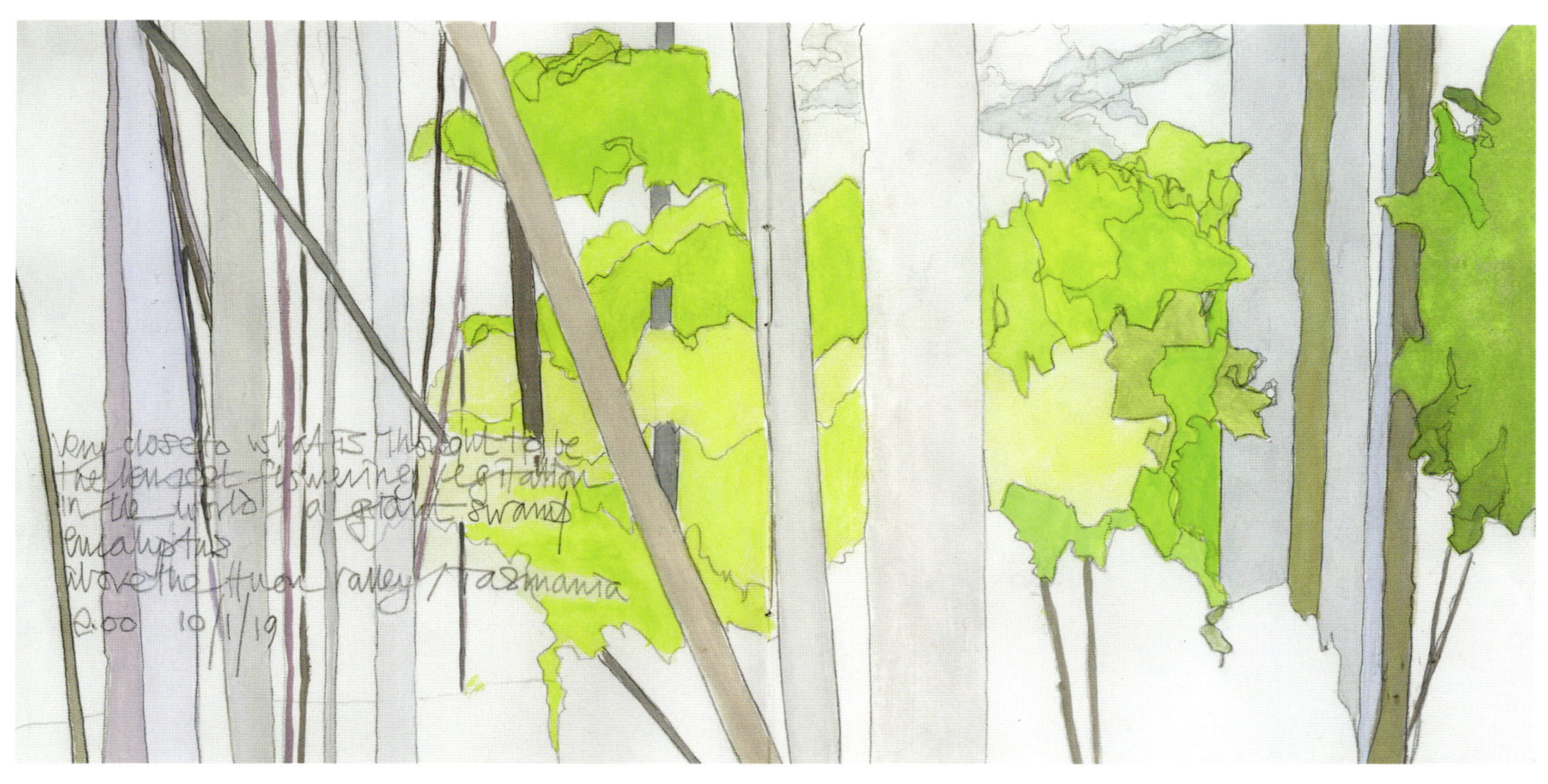


Very close to what is thought to be
the largest flowering vegetation
in the world, a giant swamp
eucalyptus
above the Huon Valley, Tasmania
12.00   10/1/19


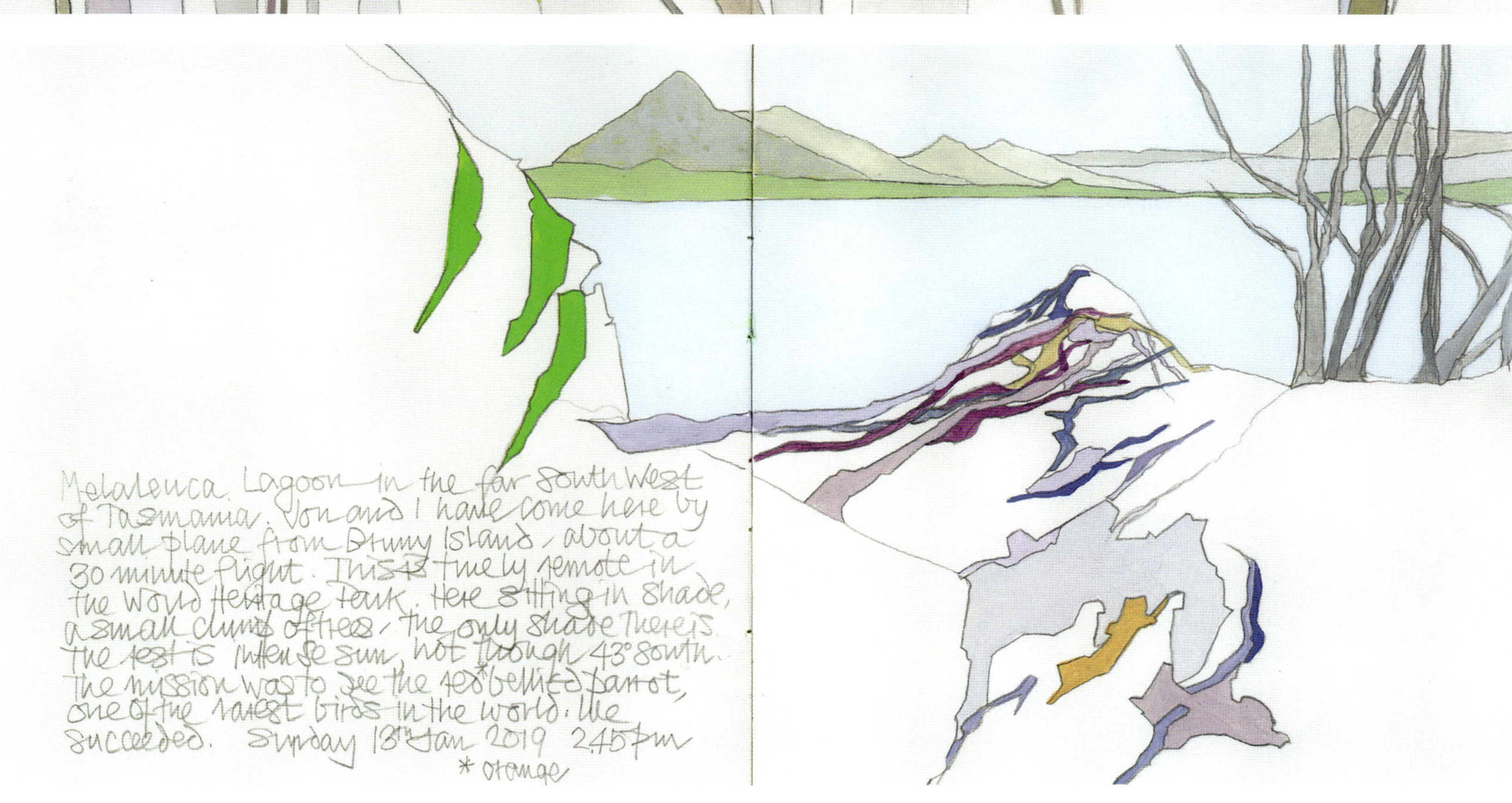


Melaleuca Lagoon in the far south west
of Tasmania. Von and I have come here by
small plane from Bruny Island, about a
30 minute flight. This is truely remote in
the World Heritage Park. Here sitting in shade,
a small clump of trees, the only shade there is.
The rest is intense sun, hot through 43° south.
The mission was to see the red*bellied parrot,
one of the rarest birds in the world. We
succeeded.  Sunday 13th Jan 2019  2.45pm
* orange

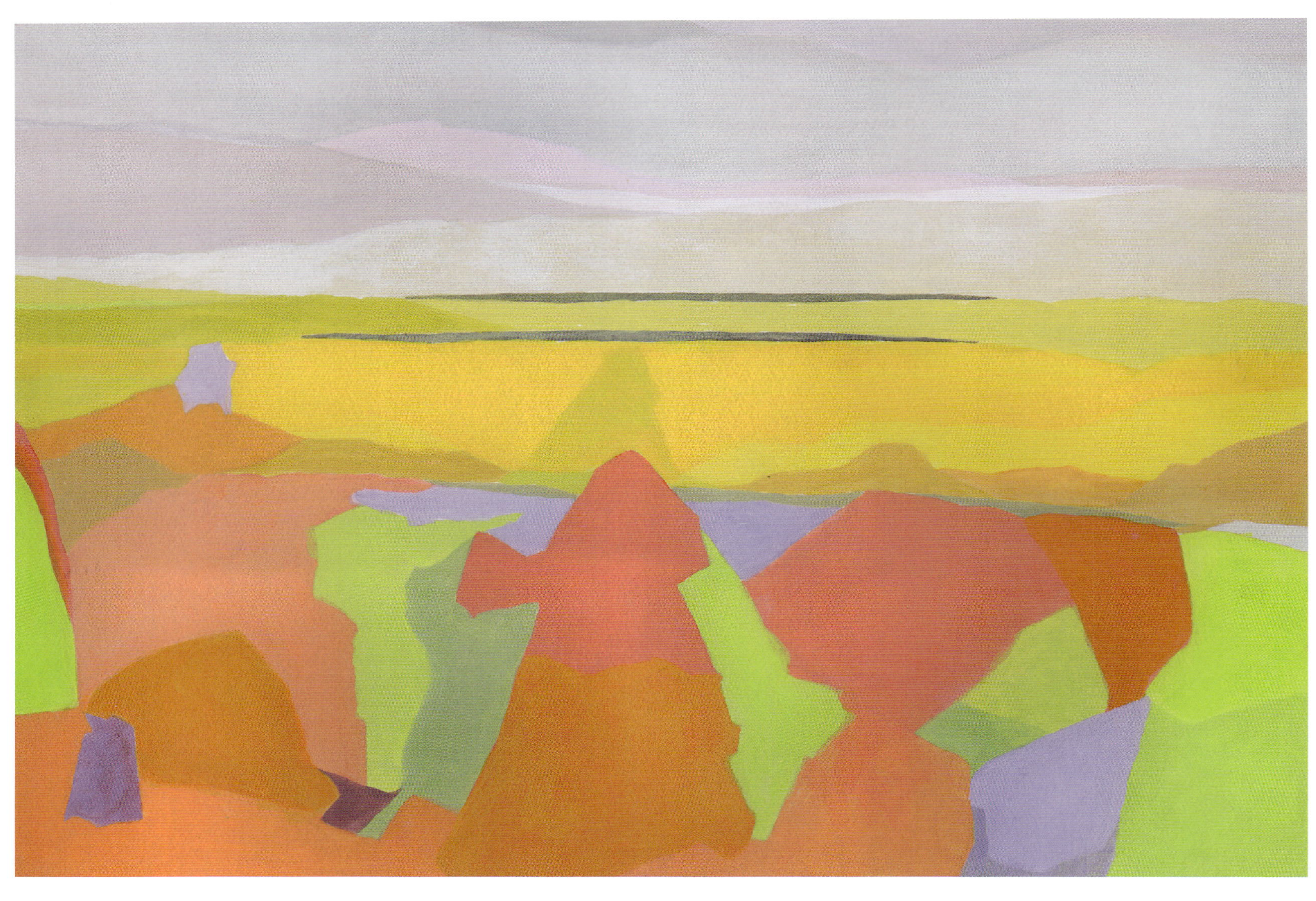

ABOVE
*Hartz Mountains*, 2019

RIGHT
*Flight to Melaleuca*, 2019

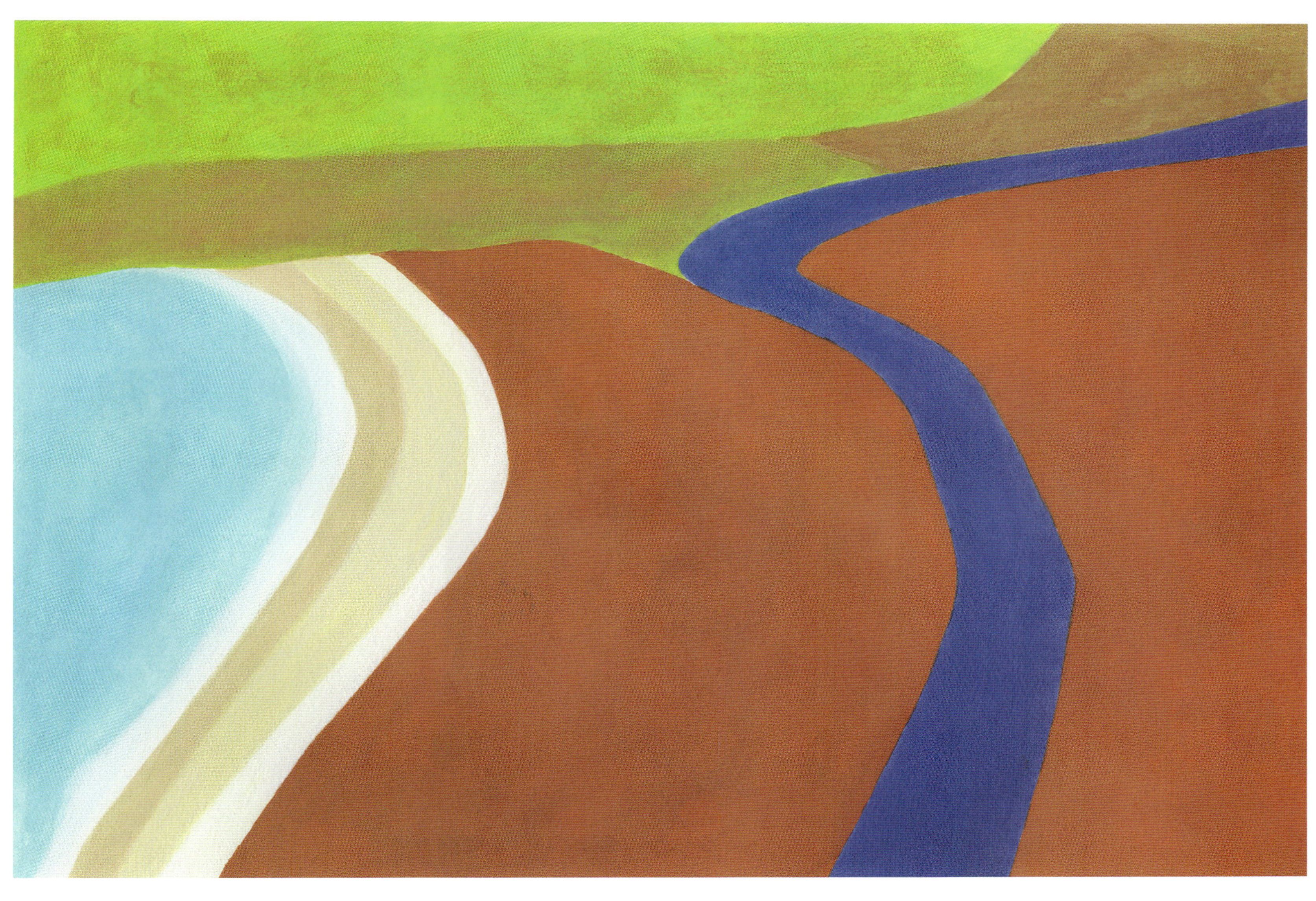

Lightning Ridge is the world
capital of black opals. Though
they are called black, they
are in fact a myriad of dark
colours: blues, greens, reds.

# Lightning Ridge,
# New South Wales

29°24'39.8"S 147°59'13.3"E
-29.411045, 147.987035

My son-in-law Jonathan, my granddaughter Ursula and I drove from Sydney to Lightning Ridge in November 2019. It is about an eleven-hour drive, north-east, inland and towards the Queensland border. The further inland we went, the drier it became, the effects of the long drought becoming more and more evident. The last two hours were frightening. Though I had read about the endless drought, I could never have imagined farmland laid to waste like this. No crops, no stock. The only animals we saw were a small group of goats.

Arriving at Lightning Ridge, there was a glimpse of green; the grassy fringes of the road in the main street were well watered, much to the joy of the kangaroos that came out to feast at night. This was the first of so many surprises in Lightning Ridge. There is plentiful water supplied by artesian wells – free to all, as are the associated thermal baths. The main street is lined with numerous motels, for this town of about 2500 inhabitants has, I was told, some 100,000 visitors a year. But we saw none. The season was already over, and as the fierce heat had set in.

Lightning Ridge is the world capital of black opals. Though they are called black, they are in fact a myriad of dark colours: blues, greens, reds. They contrast with the milky white or pale opals coming largely from Coober Pedy in South Australia. I was there to see the human-created landscape produced by the opal miners. I was told about Lightning Ridge by architects Glenn Murcutt and Wendy Lewin. They have visited often in recent years as part of their work designing the Australian Opal Centre, a large museum and cultural centre. They are so enthusiastic about the town, its people and the strange mined landscape. The local inhabitants who conceived this plan for a cultural centre have been working for years to raise sufficient money. Now, at last, they have enough to build. Detailed design is underway. The building will be largely underground, the evidence of which is the huge excavation among the mines outside the town. I made drawings of this, working in 40 °C heat.

Unlike most mining ventures around Australia (see Mount Tom Price mine, page 2) and the world in general, this is mining by individuals on tiny plots. There are dozens of mines, perhaps hundreds. Each mining concession is limited to a couple of 50-by-50 metre plots. The miners, who come from all over the world, often live beside their mines in a great variety of habitations. The mines are unseen, situated below ground. The only traces are the pyramids of white kaolinite-rich claystone that punctuate the landscape. In among this are old-looking machines and abandoned trucks, some rusting away. It is surreal. I have tried to capture this strange land in the paintings here.

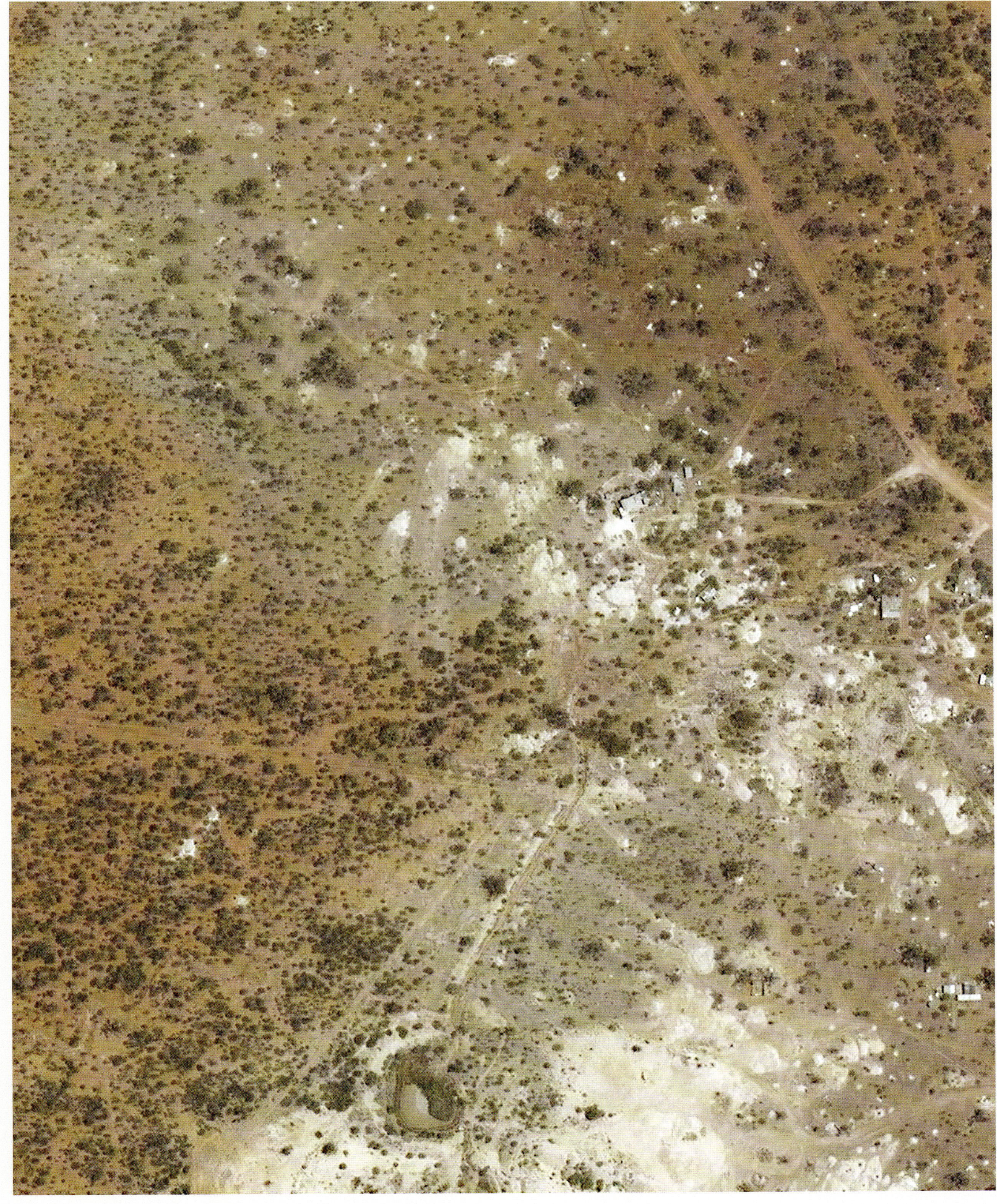

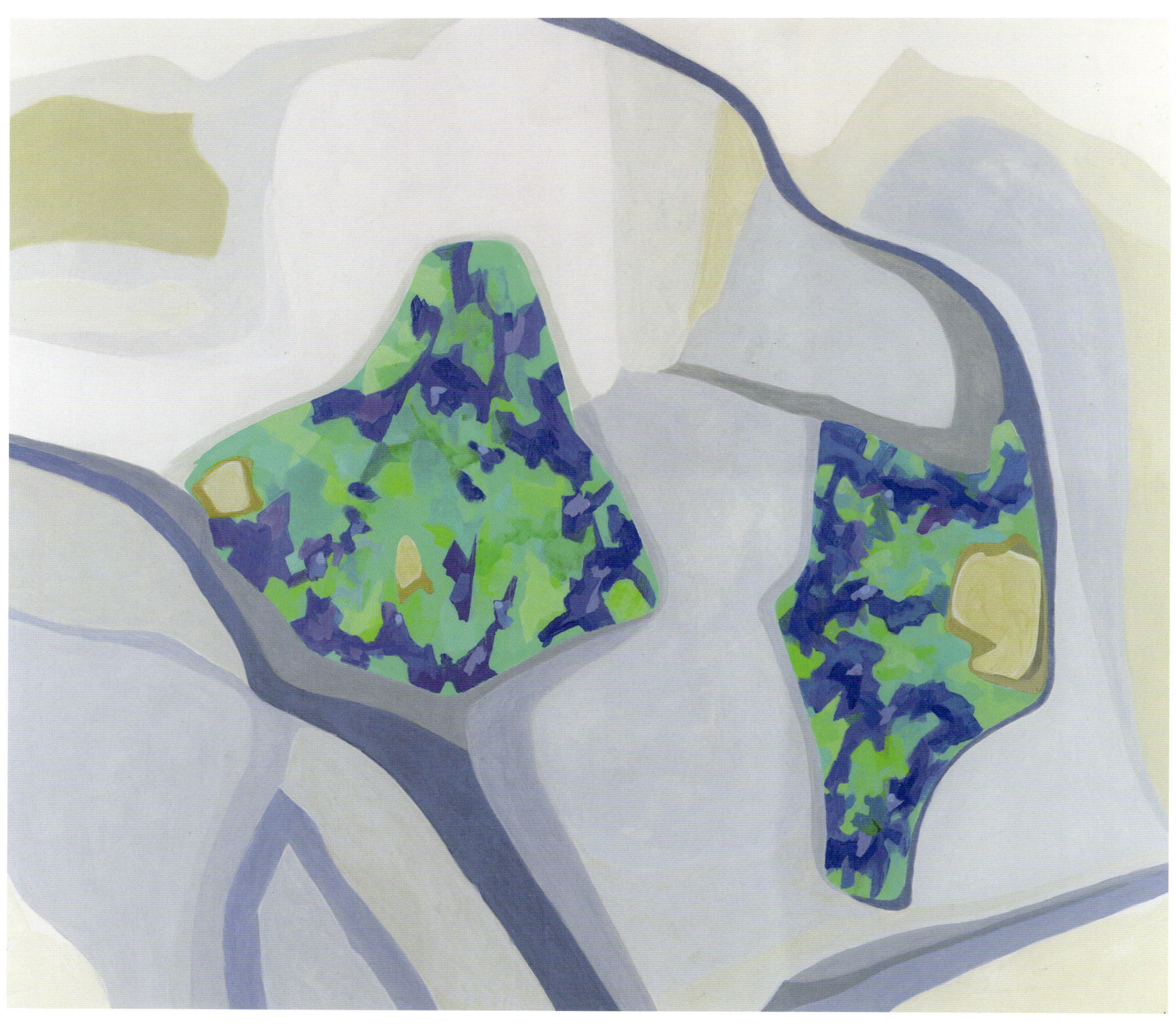

**ABOVE**
*Opal*, 2020

**RIGHT**
*Lightning Ridge: Miner's Hut*,
2019–20

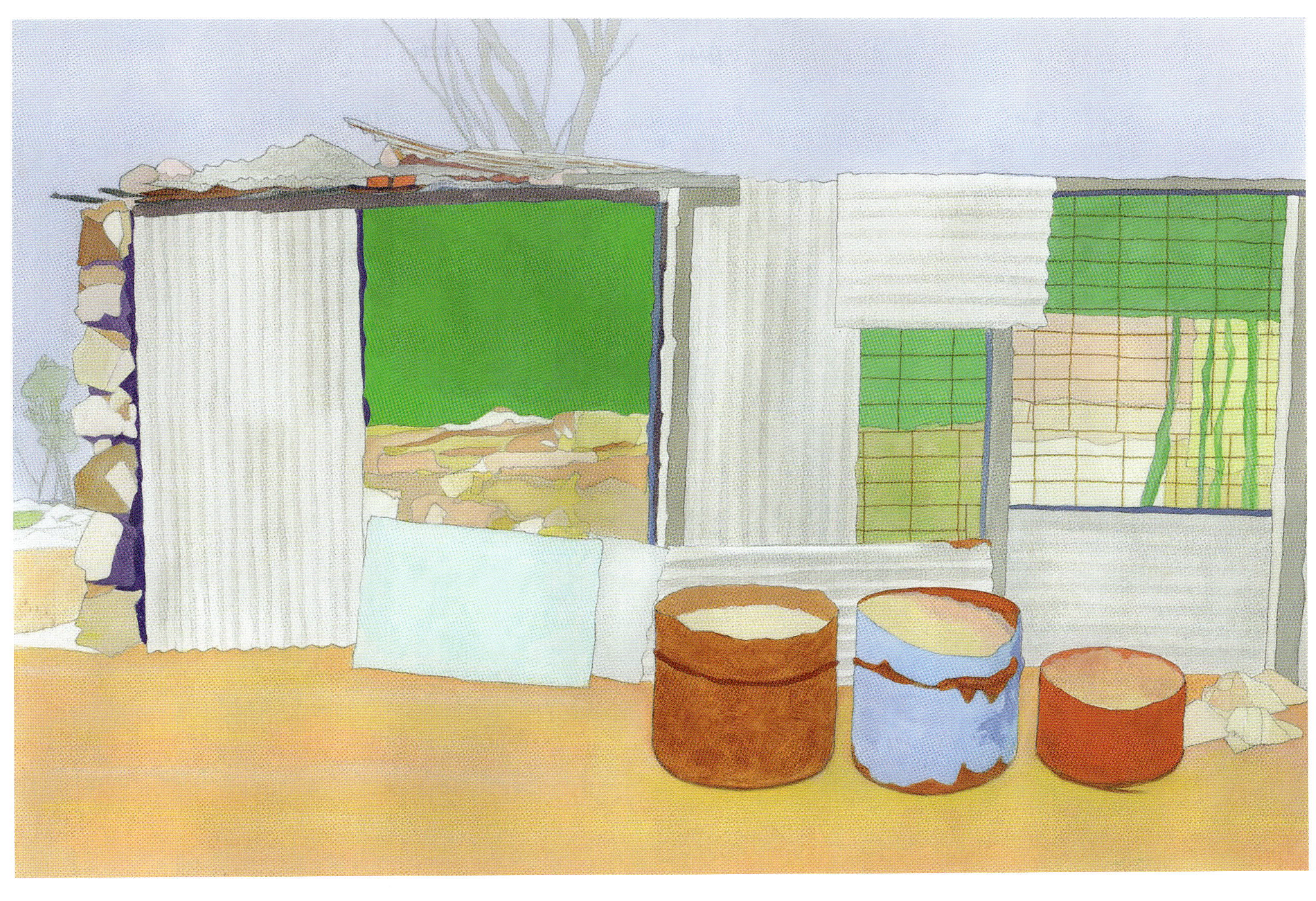

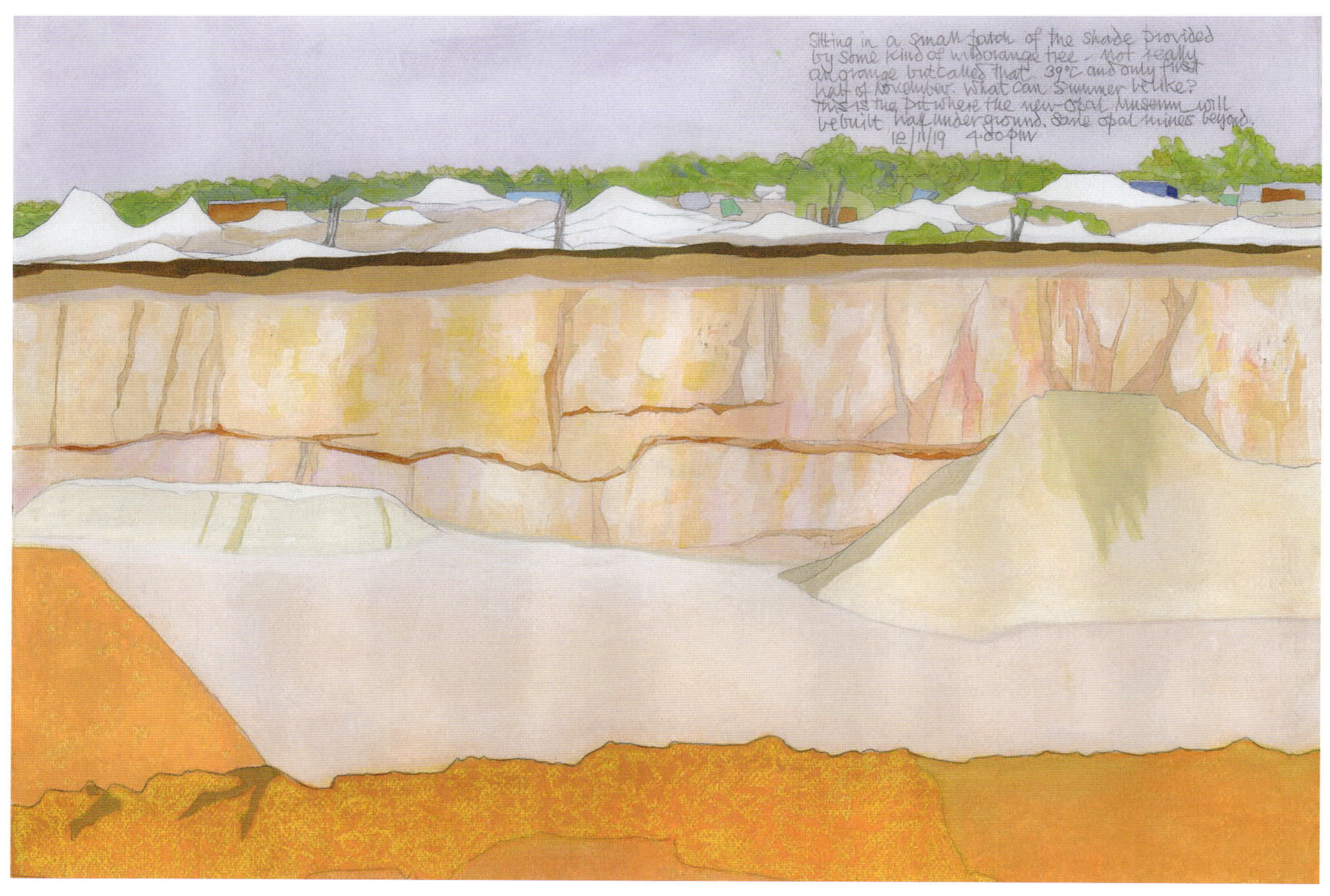





*Lightning Ridge: The Giant
Excavation*, 2019–20



*Lightning Ridge: The Mines*,
2019–20

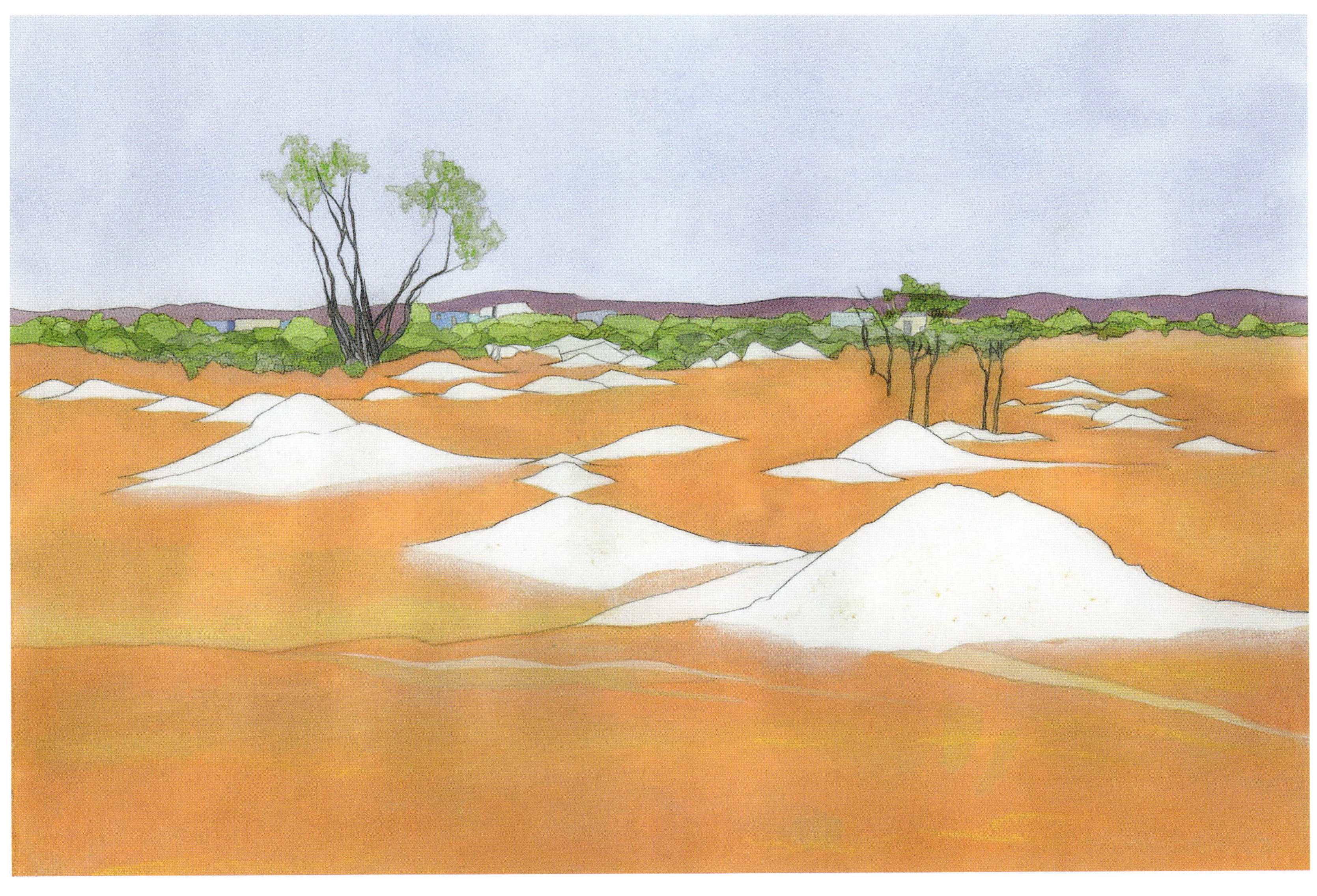

# Bundanon, Shoalhaven River, New South Wales

34°53'25.7"S 150°30'08.7"E
-34.890481, 150.502429

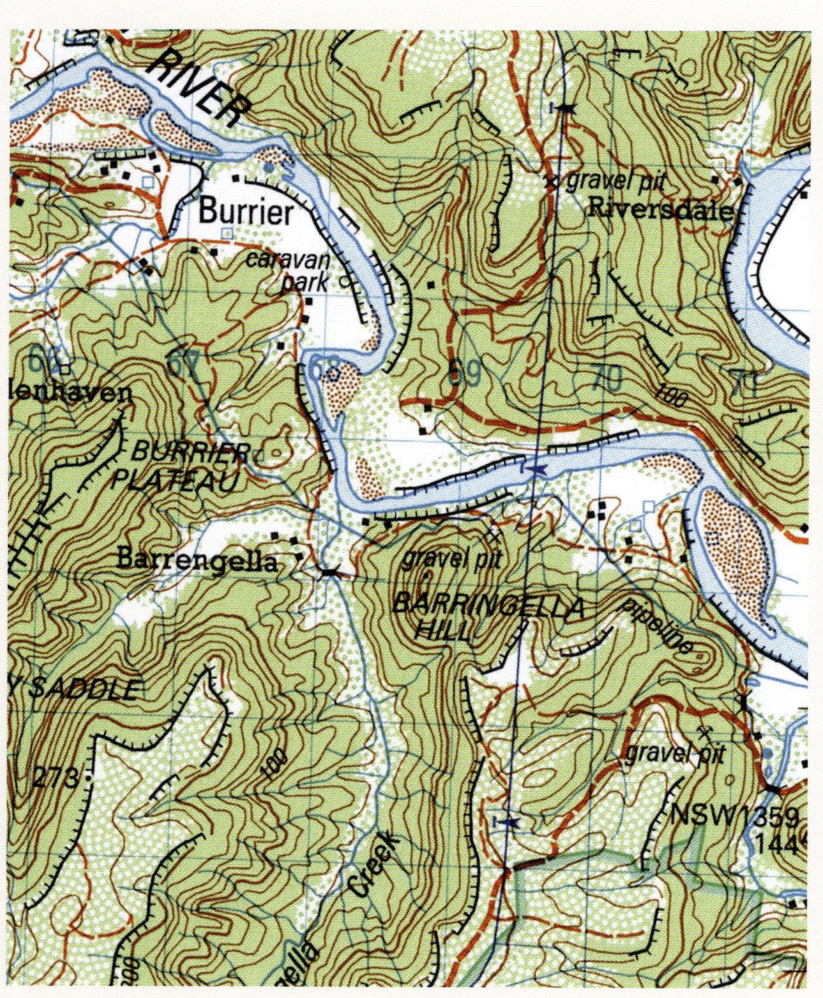


Arthur and Yvonne Boyd donated Bundanon to the people of Australia in 1993. It is a fine house in extensive bushland bordering the Shoalhaven River, near the town of Nowra. Also included in the Bundanon Trust is the superb Boyd Education Centre at Riversdale, designed by Glenn Murcutt, Wendy Lewin and Reg Lark, which opened in 1999. Near the Shoalhaven are a number of artists' studio residencies and a small cottage that serves as a writers' residence. The program through which artists and writers can apply for residencies continues.

Psiche and I were invited to stay, and we lived in the writers' cottage for a week. This period allowed me to work intensively in the immediate surrounds: in the forest behind the cottage and down on the banks of the Shoalhaven River. The site has special artistic significance in the work of Arthur Boyd, who so often painted views of the river – particularly incorporating Pulpit Rock, the cliff located on the riverbank opposite Bundanon homestead, into many of his works. I did a number of drawings while sitting on the large sandbank beside the river. Alas, the peace of this beautiful scene was disturbed by very noisy motorboats speeding past.

As well as giving me a chance to work in the Shoalhaven landscape, this visit led to us spending time with the other visiting artists, who were there for longer periods. In particular, we became friends with Cresside Collette, the tapestry weaver. She incorporates landscape into her work, to amazing effect, by weaving in situ, the way others would draw or paint.

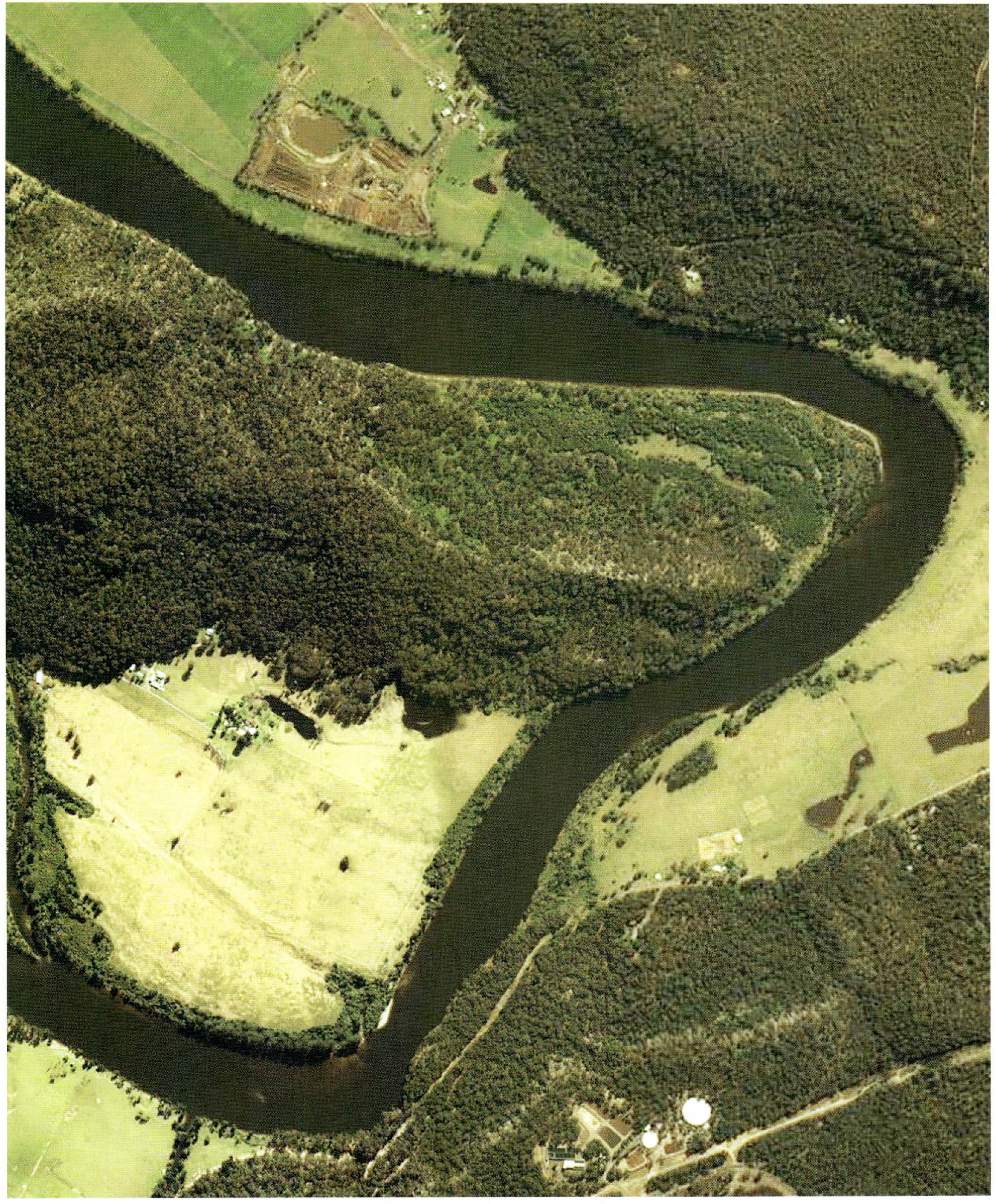

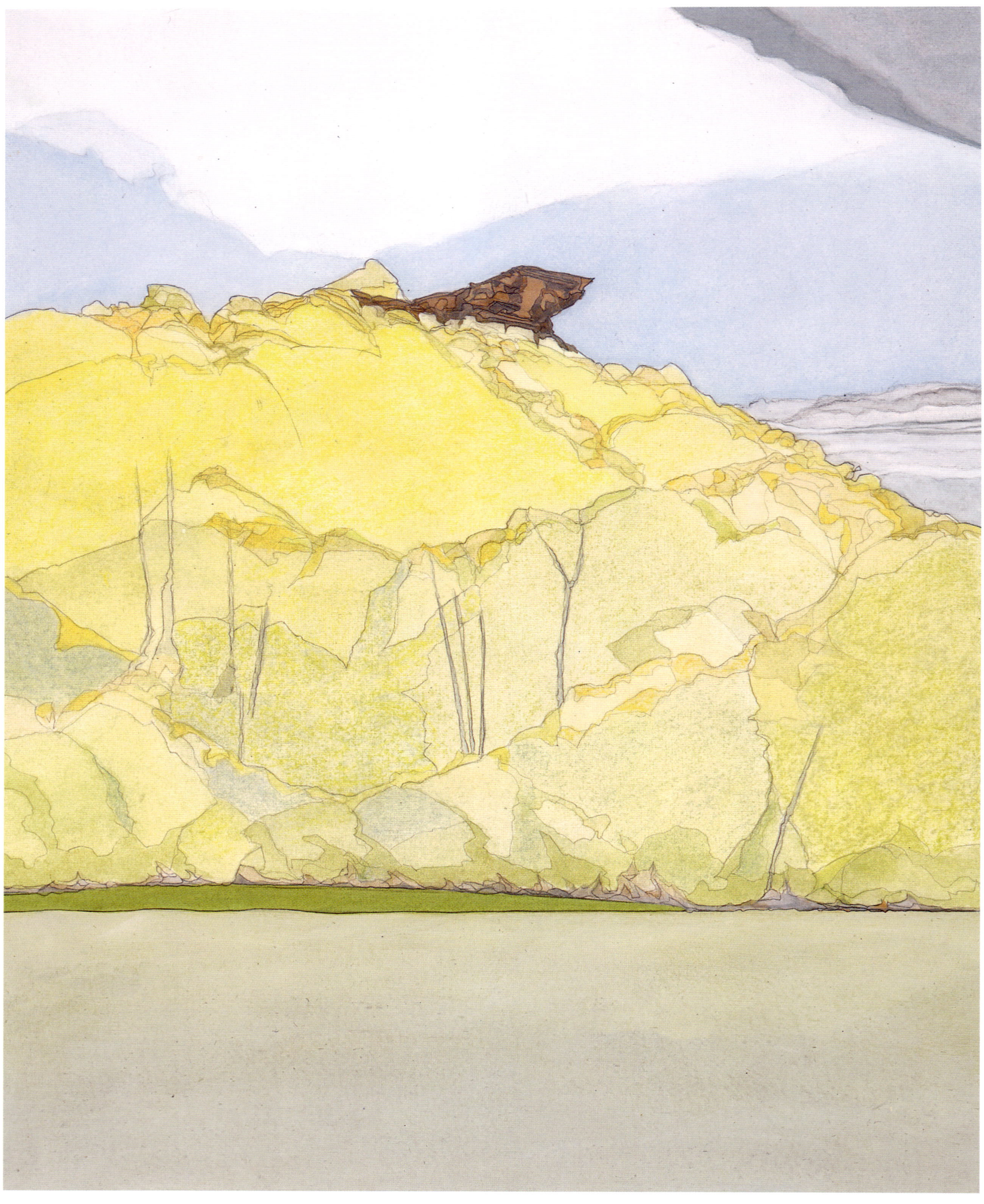

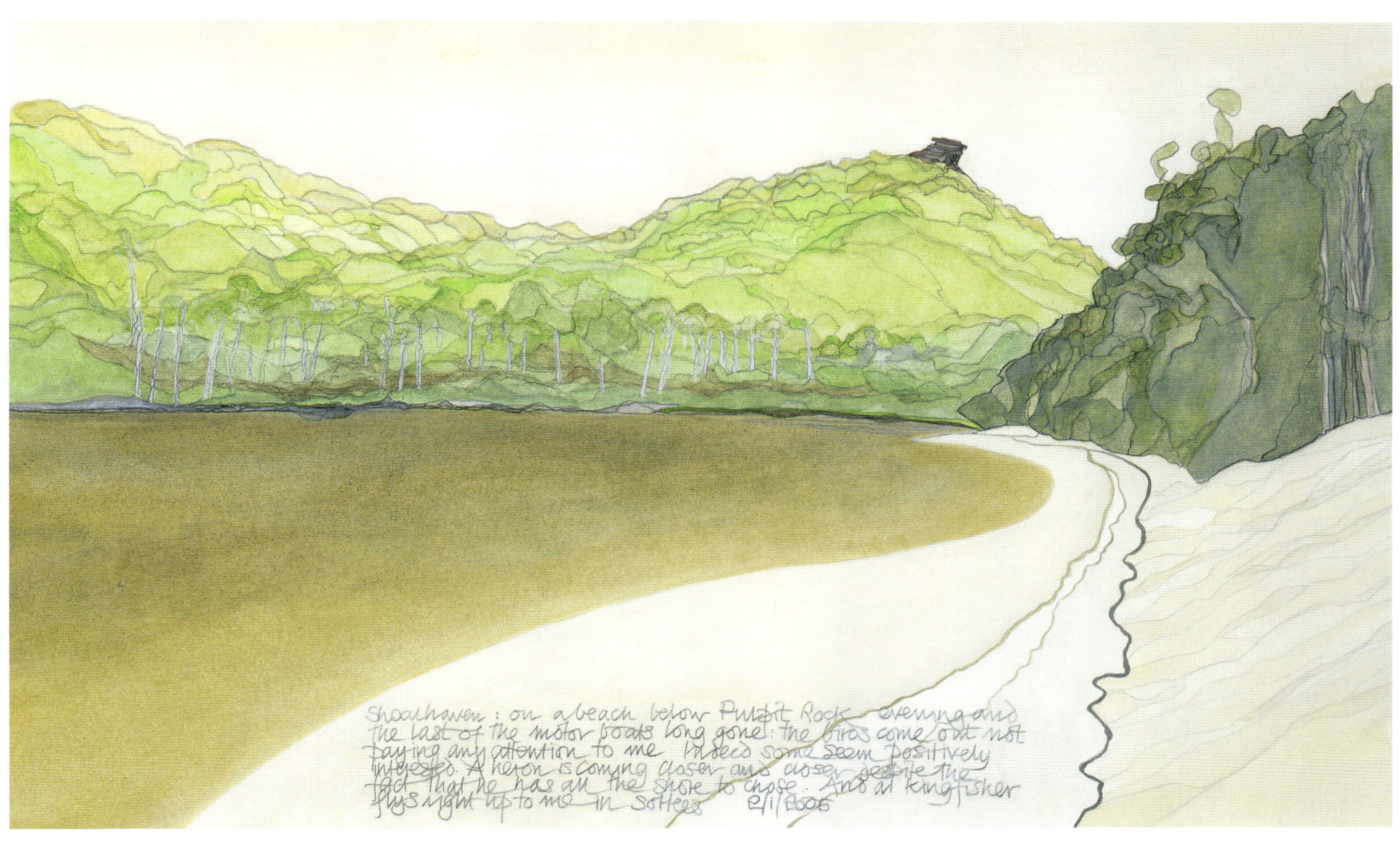


**LEFT**
*Pulpit Rock, 31 December,*
2005

**ABOVE**
*Shoalhaven in the evening,*
2005

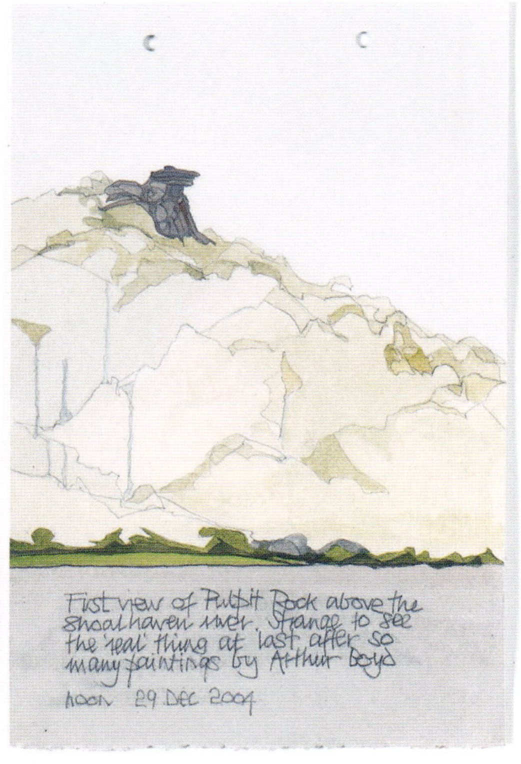

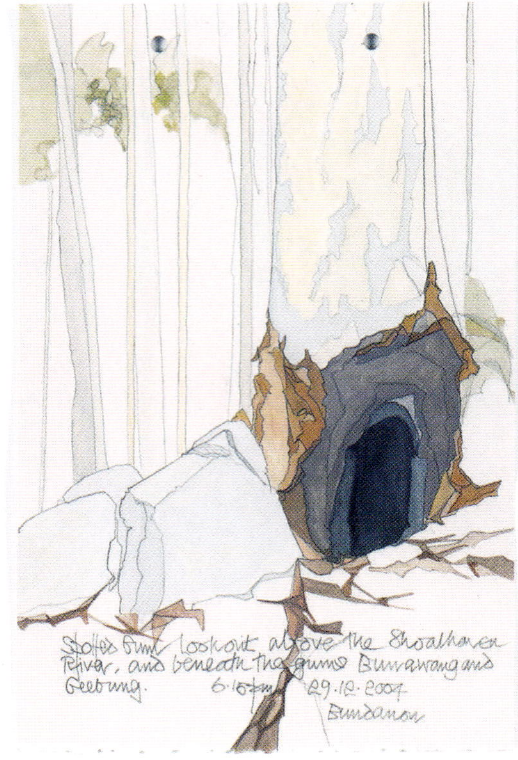

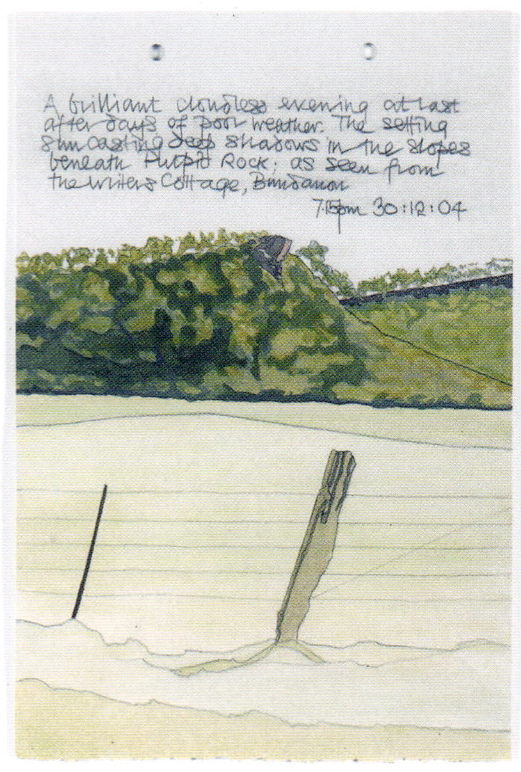

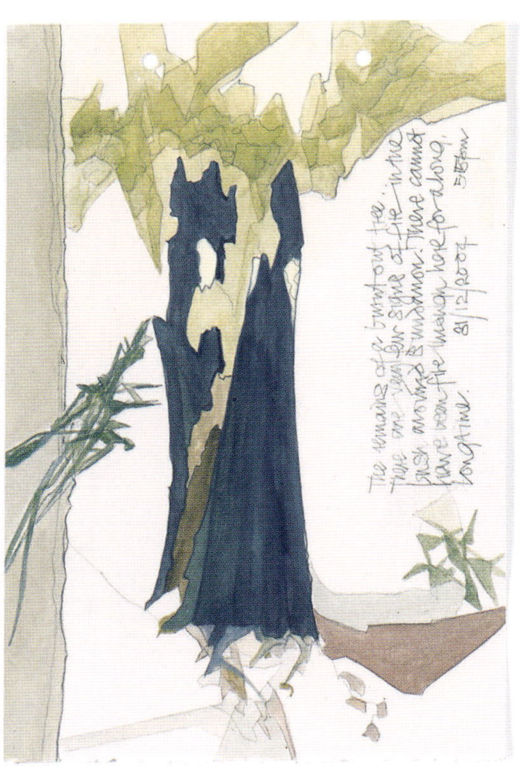

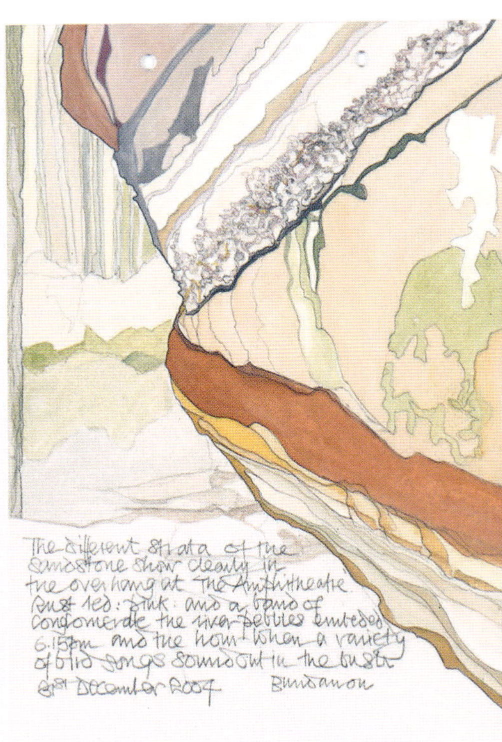

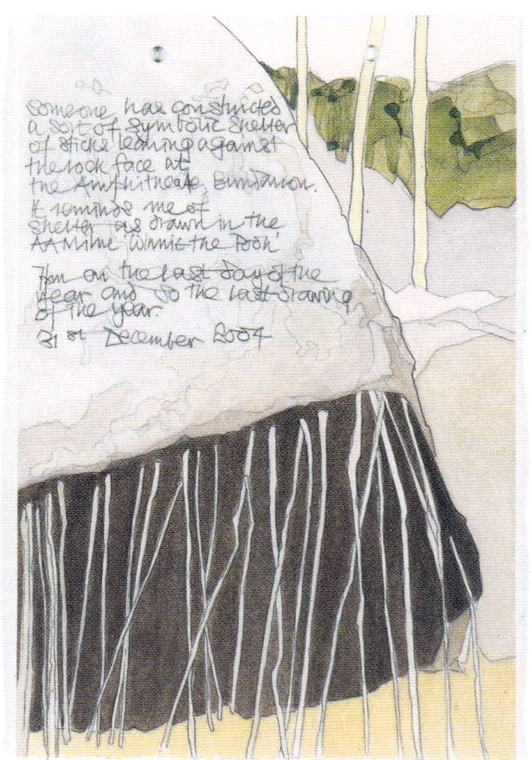



**ABOVE**
*Bundanon: the last three days
of 2004*, 2004

**RIGHT**
*Spotted Gums*, 2005

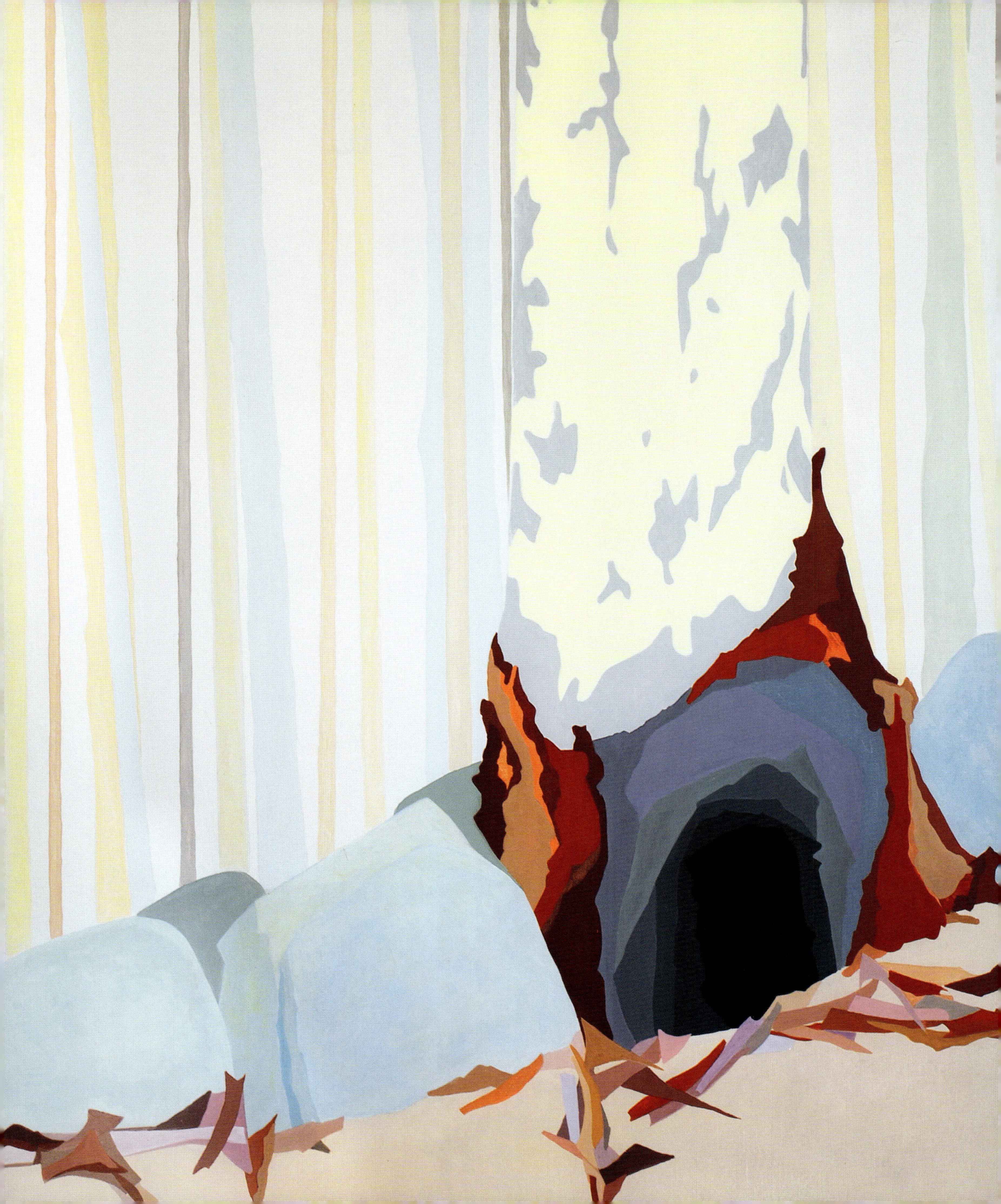

# Blue Mountains,
# New South Wales

33°34'32.7"S 150°20'18.8"E
-33.575754, 150.338559

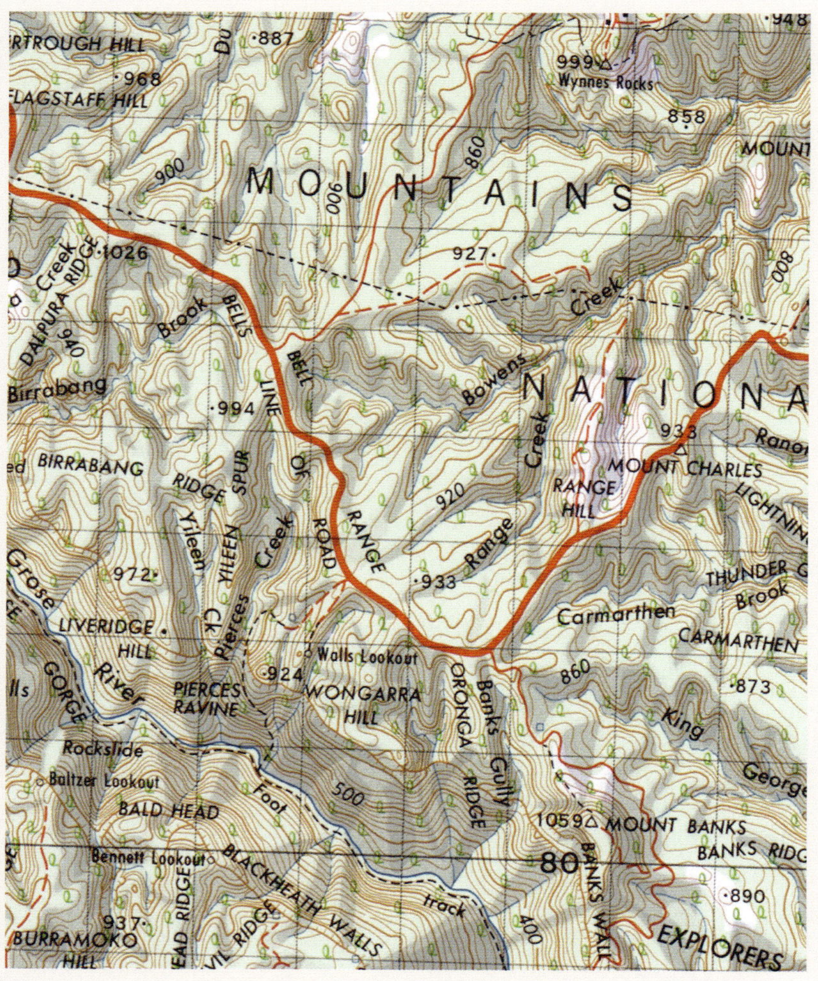



These mountains are indeed blue, whether seen on approach from Sydney in the east or from the summit ridges overlooking the valleys. But they are not conventional mountains in the general sense of the word. They are quite high at over 1000 metres, but if you approach from the east, as most people do, the road rises gradually and you do not have the impression of climbing a mountain. There are no real peaks – it is only when on the plateau, looking down at the gorges, that you realise you have climbed to the highest points.

Much of the mountains are cultivated, in places, built over with linked small towns. But you can get a real sense of wildness in two ways. One way is to walk from the base of the mountains into the valleys, with their magnificent blue gum forests. The other is to start from a road on the summit plateau and walk to one of the lookouts, where you can see the huge ravine below. The most stunning of these overlooks Grose Valley, which is some 500 metres deep, hemmed in by gigantic rock faces. The works included here show both aspects – the deep gum forests of the valleys and the views of the valleys from above.

Returning to Sydney from Lightning Ridge in November 2019, after nine hours of driving, we started to cross the mountains, coming up from Lithgow. We had to choose this route to avoid the bushfires occurring in parts of New South Wales that day, including the Blue Mountains.

Even though it was getting late, we stopped and walked on the Walls Lookout track that runs off Bells Line of Road. The track was beautiful, swathed in a proliferation of wildflowers, the route itself made of worn, pale yellow sandstone. Then, after twenty minutes, the panorama opened up and the rock wall of Grose Valley stretched across. It appeared dark, dark blue – as we were looking into the setting sun, it was nearly all in shade. A dramatic sight.

Just a few weeks after walking this track, it and all the surrounding forest were devastated by fire. I have done a multi-panel work illustrating the track (page 137), firstly as I saw it in November 2019 and then adding a last panel, showing the burnt-out scene as it was in early 2020.

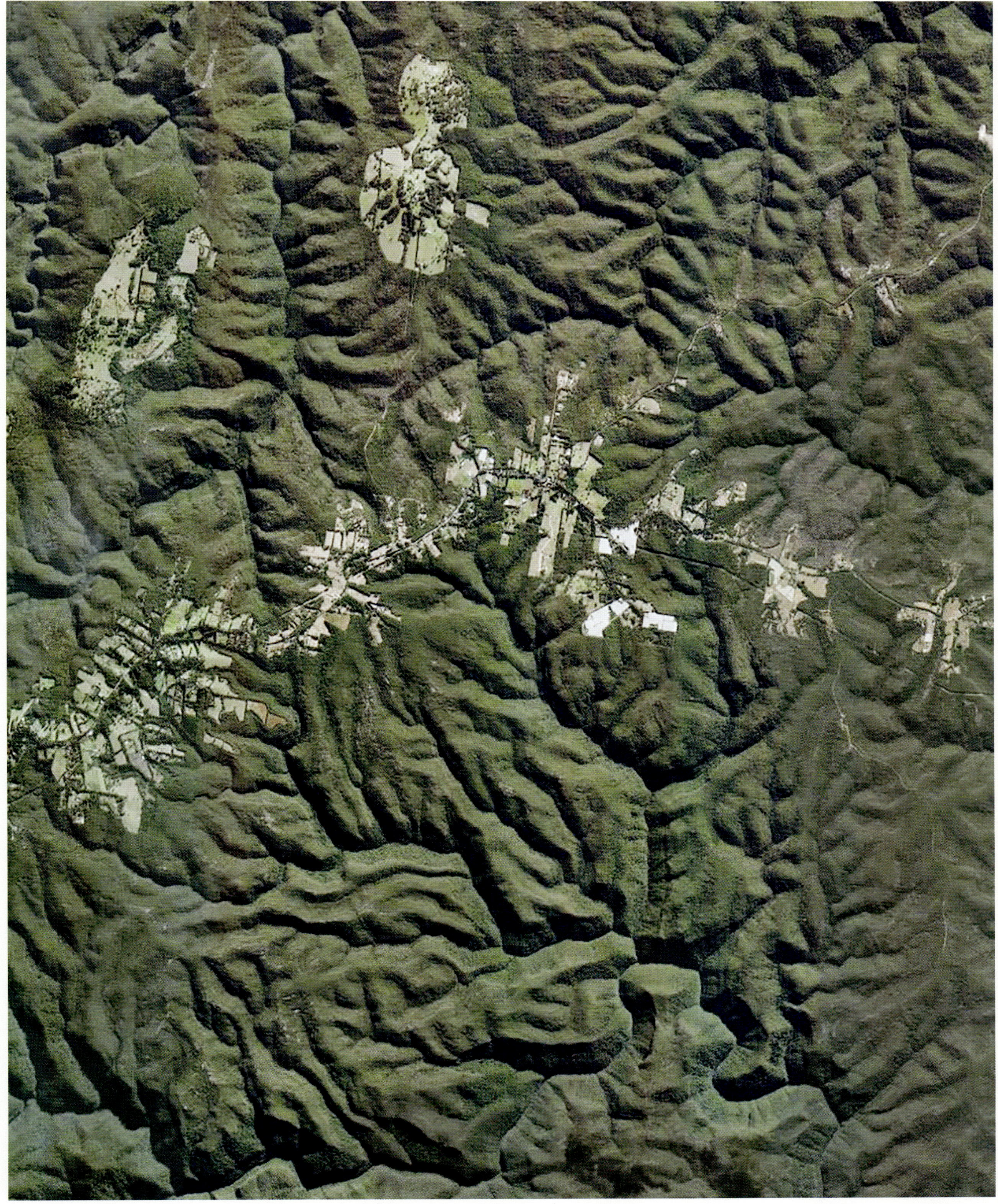

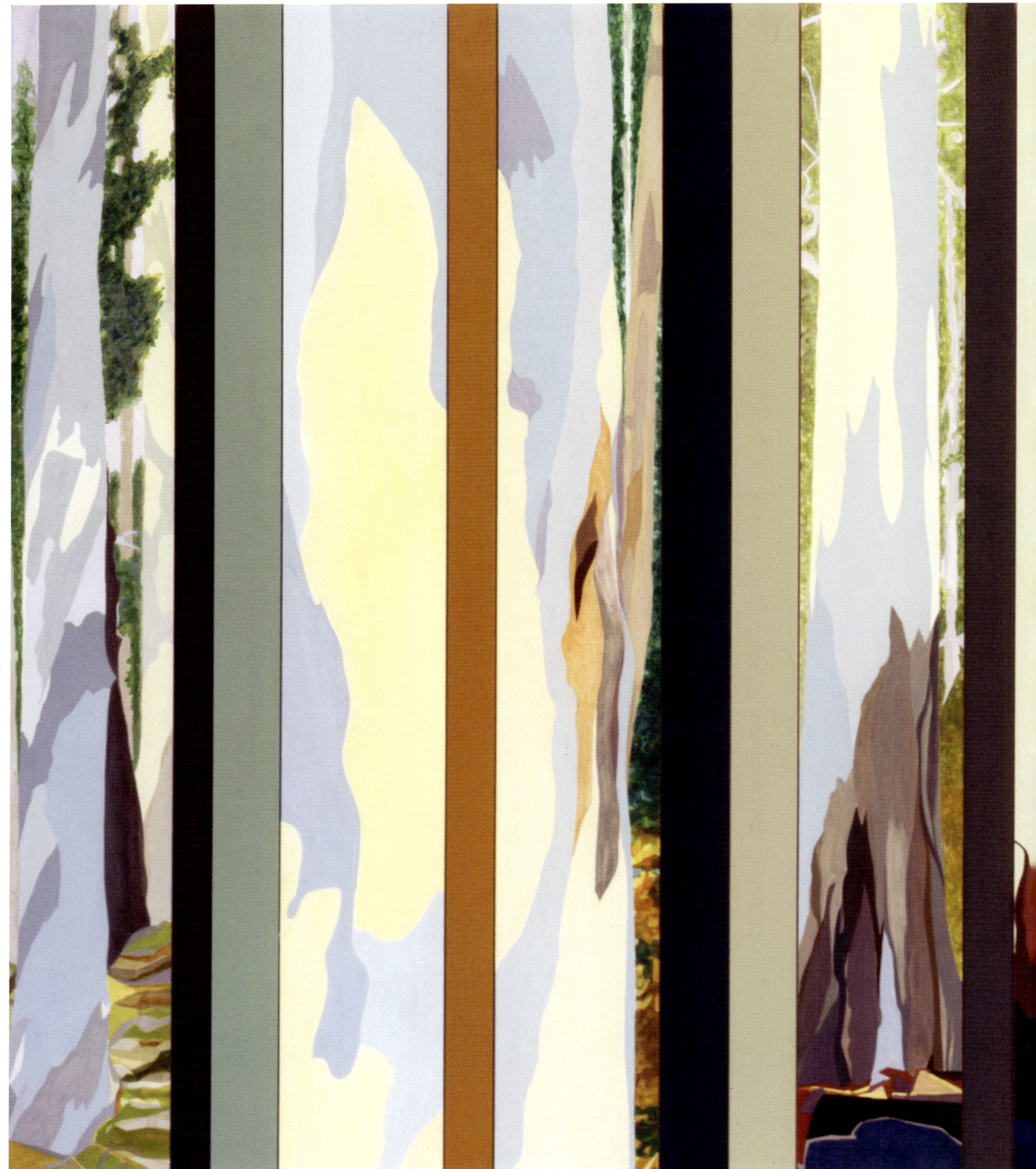

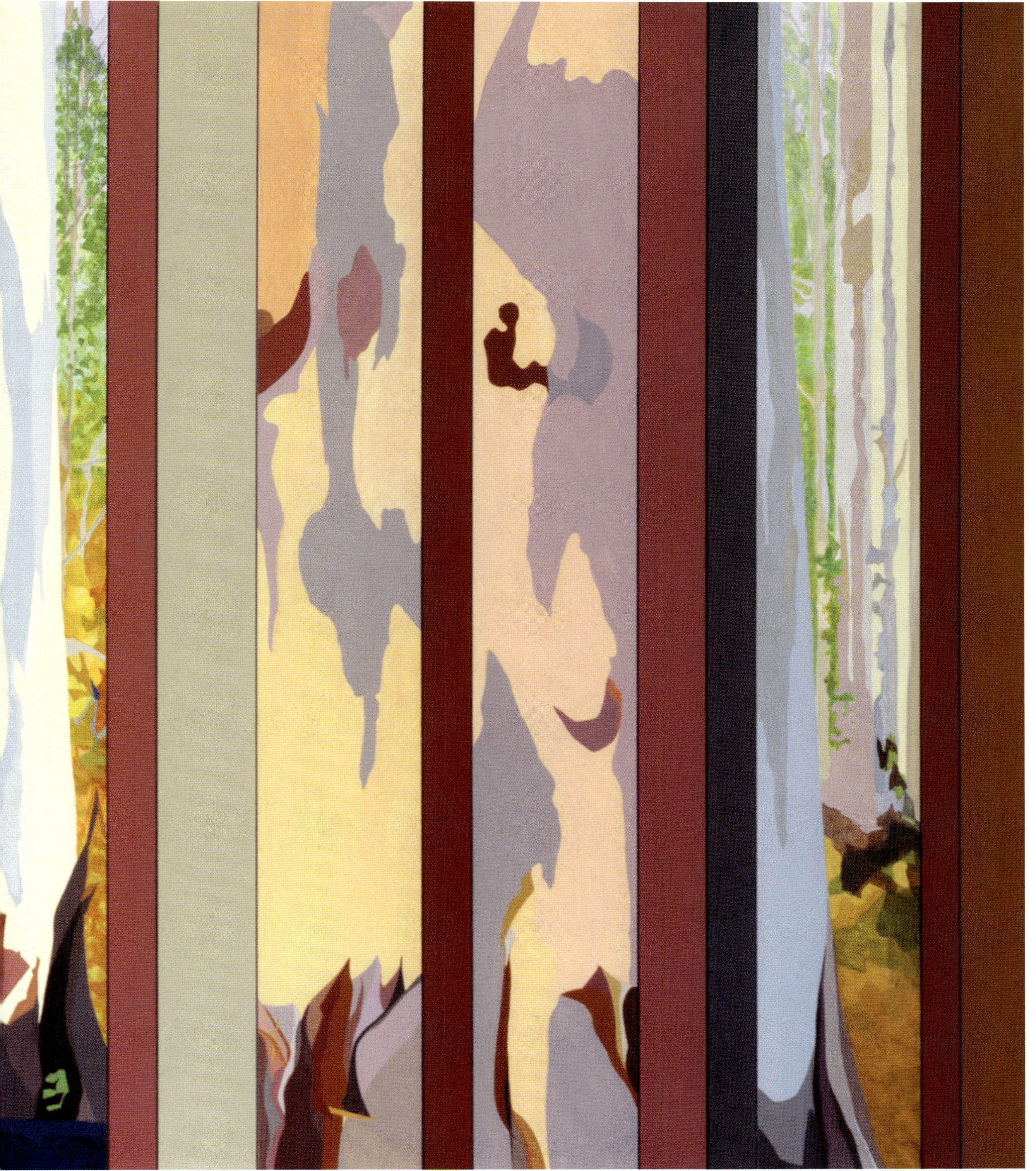

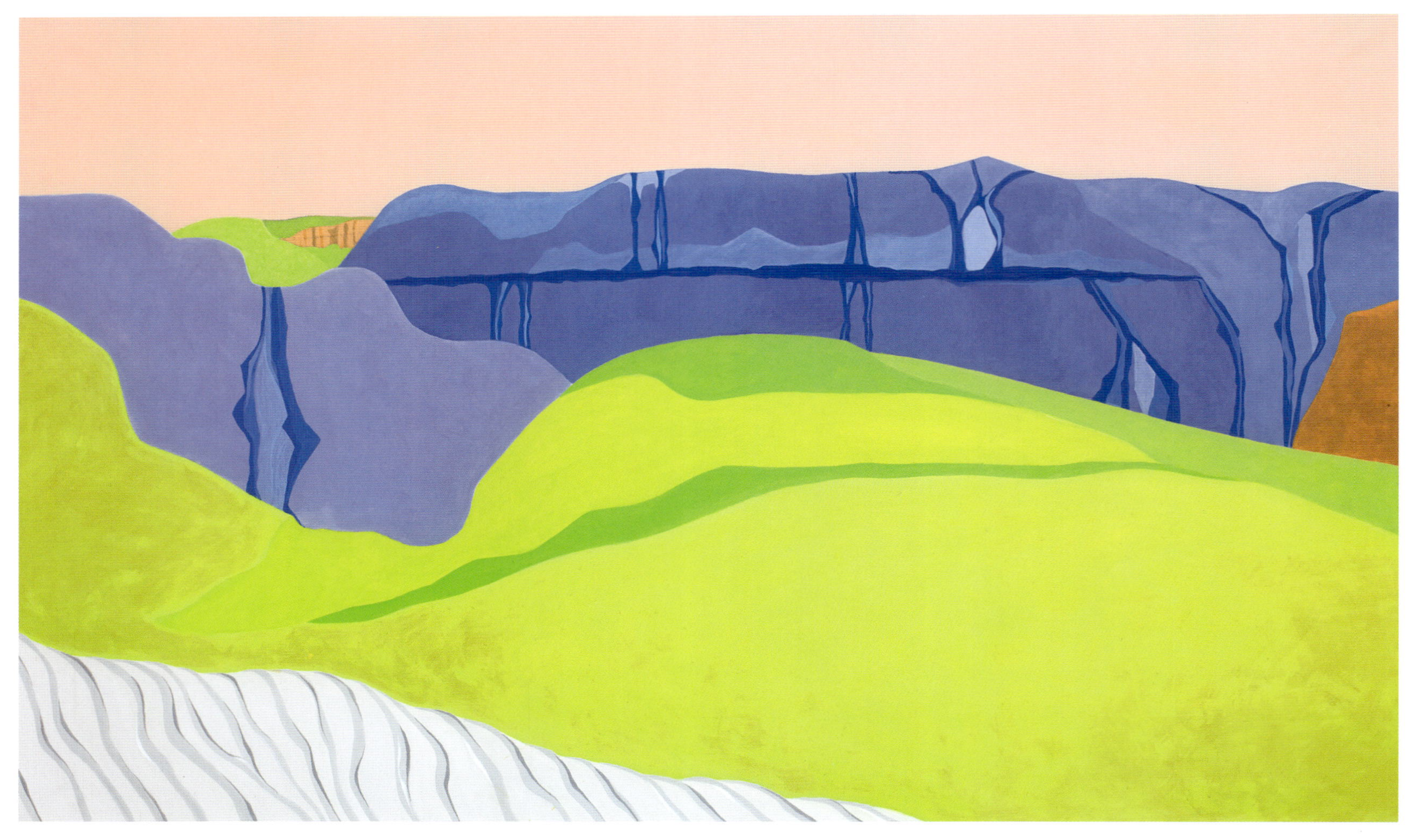

**PREVIOUS SPREAD**
*In the Blue Gum Forest I*, 1995

**ABOVE**
*Blue Mountains*, 2019–20

**RIGHT**
*Walls Lookout Track*, 2020

**FOLLOWING SPREAD**
*Blue Gum Forest*, 1987

136

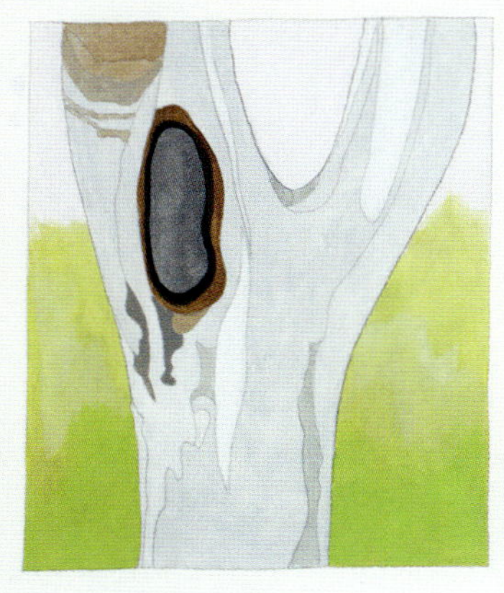

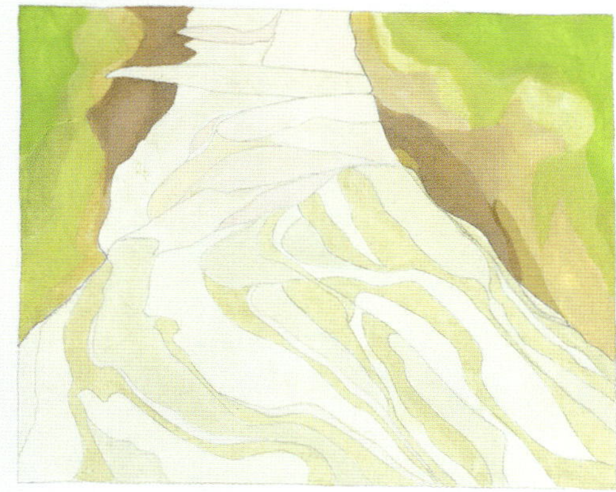

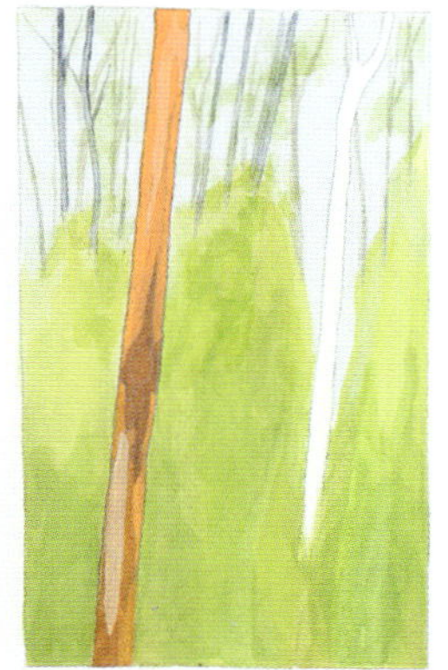

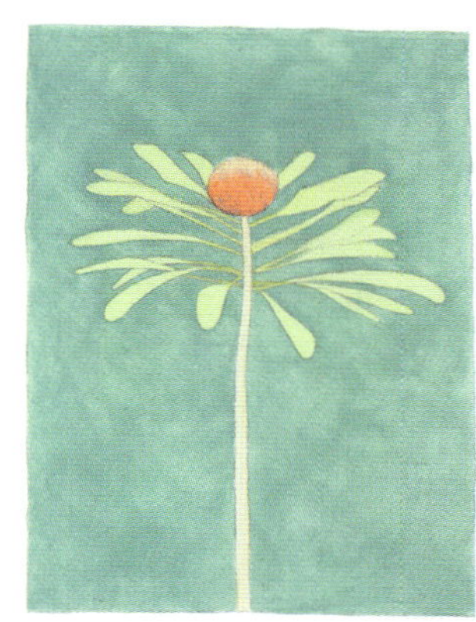

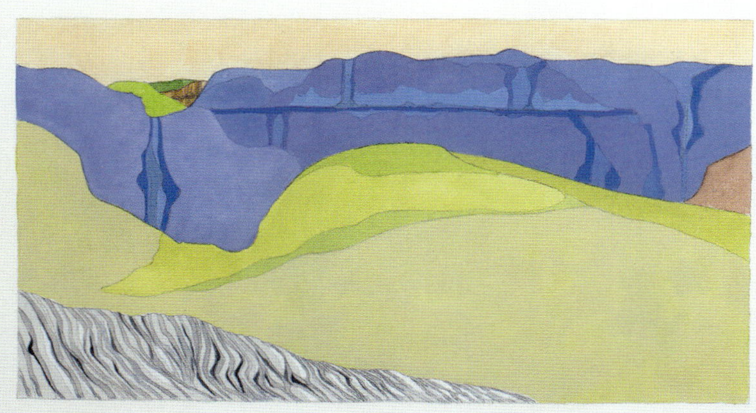

The Blue Mountains 14th Nov. 2019

The track at Pierces Pass
to Walls Lookout.

It was a mass of flowers and
a variety of trees. At the end,
a huge panorama opened up
facing the rock wall that towers
above Grose Gorge. We reached
there after 6pm and looking west
the rock face was in deep shade.

A few weeks later the whole
region was devastated by the fires
that swept through the Blue Mountains

I mark these fires with a burnt
out tree beside the track.

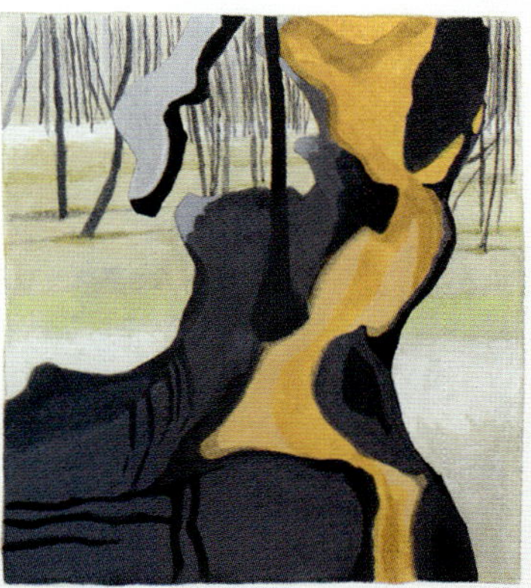

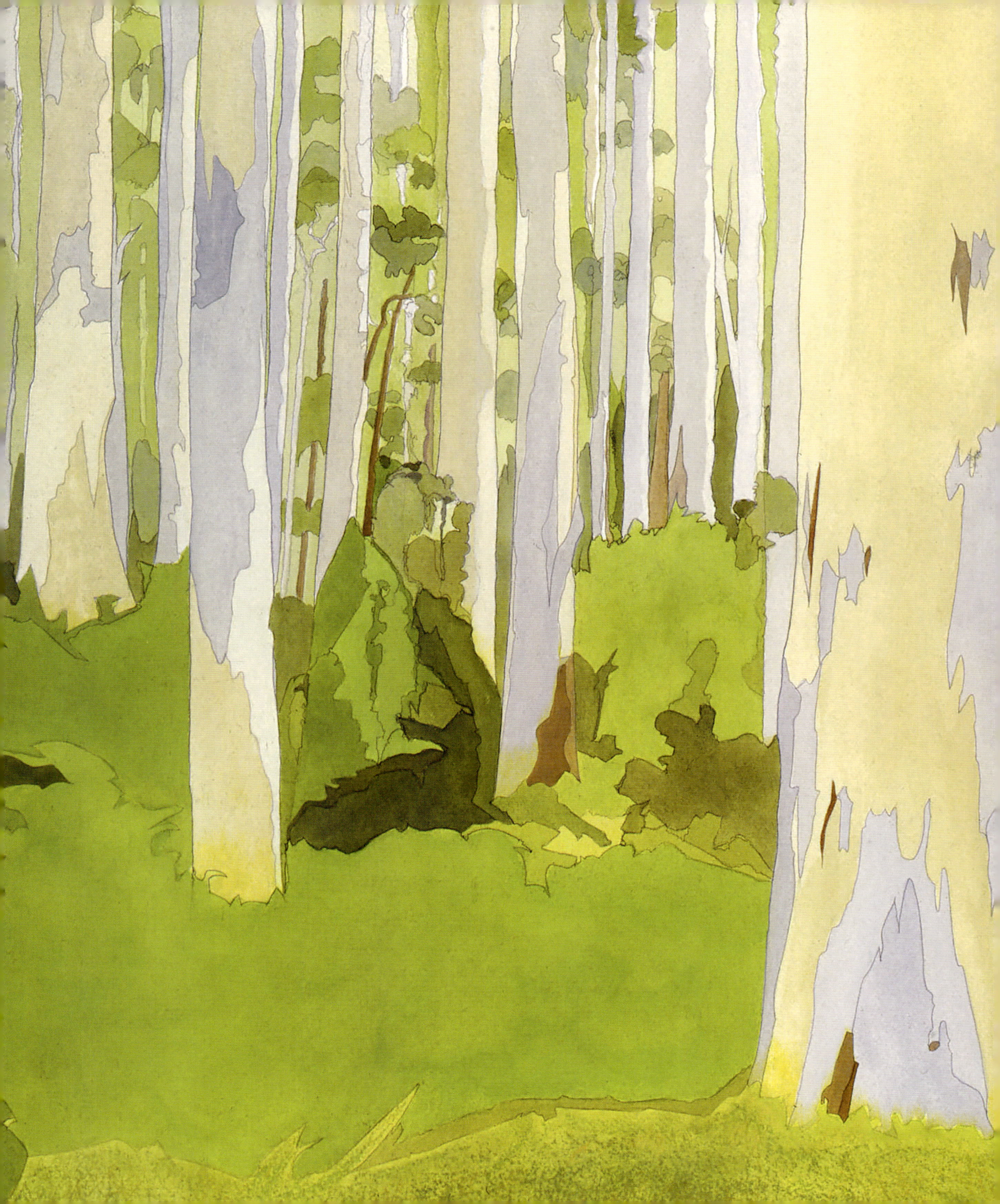

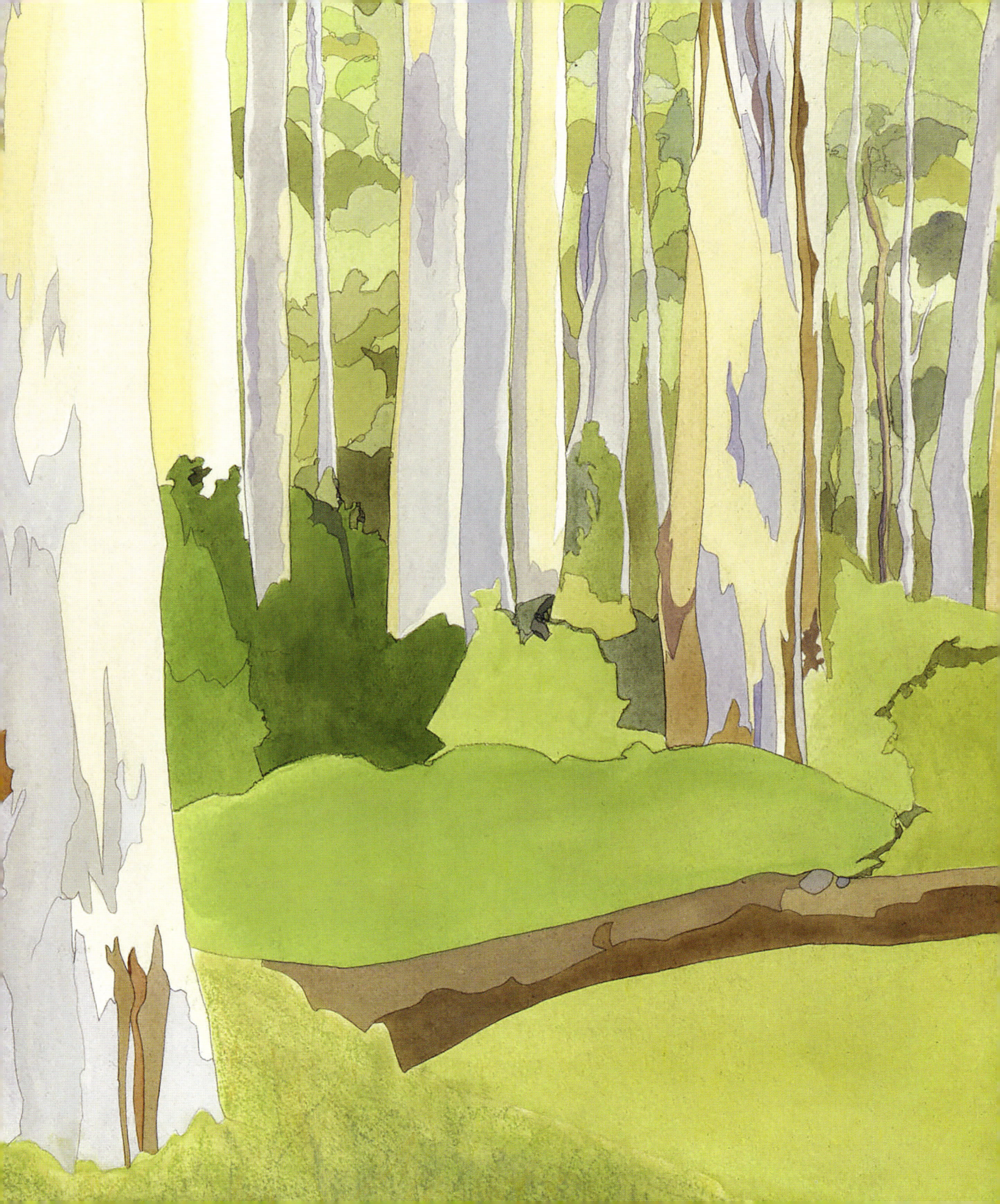

# Bouddi, New South Wales

33°31'22.9"S 151°23'25.6"E
-33.523032, 151.390430

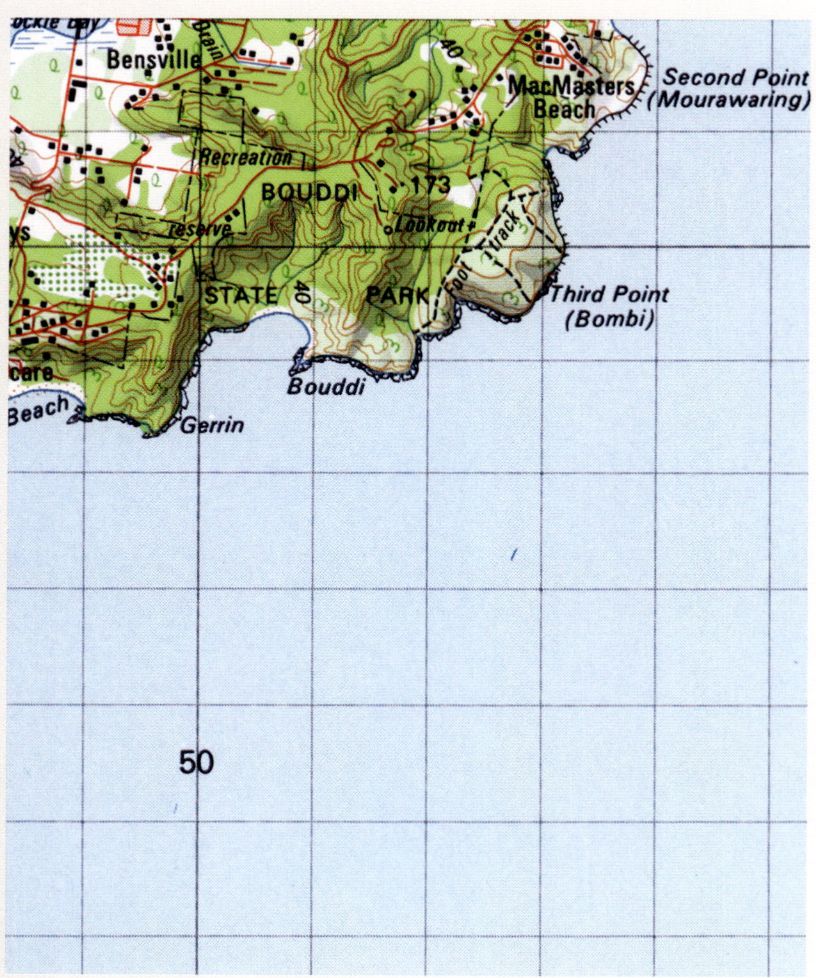


My parents had a single-storey house in Macmasters Beach, a small seaside town north of Sydney. I went and stayed there many times during my visits from the UK. Just at the end of their road was the edge of Bouddi National Park. I often walked and drew there. The park is small, but has magnificent temperate rainforest leading down to Maitland Bay. This spectacular beach and bay can only be reached by foot, so it is a very well-protected area, less than 100 kilometres from Sydney.

I was intrigued by a particular tree, an *Angophora costata*, commonly known as a Sydney red gum, with a contortion of twisted branches. Each time I stayed with my parents, I went to study this tree, sitting on the large pink-coloured rock outcrop nearby. Often, I would do a new drawing. And I would take the walk down to Maitland Bay.

One time, I found in the sand an extraordinary rock, like a cube, with sides of about 60 to 70 centimetres. One side was black, while the other sides were different deep reds, graduating to pale grey and finally to the yellow of the original sandstone. All these different tones were, I assume, caused by different levels of oxidation. This is just as in Uluru, where the caverns at the base of the rock are pale grey or yellow, not the familiar red. I drew and painted this rock, and I would have liked to have kept it as a sculpture. Of course, I could not move it. Nor should I have. It belonged on the beach. There it should have remained. But on my next visit, it was gone. All I have are the four paintings shown on page 146.

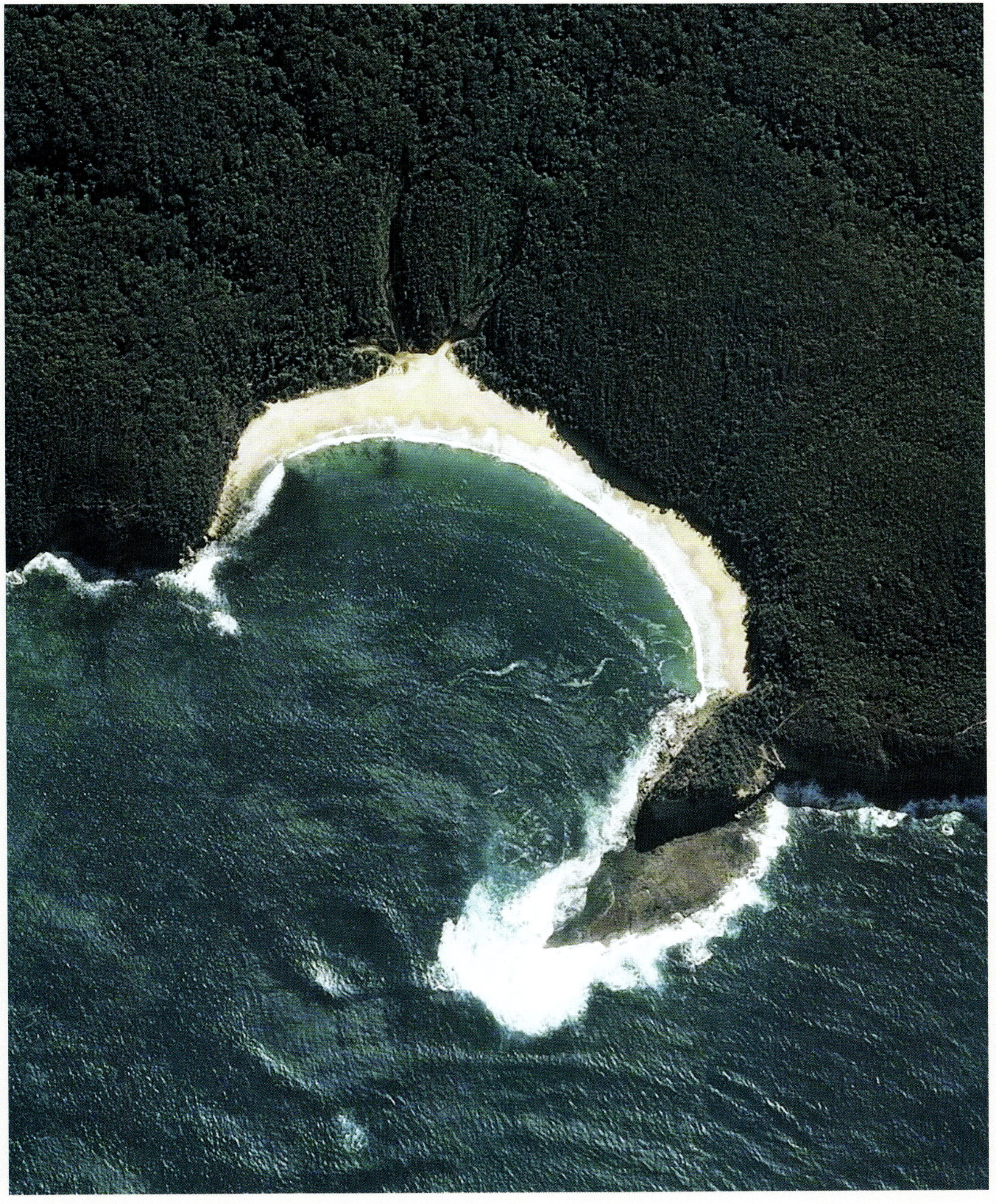

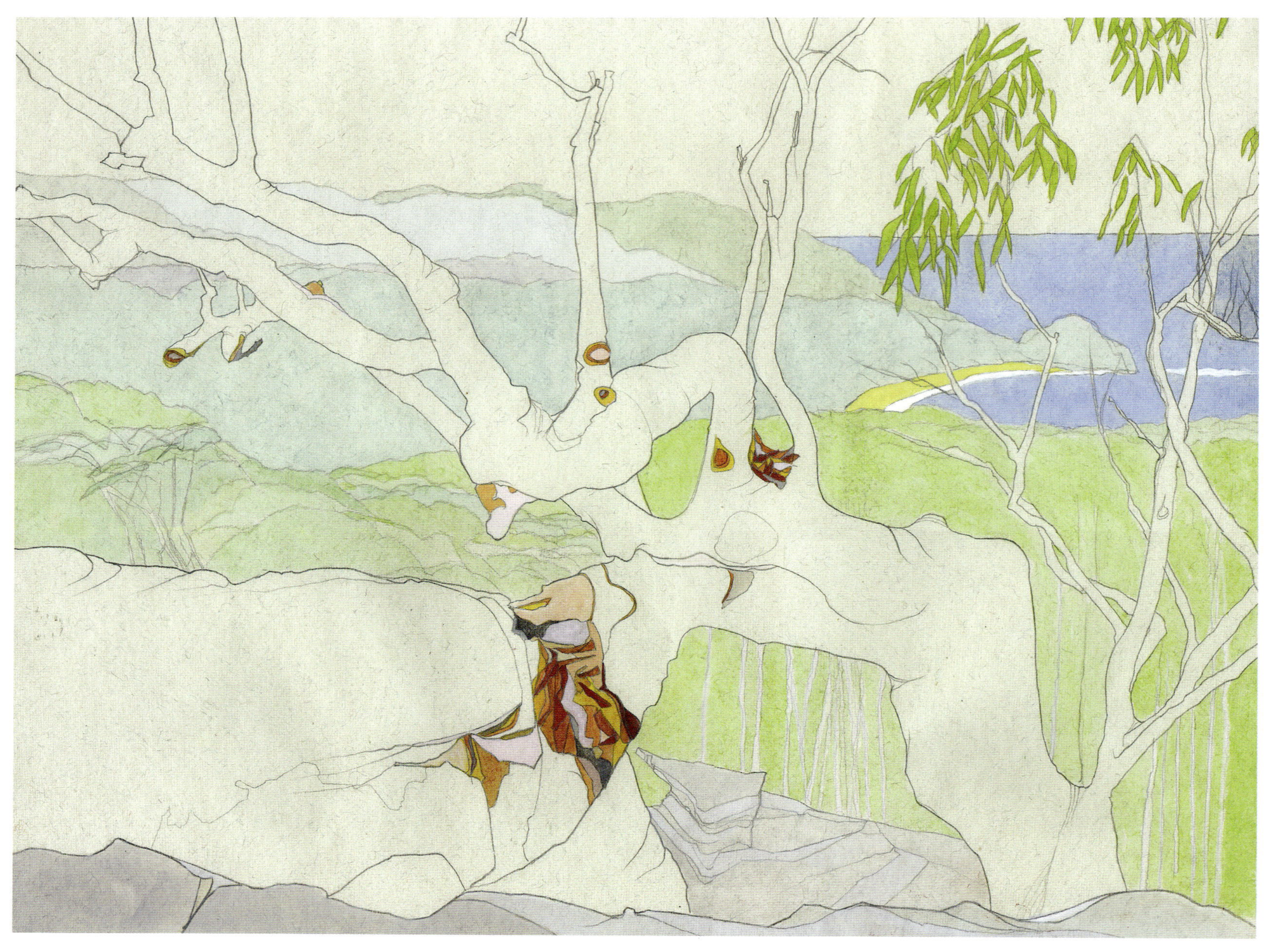

ABOVE
*Bouddi Tree 20/2/99 I,*
2019

RIGHT
*Bouddi Tree 20/2/99 IV,*
2019

FOLLOWING SPREAD
*Maitland Bay, Bouddi National Park,*
1990–1

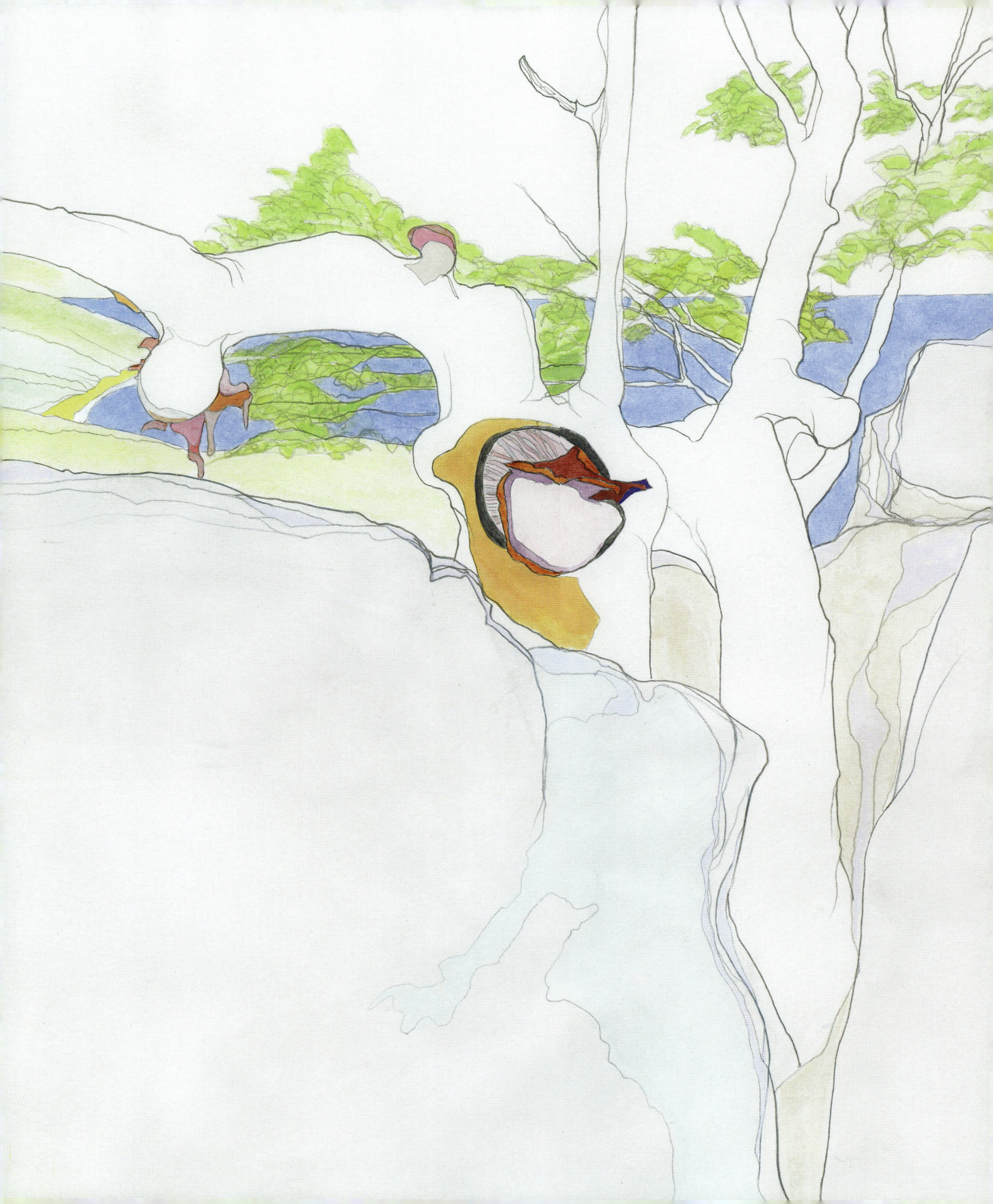

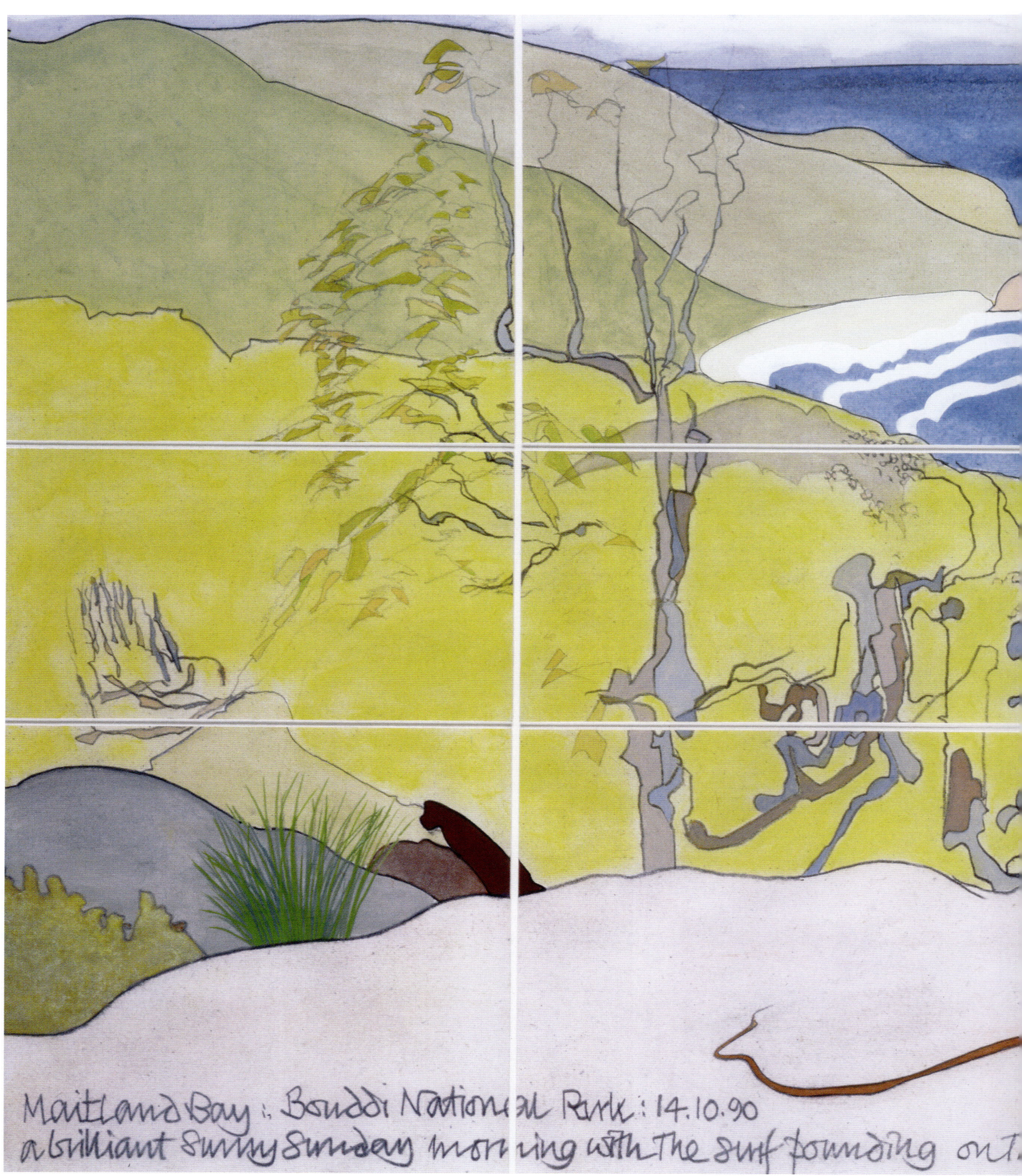

Maitland Bay : Bouddi National Park : 14.10.90
a brilliant sunny Sunday morning with the surf pounding ont.

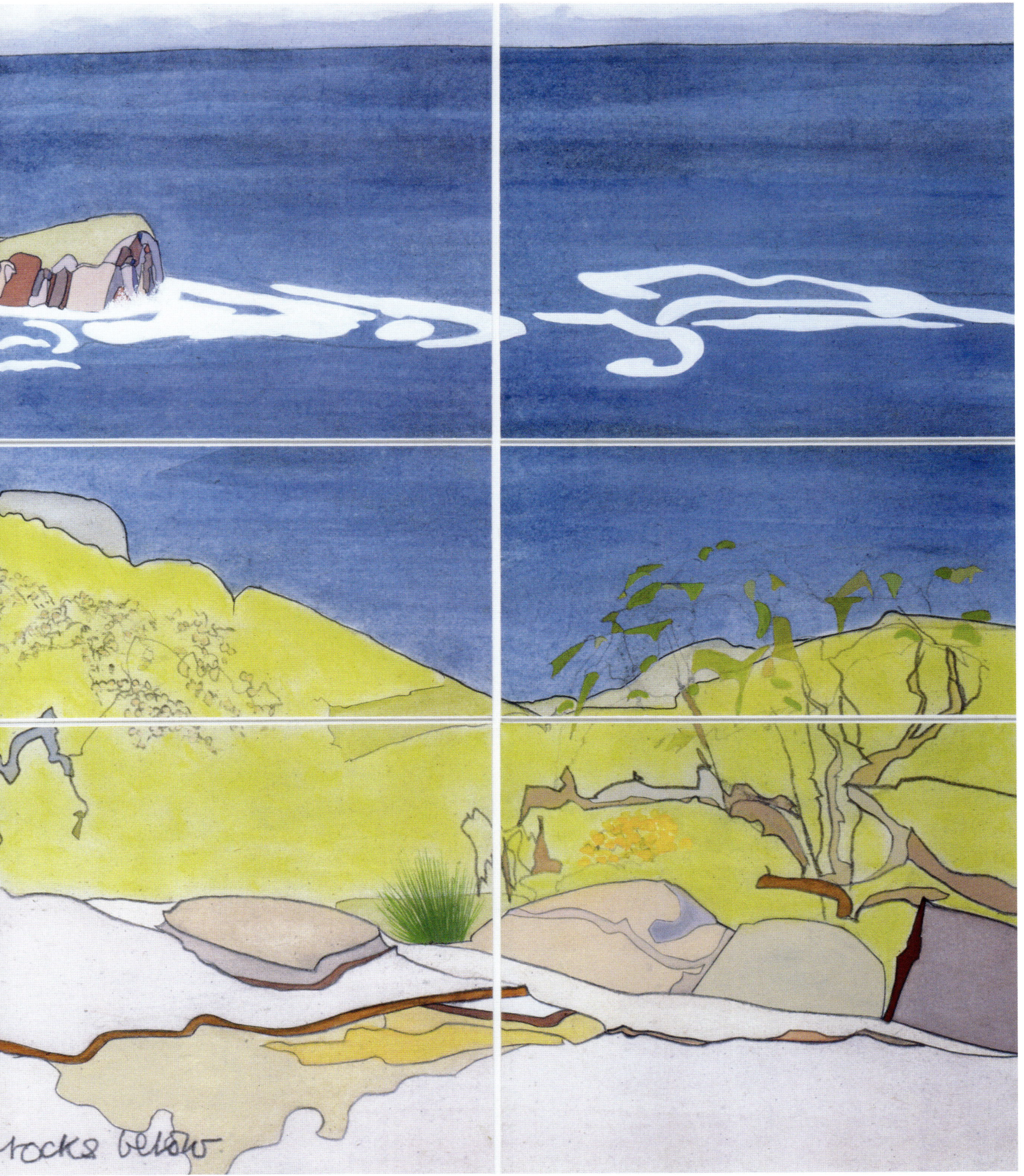

rocks below

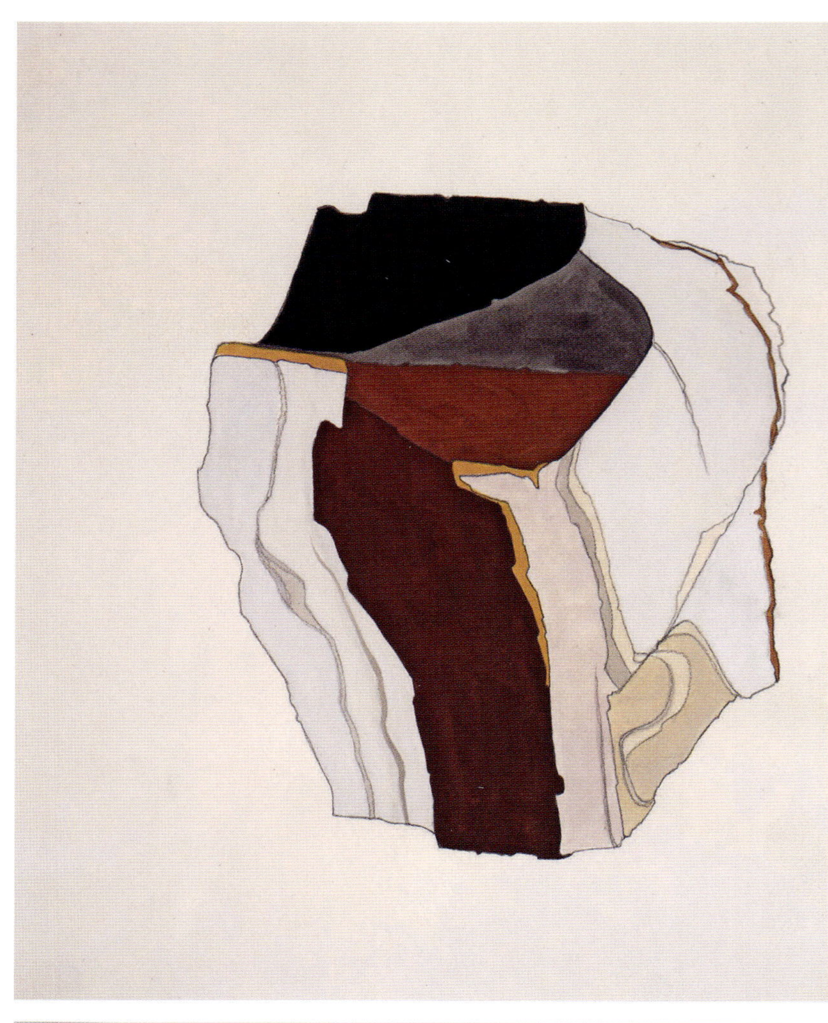
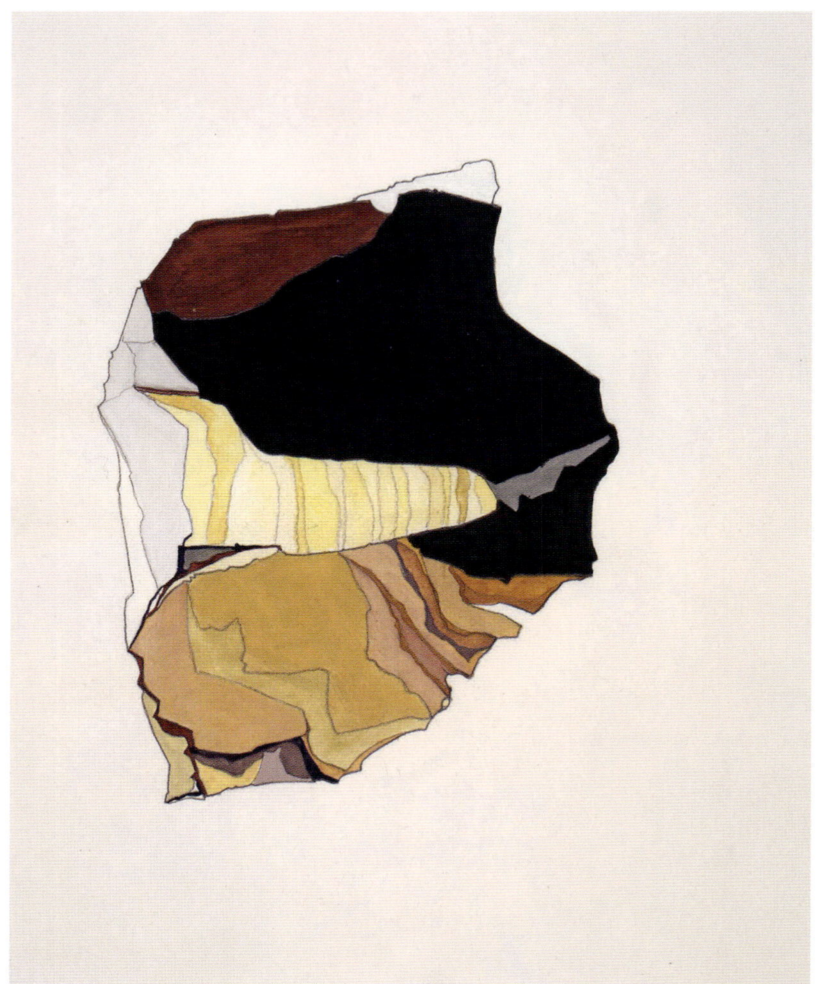
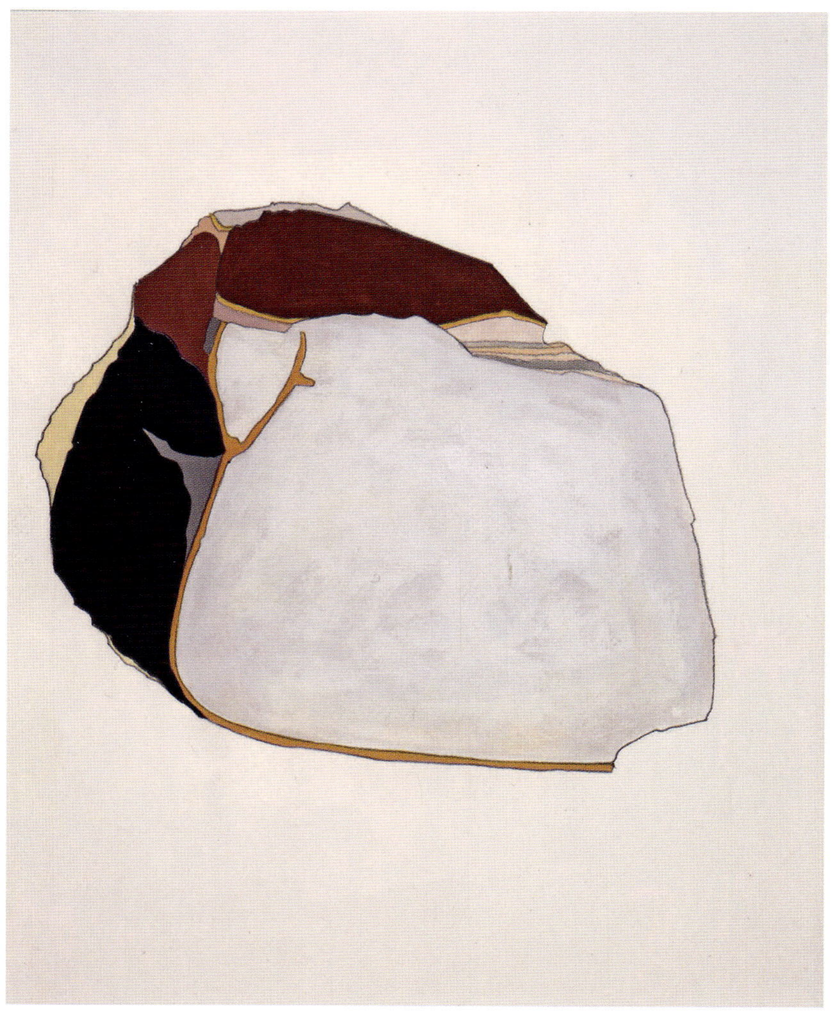
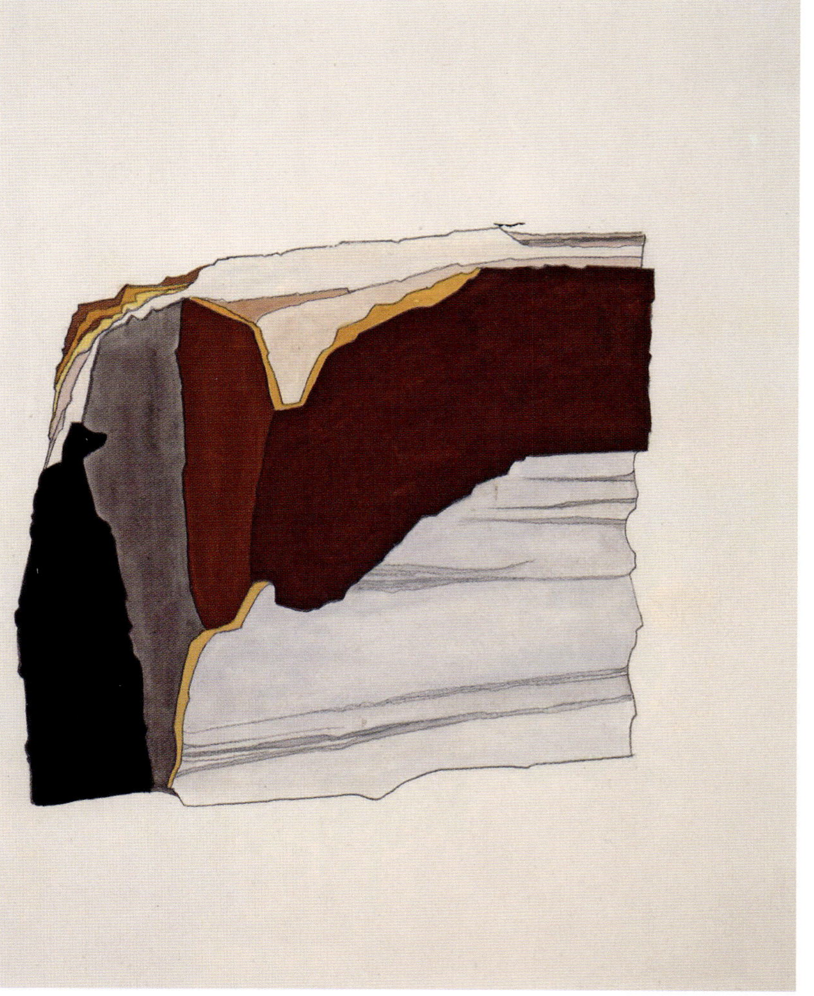

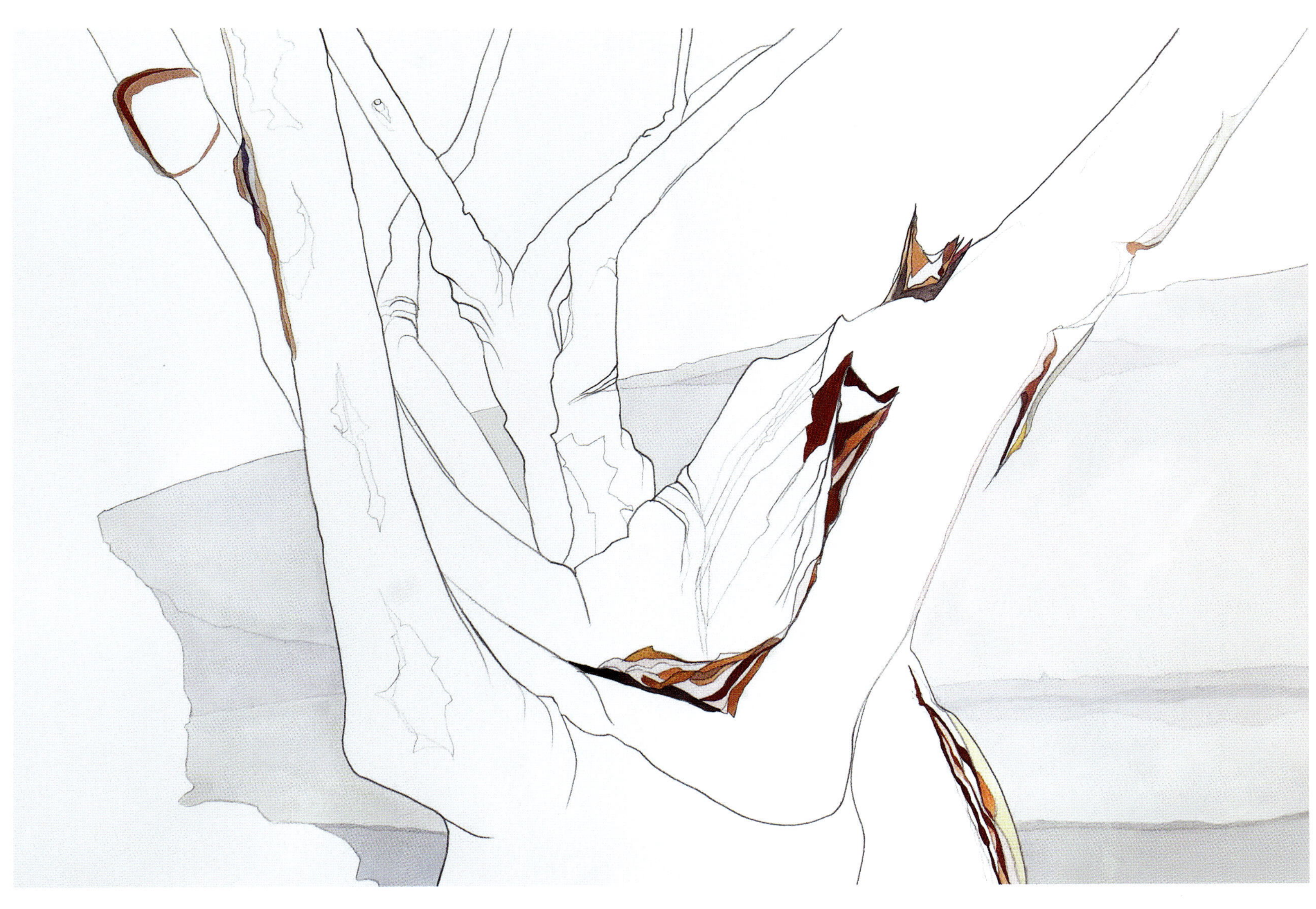

LEFT
*Macmasters Stone I–IV,*
1997

ABOVE
*Bouddi Tree,* 2019

# Fraser Island, Queensland

**25°26'04.2"S 153°09'07.6"E**
**-25.434492, 153.152104**

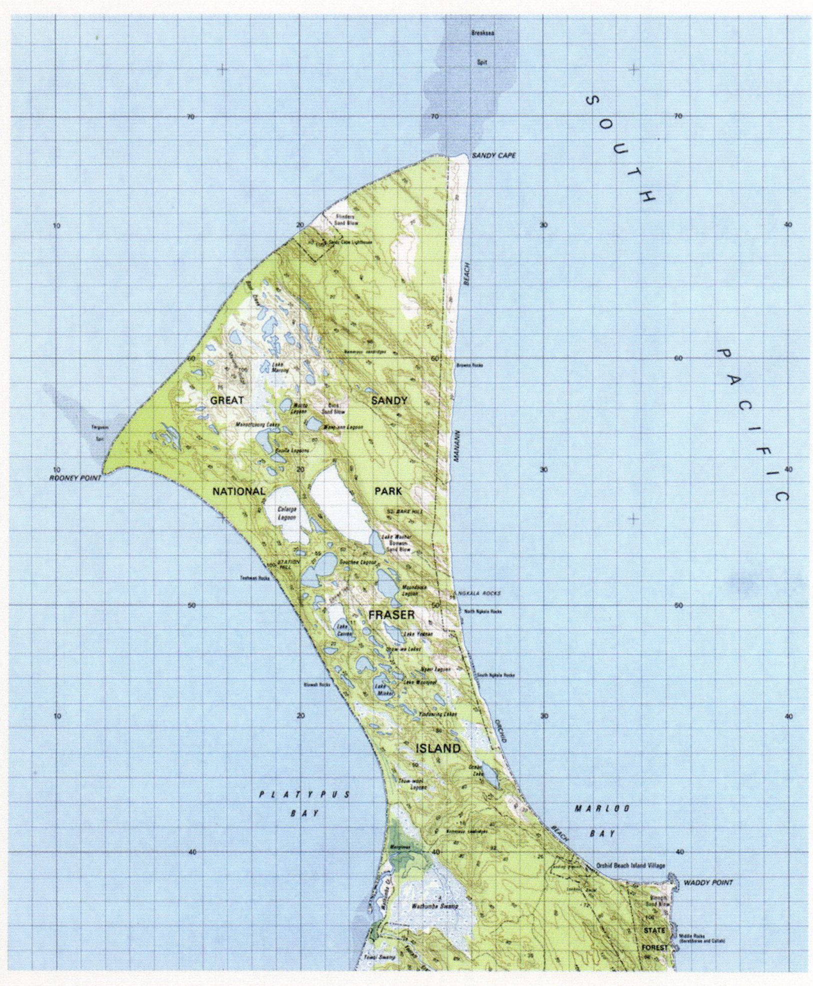

Fraser Island lies just off the Queensland coast. There is easy access by ferry from Hervey Bay. It is the largest sand island in the world, over 120 kilometres long, with sand dunes rising to over 200 metres. Fraser Island contains a number of 'perched lakes'. It seems unnatural that on an island entirely made of sand, large bodies of water can sit well above sea level. This is possible because, over time, fallen and decayed vegetation has lined the bottom of the lakes, preventing water from seeping through into the sand. The water of these lakes is very clear. To sit beside them alone, if you can, is magical.

The island is a World Heritage site, like a number of other locations in this book. After sand mining on the island ceased in 1976, it was the first site to be nominated for World Heritage status locally, by Australia. Travel on the island has to be done by four-wheel drive. When I went there over twenty years ago, it was calm, seemingly empty. I am told that this peace no longer exists, at least in the main part of the island, because of a proliferation of dune buggies.

Strangely for a sand island, it has a lot of deep rainforest. The striking contrast of the huge dunes and the vegetation is best seen from the air, and I have shown this in the aerial photograph opposite. I have developed a painting, included on page 151, that is based on an aerial view of the far-northern tip of the island.

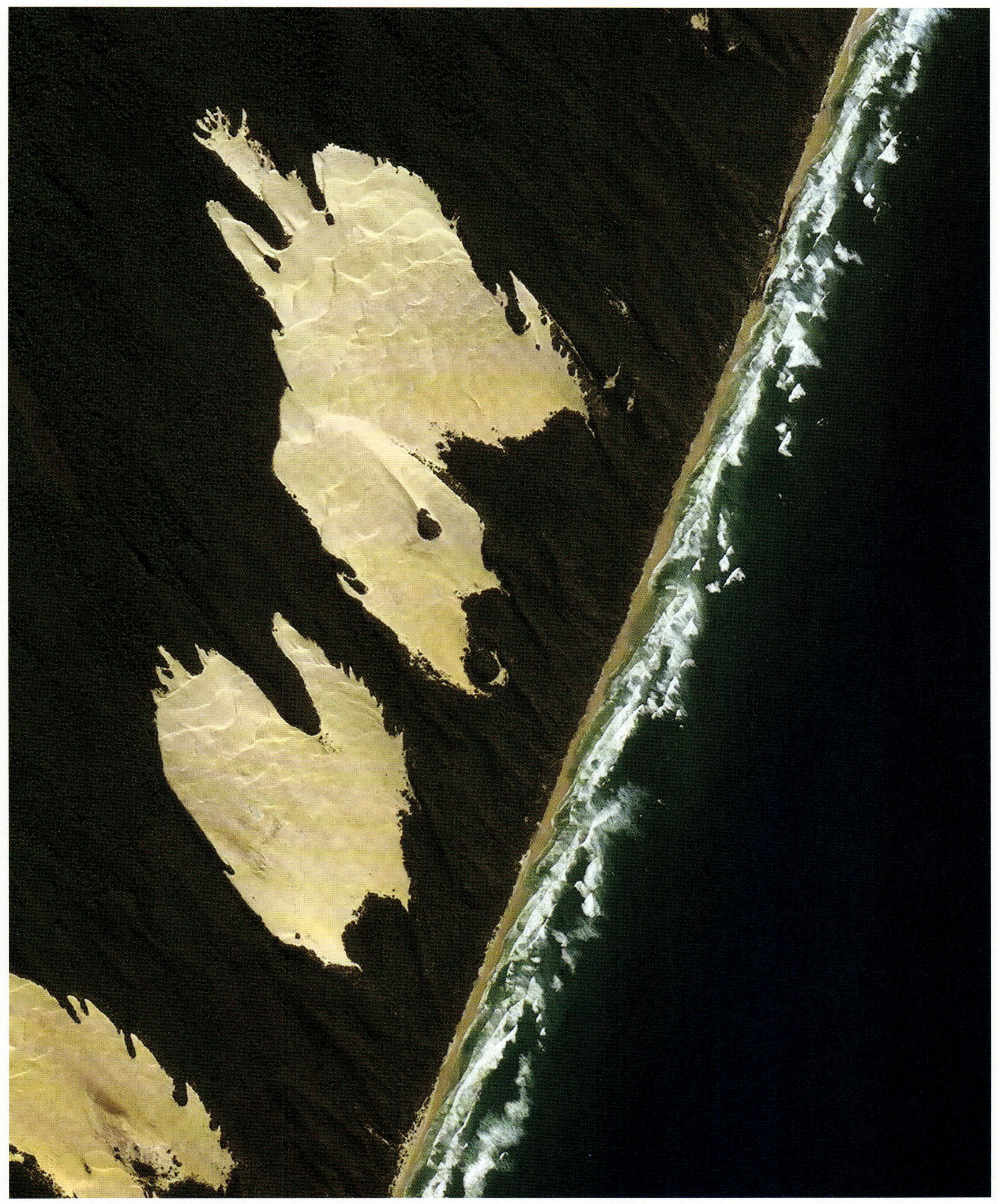

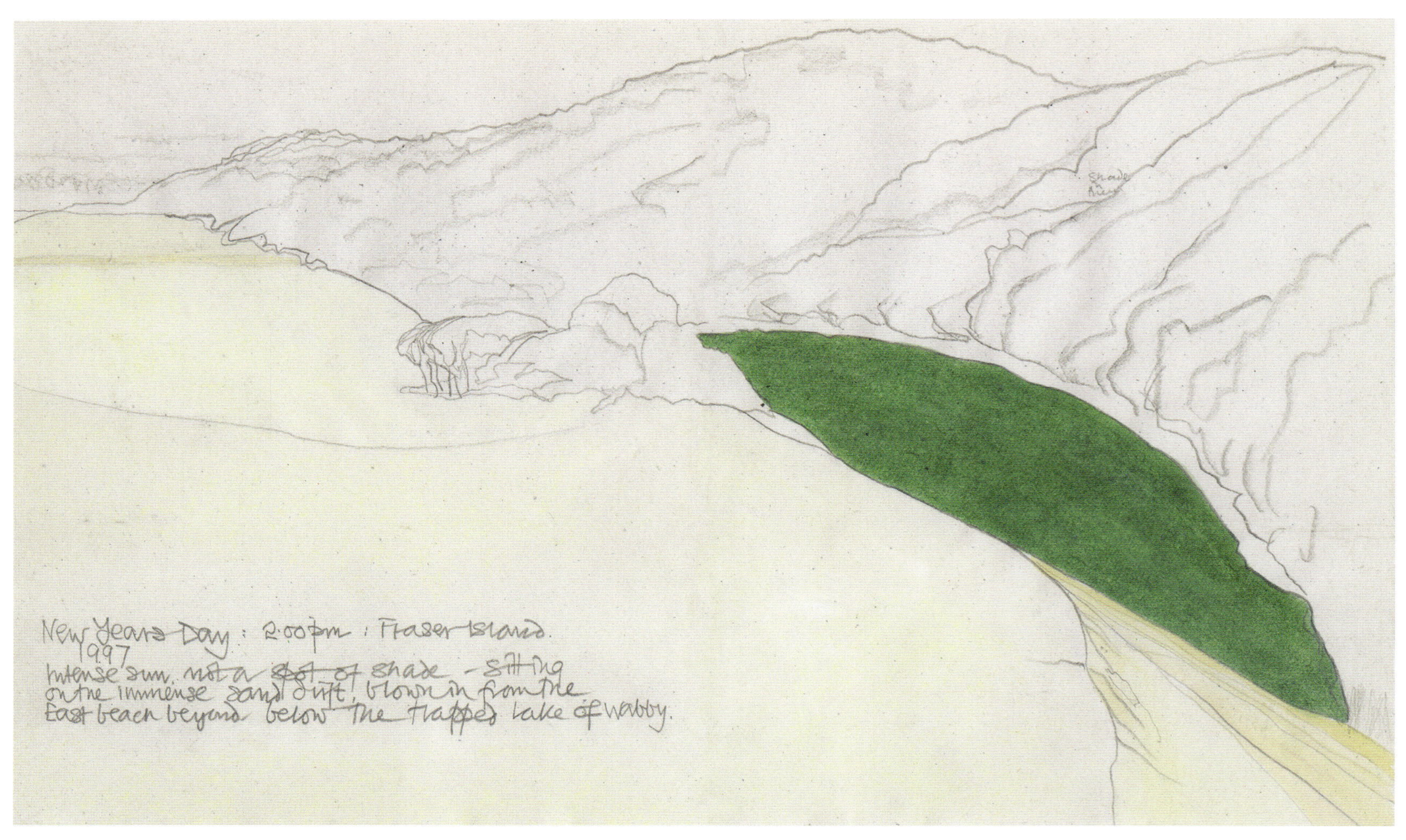

New Years Day : 2.00pm ; Fraser Island.
1997
Intense sun, not a spot of shade - sitting
on the immense sand drift, blown in from the
East beach beyond below the trapped Lake of wabby.

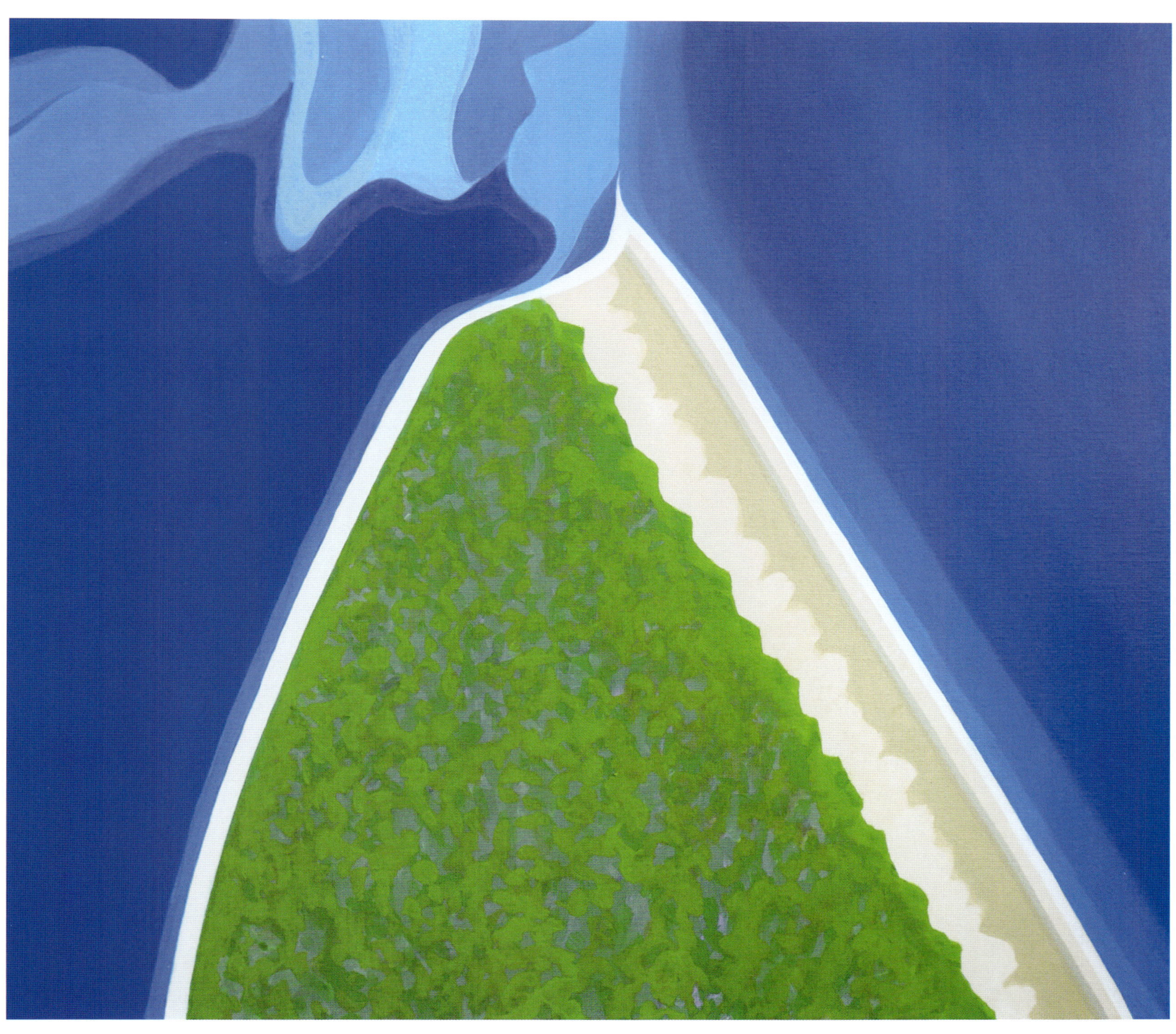

# Lord Howe Island, New South Wales

31°30'49.2"S 159°03'04.7"E
-31.513666, 159.051315

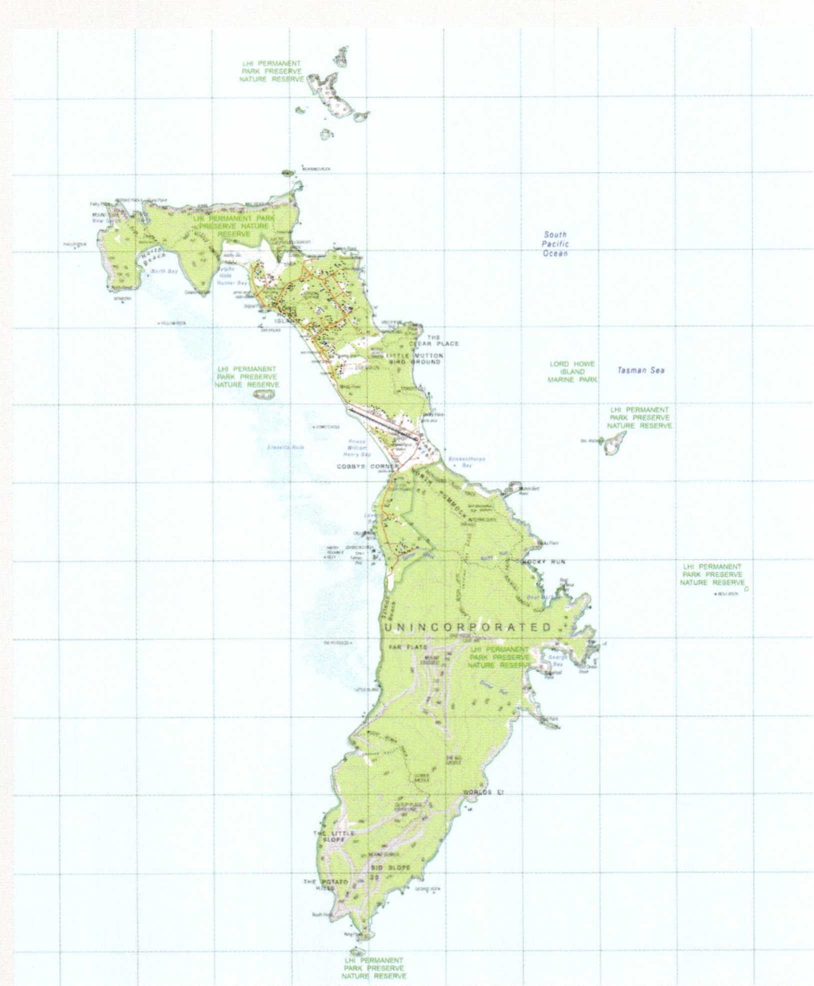


Lord Howe Island is situated in the Tasman Sea, just under 600 kilometres due east of Port Macquarie and roughly equidistant from Brisbane and Sydney. It is a UNESCO World Heritage site of global natural significance. The island is about 10 kilometres long, dominated by two peaks, Mount Gower and Mount Lidgbird. On the eastern coast is a lagoon that contains the world's southernmost coral reef. The island has important animals and plants, some found nowhere else in the world.

I have been there twice – first with Psiche, and a second time when we were joined by my sister Sally and family. It is a wonderful location for a holiday. There are so many different aspects to this small island: the coral reef and lagoon, and on the eastern side a surf beach. Also on the eastern coast is a beach where the mutton birds come ashore at dusk, hundreds walking up the beach to their burrows. The volcanic origin of the island is clear in the basalt rocks and the dramatic steepness of Mount Gower. It is a difficult climb, so steep that a rope has been installed along the track to the peak, which you cling to and use to pull yourself up. The vegetation on the climb and at the peak is dense subtropical forest. The panoramic painting illustrated overleaf is the view from Mount Eliza in the south towards the two large peaks at the northerly extreme. The other, on pages 158–9, is a large work on wooden panels, based on a basalt outcrop by the lagoon.

Part of the attraction of the island is its very small population. There are very few cars, though numbers did grow between my first and second visits. Cycling is the preferred form of transport. Tourist numbers are strictly limited by the capacity of the small plane that flies there from Sydney. The second time we went, the flight passed over an incredible pinnacle of rock in the sea, Ball's Pyramid, about 25 kilometres to the east of the island. When I saw it, I could not believe my eyes – it was so sharply pointed, steep and tall. Like Lord Howe Island, Ball's Pyramid is volcanic, and at 582 metres high – and 110 metres long by 300 metres wide at the base – it is the highest volcanic stack in the world. We planned to go there from Lord Howe Island by boat, but it was too rough. Instead, we got a closer look with a flight in a small plane.

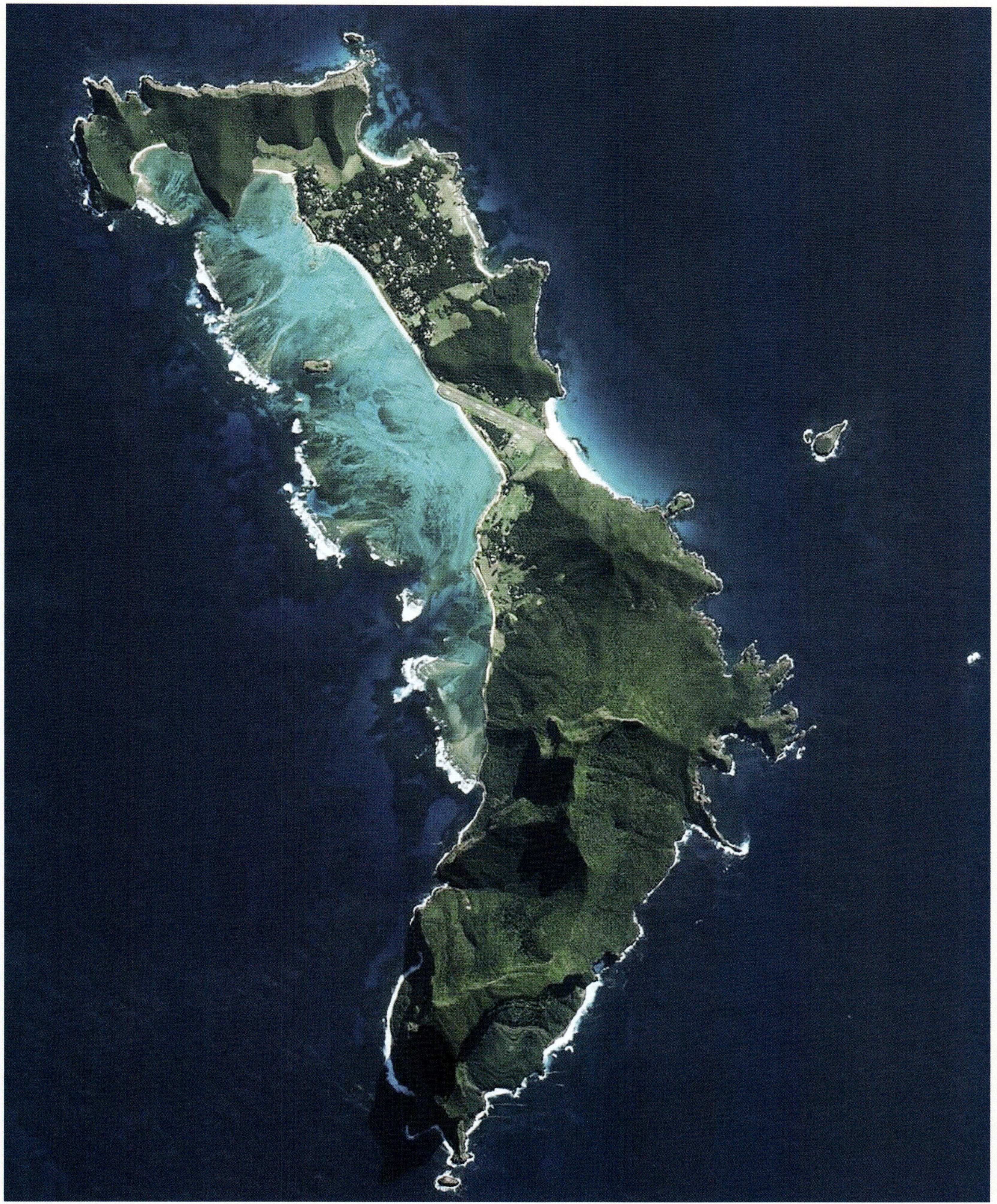

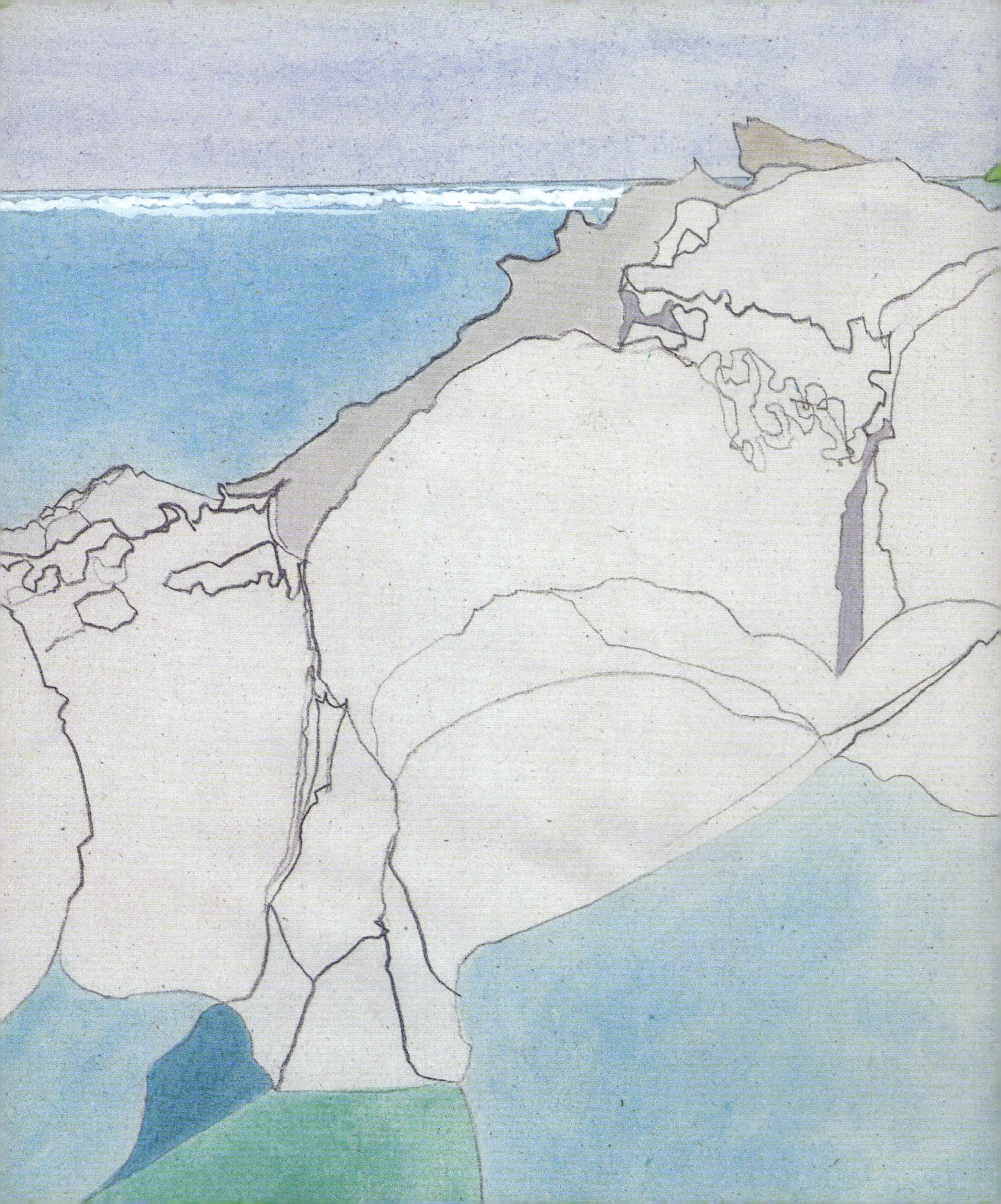

Lord Howe Island : Old Settlement Beach,
the volcanic rock outcrops at the edge
of the Lagoon : a brilliant turquoise sea
Midday   18:12:92

There are so many different aspects to this
small island: the coral reef and lagoon, and
on the eastern side a surf beach. Also on the
eastern coast is a beach where the mutton
birds come ashore at dusk, hundreds
walking up the beach to their burrows.
The volcanic origin of the island is clear in
the basalt rocks and the dramatic steepness
of Mount Gower.

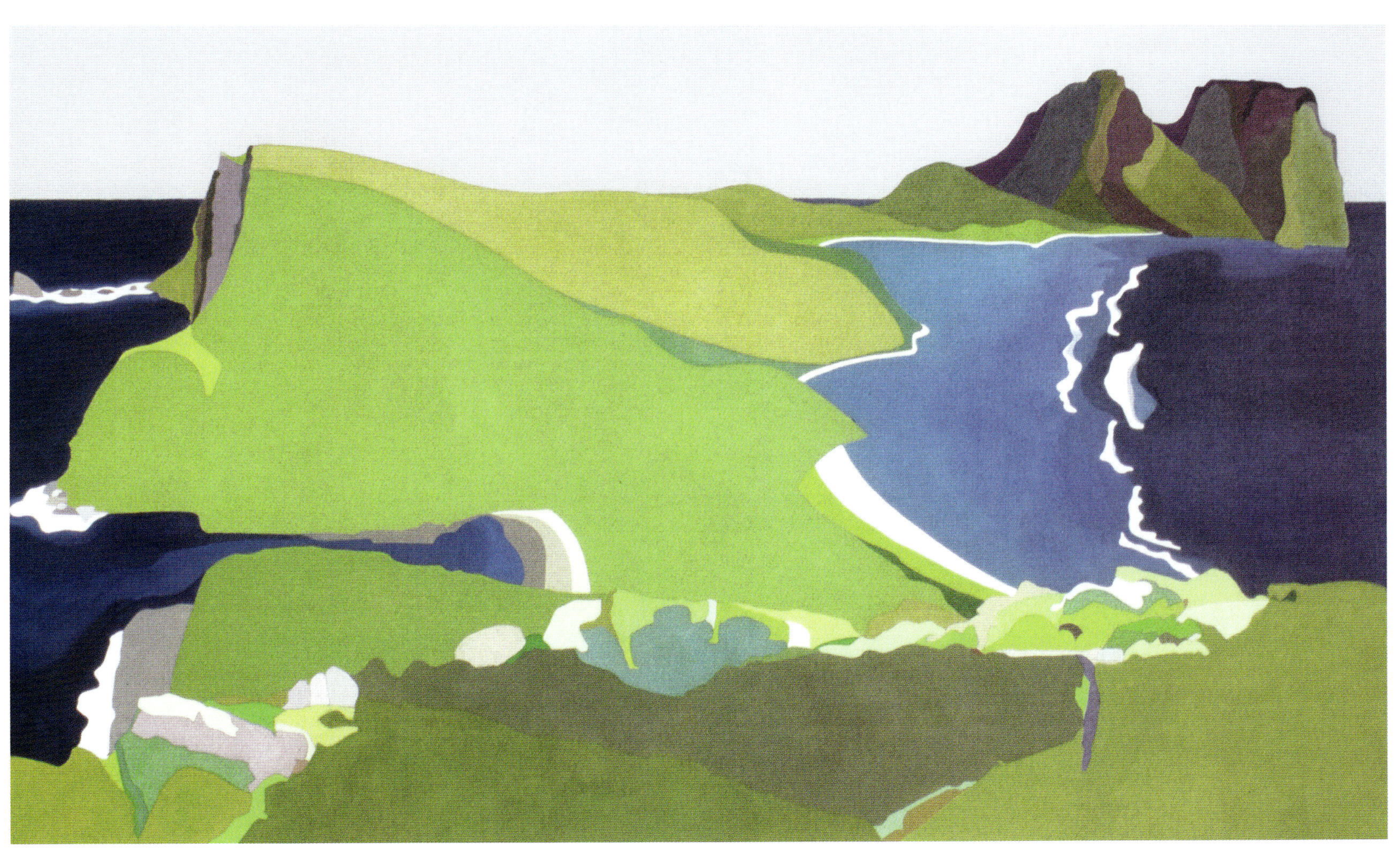

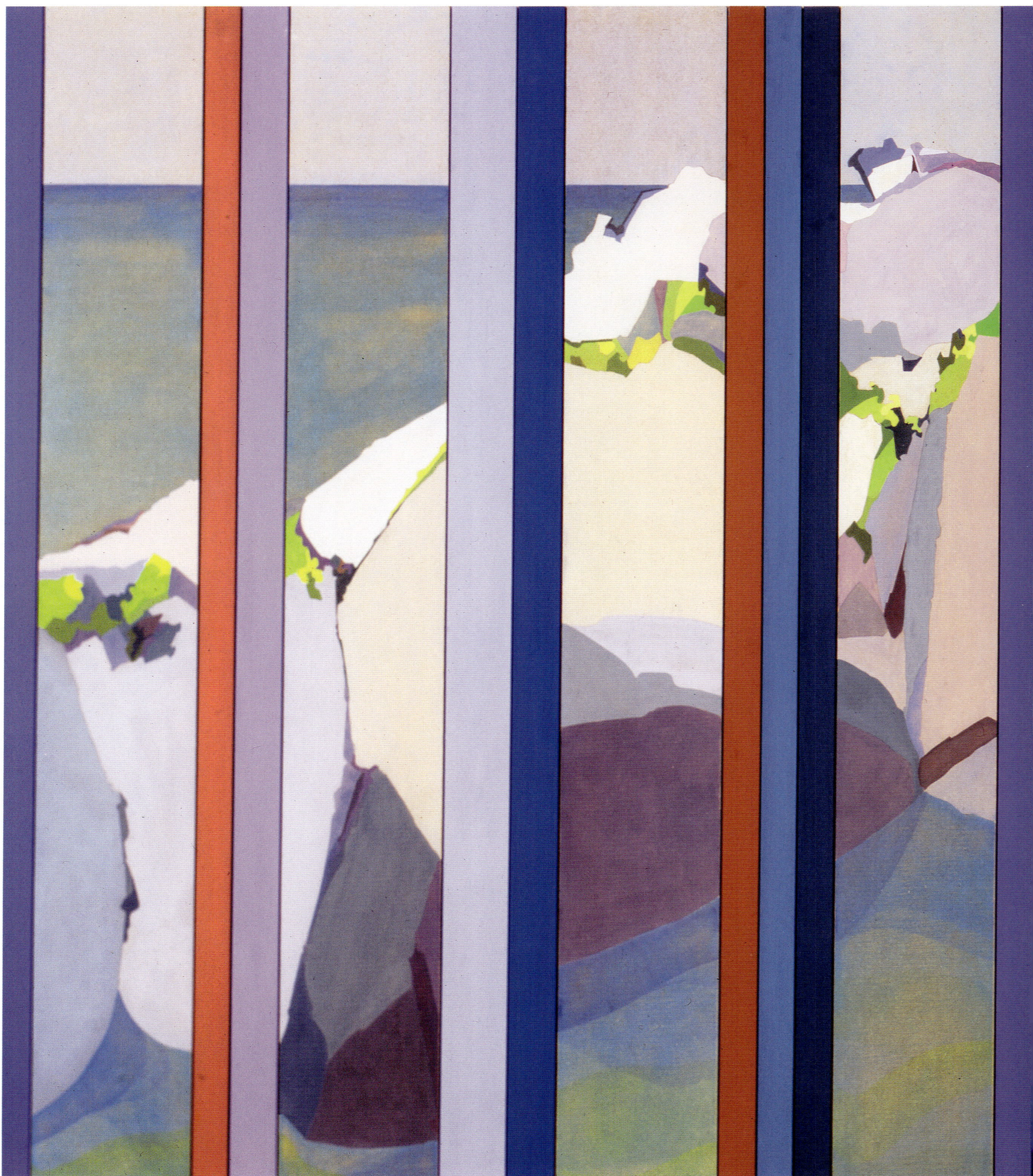

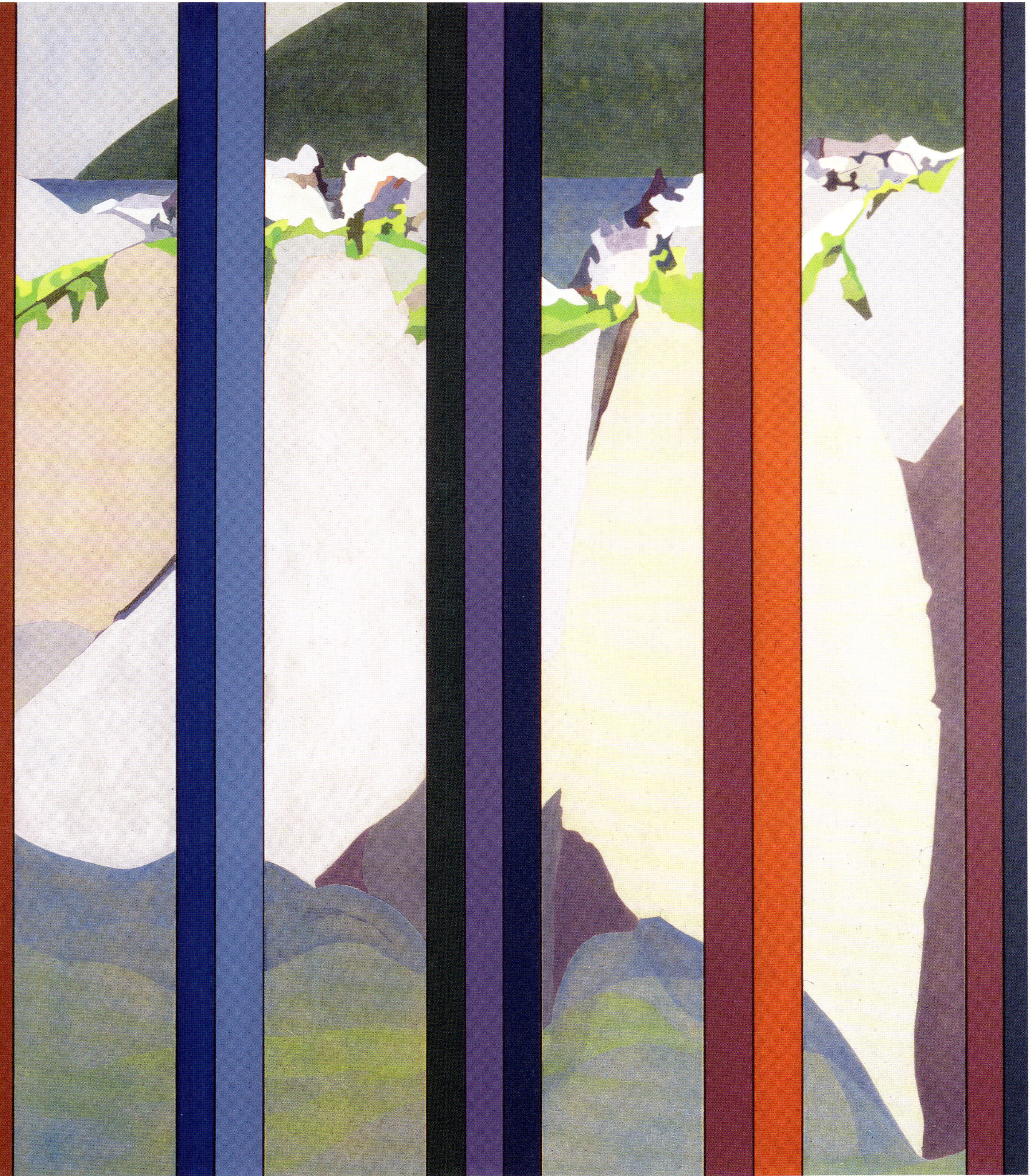

# Acknowledgements

Many people have provided so much help in the preparation of this book. I would particularly like to thank Amy Petra Woodward, who has done the major task of putting together all of the images at the quality required and provided so much other assistance. I also thank Ursula Meyer, who did the research for and sourcing of the maps and aerial photographs. I thank both Glenn Murcutt and Jonathan Meyer for their invaluable written contributions. In addition, each helped in suggesting and planning journeys to certain locations, as did Sally Rose. Thank you to Sam Palfreyman, Claire Orrell and Diana Hill for their amazing work in putting the whole book together. Finally, I thank Paulina de Laveaux, who had the idea for this book and without whom it would not have happened.

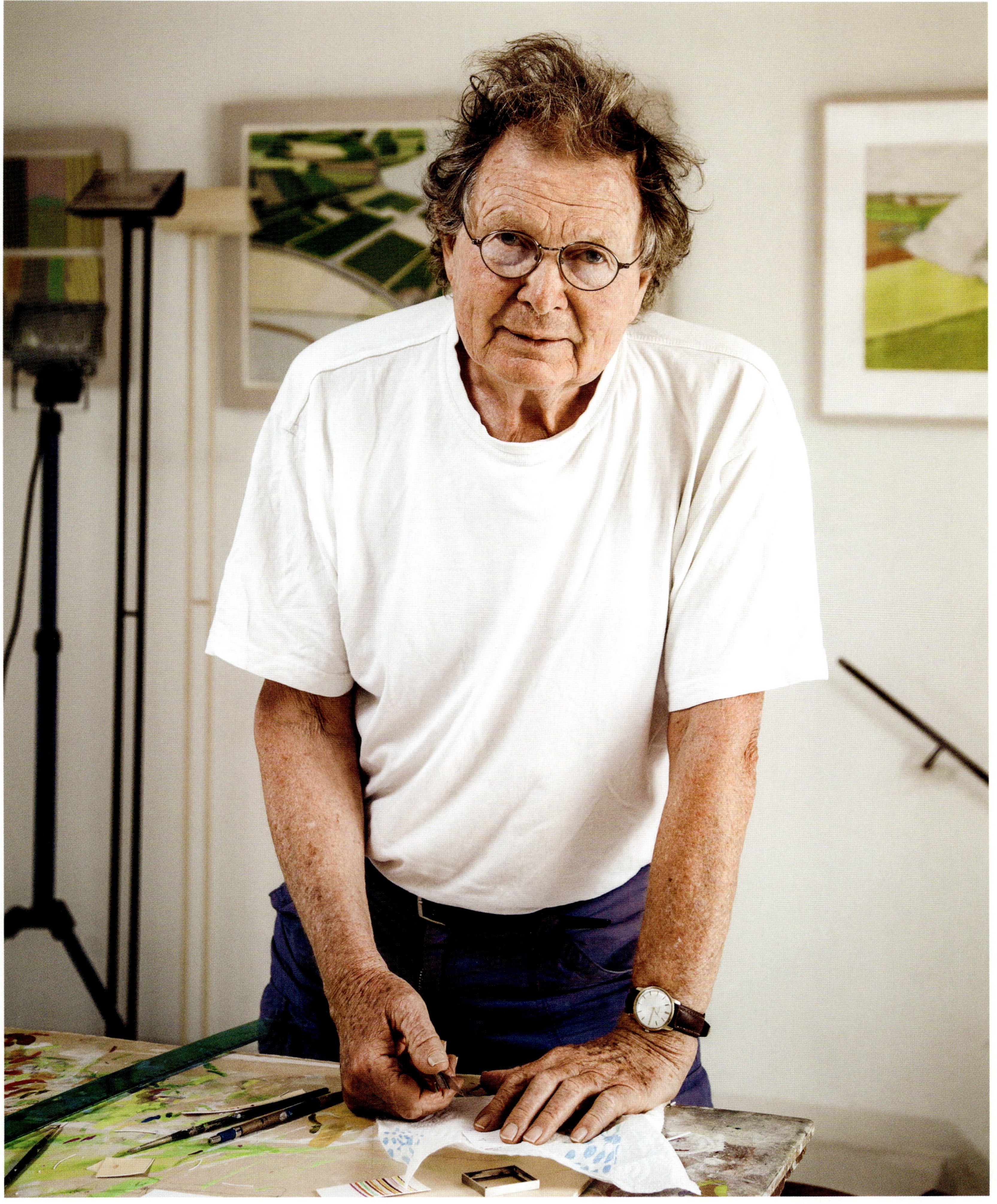

# Exhibition List

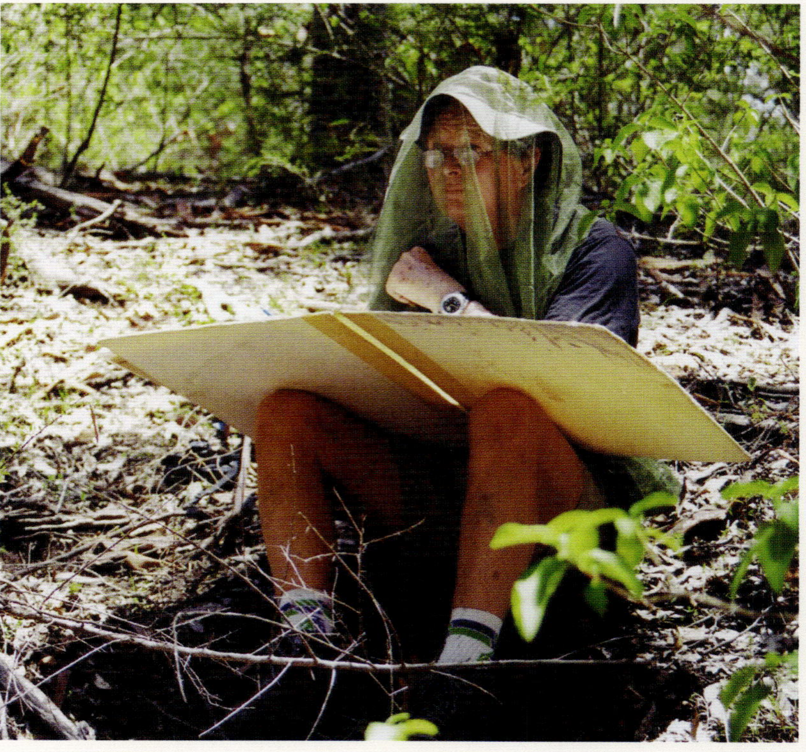

# Publications

Carmen Boullosa, Philip Hughes and Amy Petra Woodward,
*Alchimia de los Planetas* (Alchemy of the Planets), transl. by Psiche Hughes,
The Old School Press, Seaton, England, 2018.

Philip Hughes, *Tracks: Walking the Ancient Landscapes of Britain*, Thames & Hudson,
London, England, 2012 (paperback edition released in 2019).

Carmen Boullosa and Philip Hughes, *Jump of the Manta Ray*,
transl. by Psiche Hughes, The Old School Press, Seaton, England, 2002.

Philip Hughes, *Patterns in the Landscape: The Notebooks of Philip Hughes*,
Thames & Hudson, London, England, 1998.

Carmen Boullosa and Philip Hughes, *Elysian Garden*, transl. by Psiche Hughes,
Taller Magenta, Monterrey, Mexico, 1997.

# Collections

The British Library, London, England
The British Museum, London, England
Clare College, Cambridge University, Cambridge, England
Columbia University, New York, USA
Library of Congress, Washington, DC, USA
Musée du Pays Châtillonais, Châtillon-sur-Seine, France
The Museum of Fine Arts, Houston, USA
National Gallery of Australia, Canberra, Australia
The New York Public Library, New York, USA
The UK Government Collection, London, England
University of Georgia, Athens, USA
University of Iowa, Iowa City, USA
University of Stirling, Stirling, Scotland
The Victoria and Albert Museum, London, England
Washington University, St Louis, USA

# Picture Credits

**MAPS**

p. 2    2452-1 Tom Price Mine Topographic Map 1:50 000 (1988).
Source: Geoscience Australia

p. 10    2553 Wittenoom WA Topographic Map 1:100 000 (2nd Edition, 1990).
Source: Geoscience Australia.

p. 20    4565-2 Carr Boyd Range Topographic Map 1:50 000 (1992).
Source: Geoscience Australia.

p. 28    4563-2 Bungle Bungle Topographic Map 1:50 000 (1993).
Source: Geoscience Australia.

p. 38    SH52 Nullarbor Plain Topographic Map 1:1 000 000 (1st Edition, 2012).
Source: Geoscience Australia.

p. 42    SG5208 Ayers Rock NT Geological Map 1:250 000 (2nd Edition, 2002).
Source: Geoscience Australia.

p. 48    SG5208 Ayers Rock NT Geological Map 1:250 000 (2nd Edition, 2002).
Source: Geoscience Australia.

p. 56    SF5313 Hermannsburg NT Geological Map 1:250 000
(2nd Edition, 1995). Source: Geoscience Australia.

p. 62    WGS84 Cannon Hill NT Topographic Map 1:50 000 (1997).
Source: Geoscience Australia.

p. 68    SI53-16 Kangaroo Island Special SA Topographic Map 1:250 000
(2nd Edition, 2004). Source: Geoscience Australia.

p. 74    © Philip Hughes.

p. 88    SH53-04 Lake Eyre SA Topographic Map 1:250 000 (2nd Edition,
1999). Source: Geoscience Australia.

p. 96    6634 Wilpena SA Topographic Map 1:100 000 (1st Edition, 1984).
Source: Geoscience Australia.

p. 102    7420 Port Campbell VIC Topographic Map 1:100 000 (1st Edition,
1978). Source: Geoscience Australia.

p. 108    3828 D'Aguilar Topographic Map 1:25 000 (1st Edition, 1991).
Base image reproduced with the permission of TASMAP
(www.tasmap.tas.gov.au) © State of Tasmania.

p. 126    8928 Moss Vale NSW Topographic Map 1:100 000 (3rd Edition,
2000). Source: Geoscience Australia.

p. 132    9030 Penrith NSW Topographic Map 1:100 000 (1st Edition, 1980).
Source: Geoscience Australia.

p. 140    9130 Sydney NSW Topographic Map 1:100 000 (1st Edition, 1976).
Source: Geoscience Australia.

p. 148    9548 Waddy Point QLD Topographic Map 1:100 000 (1st Edition,
1981). Source: Geoscience Australia.

p. 152    NSW 0735-4N Lord Howe Island 1:25 000 (2016). © State of New
South Wales (Spatial Services, a business unit of the Department
of Customer Service NSW). For current information go to
spatial.nsw.gov.au.

**AERIAL IMAGES**

p. 83    Image reproduced courtesy of Kalamurina Homestead.

All other aerial images were sourced from Bing Maps.
Microsoft product screenshots reprinted with permission
from Microsoft Corporation.

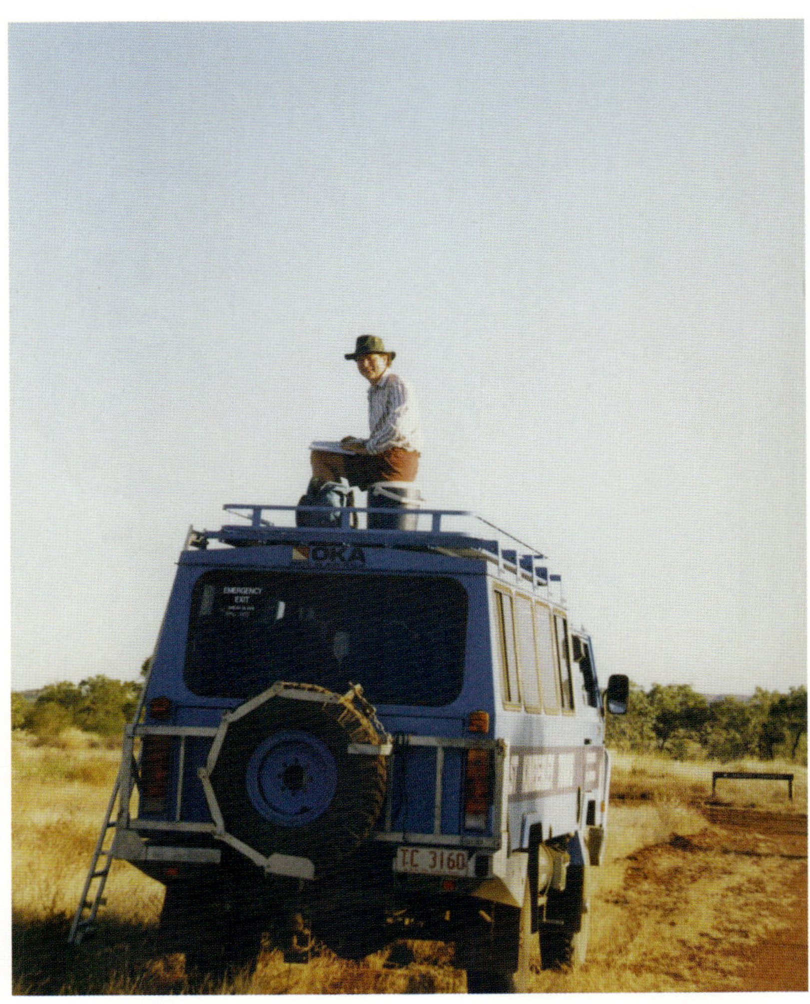

# List of Works

p. 77 (top)
*67 miles to Kalamurina*
20 April 2011
(Notebook)
22 x 44 cm

p. 77 (bottom)
*44 miles to Kalamurina*
20 April 2011
(Notebook)
22 x 44 cm

p. 78–9
*Lake Griselda II*
2012
Acrylic, gouache
and pastel on paper
38 x 57 cm

p. 80
*Lake Griselda*
2012
Acrylic on canvas
86 x 148 cm

p. 81
*Flight from Alice Springs
to Kalamurina*
2011
Gouache and
acrylic on paper
95 x 150 cm

p. 84
*Salt Lake en route
to Kallakoopah*
2012
Acrylic, gouache
and pastel on paper
60 x 60 cm

p. 85
*Lake and sand dune
en route to Kallakoopah*
(crop)
2012
Acrylic, gouache
and pastel on paper
60 x 60 cm

p. 86
*Flight to Kallakoopah*
(crop)
2011
Acrylic on canvas
97 x 70 cm

p. 87 (top)
*Flight north-west
of Kalamurina*
23 April 2011
(Notebook)
22 x 44 cm

p. 87 (bottom)
*Warbuton Creek en
route to Lake Eyre*
22 April 2011
(Notebook)
22 x 44 cm

p. 90
*Warburton Groove*
2012
Gouache on card
50 x 50 cm

p. 91
*Lake Eyre, Shore*
2012
Acrylic, gouache
and pastel on paper
mounted on board
60 x 60 cm

pp. 92–3
*Edge of Lake Eyre* (crop)
2012
Acrylic on canvas
70 x 97 cm

p. 95 (top)
*Lake Eyre: First View,
9.55 am*
22 April 2011
(Notebook)
22 x 44 cm

p. 95 (bottom)
*Lake Eyre from above
Warburton Gap, 11.57 am*
22 April 2011
(Notebook)
22 x 44 cm

pp. 98–9
*Grass trees at Bridle Gap*
1989
Acrylic on canvas
83 x 143 cm

p. 100
*Bungaroo Creek*
1989
Acrylic on canvas
83 x 143 cm

p. 101
*Approach to Arkaroo Rock*
1 December 1998
(Notebook)
28 x 48 cm

p. 104
*Twelve Apostles,
Port Campbell*
1992
Acrylic on paper
37 x 55 cm

p. 105
*Broken Head,
Port Campbell*
1991
Mixed media on board
66 x 85 cm

p. 106
*Loch Ard Gorge,
Port Campbell*
8 October 1990
(Notebook)
28 x 48 cm

p. 107
*The Grotto, Port Campbell*
1991
Acrylic and pastel
on board
126 x 131 cm

p. 110
*Just Before the Site
of the Dam*
1983
Gouache and acrylic
on paper
24 x 30 cm

p. 111
*Beside Butler Island*
1983
Gouache and acrylic
on paper
24 x 30 cm

p. 112
*Warners Landing, building
the access road*
1983
Gouache and acrylic
on paper
24 x 30 cm

p. 113
*Meeting Tent in
TWS Camp*
1983
Gouache and
acrylic on paper
24 x 30 cm

p. 117 (top)
*Above the Huon Valley*
10 January 2019
(Notebook)
22 x 44 cm

p. 117 (bottom)
*Melaleuca Lagoon*
13 January 2019
(Notebook)
22 x 44 cm

p. 118
*Hartz Mountains*
2019
Acrylic on paper
62 x 77 cm

p. 119
*Flight to Melaleuca*
2019
Acrylic on paper
62 x 77 cm

p. 122
*Opal*
2020
Acrylic on board
49.5 x 60.5 cm

p. 123
*Lightning Ridge:
Miner's Hut*
2019–20
Acrylic and pastel
on paper
56 x 76 cm

p. 124
*Lightning Ridge: The Giant
Excavation*
2019–20
Acrylic and pastel
on paper
56 x 76 cm

p. 125
*Lightning Ridge:
The Mines*
2019–20
Acrylic and pastel
on paper
56 x 76 cm

p. 128
*Pulpit Rock, 31 December*
2005
Acrylic and aquacryl
on paper
44 x 31 cm

p. 129
*Shoalhaven in the evening*
2005
Acrylic and aquacryl
on paper
30 x 49 cm

p. 130
*Bundanon: the last three
days of 2004*
2004
Acrylic and gouache
on paper
60 x 60 cm

p. 131
*Spotted Gums*
2005
Acrylic on canvas
84 x 70 cm

pp. 134–5
*In the Blue Gum Forest I*
1995
Acrylic on board
120 x 220 cm

p. 136
*Blue Mountains*
2019–20
Acrylic on canvas
85 x 150 cm

p. 137
*Walls Lookout Track*
2020
Acrylic on paper
80 x 126 cm

pp. 138–9
*Blue Gum Forest* (crop)
1987
Acrylic on paper
76 x 107 cm

p. 142
*Bouddi Tree 20/2/99 I*
2019
Acrylic on paper
56 x 76 cm

p. 143
*Bouddi Tree 20/2/99 IV*
2019
Acrylic on paper
76 x 56 cm

pp. 144–5
*Maitland Bay, Bouddi
National Park*
1990–1
Mixed media on board
76 x 125 cm

p. 146
*Macmasters Stone I–IV*
1997
Gouache on paper
33 x 40 cm (each)

p. 147
*Bouddi Tree*
2019
Acrylic on paper
67 x 100 cm

p. 150
*Fraser Island,
New Year's Day*
1 January 1997
(Notebook)
28 x 48 cm

p. 151
*Fraser Island*
2020
Acrylic on canvas
65 x 80 cm

pp. 154–5
*Old Settlement Beach*
18 December 1992
(Notebook)
28 x 48 cm

p. 157
*Lord Howe Island*
1993
Acrylic on canvas
86 x 148 cm

pp. 158–9
*Lava Flow*
1995
Acrylic on board
120 x 334 cm

First published in Australia in 2020
by Thames & Hudson Australia Pty Ltd
11 Central Boulevard, Portside Business Park
Port Melbourne, Victoria 3207
ABN: 72 004 751 964

First published in the United Kingdom in 2021
by Thames & Hudson Ltd
181a High Holborn
London WC1V 7QX


Thames & Hudson Australia wishes to acknowledge that Aboriginal
and Torres Strait Islander people are the first storytellers of this nation
and the traditional custodians of the land on which we live and work.
We acknowledge their continuing culture and pay respect to Elders
past, present and future.

ISBN 978-1-760-76071-7

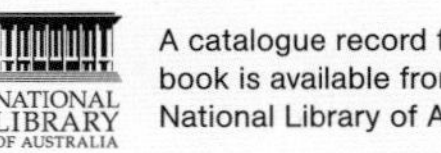

A catalogue record for this
book is available from the
National Library of Australia

British Library Cataloguing-in-Publication Data
A catalogue record for this book is available from the British Library.



Front cover: *Mesa*, 2005
Back cover: *Tom Price Mine II*, 2005

Design: Claire Orrell
Editing: Diana Hill
Printed and bound in China by RR Donnelley

Be the first to know about our new releases,
exclusive content and author events by visiting
thamesandhudson.com.au
thamesandhudson.com
thamesandhudsonusa.com

FSC® is dedicated to the promotion of responsible forest management
worldwide. This book is made of material from FSC®-certified forests
and other controlled sources.